THE HISTORY OF PATTEN AND MOUNT CHASE

By Debbie Coolong

The sale of this book without its cover is unauthorized. If you purchased this book without a cover, you should be aware that it was reported to the publisher as "unsold and destroyed." Neither the author nor the publisher has received payment for the sale of this "stripped book."

Published by Oliver Press
1274 Shin Pond Rd., Mt. Chase ME 04765

Copyright © 2017 by Debbie Coolong

All rights reserved, including the right to reproduce this book or portions thereof in any form whatsoever.

For information address Oliver Press
1274 Shin Pond Rd., Mt. Chase ME 04765

ISBN – 13: 978-1-541-27845-5
ISBN – 10: 978-1-541-27845-3

First printing August 2017

Town of Patten photograph by Diane Peck
Mt. Chase photograph and cover design by Debbie Coolong

Printed in the U.S.A.

THE HISTORY OF PATTEN AND MOUNT CHASE

DEDICATION

This history is dedicated to <u>people past</u>  (those who created this history),

<u>people present</u> (those who helped me write it down),

Don Campbell

Tellis Coolong

Kemp Coolong

and <u>people future</u> (those who will read it in years to come).

(including my grandson Oliver Kempton Probert, who was born during the revising/editing stage)

CONTENTS

Author's Notes	i
Introduction	v
Chapter One: Geography and Climate	1
Chapter Two: The Towns from 1828-1865	12
Chapter Three: The Towns from 1866-1889	44
Chapter Four: The Towns from 1890-1917	62
Chapter Five: The Towns from 1918-1945	99
Chapter Six: The Towns from 1946-1968	132
Chapter Seven: The Towns from 1969-1999	167
Chapter Eight: The Towns from 2000-2016	208
Chapter Nine: Up and Down Main Street	233
Chapter Ten: Schools and Libraries	257
Chapter Eleven: Health Care and Emergency Services	301
Chapter Twelve: Churches, Organizations, and Recreation	338
Chapter Thirteen: Recollections	358
Chapter Fourteen: Logging, the Mills, and the Museum	369
Chapter Fifteen: Farming	394
Chapter Sixteen: Outsiders and Outdoorsmen	410
Conclusion	438
Appendix A: Timeline of Mount Chase Development and Government	442
Appendix B: Timeline of Patten Development and Government	444
Appendix C: The Populations of Patten and Mount Chase According to Census Figures	451
Appendix D: Honor Roll Lists	452
Bibliography	464

AUTHOR'S NOTES

My first serious study of the history of Patten dates back to the 1980's, when I was a third-grade teacher at Patten Grammar School. At that time, Maine second-graders learned about neighborhoods, fourth-graders learned about the state of Maine, and fifth-graders studied the United States. And third-graders were supposed to learn about their communities. There was only one problem: there were no published histories of the towns of Patten and Mount Chase.

But I had a great resource in the person of Irene Olsen Bradford, who had been the town's historian for much of the 20th century. Her *History of Patten Academy*, written in 1947, is an excellent account of the town's achievements in establishing a school of the highest quality. Mrs. Bradford also wrote *It Took a Miracle*, which related the history of her beloved Stetson Memorial United Methodist Church. Mrs. Bradford also shared her knowledge about Patten's history with the young people in her Sunday School class, which included me. Using all the work Irene had done and a History of Patten research paper written by Rita Harrington that I found at the library, I put together a teaching unit. (This photo shows Mrs. Bradford on the occasion of the town's 150th birthday.)

After retiring from teaching in 2014, I finally had time to do some writing, and I decided to tackle the history of Patten. I whipped up several chapters in no time, using my teaching unit as my primary resource. I then contacted Donald Campbell, who I knew had a collection of photos taken throughout Patten's history. One evening, Donnie drove into my dooryard and handed me four photo albums. I wasted no time opening one of them up. What I discovered was astounding. Not only did Donnie have all those photos, but he also had a tremendous amount of information about Patten's history. So my initial few short chapters morphed into sixteen extensive chapters!!! Thank you so much, Donnie. You are a fantastic historian, and I could not have written this book without you. (This photo shows three of the albums with Post-It notes marking the pages which had photos I decided to use!)

As I worked on the history of Patten, I found I was including a lot of information about its sister community, Mount Chase, and I decided to expand my history to include Mount Chase. I visited Lora Ryan at the Mount Chase Town Office to see what she had on hand for information. Once again I had hit the jackpot, and I came home with two binders and a handful of plastic sleeves with lots of new information which had been organized by Rhoda Houtz, a former administrative assistant for the town of Mount Chase. Thank you, Rhoda, for all the time and effort you put into doing this.

I turned to social media at times with appeals for information, especially on the *You Know You're From Patten* Facebook page. Thanks go to those who supplied information and photos on this site. Extra special thanks go to Eleanor Sargent Hunter, a Mount Chase and Patten success story. Eleanor helped me clarify some information and graciously granted me permission to use her photos.

Another helpful discovery was *An Informal History of the Town of Patten, Maine*, written by Juanita Bates Finch and published in the Millinocket Journal in 1950 and 1951. Mrs. Finch included a lot of anecdotal history in her book; I have included a couple of her stories in my history. You can buy a copy of Mrs. Finch's history (put into booklet form by her niece, Jennifer Bates Ryan) at the Veteran's Memorial Library.

The library also had a series of scrapbooks compiled by Wayne Brown. These scrapbooks contained all the newspaper articles that Wayne had written about events in Patten and Mount Chase.

The Mount Chase and Patten Town Reports and the Patten Academy yearbooks were very helpful. Veteran's Memorial Library had copies of the Patten Town Reports from 1892 to 2016 and the yearly editions of the Mirror (the P.A. Yearbook) from 1906 to the present. I was able to get the Mount Chase Town Reports at the Mount Chase Town Office. Thank you, Doris DeRespino at the library, Ray Foss at the Patten Town Office, and Lora Ryan at the Mount Chase Town Office.

I also discovered that the state of Maine has published annually a book called "The Annual Register of Maine." I found quite a few of the registers online under Google Books, found a few more in hardcopy at Veteran's Memorial Library, and then found all the editions of the Register at Cary Library in Houlton. These registers go back to the early 1800's and were very helpful in learning more about the businesses and organizations of Patten and Mount Chase.

A particularly helpful book was *The History of Penobscot County*, which I accessed online through Google Books. It contained information about the towns and many of the early settlers, tracing family lines over several generations. It also had a section on military history which contained listings of Civil War Maine Volunteer units.

I sent out over 60 letters to people and businesses explaining my project and what I was writing about that affected them, asking permission to use the information and/or photos, and asking them to correct any errors I had made. I heard back from most of these. Thank you so much for your responses and support. You helped me straighten out errors and provided new information and photos.

Writing this history turned out to be a family affair as well. I got some information from papers collected by my husband's parents, Hadley and Patricia Coolong, and his grandfather, Wesley Cunningham. My husband, Kemp Coolong, answered question after question about Patten and Mount Chase for me. He has a fantastic long-term memory and can recall events and information dating back to the 1950's. If he got stumped on something, he asked the guys from the early-morning gang at Scotty and Louise Skinner's Wilderness Variety for help.

Special thanks go to my talented son, Tellis Coolong, an author in his own right. Tellis helped me edit and publish this book through CreateSpace on Amazon. Couldn't have done it without ya, Tellis.

I have tried to document any printed resources I used in my bibliography, although some of my resources were just photocopies of random articles which were not annotated. The bibliography also lists websites through which I found information.

All photos, unless otherwise noted, came from the collections of Donnie Campbell or myself. The beautiful photo of Patten which appears on the cover of this book was taken by Diane Peck, who graciously granted me permission to use it. I took the cover picture of Mount Chase as seen from Bumpus Hill in October 2016. The untagged photos on the dedication page are of Henry Rowe on the left and Telesphore Coulombe (Tellis Coolong) on the right. I wonder what Grampie Tellis would think about being mentioned several times in a history book and having his picture on a dedication page along with his grandson, great-grandson, and great-great grandson!

I am going to apologize in advance for any errors and omissions in this book. I know there are some of both! You will find a variety of errors, including spelling mistakes, typos, etc. In my defense, things tended to get kind of confusing at times, with various resources giving conflicting information about names, places, and dates. Where there was disagreement, I have either provided both versions or have used my judgment to decide which version was the most accurate. I also know that the information I have recorded here is not the whole story. I would love to learn more—if you know other facts about Patten history, please let me know! Maybe something you read in these pages will jog your memory about more people, places, and things related to this history, or maybe you noticed an error. I may in the future issue an addendum to the book with corrections and additions to this history. You can contact me by snail-mail at 1274 Shin Pond Road, Mount Chase, Maine 04765 or by e-mail at kdcoolong@gmail.com.

THE HISTORY OF PATTEN AND MOUNT CHASE

INTRODUCTION

Patten and Mount Chase, two small towns in northern Maine, have an intertwined history. Since Mount Chase is a more rural town and doesn't have a "downtown" area, its citizens consider Patten to be their community in many ways. Likewise, you can't talk about Patten's history without mentioning Mount Chase names, places, and events.

This history traces the growth of the Patten and Mount Chase area over a period of almost two hundred years, from the time when only Wabanaki Native Americans walked through its forests, until 2016. As in most towns, history is tied closely to economy. For Patten and Mount Chase, that economy has always had its roots in the forests and fields which surround the town. The area businesses depend on the forests in two respects: the money generated by cutting of those forests and the tourist industry which is based on "outsiders" coming to the area to enjoy being in the forest. In addition, farming was once a vital part of the area's economy.

I will be using the word *community* a lot in this history. The word community implies more than a group of houses built in close proximity. A community is really a collection of people with similar goals and interests. The earliest residents of Patten wanted a real community, with businesses, schools, and churches. Although Mount Chase took a different path to development, it too was made up of people who had similar goals and interests. Over the years, the two towns have become one community, and they share much more than a ZIP code, a phone number prefix, and the same page in the atlas.

It is my hope that this history will give you not only the facts, but also the flavor of the communities of Patten and Mount Chase. I hope it will help you appreciate the pioneering spirit which created the towns and the hard work which has kept them alive for almost two hundred years. Hopefully, that will result in a lively enthusiasm for efforts to keep our community vital and thriving.

CHAPTER ONE: GEOGRAPHY AND CLIMATE

We can't begin a history of Patten and Mount Chase without talking about townships and ranges. Before Maine separated from Massachusetts and became a state in 1820, northern Maine had been divided into a grid as shown in the map here. The T stands for township, and the R stands for Range; the townships go from 1 in the south to 20 in the north, and the ranges go from 1 in the east to 19 in the west. Massachusetts and later Maine sold off these sections of land. T5R6 became Mount Chase, and T4R6 became Patten.

Patten and Mount Chase lie in the wooded foothills to the east of Mount Katahdin. The towns are located near the northern border of Penobscot County, with Aroostook County to the north and east and Piscataquis County to the west. Mount Chase is actually the northernmost town in Penobscot County.

Patten is located at -68.5° longitude and 46° latitude. It is about 90 miles by car north of Bangor, and 60 miles by car south of Presque Isle. The Canadian border lies only about 40 miles east, just beyond the town of Houlton. The closest exits off Interstate 95 are in Sherman and Island Falls. Patten and Shin Pond (an area within Mount Chase) are the northern gateway to Baxter State Park and Mount Katahdin, which lie in Piscataquis County to its west.

Patten forms a triangle with the neighboring communities of Sherman and Island Falls, with the town of Stacyville lying between Patten and Sherman and Crystal lying between Patten and Island Falls. As you approach Patten from the south, Route 11 brings you down a long, steep hill (Finch Hill) and up a short, steep hill (Mill Hill) into the business district; the next several miles as you continue traveling north are on relatively flat land before getting into hilly terrain as you enter Mount Chase. Mount Chase can also be reached by turning left at the intersection of Route 11 and Route 159; the road that travels northwest from there is called the Shin Pond Road. The Owlsboro Road connects the two parts of Mount Chase north of Patten.

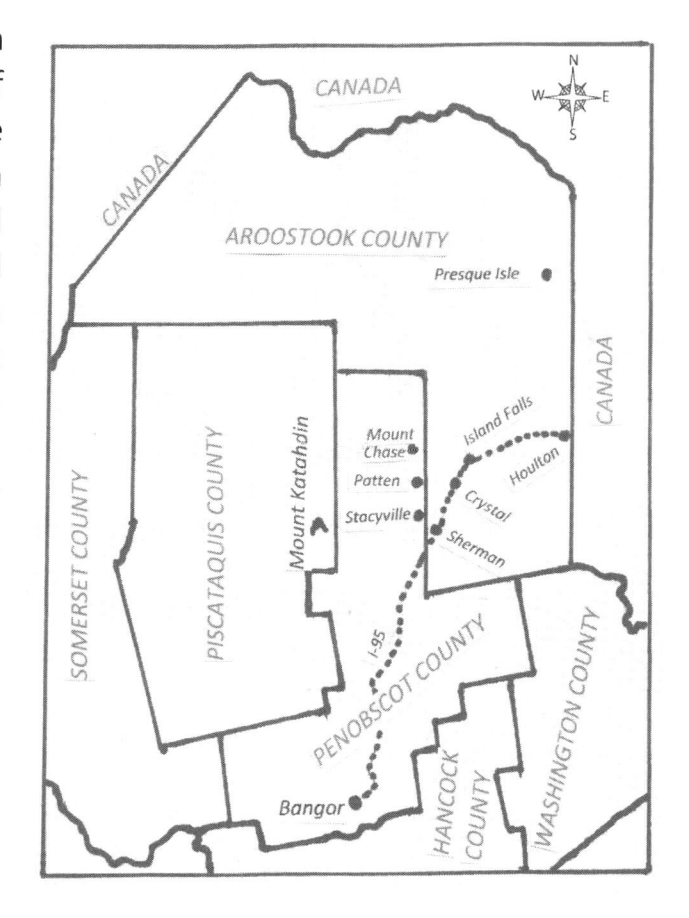

An aerial view of Upper (right) and Lower (left) Shin Pond.

There are several brooks which run through Patten and Mount Chase. Additionally, there are two large rivers to the west of the towns. The chart below gives information about these bodies of water. The map on the next page might or might not help you locate them in your mind!

NAME	WHERE IT ORIGINATES	WHERE IT FLOWS	WHERE IT DUMPS
Willett, Kimball, and Sargent Brooks	Mount Chase	Southeast through Mount Chase	Crystal Brook
Houston and Mill Brooks	Mount Chase	Southeast through Mount Chase and Hersey	Crystal Brook
Crystal Brook	Mount Chase	Southeast through Mount Chase, Hersey, and Crystal	Fish Stream
Rowe Brook	Patten, just west of Rte. 159	Southeast to near Peavey Corner	Peasely Brook
Peasley Brook	Near the Owlsboro Road in Mount Chase	Southeast to Peavey Corner/Peasley Dam, then southeast to Fish Stream on the west side of Patten	Fish Stream
Weeks Brook	Mount Chase	Southeast on east side of Patten	Fish Stream
Webb Brook	Near the Clark Road in Patten	Southeast through town	Fish Stream
Fish Stream	West of Patten near border with Mount Chase	Southeast through Patten at the foot of Mill Hill, east to Crystal and Island Falls	W. Br. Of Mattawamkeag River, then Penobscot R.
Sebois River	Grand Lake Sebois, Snowshoe Lake	Southeast through T7R7, T6R7, T5R7, T4R7, T3R7	East Branch of Penobscot R.
East Branch of Penobscot River	Matagamon Lake in T6R8	Southeast through T5R8, T4R8, T4R7, T3R7, Soldiertown, Grindstone, East Millinocket, Medway	Penobscot River, then Atlantic Ocean

BODIES OF WATER AND ROADS IN PATTEN AND MOUNT CHASE

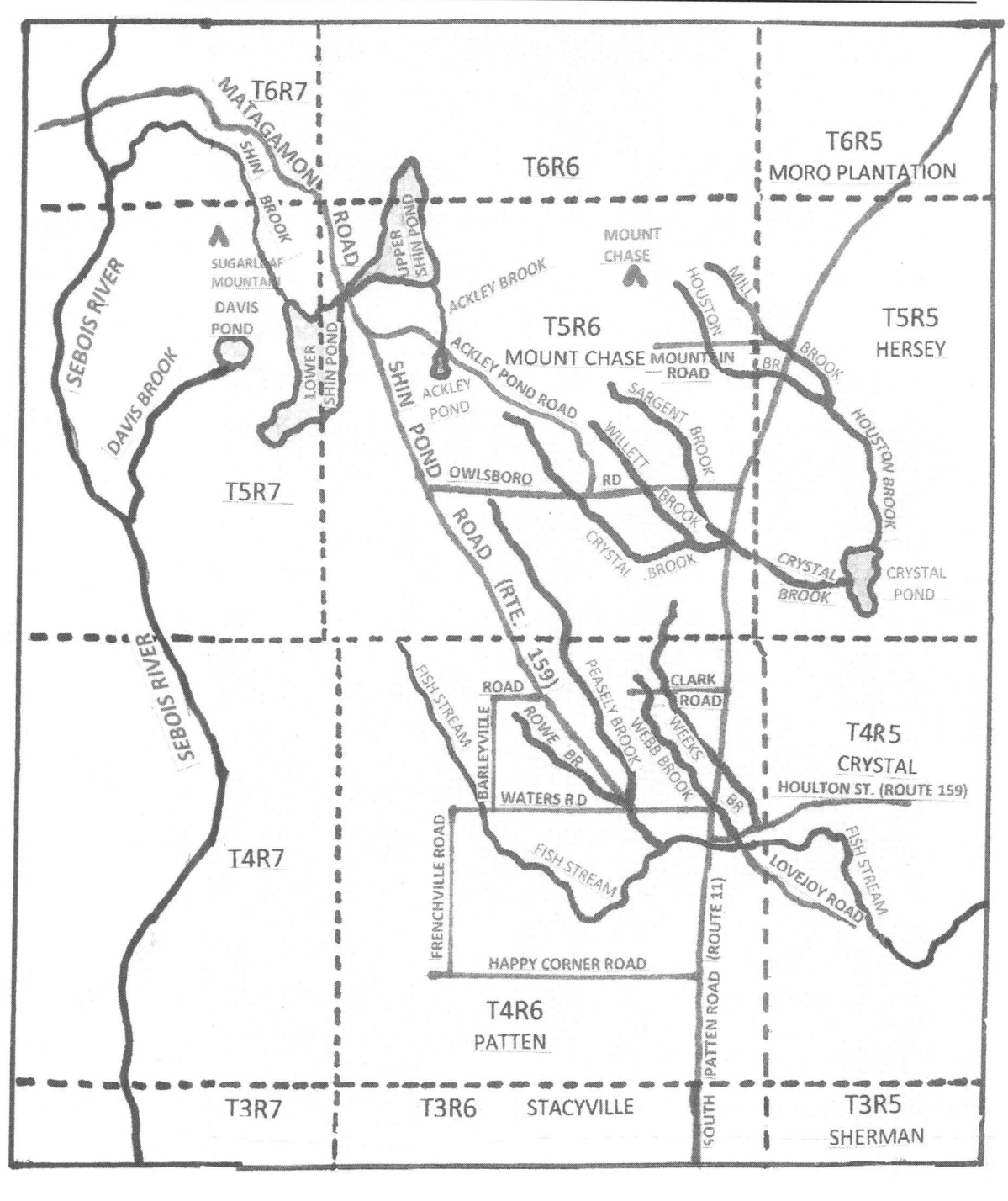

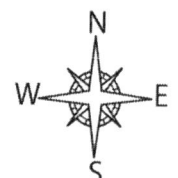

The largest bodies of water in the area are Upper and Lower Shin Pond, located in the northwestern corner of Mount Chase and in the unorganized territories of T6R6 and T5R7. Upper Shin Pond covers 544 acres and has a maximum depth of 64 feet. Lower Shin Pond covers 560 acres but is shallower, with its deepest point being 25 feet. They are connected by a narrow thoroughfare over which the Shin Pond Bridge was built. Ackley Pond, in Mount Chase on the east side of the Shin Pond Road, covers 19 acres and has a maximum depth of 5 feet. Davis Pond (also called Wapiti Pond) in T5R7 lies west of Lower Shin Pond, covers 58 acres, and has a maximum depth of 54 feet. The Gardner Point Road (just before the bridge) and the Black Point Road (about a mile beyond the bridge) are east of the Shin Pond Road, and the Wapiti Road (just beyond the bridge) and the Grondin Road (about four miles before the bridge) are west of the Shin Pond Road. There are many other roads as well which lead to camps on or away from the water.

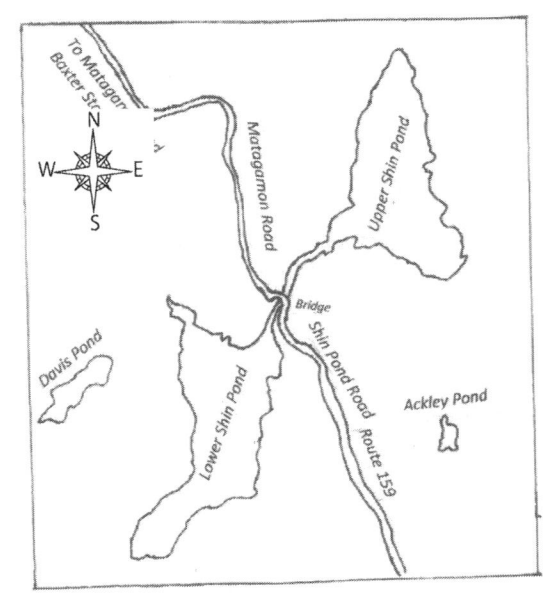

The photo at left shows the Shin Pond Bridge in the early 1900's.

The land around Patten and Mount Chase consists of forests and open fields, including farm land. From the lookout at the top of Ash Hill (about five miles south of Patten's Main Street), mountains can be seen to the west and north, including Mount Katahdin (elevation 5,269 feet), Traveler Mountain (elevation 3,540 feet), Trout Brook Mountain, Horse Mountain, Sugarloaf Mountain, Mount Chase (elevation 2,440 feet), and several smaller mountains east of Mount Chase. Looking east from the lookout, you can see the windmills in the community of Oakfield. Patten is 541 feet above sea level.

I took this picture of Mount Katahdin in March, 2009. Katahdin is usually snow-covered from October through May. The peaks of Katahdin (which include Baxter and Pamola) are accessible using several different trails; no matter which trail you take, it is considered a challenging climb.

This photo of Mount Chase as was taken by Sherri Skinner in 2006. It is titled *Mt. Chase Sunset from Upper Shin Pond*. Mount Chase is a moderately difficult climb; it can be done in a few hours. There was once a fire tower situated at the top of the mountain; this tower has been relocated to the Lumberman's Museum in Patten.

The climate of the Patten and Mount Chase area is considered *humid continental climate*. That means the summers are warm with an average high temperature in the 70s and a monthly average rainfall of close to four inches. The spring season can bring wide variations in weather, but gradually warming temperatures in March and April bring on a mud season as snow melts and the ground thaws. (Unfortunately, warmer weather in May also brings hordes of blackflies.) Summer days can be humid, and thunderstorms are not unusual. Autumn brings warm days with little humidity and cool nights, prompting a gorgeous display of fall foliage.

Winters are cold and snowy, with average temperatures in the 20's, although below zero temperatures are not unusual. The coldest recorded temperature in Patten in the last 100 years was -38° on January 20, 1994. On that day, Sherman froze at -48° and Island Falls chilled out at -56°! The ground freezes hard, and lakes and ponds in the area have enough ice to be considered safe for snowmobiling and ice fishing.

Snow may fall as early as October and as late as May; that means winters could conceivably be up to eight months long! (My grandmother even remembered it snowing at a Fourth of July parade in Sherman.) Snowfall amounts vary from winter to winter, but the average annual snowfall is around 92 inches. The highest recorded annual snowfall since 1916 was 156.5 inches in the winter of 1970-71, and the lowest since 1916 was 48.3 inches in 2005-2006. The largest recorded snowfall in one storm since 1916 was 37 inches, falling on the last day of December, 1962 and continuing into New Years Day, 1963. When I looked at snowfall records, I expected to see drastic changes over time, as it seems like we don't get as much snow now as we used to when I was a kid. I did not find that to be true; I think perhaps we just have better snow removal equipment now than we used to. Also, the road crews nowadays keep the ditches dug deep beside the roads—those ditches have to fill up before you see a snowbank. The photo at the right shows what Main Street in Patten looked like after a significant storm in the 1940s. You wouldn't see snow piled up like that on Main Street in modern times!

As in most small towns, the weather is probably the most common topic for casual conversation. In Patten and Mount Chase, people always complain about the heat and humidity in the summer, and the cold and snow in the winter. (Check out "another note" below for some weather that really did warrant lots of complaints.) In the spring, they add blackflies and mud to their complaints. But most locals enjoy the various challenges of the seasons. After all, you can always sit in front of a fan or go to Shin Pond in the summer, you can wear a sweatshirt or jacket in the fall, you can either bundle up or sit by the stove in the winter, and you can buy fly dope (known to outsiders as insect repellant) at any store. For most natives the assets of the natural environment makes living here a rewarding experience, well worth any aggravation the climate brings!

Note: see Insect Guide on page 12 for advice on dealing with insects that inhabit the Patten and Mount Chase area.

Another note: As I was researching weather patterns for Patten and Mount Chase, I came across the expressions *1800 and Froze to Death* and *The Year Without a Summer*. This sparked my interest, so I did a little more research and discovered that a major weather anomaly occurred in the years 1815 and 1816. In 1815, a colossal eruption of Mount Tambora, a volcano on Sumbawa Island in the Dutch East Indies (now Indonesia), spewed ashes 27 miles into the air. The eruption sheared the top off the mountain, killed all the vegetation on the island, wiped out villages on the island, caused a tsunami, and directly killed at least 10,000 people. Around 90,000 people in that region died later of starvation and disease. The volcanic cloud, which lingered in the atmosphere for several years, also affected many other parts of the world, including the New England states. During spring and summer of 1816, a dry, reddish-colored fog covered Maine, preventing sunlight from reaching the ground. As a result, winter weather continued on throughout the spring and summer months and into the fall. There was frost in every month, and snow in almost every month. There were disastrous crop failures, prompting many Mainers to emigrate to warmer climates. Similar situations occurred in many other places, including Ireland, Great Britain, Germany, and the Canadian Maritime provinces. There were no towns of Patten and Mount Chase in 1816, but they were probably still talking about the year without a summer twenty years later in downtown Patten.

The map on the next page shows Patten's streets. The chart below provides former or alternate names of roads and streets in Patten and Mount Chase.

ROAD	FORMERLY OR ALSO KNOWN AS	STREET	FORMERLY OR ALSO KNOWN AS
Route 11 north of Patten	North Road, Aroostook Road, Aroostook Scenic Highway	Main Street	Aroostook Road Route 11
Route 11 south of Patten	South Patten Road	Founders Street	School Street
Mountain Road	Lookout Road	Gardner Street	Cedar Street
Owlsboro Road	Allsbury Road*	Katahdin Street	Mechanic Street
Shin Pond Road	Matagamon Road, Shin Pond Tote Road, Waters Road (as far as Peavey Corner)	Dearborn Street	Fish Lane
Lovejoy Road	Extends to Cow Team Road, which goes through Crystal to Golden Ridge Rd. in Sherman	Houlton Street	Parsonage Street
Winding Hill Road or road at bottom of Bumpus Hill	Upper Crystal Road	?—Possibly the south end of Pleasant St.	Maple Street

*Allsbury Road may have been its intended name since a man named Charles Allsbury once ran a clapboard lathe mill near Sargent Brook on that road.

I took this photo with a view of Mount Chase from the top of Finch Hill. The smaller mountains east of Mount Chase are Bald, Davis, Long, and Pickett Mountains.

PATTEN'S STREETS

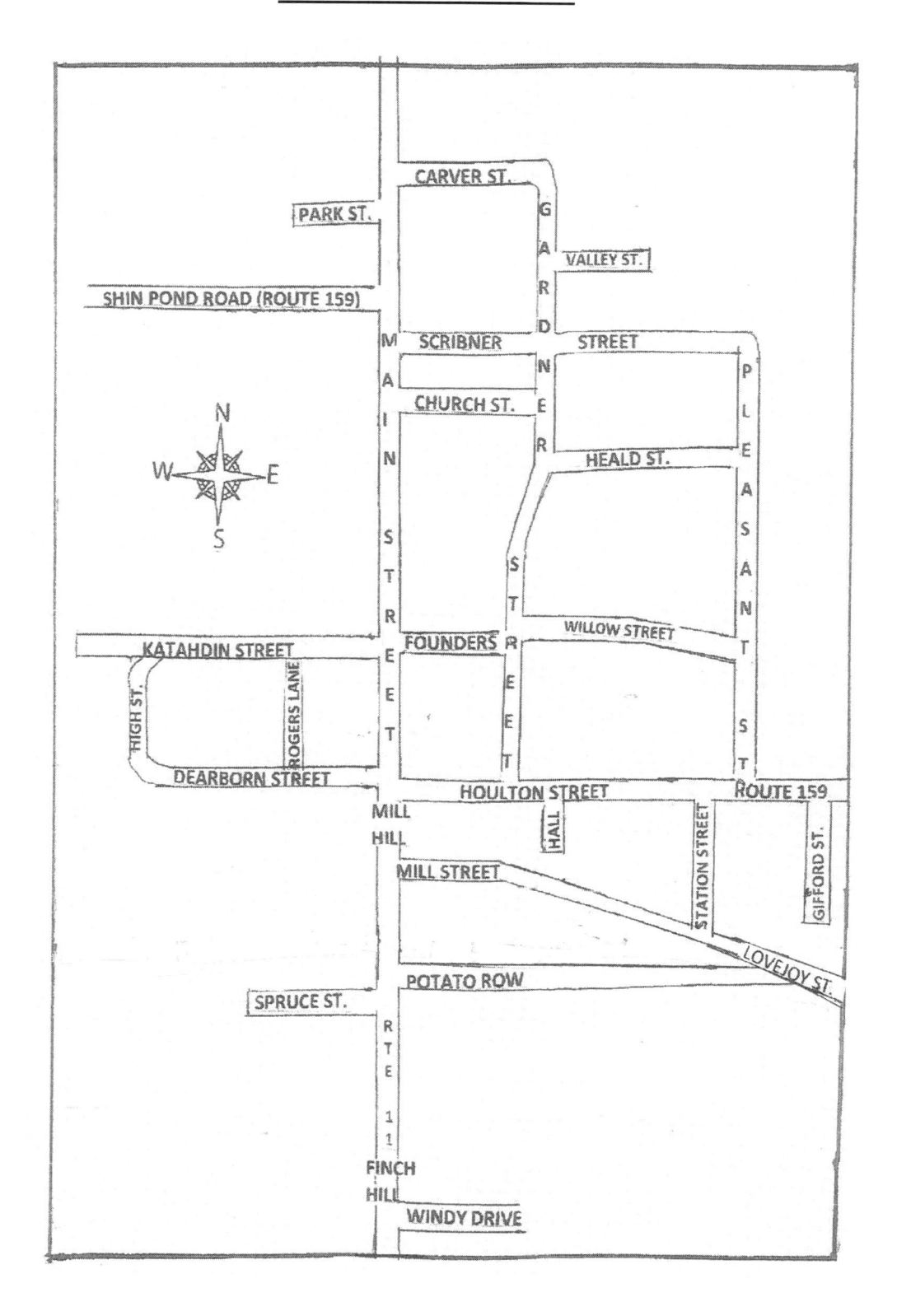

YOUR GUIDE TO DANGEROUS INSECTS IN PATTEN AND MOUNT CHASE

Warning: Size does not indicate the degree of hurt or havoc the insect can cause.

PHOTO ID	INSECT	HURT OR HAVOC	WHAT TO DO ABOUT IT
	Midge or mingie	Causes extreme itching, drives you crazy	Do not use lights after dark, sleep with all parts of body covered.
	blackfly	Swarms and overpowers you, bite causes bleeding, leaves blotch for days, itchy, drives you crazy	Do not go outside. Do not come to area in May, June, or July. Cover all parts of body. Secure pant legs with elastics. Use fly dope.
	mosquito	Leaves large bump, very itchy, makes an annoying whining sound, especially when trying to get to sleep, drives you crazy	Cover all parts of body. Don't go out after sunset or before 9:00 a.m. Slap to kill. Use fly dope.
	housefly	Appears when fly swatter is not handy, disappears when you have fly swatter in hand, drives you crazy	Carry fly swatter at all times, especially when sitting down. Doesn't do any good to keep windows closed—they breed everywhere.
	Horse fly, moose fly, deer fly	Bite causes huge itchy welt. Insect follows you around outdoors, everywhere you go, drives you crazy	See if you can outrun it. If you can't, slap fly hard enough to leave bruise (on yourself, not on fly).

CHAPTER TWO: THE TOWNS FROM 1828-1865

Americans often forget that the Native Americans were here first. The first humans to visit the Patten and Mount Chase area were the Wabanaki, specifically members of the Penobscot and Maliseet Tribes. The Maliseet reservation is in the Houlton area, and the Penobscot Reservation is located in Old Town, but in the times before white men arrived, the tribes moved around from season to season. They visited coastal areas for fishing and clamming, traveled up and down the rivers fishing, and used the Penobscot and other waterways to access forest areas for hunting. Many of the place names throughout Maine are Wabanaki words which describe a physical attribute of an area. For example, the word Katahdin comes from the Wabanaki word for "the greatest mountain." Penobscot means "where the rocks open out."

Thus we know that the Wabanakis were familiar with the area long before it was claimed by Massachusetts. As I mentioned in Chapter One, both Massachusetts and Maine (after 1820) sold the township/range parcels of land. Not all of the parcels sold developed into towns; many of them were purchased solely for logging operations. The areas west of Mount Chase had been opened up to logging in the early 1800s. Since that time, many of these parcels of land have been resold and relogged several times, but still remain unorganized territories.

Around 1828, Amos Patten of Bangor bought the section labeled Township 4 Range 6 for twenty cents an acre. Mr. Patten was considered one of those successful businessmen known as *lumber barons*. As early as 1805, he had been buying land for the purpose of logging it. Shortly after purchasing T4R6, Mr. Patten sent three men north to survey the land. In the spring of 1828, Eli Kellogg, Ira Dearborn Fish, and Samuel Wiggins travelled by canoe up the Penobscot to the Indian village of Mattawamkeag, and then up the Mattawamkeag River and Fish Stream to T4R6.

They proceeded to survey the area and prepare a report for Mr. Patten. The report stated that the purchase was made up of prime woodland and possible farmland and noted white pine trees standing 150-200 feet tall (worth a fortune, as Amos Patten would have known). The surveyors would have also discovered that Amos Patten may have gotten cheated on his purchase. Most of the Township/Range lots measured exactly six miles square, for a total of 23,000 acres. For some reason, T4R6 fell short of being six miles square and only had 22,400 acres. Mount Chase, however, has 37.73 square miles and more than 23,000 acres.

Still, the surveyors must have been very impressed with the tract of land, since they accepted ownership of lots within T4R6 as payment for their services. Before returning to Bangor for the winter, they hired David Lowe and Jonathan Clay to help them clear land. They returned in 1829 and built the first homes in T4R6.

The photo at left shows Ira and Abra Fish. He died in 1872 at the age of 82. He would have been about 38 years old when he first came to T4R6. He was a town leader and was known as "Squire Fish." He served in the State Legislature at one point.

The photo at right shows Eli and Fanny Kellogg. He died in 1886 at the age of 73. That makes him only 15 years old when he first came to T4R6.

The photo at left shows Samuel Wiggins. He died in 1875 at the age of 76, making him 29 years old in 1828.

All three surveyors are buried in the Patten cemetery along with their wives and other family members.

The word pioneer has most often been applied to those people who settled the American West, but the first settlers of T4R6 and T5R6 were truly pioneers as well. This area was little more than wilderness in the early 1800s. The first settlers arrived here on foot or on horseback, with only the most basic of belongings. They then had to build a cabin for themselves and outbuildings for livestock. They had to prepare the soil and plant a garden, not an easy task when contending with all those trees and Maine's rocky soil. The first year they probably burned some of the trees and planted around tree stumps, using ashes as fertilizer. They supplemented garden crops with wild game and what they could gather, including berries and fiddleheads. Water had to be lugged and firewood had to be cut and toted. The winter weather was unforgiving, making every task even more difficult. Supplies were hauled in from downstate, and if a family hadn't stocked enough supplies for the long winter, they went without. Spring brought mud and blackflies. Planting summer crops was a guessing game: they had to be planted after the last frost but early enough to mature throughout the short growing season. Life was very basic—no schools, no churches, no social organizations. There was no doctor to treat their illnesses and injuries, and there was little communication with the outside world.

Evidently the first settlers were a hardy lot, though, because the community grew and even thrived. As I noted in the introduction, the word community implies more than a group of houses built in close proximity. A community is really a collection of people with similar goals and interests. I also stated that the residents of T4R6 quickly established that they wanted a real community, with businesses, schools, and churches. Some important events during these developing years are as follows.

1830: A spotted trail called the Aroostook Trail was blazed through the woods between Mattawamkeag and T4R6, and other settlers soon arrived in T4R6.

Andrew Jackson was the president of the United States, and Jonathan Hunton was the governor of Maine.

1831: A grist mill was built at the foot of Mill Hill, along Fish Stream.

Samuel Smith was governor of Maine from 1831-1834.

1832: Ira Dearborn Fish built a home on Fish Lane (now Dearborn Street; photo at right). He later built three large barns on his property. This home still exists and is part of another home which stands on Dearborn Street. (At one time, Laurel "Pop" Johnson owned this home.) Ira and his wife Abra had three children: Ira D., Charles, and Luisa. Patten was at this time referred to as Fish's Township, Fish's Village, or Fish's Mills.

1833: David Haynes established a lumber and floor business. He bought the property on which the Bradford house now stands. By 1840, he had built a barn on this property. The family of William Leslie settled in T4R6.

1834: Henry and Ellen (Cushman) Blake (photos at left) and their two children moved to T4R6. Ellen was the first woman to settle in Patten. She rode a horse to get here.

Robert Dunlap was the governor of Maine.

Jonathan Palmer built the first framed house. It was located on the south corner of Main and Dearborn Streets. Jonathan's wife died just before he moved to Patten, but he raised his large family in Patten, including three sons and a daughter who married four siblings from the Darling family. His daughter Amanda is mentioned on page 18.

1835: Captain Samuel Chase Leslie of Lincoln, son of William and Mary Leslie, built a sawmill/gristmill for Ira D. Fish. Mr. Leslie also owned one of Patten's first taverns. (Note: My resources spelled Mr. Leslie's last name with one *s*, but I noticed in my cemetery wanderings that his headstone spelled his last name *Lesslie*. I'm going to stick with the one *s* version. You can read more about the Leslie family at the end of Chapter Four.)

1835, cont.: New names in town included Andrew Grant, Daniel Whitehouse, John Carpenter, and Henry Pike Buzzell, Sr. Mr. Buzzell and his wife Comfort (nee Frost) had twelve children. Their first eight children were born in Middleton, New Hampshire, and the next three were born in Lincoln, Maine. Their last child, Eliza, was born on June 16, 1835 in Patten, making her the first child to be born in Patten. (Another resource puts her birth year at 1830.) Eliza later married Alfred Gates and spent the rest of her life in Lincoln Center. Henry and Comfort Buzzell's son Samuel died in Patten in 1838 at the age of fourteen, and their son Henry Pike Buzzell, Jr., married Emily Myrick, daughter of Thomas Myrick (who was Mount Chase's first settler). Henry and Emily, who were the first couple to be married in Patten, were living in Patten in 1850 and in Sherman in 1870.

1836: The Blakes added to the population when their son Ezra (photo at left) became the first male baby born in T4R6. Their older son, Levi is pictured at right. He married Samuel Leslie's daughter, Mary.

Calvin and Kesiah Bradford moved to Moro from Turner, ME and opened an inn. A much improved road called the Aroostook Road connected the area to other communities in Maine and made it easier to travel and transport supplies into the area. By now, David Haynes was operating the first stage between Mattawamkeag and T4R6. After his death James Hill, then Laing and Jones operated the stage.

1837: The Baptists had begun to meet for worship. Henry Blake built a brick kiln. This was the first manufacturing industry in Patten.

A special Maine census included these names of Patten residents in addition to those I have already mentioned: M.M. Eveleth, Joseph Hersey, Isaac Lewis, David Leavitt, Sylvanus Leslie, Ichabod Morrill, Jacob Perley, J.M. Page, Samuel Robbins, Oliver Robinson, H.Y. Twombley, and Abner Weeks. The population of Patten in 1837 was 114. Included in the census count were 11 members of the Jonathan Palmer household.

1837, cont.: The earliest settlers in Mount Chase arrived. They were Thomas Myrick and Hartson Weeks. They were soon followed by Ezra Myrick, Francis Weeks, John Crommett, John Fish, and David Bumpus. Mr. Bumpus settled on what is now called Bumpus Hill. The Myricks also settled on the North Road; in later years the Mount Chase school in that area was named Myrick School and the cemetery was called the Myrick Cemetery. You can read more about the Myrick and Fish families at the end of Chapter Four.

Martin Van Buren was the president of the United States from 1837-1841.

1838: By 1838, the residents of T4R6 had formed a Methodist Society.

The residents had hired a school teacher, Miss Amanda (or May or Mary) Palmer (photo at right). A one-room schoolhouse was built on the North Road on the site where the cemetery now exists. Miss Palmer was the daughter of Jonathan Palmer; she married Solomon Read and died in North Chesterville.

The Bloodless Aroostook War took place between 1838 and 1842. About 500 soldiers camped at the corner of Main and Houlton Streets during 1838-1839. Men from Patten who were involved in this event were Ephraim Bailey, George Buzzell, John Carpenter, John Carpenter, Jr., Sewall Jackman, and A.G. Baker. You can read more about this strange war in Chapter Fifteen.

Edward Kent was the governor of Maine from 1838-1839.

1839: On October 5, 1839, Reverend John Gilman Pingree (photo at left) was appointed as the community's first circuit preacher. He rode into Patten on October 12 to hold the first official Methodist church service in Elbridge Stetson's cabin.

Rhoda Freeman Rigby passed away along with her two daughters, Irena and Mary. She was the wife of George Rigby and was 37 years old. Her daughters were three and 11. This was the first burial in the Patten Cemetery; their gravestone is located in the northeast corner of the cemetery.

John Fairfield was the governor of Maine from 1839-1841.

1840: The Congregationalists began to meet for worship.

Calvin and Kesiah Bradford became parents of a son named Calvin.

Jacob Frye showed up in Patten with a peddler's wagon and wound up becoming a prominent businessman in town; among other accomplishments which will be mentioned later, he built a hotel and had a machine shop with Samuel Darling. At some point before 1860, he bought the property later called the Bradford Farm and the lots on both sides of this property.

By 1840-41: Businesses in Patten included a general store owned by Ephraim Fairfield (located where the bank is now), another general store owned by John Gardner (on the south corner of what are Main and Founders Street), two taverns (owned by Captain Samuel Leslie and Ichabod Morrill), two blacksmiths (one was Ichabod Morrill, and the other may have been John Twitchell), a tailor, and a tannery. Dr. Luther Rogers had opened a doctor's office on the north corner of Founders and Main Streets, and Minerva True had opened a millinery shop on the corner where Patten Drug is now. A sheriff had been hired to keep the peace, and Horace Miles was the town cordwainer (shoemaker). Town meetings were held in Ichabod Morrill's tavern. One resource stated that the Gardner and Stetson store was located on the Steve Caro lot. She may have been referring to the S. Carreau lot shown on the map on page 56. The resource also said Joseph Heald had a building, later occupied by Irving Bragg, behind Minerva True's.

Ichabod Morrill   Dr. Luther Rogers

Minerva True    Horace Miles

1839-1841: New settlers included S. Waters, Amasa Parker, John Twitchell, and Joseph Hasey. Mr. and Mrs. Oliver Blackwell were the first settlers on the Happy Corner Road. Elbridge Gerry Stetson and his wife Electa had built a house, and Mr. Stetson had opened a store with Mr. Gardner. He later operated the store on his own for six or seven years before becoming a farmer. Dr. Luther Rogers and his wife became parents of a son named Luther Bailey Rogers.

The Happy Corner Road School was taught by Mr. A. G. Baker, a "veteran" of the Bloodless Aroostook War. In her history of Patten, Mrs. Juanita Bates wrote that the Happy Corner Road was so named because Mr. Baker and two friends (Mr. Page and Mr. Coburn) formed a trio of merry musicians.

Samuel and Hannah Darling had eleven children, including Horatio Nelson Darling and three daughters who married Palmers from Patten. You can read more about the Darling family at the end of Chapter Four.

Eli Kellogg and his wife Fanny Coburn Jameson were helping Patten's population grow as well. They had at least eight children, including Sarah Jane, Nathan Putnam, Adaline Hazen (who married Ephraim Bailey), Esther Leslie, Elvira (who married Captain Charles Perry), Marcellus Reed (who was wounded and presumed dead during the Civil War), Horace, and Winfield Scott. Winfield (or W.S., in the fashion of men using their initials instead of their first names) married Emma Jewell, then John Gardner's daughter Almy. W.S. was a Patten success story. He was active in Patten government and business, was a prominent Penobscot County lumberman, and served in the Maine Senate.

The governorship of Maine was in a constant state of change. John Fairfield resigned in 1841 and was replaced by Richard Vose (acting governor) then Edward Kent. In 1842, James Fairfield came back and served until 1843. On the national scene, William Henry Harrison died in 1841 during his first year as president of the United States. He was replaced by John Tyler, who served from 1841-1845.

The first settlers of Patten established early on a town government of sorts. (Naturally, women could not be considered voters, but one can imagine that these hardy females would make their opinions heard in other ways!) By 1840, there were 82 registered voters in T4R6, and the decision was made to apply to the Court of County Commissioners for T4R6 to be made a plantation. John Biddeford and Lorenzo Wadlin headed up a committee to submit the application.

I was very excited to find a piece of Patten's history at the town office. It was a set of papers, folded into thirds, with this written on the outside: Petition to County Commissioners to organize No. 4 Plantation into a town—1840. However, the beautifully handwritten document inside seems instead to be a letter informing the residents of T4R6 that their application to the state to become a plantation had been approved, and Mr. Wadlin and Mr. Biddeford were instructed to issue a warrant for a plantation meeting to be held for the purpose of electing a clerk and three assessors. Still pretty exciting news for T4R6! You can see a section of the handwritten application on this page and a typed version of the whole document on the next two pages.

-20-

State of Maine

Penobscot Co.

To Lorenzo Wadlin of Township No. 4 in the sixth range of townships west from the East line of the State   Greeting~

Whereas John Biddeford, Lorenzo Wadlin, and five other inhabitants of said township by their application in writing represent that their situation is such, being distant upward of forty miles from any town or organised plantation by any passable roads, that it is extremely inconvenient and expensive for them to attend the elections, that they are desirous of enjoying in common with other citizens of the State the privilege of voting for public officers and asking to be organised as a plantation. This petition was entered at the April term of the Court of County Commissioners for said county A.D. 1840 when it was ordered by said Court that the Petitioners give public notice to all interested to appear at the then next August term of said Court to shew cause if any they had why the prayer of said Petitioners should not be granted. And that said Petitioners cause their petition with the order of notice thereon to be published in a Newspaper printed in Bangor in said County three weeks successively: the last publication to be two weeks at least before the then next session of said Court and said Petition was thence continued to said August term and it appearing to the Court that said notice had been given as was ordered and no person appearing to shew cause why said Plantation should not be organised, said Court of County Commissioners organised the Inhabitants of said Township No. 4 within the territorial limits of the same and granted a warrant to said Lorenzo Wadlin one of said Petitioners, authorizing him to call the first meeting of said Inhabitants. You will therefore as soon as may be all in manner prescribed by law said first meeting for the purpose of choosing plantation officers and transacting such other business as Plantations in this State are allowed to do agreeably to the 275th Chapter of the laws of this State passed March 25, 1837.

Witness Frederick A. Fuller, Esquire, at Bangor this fifth day of August in the year of our Lord one thousand eight hundred and forty.

Charles Stetson, Clerk

Pursuant to the above warrant, the inhabitants of Township 4 such as are legal voters are hereby notified and warned to meet at the tavern of I. Morrill on Thursday the 20th day of August ...at 2 o'clock in the afternoon to act on the following business
> 1) *To choose a moderator to govern said meeting*
> 2) *To choose a plantation clerk*
> 3) *To choose three assessors*

Given under my hand at No. 4
the 11th day of August A.D. 1840.
Lorenzo Wadlin

Agreeable to the within warrant I have notified the Inhabitants of said Plantation according to Law to meet at the time and place and to act on the business therein warned. August 20th, 1840

Lorenzo Wadlin

So T4R6 was officially a plantation, probably known informally as Fish's Village, Fish's Township, or Fish's Mills at the time. This was only a preliminary step, however. The real goal of the community was to be founded as a town. Immediately after becoming a plantation, a petition was submitted to the state to set this procedure in motion.

Finally, on April 16, 1841, T4R6 became a town! The citizens named their community *Patten* in honor of the original owner of the land, Amos Patten (in picture at right). The first order of business was to elect town officials. E.C. Fairfield was appointed as town clerk, James Mitchell as treasurer, and Henry Blake, Jacob Perley, and H.N. Darling as selectmen (or assessors, as they were often called).

Thirteen years. That doesn't seem like a very long time for a clearing in the wilderness to become an established community. Think of the changes Patten's citizens saw and experienced during those years as Main Street developed, mills were built, and neighborhoods came into being. Their children now attended school, and politics and religion brought the citizens together with common interests and goals. And that's what a community is.

Now let's see what the latest news was in the *town* of Patten.

1842: The home that is now the Bradford House was built on the property owned by David Haynes, then Jacob Frye. One resource stated that Joshua Goodwin built the buildings on this property; if so, he was the carpenter who built them, not the owner of the property... yet.

The first Patten House was built and was operated by Mr. and Mrs. Lucius Hackett. Some resources also mention Charles Lucius Hackett as owner; they could be one and the same, father and son, or brothers.

Elder Elia McGregor, a missionary from the Maine Baptist Board, was preaching to the Baptists at the home of James Mitchell on the North Road. This home was later owned by a Drew family, Fred and Amy Curtis, Vivian and Mildred Grant, and Christine (Grant) and Donald Shorey.

1843: A new schoolhouse was built. It was on Finch Hill and was taught by Miss Cushman.

Samuel Darling (photo at left) was the first furniture maker. He also made cabinets, blinds, doors, and sashes.

1843-1844: Edward Kavanaugh was governor of Maine from 1843-1844. David Dunn and John W. Dana served briefly in 1844. Hugh J. Anderson served as governor from 1844-1847.

1844: Jerome Frye (photo at right) was the first undertaker in Patten. Jerome was the brother of Jacob Frye; their parents, Timothy and Rachel Frye, lived in New Hampshire, then Weld, Maine.

1845: Samuel E. Benjamin (photo at left; from *History of Patten Academy*) was the first lawyer in Patten. His office was on the lot that is now the Patten Community Playground. His son Charles was later a teacher and principal at Patten Academy before going on to be a college professor and an author of engineering textbooks.

1845, cont.: William Jackman built a home on Willow Street that was later owned by Fred Quint. You can read more about Mr. Jackman at the end of this chapter.

The Baptist Church was completed. This building still stands as the Veteran's Memorial Library; it is the oldest public building in Patten. You can read more about this building in Chapters Ten and Twelve.

A Social Library had been formed.

James K. Polk was president of the United States from 1845-1849.

1846: The house on Main Street that was owned through the years by Ira Fish, S. Carpenter, Laroy & Althea Miles, Frank & Cecilia (Miles) Allen, Frederick & Priscilla (Allen) Newcomb, and Al & Cecily (Newcomb) MacKinnon was built.

John Gardner (photo at left from *History of Patten Academy*) served as the representative from Patten in the Maine House of Representatives.

The Penobscot Log Driving Company was established.

1847: The Trustees of Patten Academy were incorporated by decree of Governor John. W. Dana.

John W. Dana returned as governor of Maine and served until 1850.

1848: In September, Patten Academy officially opened. You can read more about Patten Academy in Chapter Ten.

1848, cont.: Oliver Cobb was the first harness maker in Patten. He opened a shop on Main Street (photo at right). I found Oliver and Lucy Cobb's headstone at the cemetery. It also had the name of their daughter Myrtie on it; she died at age four.

1849: The California Gold Rush inspired men from all parts of the United States to leave home and head west to strike it rich. One of those men was Greenleaf "Hunter" Davis of Lincoln, who returned from the Gold Rush to become known as the Hermit of Shin Pond. You can read more about Mr. Davis in Chapter Sixteen.

Silas Coburn (photo at left) decided to harness his cows to use in place of oxen. And that's how the Cow Team Road got its name!

Zachary Taylor served as president of the United States from 1849-1850, when he died in office.

1850: Joe Heald built a grist mill on Ellis Brook (now called Webb Brook). Robert Finch drove the first four-horse team into Patten. And that's how Finch Hill got its name!

The population of Patten was 470.

John Hubbard served as governor of Maine from 1850-1853. Millard Fillmore took over the presidency after Zachary Taylor's death and served until 1853.

1851: The house on Main Street that is now the home of the Patten Historical Society was built. It was owned through the years by John & Mary Gardner, Halbert & Cora (Chapman) Robinson, Charles Vaughn & Dove (Soule) Chapman, Bill & Helen (Chapman) Garton, and Ervin & Dawn (Hotham) Tower.

1852-1858: New names in Patten include Daniel Whitehouse, Zenas Littlefield, Samuel Reed, David Cook, and Alonzo Wadlin. John Hammond came from a family of sixteen children; he married Jeannette Cushman and they had seven daughters: Susan, Dora, Adna, Mary, Florence, Nettie, and Eda. Mr. Hammond became one of Patten's most successful farmers and lumbermen. Batchelder Hussey Huston (photo at far right) came from Pittsfield, Maine, and married Lucetta Drew (photo at near right) of Patten. You can read more about the Huston family at the end of Chapter Four.

1852: The *Annual Maine Register* reported that John Gardner was the civil officer and sheriff. Justices included Samuel E. Benjamin, America T. Coburn, Horatio Darling, Samuel F. Gilson, David Haynes, James S. Mitchell (photo at left, from *A History of Patten Academy*), and Ebenezer Jackman. David Haynes was the coroner. Patten had 112 polls (people eligible to vote) and was valued at $46,447.00. The average number of pupils at Patten Academy was 60.

In the outside world, the closest post office was in Mattawamkeag, telegraph lines reached to Bangor, and the railroad had been extended to Old Town.

1853: David and Mary Bumpus of Mount Chase lost their son David, Jr., age four, and their daughter Mary, age two, just one day apart in July of 1853. I found their headstone in the Route 11 cemetery in Mount Chase.

Samuel E. Benjamin of Patten served in the Maine House of Representatives.

William G. Crosby served as governor of Maine from 1853-1855, and Franklin Pierce of New Hampshire was president of the United States from 1853-1857.

1854: The Methodist Parsonage was built. Jacob Frye was operating a hotel and Frye's Tavern. It was interesting that the town always had religion and always had taverns, although eventually religion trumped taverns. Prohibition in 1920-1933 may have had something to do with that.

1855: Jacob Frye opened a cheese factory which was located on the site where Patten Academy Alumni Park now exists.

Anson P. Morrill was the governor of Maine from 1855-1856.

1856: The Patten Rifle Company was established. This was a militia group called Company D, and it was attached to the 1st Regiment, 1st brigade, 9th Division. They met at Frye's Inn with Ichabod Morrill serving as the captain. They disbanded in 1861, when most of the militia men enlisted to fight in the Civil War.

Bela Chesley of Patten served in the Maine House of Representatives.

The *Annual Maine Register* for 1856 reported that blacksmiths in town were Ichabod Morrill, J. W. Bartlett, and Henry Perry. Horace Miles and George Hamilton were manufacturing boots and shoes. Joseph Heald was the postmaster and also had a grist mill. Ephraim H. Hall was a tinsmith, and Samuel Darling, Jr., William Jackman, and Sylvester J. Leslie (son of Samuel and Elizabeth Leslie) were carpenters. Jerome Frye, Gardner and Coburn, William Jackman, and E.G. Stetson had established "country stores." Jacob Frye and Paul Peavey operated "public houses." Frye and Peavey owned side-by-side lots on Main Street.

1857-1858: James Buchanan served as president of the United States from 1857-1861. Maine governors during this time were Samuel Wells, Hannibal Hamlin, and Joseph Williams. Lot M. Morrill served as governor from 1858-1861.

1858: The town of Sherman was incorporated. It was previously called Golden Ridge.

1858 & 1859: Patten hosted the annual exhibit for the Penobscot and Aroostook Union Agricultural Society, which had been established with Sherman in 1852 as a division of the Maine Board of Agriculture. You can read more about the exhibition and the agricultural societies in Chapter Fifteen.

By 1859: Robert Finch owned a house on the south corner of the Shin Pond Road and Main Street.

1859-60: Ira Fish of Patten served in the Maine House of Representatives.

The Masons were established in Patten as Katahdin Lodge #98.

1860: A newspaper called *The Voice* was published jointly by the communities of Patten and Sherman.

T5R6 to the north of Patten was known as Monterey Plantation and had a population of 250. The population of Patten was 639.

1861-1865: The Civil War was fought. See more about the war and Patten's soldiers at the end of this chapter.

1861: A mail coach now helped Patten citizens establish better communications with the outside world. One of the first postmasters of Patten was Joseph Heald. Mary (Stetson) and Calvin Bradford were also postmasters and owners of a tinware shop. The post office and the tinware shop were both located on Main Street.

Israel Washburn was the governor of Maine from 1861-1863. Abraham Lincoln began his presidency in 1861.

1862: Monterey Plantation became Mount Chase Plantation.

Samuel Darling, Junior, of Patten served in the Maine House of Representatives.

1863: The Scribner House on Main Street was built by Jerome Frye.

Abner Coburn was the governor of Maine from 1863-1864, when he was replaced by Samuel Cony.

1864: Charles Quincy built a store on Main Street. It burned in 1892.

Here is a sad but true story about an event that took place in our area of Maine in 1826. The story, written by Winthrop Packard, was first published in *The Boston Transcript*, and later appeared in a magazine called *the Thresherman's Review*. You will understand the significance of the article as you read on. By the way, I first heard of this incident from Irene Olsen Bradford many years ago.

AN ACCIDENTAL OFFICIAL FOREST FIRE

One of the worse fires that Maine ever saw was set, years ago, by the hand of authority, paradoxically, in an attempt to save the timber. It is known in folk lore as the "Great State Bonfire of 1826." At that time all the forests were owned by the state and the valuable pumpkin pine region up around Sebois was the favorite resort of timber thieves who went in in the spring, cut and stacked vast quantities of hay from the meadows, and used it to feed their oxen during the winter while they helped themselves to the splendid timber. The state authorities sought to stop this thievery and sent Jim Chase, a timber looker and a man supposed to be wise in woodcraft, one dry August, to burn this hay and thus block the timber pirates. Jim reached the meadows in safety, touched a match to the stacks, and sat down to smoke and muse on how easily he had outwitted the thieves and saved the timber. The stacks burned splendidly, and so did the neighboring forests, which were lighted for miles by flying embers. The wind increased and veered, and it was but a brief half hour before this authorized incendiary was fleeing wildly with the frantic denizens of the wood, in a desperate attempt to save their lives. The flames leaped hither and thither. Now with blistered face and shriveled boots, he plunged through scorching embers and choking smoke, again gained a stretch of forest yet untouched, but always fleeing toward his one point of safety, a bare slate peak half a dozen miles to the south. Strange was the companionship of that wild journey. Bear, deer, moose, everything that could run, fly, or crawl fled with him, driven by the blaze that Jim Chase had kindled in the name of the state of Maine. At last, bleeding, blistered, blazing, he sank exhausted on the great rock pinnacle which goes to this day by the name of Mount Chase. For two weeks, Jim dwelt on this bare hill, living as best he might while the woods burned in an ever widening circle of fire all about him.

On the fifteenth night, a heavy rain fell and he was able to traverse the burned and blackened hills and valleys back to Bangor. "Did you burn the hay?" asked the state agent. "Hay?" said Jim. "Gosh-a-mighty! I burnt the hay, and the woods and the ground and every living critter in 'em, and if Moosehead Lake ain't afire now, it ain't my fault."

It was found afterward that Jim's official fire had burned over five townships entire and parts of six others, a total of nearly two hundred square miles covered with the finest timber that ever grew. If the timber pirates of Sebois had been allowed to cut steadily from that day to this they could not have done half the damage that had come from this vigorous but ill-advised attempt to drive them out. That was Maine's last state bonfire.

So that's how Mount Chase the mountain got its name and how Mount Chase the town got its name, and maybe that's how Hay Lake got its name!

1864: So after Jim Chase survived the fire, and settlers moved in, and they became a plantation, Mount Chase was finally incorporated as the 415th town in Maine in 1864.

Some of the names of the families who lived in Mount Chase during those years were Bither, Bumpus, Buxton, Carver, Conant, Connor, Cooper, Darling, Davis, Elwell, Fish (no relation to Ira Fish of Patten, even though this one's name was also Ira), Getchell, Glidden, Hall, Harrison, Harvey, Hatt, Kimball, Laughton/Lawton, Libby, Lord, Myrick, Noyes, Osgood, Phelps, Purvis, Rhodes, Rider/Ryder, Sargent, Shaw, Sibley, Smith, Steen, Webster, Weeks, and Wescott. Mr. Bumpus boarded a school teacher at his home.

I mentioned earlier that Mount Chase's development was different in some ways from Patten's development. Perhaps it was because Patten was already an established settlement by the time Mount Chase's first permanent residents arrived. It might be due in part to the way Mount Chase has three almost separate parts: the north road, the Owlsboro Road, and Shin Pond. It may be because Mount Chase never had an industry that employed a significant number of people. Whatever the cause, Mount Chase never did develop a Main Street area like Patten did. But Mount Chase could and still can be called a community, since its residents had and still have similar goals and interests. And from a broader perspective, over the years Mount Chase and Patten have really become one community with two parts which complement each other.

1864, cont.: In 1864, a list of names of men from Patten who were eligible for military duty was made. The list included 48 names of men between the ages of 19 and 44, including Samuel Benjamin, Ezra and Levi Blake, Albion and Calvin Bradford, three Carpenters (Clinton, Albion, and Simeon), William Chase, Joseph and Moses Clark, America Coburn, Albert Farewell, Charles and Ira Fish (Jr.), William Gifford, Hiram and Andrew Grant, James Guptill, Joseph Hall, Ephraim Hall, John Hammond, Joseph Hunt, Ephraim and Edmund Joy, James and Sylvester Leslie, John McKenney, four Mitchells (William, Jonathan, Roscoe, and John), Eli and Joel Morrill, Hiram Neal, Charles Palmer, James Parker, Paul Peavey, Leverett Peters, Annis Potter, Benjamin Reed, B. H. Ricker, Lorain Stanford, John Twitchell, William Waters, Nathan Weymouth, and Benjamin and Henry Whitehouse. Since the Civil War was over in 1865, this list doesn't include most of the young men who served in the Union Army. However, you can see some of the family names of people who lived in Patten at that time; by this time, some second-generation residents had reached adulthood.

1865: Samuel Leslie's mill closed.

The Congregational Church was built. The first minister was E.G. Carpenter. This building later became the Grange Hall and then a community center. It was located on the site where the Bartlett's Lodge building now stands on the corner of Church Street and Main Street.

We will end this era in the history of Patten and Mount Chase with an event that no doubt shocked and saddened the citizens. In 1865, just a few days after the conclusion of the War which accomplished his goal of ending slavery, President Abraham Lincoln was assassinated.

The Civil War had been fought for the best of reasons, but it was very costly in terms of human life and suffering, especially for the Southern States. In total 620,000 lives were lost, an average of 504 deaths per day or about 2.5% of the American population at the time. While the death toll from battle fatalities was high, even more soldiers died of typhoid fever and dysentery caused by unsanitary conditions. Around 110,000 fatalities were from the northern states. Of the northern states, Maine soldiers accounted for the highest proportion to population of soldiers; with its first 10,000 enlistees, it formed 31 infantry regiments, 3 cavalry regiments, and a heavy artillery regiment, besides some sailors and sharpshooters and other special units. An additional 63,000 men enlisted at later dates. Around 9,400 Maine men died in the war. Patten and Mount Chase sent off more than their fair share of soldiers: around 177 men (20% of the population) enlisted to fight with the Union soldiers against the evils of slavery. Thirty-five did not return.

The Civil War military was different from today's military in several ways.
- Most civilians joined the army in groups. For example, the first wave of volunteers from Patten all wound up serving in the same company and regiment of the Maine Volunteers. (The term *Maine Volunteers* means the regiment was formed as a response to war; the opposite was *Regular* Army, meaning a regiment that was already in place before the war began.)
- The draft was enacted in the Confederate States in 1862 and in the Northern States in March 1863. It was the first time the draft was used in the United States. The Enrollment Act, as it was called, was passed by Congress to recruit more soldiers for the war effort. You were eligible for draft if you were 20-45 years old and in good health. It was possible to pay someone to be your *substitute*, or you could pay the government $300.00 to get out of going off to war. Some wily fellows became *career jumpers*. They would get paid to be someone's substitute, get assigned to a unit, then desert before going into battle. Then they would repeat the process as many times as they could get away with it.

- Deserters were dealt with very harshly, usually in one or more of three ways: court martial, execution, or branding (in which an initial—C for coward, D for deserter, etc.—was branded into the soldier's forehead with a tattoo or branding iron). Execution was usually by a firing squad. It was public so that other soldiers would not be tempted to desert. In some cases, if there was a specific reason for desertion, leniency might prevail.
- The enlistees were often married men with families and many were older than privates are today.
- Your chances of survival in a prisoner-of-war camp were slim, as death from illness, starvation, or battle wounds was a distinct possibility.
- There was no standard tour-of-duty. Many of the soldiers stayed in the army until they died, were wounded too badly to fight any more, or mustered out at the end of the war.
- A soldier might have the rank of *farrier*, *wagoner*, *musician*, or *bugler* rather than private or a higher office.
- Many of the men from Patten were killed near the end of the war, in battles in Winchester and Cold Harbor, Virginia.
- It wasn't unusual for several brothers to be off fighting at the same time, often in the same company and regiment. And of course, there were some brothers who fought on opposite sides.

Three men from Patten with the last name Bigger went off to war, but only one came back. Alexander and Ebenezer both died in 1864, while Archibald survived the war.

Charles Wescott of Patten lost two older half-brothers in the conflict. Daniel Wescott died of disease, and John Wescott died of wounds received in battle. Another brother, William, was due to be mustered in but the war ended; tragically, he later drowned in Matagamon Lake.

Jemima (Scribner) and Lorenzo Wadlin of Patten sacrificed two sons to the war. Loammi Hooper Wadlin, died at Cold Harbor in 1864. He was 17 years old and a member of Company H, 31st Regiment, Maine Volunteers. His brother, Private Ira Fish Wadlin, age 21, died Sept. 9, 1864, of disease in New Orleans. He was a member of Co. A, 2nd ME Cavalry. Both young men are buried in the Patten Cemetery. Jemima's sister Hannah lost her husband, John Troop, at Cold Harbor also.

Unbelievably, there was yet another Civil War fatality for the Scribner family. Jemima and Hannah's nephew, Miles Sampson Scribner, died in Washington, D.C. in 1864. He served with the 8th Regiment Infantry. Miles's father, Miles Sampson Scribner, Sr. served in the same unit as his son.

Miles, Hannah, and Jemima's brother Daniel Sampson Scribner was a member of Company I, 14th Regiment Infantry, Maine Volunteers. He was captured at Winchester and was a prisoner-of-war at Libby prison and Belle Isle Stockade, but survived to return home after the war. You can read more about the Scribner family at the end of Chapter Four.

Timothy Johnson Woodbury enlisted with his father William in 1863; he had two brothers, William Worthly and Edwin, who had previously enlisted.

One of the young men from Patten who enlisted was 2nd Lieutenant Edwin Searle Rogers (photo at right). Edwin was a junior at Bowdoin College when he enlisted in the Union Army. He was a member of Company E, 31st Regiment Infantry, Maine Volunteers. Tragically, his parents, Luther (the town doctor) and Mary, received a letter from President Abraham Lincoln in 1864 stating that he had been killed at Cold Harbor, Virginia, in an act of courage and patriotism while refusing to surrender to a Southern officer. He was buried in Cold Harbor.

Edwin Rogers's brother, Colonel Luther Bailey Rogers, fought in the same Cold Harbor battle that claimed his brother Edwin's life. Just eleven days later, he was wounded in action in Petersburg. Rogers returned to Patten where he became an important member of the community. He owned logging operations and built camps at Shin Pond and on the East Branch of the Penobscot. He was nicknamed "the Colonel". He lost his first wife (the mother of his daughter Matilda), but remarried and had seven more children, including his son Lore. Luther is shown in the photo at right. You can read more about the Rogers family at the end of Chapter Four.

Another enlistee from Patten was Ira Gardner, the son of John and Mary (Coburn) Gardner. Ira became the youngest colonel in the Union Army. He lost his right arm in the battle of Opequan Creek, near Winchester, Virginia. He returned home from war, married Helen Darling, and became a leader in the community. You can read more about the Gardner family at the end of Chapter Four.

At left is a photo of 1st Lt. Edward Cunningham, who was killed in action at Gettysburg in 1863. He served with Company D, 19th Regiment Infantry, Maine Volunteers.

1st Lt. William Jackman was a member of Company I, 14th Regiment Infantry, Maine Volunteers. Below is a typed reproduction of a letter he wrote to his wife Nancy, who was living in Patten with their children. (I have added punctuation to the letter to make it easier to read.) The URL for this site is http://louisdl.louislibraries.org/cdm/ref/collection/AAW/id/994

Berwick City, September 22, 1863

Dear Nancy,

This place is at the end of the railroad, about eighty miles west of the city of New Orleans. I think there are only two families here now. The place is partly burnt. I don't think it ever was larger than Patten. It is on the west side of the bay. Brushean City is opposite and it is some larger. As near as I can calculate, there is about 15,000 troops in the two places. Then there is another force of about 5,000 coming down the bayou, making in all about 20,000, which I think is force enough for the object. As near as I can find out, this force is to subdue the rebels in the western part of Louisiana and Texas. Probably we shall stay here a week or ten days—can't tell how long. It takes time to get together and move an army.

I have received yours of the 6th—just fourteen days from Patten. Very glad again to hear that you are all well. It is getting quite cool down here. The weather has changed within a few days. Amazingly we can stand a march a good deal better than we did last June.

I wish you and the children could see how soldiers have to fare and see where they are obliged to rest their bones at night. Each soldier has a piece of cotton sheeting about as large as a tablecloth which he carries with him, makes a shade of it in the day, and sleeps under it at night. I suppose Adelbert and Jon would think it sport, but to follow it up for two years would make them desire a better shelter. But we have got used to it. We look for and expect nothing better, but every soldier longs to see the end of this war. Every victory gained causes him to rejoice to the bottom of his soul. For my part I stand it well. I do not suffer any, nor do I take any comfort, nor don't expect to till I can get back to my home, which I shall try to do the first of next year, either on a furlough or get discharged. I think it will take till that time to finish up this campaign. I am anxious to hear from that money that I sent and to know all about Patten Conscripts, where they go and who goes. I do not think they will have much fighting to do. After Charleston is taken (which must soon fall into our hands), the rebs will begin to cave in faster than ever. Bragg's army has become so weak that it did not dare to fight Rosecrans, so you may conclude that the fighting is about done in that region. A retreating army never becomes any stronger. Charleston taken and the army on the Potomac strengthened, the war is at an end. I have prophesied before and almost always was wrong, but I have reason to believe that I shall be right this time. Do not borrow any trouble about me. Take no thought of the morrow. I do not. But take what comes and make the best of it. October, November, and December will soon pass away, then I shall hope soon after to see you. Take care of yourself and children.

Truly Yours
William Jackman

Even though he was quite hopeful in his prophecy that the war would be over soon, 1st Lt. Jackson was wrong once again. He did not make it home in December, nor in any of the eight months after that. Even then Mr. Jackman didn't have the reunion with his family he had so wanted: he was killed in action on September 19, 1864, in Winchester, Virginia.

The chart on the following pages lists the fates of many of the soldiers from Patten who were injured or killed, died of disease or wounds, were discharged for an unnamed disability, or deserted. Surprisingly, records were pretty well kept and many are available online. Most of the information in the chart comes from annual reports written by company commanders to the Maine Adjutant General. I stumbled across these reports while doing research online. You can access the reports, which are digitized versions, at the site
    https://books.google.com/books?id=duiE2cQSnvcC&pg=PA466&lpg=PA466&dq+%20Patten%20+%20Maine#v=onepage&q&f=false

Once you're on the site, there is a search box on the left side if you want to type in more specific information.

There were some pages missing from the documents, which were over a thousand pages each, so there may be some omissions. Some of the information comes from other resources and may be less detailed. There are a few men who were listed in one of my resources as fatalities in the war, but I was unable to find any information on them.

My chart uses these codes:

W= Wagoner
CO = Commissioned Officer
MS= Marital Status
Inf= Infantry
MV= Maine Volunteers
MI=Mustered In
KIA= killed in action
Wnd.= wounded

F= Farrier
Age=age at time of mustering in
Rgt.= Regiment
Cav= Cavalry
MVV= Maine Veteran Volunteers
Disch= discharged
WIA– wounded in action

Some soldiers seem to have been discharged for a disability and then reenlisted at a later date. There may have been transfers from one unit to another or promotions in rank that I did not discover.

Please refer to Appendix C for a list of all area veterans of the Civil War.

NAME	RANK	AGE	MS	COMPANY	MI	COMMENTS
Akley, Caleb	Pvt.	29	M	Co. E, 22nd Rgt. Inf. MV	10-10-62	Disch. for disability; New Orleans
Bigger, Alexander	Pvt.	32	S	Co. A, 2nd Rgt. Cav. MV	11-30-63	Died 8-8-64 at Ft. Schyler, NY
Bigger, Ebenezer	Pvt.	22	S	Co. A, 2nd Rgt. Cav. MV	11-30-63	KIA 1864 in New Orleans, LA
Blackwell, Joshua	Pvt. Sgt.	20	S	Co. B, 8th Rgt. Inf. MV Co. A, 2nd Rgt. Cav. MV	9-7-61	Disch. for disability 11-23-62, reinlisted
Blackwell, Wallace	Pvt.	21	S	Co. E, 31st Rgt. Inf. MV	3-11-64	Died 5-19-64 in hospital
Brackett, Elijah	Pvt.	29	M	Co. H, 30th Rgt. Inf. MVV	1-1-64	WIA 4-23-64
Bradford, Columbus	Pvt.	18	M	Co. H, 19th Rgt. Inf. MV	9-21-63	Disch. for disability 1-18-64
Brown, Bradish		40	M	Co. E, 31st Rgt. Inf. MV	3-11-64	Died 8-29-64 in RI hospital
Brown, Orin (Orrin)	Pvt.	22	M	Co. L, 1st Reg. Cav. MV	11-1-61	Taken prisoner 10-12-62
Chesley, Hiram	Pvt.	19	S	Co. H, 20th Rgt. Inf. MV	8-29-62	Disch. for disability 4-29-64
Chesley, John						
Clark, Alonzo	Pvt.	19	S	Co. E, 31st Rgt. Inf. MV	3-11-64	Died in hospital 5-23-64
Crommett, Samuel	Sgt.	29	M	Co. E, 31st Rgt. Inf. MV	3-11-64	KIA 12-1-64 at Fort Francis
Cunningham, Edward	1st Lt.	22	S	Co. L, 1st Reg. Cav. MV	11-1-61	KIA 7-3-63 at Gettysburg
Cunningham, Owen	Pvt.	18	S	Co. A, 16th Rgt. Inf. MV	8-14-62	KIA 12-13-62 at Fredericksburg
Curo, Edward	Pvt.	30	M	Co. E, 31st Rgt. Inf. MV	3-11-64	Deserted 8-64
Dolloff, Lyman	Pvt.	21	S	Co. E, 8th Rgt. Inf. MV	3-8-62	Died 6-15-64 at Pt. Lookout, MD
Donham, Isaac	Pvt.	44	M	Co. E, 31st Rgt. Inf. MV	3-11-64	Died 7-13-64 at City Pt.
Fairfield, Hadley	Corp.	21	S	Co. A, 7th Rgt. Inf. MV	8-21-61	WIA--discharged

NAME	RANK	AGE	MS	COMPANY	MI	COMMENTS
Fairfield, James				Co. A, 14th Rgt. Inf. MV		Died of fever
Farewell, Jeremiah	Pvt.	21	S	Co. A, 2nd Rgt. Cav. MV	11-30-63	Died 9-12-64 in Barrancas, FL
Fitzpatrick, John	Pvt.	42	S	Co. B, 8th Rgt. Inf. MV	9-7-61	Deserted 9-18-61 or 9-26-61
Fowler, Timothy	Pvt.	24	S	Co. A, 7th Rgt. Inf. MV	8-21-61	Disch. for disability 8-16-62
Gardner, Ira	Col.	19	M	Co. I, 14th Rgt. Inf MV	12-14-61	WIA 9-19-64, disch.
George, John	Pvt.	32	S	Co. A, 2nd Reg. Cav. MVV	11-30-63	Disch. for disability 6-27-65
Gilman, Charles	Pvt.	21	S	Co. C, 16th Rgt. Inf. MV	8-14-64	POW paroled
Goff, Edmund	Pvt.	21	S	Co. H, 20th Rgt. Inf. MV	8-29-62	Wounded 5-5-64, disch.2-16-65
Gonier, David*	Pvt.	20	S	Co. E, 31st Rgt. Inf. ME	3-11-64	Deserted 9-24-64 from hospital
Hackett, Alden	Pvt.	18	S	Co. B, 16th Rgt. Inf. MV	8-14-62	Died of disease 12-17-64
Harriman, Walker						Not accounted for at muster-out
Haynes, Thomas II	Pvt.	34	M	Co. B, 8th Rgt. Inf. MV	8-17-63	Wnd. 5-20-64, Disch. 6-1-65
Heald, Charles	Pvt.	22	M	Co. B, 8th Rgt. Inf. MV	8-18-62	KIA 12-19-64
Jackman, William	Lt.	40	M	Co. I, 14th Rgt. Inf. MV	12-21-61	Wnd. 8-25-64, supposed dead
Kellogg, Marcellus	Pvt.	20	S	1st Maine Cavalry	10-15-63	Died 9-14-64 at Barrancas, FL
Kimball, Charles	Pvt.	19	S	Co. A, 2nd Rgt. Cav. MV	11-30-63	Died 7-19-62
Kimball, Martin		20		Co. B, 8th Rgt. Inf. MV	9-7-61	Disch.?
Kimball, Samuel	Corp.	21	S	Co. A, 7th Rgt. Inf. MV	8-21-61	Wounded 4-2-65; disch.
		26	M	Co. A, 2nd Rgt. Cav. MV	4-9-64	
Kyle, James	Pvt.	25	S	Co. A, 16th Rgt. Inf. MV	8-14-62	Died 10-21-62 in hospital
Legrow, Erastus	Pvt.	22	S	Co. B, 8th Rgt. Inf. MV	9-7-61	Disch. for disability 11-23-62

NAME	RANK	AGE	MS	COMPANY	MI	COMMENTS
Lincoln, George	Pvt.	33	M	Co. E, 31st Rgt. Inf. MV	3-11-64	Disch. for disability 5-4-65
Lurvey, Joseph	Pvt.	26	M	Co. B, 16th Rgt. Inf. MV	8-15-64	Died of disease 3-19-65
Marshall, Jimmo		33	M	Co. H, 1st Rgt. Inf. MV	2-24-64	Disch. for disability 7-25-64
McKeen, John		20	S	5th Btty of Mtd Artillery	8-14-64	Died of wounds in '64 or '65
Morgridge, Wyman				Co. I, 14th Reg. Inf.	12-14-61	Family lived briefly in Patten, then moved to Island Falls, died while serving
Morrill, Ira	Pvt.	29	M	Co. E, 1st Reg. Cav. MV	10-19-61	Disch. for disability 11-20-62
	F	32		Co. A, 2nd Rgt Cav. MV	12-23-63	KIA 7-28-64 in New Orleans, LA
Morrill, Winslow	Sgt.	29	M	Co. A, 16th Rgt. Inf. MV	8-14-62	W. at Gettysburg, died 8-12-63
Palmer, Moses Jr.	Sgt.	21	M		12-14-64	Taken prisoner
Palmer, Uriah	Pvt.	27	S	Co. D., 7th Rgt. Inf. MV	8-21-61	Taken prisoner 5-4-63
Parker, James	Pvt.	24	S	Co. B, 8th Rgt. Inf. MV	9-7-61	Disch. for disability 5-17-63
Perow, Benjamin	Pvt	21	S	Co. E, 31st Rgt. Inf. MV	3-11-64	WIA
Perry, Jonathan	Pvt.	23	M	Co. E, 8th Rgt. Inf. MV	2-11-62	Disch. for disability 5-4-63
Pierce, Gardner	Sgt.	30		Co. E, 1st Rgt. Cav. MV		Died in 1862
Preble, Joseph	Corp.	18	S	Co. I, 14th Rgt. Inf. MV	12-14-61	Died 8-2-63
Ricker, Henry	Pvt.	26	M	Co. B, 8th Rgt. Inf. MV	8-27-62	KIA 5-20-64
Rogers, Edwin	2nd Lt.	21	S	Co. E, 31st Rgt. Inf. MV	3-12-64	KIA 6-7-64 at Cold Harbor, VA
Rogers, Luther	Col.			Co. B, 8th Rgt. Inf. MV	9-7-61	WIA 6-18-64 at Petersburg
Sargent, Edward						
Savage, Cyrus	F	40	M	Co. A, 2nd Reg. Cav. MVV	12-22-63	Disch. for disability 5-19-65

NAME	RANK	AGE	MS	COMPANY	MI	COMMENTS
Scribner, Daniel	Sgt.	30	S	Co. I, 14th Rgt. Inf. MV	6-7-62	Taken POW at Winchester, VA, '64, sent to Libby and Belle Island
Scribner, Francis	Corp.	27	S	Co. D, 14th Rgt. Battalion Co. B, 8th Rgt. Inf. MV	9-7-61	Disch. 10-5-61
				Co. F, 31st Rgt. Inf. MV	3-15-64	Disch. for disability 8-15-64
Scribner, Miles, Jr.		30	M	Co. B, 8th Rgt. Inf. MV	9-7-61	Died 6-7-64 in Washington D.C.
Scribner, Miles, Sr.			M	Co. B, 8th Rgt. Inf. MV		Wounded, disch.
Shaw, Joshua	Pvt.			Co. B, 8th Rgt. Inf. MV	9-7-61	Disch. or deceased 1862
Smart, Robert	Pvt.	24	S	Co. B, 8th Rgt. Inf. MV	2-29-64	Wounded 5-20-64
Tripp, Alonzo	Pvt.	22	S	Co. A, 16th Rgt. Inf. MV	8-14-62	Disch. for disability 8-10-63
Troop, John	Pvt.	28	M	Co. B, 8th Rgt. Inf. MV	9-7-61	KIA 5-20-64 at Cold Harbor, VA
Vance, Robert	Pvt.	21	S	Co D, 7th Rgt. Inf. MV	8-21-61	Deserted 1863
Wadlin, Ira	Pvt.	21		Co. A, 2nd Rgt. Cav. MV	11-30-63	Died of disease in LA 9-9-64
Wadlin, Loammi	Pvt.	17	S	Co. H, 31st, Rgt. Inf. MV		KIA 1864 At Cold Harbor, VA
Waters, Byron	Pvt.	18		Co. H, 19th Rgt. Inf. MV	8-19-63	Wnd. 10-13-64, died 4-28-65
Weeks, Hartson		33		Co. B, 8th Rgt. Inf. MV	9-7-61	Died 8-16-62
Wescott, Daniel	Pvt.	18	S	Co. I, 14th Rgt. Inf. MV	12-14-61	Died of disease 12-23-62 or 12-25-62 at Carrollton, LA
Wescott, John						Died of wounds
Whalon, Peter	Pvt.	19	S	Co. E, 31st Rgt. Inf. MV	3-11-64	Deserted 3-20-64
Wilson, William	Pvt.	24	S	Co. I, 13th Rgt. Inf. MV	12-12-61	Deserted 12-12-61
York, Isaac	W	44	M	Co. E, 31st Rgt. Inf. MV	3-11-64	KIA 6-7-64

In a few instances, I did not find the date the soldier mustered in. However, I assumed that he would have enlisted at the same time that other Patten and Mount Chase members of his unit did.

CEMETERIES

The Mount Chase cemetery on the Shin Pond road was established in 1867 and has only a handful of stones in the north end of a grassy area surrounded by trees. The Mount Chase cemetery on Route 11 is much larger and more populated than the Shin Pond site. It was called by various names in the resources I used: the Myrick Cemetery, the Mount Chase Cemetery, and the Wadsworth Cemetery. I believe this cemetery was established around 1852 or 1853. I found mention of an infant who died in 1852 on one stone, and another that dates from 1853 when David and Mary Bumpus's children David and Mary died in July just one day apart. One resource referred to the cemetery as the Wadsworth Cemetery. There was a Wadsworth family in Mount Chase in the mid-late-1800's who were ancestors of the Johnson family, but their death records say they are buried in "the Myrick Cemetery."

I visited the Patten Cemetery on several occasions for the specific purpose of searching for headstones of people I had been writing about. I mentioned earlier that Rhoda Freeman Rigby and her two daughters, Irena and Mary, were buried in the Patten Cemetery in 1839, when that cemetery was established. Her stone is located in the northeast corner of the cemetery. Andrew Grant seems to be the second person buried there; he died in 1842; he is situated several rows back from Mrs. Rigby.

I also found headstones for Eli and Fanny Kellogg, Ira and Abra Fish, Samuel and Marcia Wiggins, Henry, Ellen, Levi, and Ezra Blake and their sons Levi and Ezra, Samuel and Eliza Leslie (Lesslie) and their son David, Elbridge and Electa Stetson, Samuel and Mary Darling, Ira B. and Helen Gardner, Loammi Wadlin, Edwin Searle Rogers, and many other gravesites of Patten's early settlers.

In my Patten cemetery wanderings, I was curious about one of the tallest and most ornate monuments. It turned out to be John Gardner's headstone (photo at left). The Gardner family became one of the wealthiest families in Patten; Gardners for several generations owned Main Street businesses and mills, were involved in the logging industry, took part in town political affairs, and/or had successful careers in other locales.

As I read headstone inscriptions, I noticed a number of children's deaths in 1861-1862. Through further research, I learned that Patten and Mount Chase were hit with an epidemic of illness at that time. In Mount Chase, Elias Cundy lost his seven-year-old son Willis and his five-year-old daughter Mary Ella in May of 1861. Then his wife Sarah, age 32, died in June. (Tragically, this family had already lost a son William in 1852 when he was ten months old.) Also in the Mount Chase cemetery, a little headstone that says *Our Babies* on its rounded top marks the graves of seventeen-month-old Alice May and nine-month-old Paulina, daughters of Samuel and Betsey Ann Willey. They died in September and October of 1861. In 1862, Amasa and Rosanna (Ellis) Parker lost four children to a diphtheria epidemic. Another son, James, was wounded while fighting in the Civil War. After returning home, James married Abigail Sargent of Mount Chase; they also lost their daughter Harriet to diphtheria.

In Patten, Jerome Frye and his first wife Nancy lost two little girls in 1861. In October, just eleven days apart, Abby died at the age of six and Josephene died at age two. Ironically, Mr. Frye was Patten's undertaker. Josie's and Abby's headstones in the Patten cemetery are shown in the photo at the right. All of the children's headstones have loving messages from their parents inscribed on them. These monuments are a stark reminder that life was very hard for the early settlers. And the parents who lost those children certainly grieved just as deeply as a parent would in modern times.

After spending so many hours learning about and writing about the people of Patten and Mount Chase, I felt like I knew these folks even though they had died before my grandparents were even born. But at the same time, I wondered about their lives. What made them happy? Did they think their lives were hard? What were their marriages like? How did they treat their children? How did they handle their heartaches? Histories and headstones can provide names and dates and places and events, but they don't always tell you much about the people themselves.

-43-

CHAPTER THREE: THE TOWNS FROM 1866-1890

The Civil War had been an interruption in the lives of Patten and Mount Chase citizens, but with the return of the soldiers who survived the war, the focus turned back to the development of the communities. Lumbering, farming, retail, manufacturing, and the development of sporting camps all contributed to the booming economy of the region. This chapter includes some of the major events in the towns between 1866 and 1890.

1866: Andrew Johnson had replaced Abraham Lincoln as president and served until 1869.

1867: A stage coach now traveled between Patten and Mattawamkeag. In 1867, it was operated by George Scribner, and in 1869, it was called Heald's Express. In 1870, Paul Peavey took it over (photo at right from Eleanor Sargent Hunter collection). It took ten hours to make a one-way trip.

William Gifford bought Samuel Leslie's grist mill and made it into a steam lumber mill. He later sold it to F.F. Weymouth, who later sold it to Jerry Foote. Patten's first exported products were probably clapboards and shingles.

Jacob Frye sold the part of his Main Street property now called the Bradford House to Joshua Goodwin. The business census of 1870 showed that Mr. Goodwin was a successful farmer. He raised oats, buckwheat, hay, and potatoes to sell (perhaps to the lumber camps) and also sold milk and butter.

An issue of *The Voice* included articles on reorganizing a militia and a meeting of the Penobscot and Aroostook Union Agricultural and Horticultural Society hosted by the town of Patten.

Fire destroyed buildings on Houlton Street owned by Ira Fish and Samuel Wiggins. Only the work of a bucket brigade saved other buildings in the area.

The Mount Chase Cemetery on the Shin Pond Road was established.

1867, cont.: David N. Rogers of Patten (the brother of Dr. Luther Rogers) served in the Maine House of Representatives.

Maine Civil War hero Brigadier General Joshua L. Chamberlain of Bangor became the governor of Maine. He served until 1871.

1869: Civil War hero General Ulysses S. Grant served as president from 1869-1877.

1870-1871: Jacob Frye built a steam lumber and grist mill on the north side of his cheese factory, about where the parking area for the ball field now exists. Main Street included businesses owned by Jerome Frye, Stetson & Gardner (or Stetson and Coburn), William Jackson, E. H. Hall, and Bither's Barber Shop. In 1871, S.S. Thompson was operating a hotel called The Patten Exchange. Lumbermen in Mount Chase were S.L. Kimball, Ezra Myrick, S.L. Hackman, and Samuel Harvey. Dr. Benjamin C. Woodbury, Sr. opened a medical practice around this time. Charles Sibley was operating the Shin Pond House.

Horatio Darling of Patten served in the Maine House of Representatives.

The 1870 census determined that the population of Patten was 704 and the population of Mount Chase was 262.

1871: The Jonathan Flanders farm buildings burned.

The Methodists built a church on the site of Ira Fish's sheep barn, on the west side of the parsonage. The picture on the left is a photo of Elbridge Stetson, for whom the Methodists named their church. Remember, he was the fellow who let them use his cabin for services in the early days. I found Elbridge and Electa Stetson's headstones in the Patten Cemetery. He died in 1886, and she died in 1872.

Sidney Perham served as governor of Maine from 1871-1874.

1871, cont.: The deadliest wildfire in recorded history claimed 2,500 lives near Peshtigo, Wisconsin. The Great Chicago Fire killed 300 people and left 100,000 homeless.

1872: Island Falls was incorporated.

1873: Samuel Kimball, a resident of Mount Chase, served in the Maine House of Representatives.

1874: Another Jonathan Flanders building burned.

Nelson Dingley, Jr. was Maine's governor from 1874-1876.

1875: Perhaps the two Flanders fire were a stimulus that moved the community to action, as the first fire company, complete with uniforms, was established.

The town of Medway (originally known as Nicatou) was incorporated.

1876: The *Maine Annual Register* for the year 1876 included this information. Hugh Anderson was a wheelwright. I. B. Bolton was practicing medicine in Patten. John Putnam Leslie had opened a store, and the Bragg Brothers had opened a blacksmith shop. C.L. Hackett was operating the Patten House. W.E. Myrick was a lumberman in Mount Chase. I could not find out for sure who W.E. Myrick was. Thomas Myrick had a son Willis, who was born in 1869, but he would only have been about seven years old in 1876. Other possibilities would have been Ezra (b. 1802), Edwin (b. 1847), or Uriah Myrick (b. 1836),

Selden Connor was Maine's governor from 1876-1879.

1877: Rutherford B. Hayes served as the U.S. president from 1877-1881

Ira Fish's mill burned.

1878: An issue of the *Katahdin Kalendar* included articles about *the Scourge of Memphis* (a deadly epidemic that hit Memphis, Tennessee) and a grave robbing in New York. Evidently there wasn't much going on in Patten at the time. However, the local ladies could get a stylish new hat from a new milliner in town, Mrs. Cora (Leslie) Wescott. You can read more about the Leslie and Wescott families at the end of Chapter Four.

1879: John Gardner and his son Ira B. Gardner built a starch factory at the foot of Mill Hill on the south side of Fish Stream. The factory processed potatoes to make starch, which was hauled to Kingman.

Around this time, the Independent Order of Oddfellows established the Patten Lodge, which was named Pamola #87.

Alonzo Garcelon was Maine's governor from 1879-1880. He was replaced by Daniel Davis, who served until 1881. Davis was replaced by Harris M. Plaisted, who served from 1881 to 1883.

1880: The census count determined that the population of Patten was 716 and the population of Mount Chase was 310. This was Mount Chase's highest recorded census count. Appearing in the 1880 Census were Paul and Martha Peavey and their seven children, Clarence, Mattie, Charles, John, Linnie, Harry, and Mary.

The Department of Fish and Game was established, thereby creating the Maine Warden Service.

1881: Mount Chase had a Methodist Society.

Jacob Frye died suddenly at the age of 68; he was survived by his second wife. At the time of his death, all six of his children by his first wife, Paulina, had died: Augusta (Hersey) died in 1872 at age 25, Delia (Heald) died in 1855 at the age of 16, Rachel died in 1846 at the age of 2, Laroy died in 1846 at the age of 5, Leroy died in 1861 at the age of 10, and Fernando died in 1858 at the age of 2. The children's mother Paulina died in 1873.

James Abram Garfield only served a half year as president of the United States before he was assassinated. He was replaced by Chester Alan Arthur, who served until 1885.

1881-1882: Samuel Waters served in the Maine House of Representatives.

1883: H.A. Bascom was the principal at Patten Academy. He later briefly practiced medicine in Patten. His greatest service to Patten, however, was to devise a way to pipe water from springs at the top of Finch Hill to Patten's Main Street area.

1883, cont.: The eruption of the volcanic island Krakatoan what is now Indonesia killed 40,000 people and disrupted weather patterns for the next five years.

Frederick Robie was Maine's governor from 1883 to 1887.

1884: The Patten Silver Cornet Band (see photo on next page) was organized under the direction of Professor Isaac T. Maddocks. A great supporter of the band was T.J. Woodbury, who earned the nickname *the Father of the Band.* The band provided music for Decoration Day for thirty-three years, with the exception of one year. The band was also known as the Patten Brass Band.

The Huston family was active in the band; Loren Huston (photo at left) played in the band, and his brother Sylvester (photo at right) played in the band and was the band leader at one point. You can read more about the Huston family at the end of Chapter Four.

1885: The Patten Bottle Company was built by Irving Bragg on the site behind the location where Patten Drug Company was built a few years later.

A third story was added to the Patten House.

The Gardner and Coburn Store burned.

@1885: Charles Quincy's *Oyster Saloon*, residence, and barn burned.

Grover Cleveland was the U.S. president from 1885-1889.

1885-1886: Daniel Scribner of Patten served in the Maine House of Representatives.

1886: The Ira B. Gardner store was built. This building housed general stores for many years until it burned down in 2008. You can see the store along with the Patten Silver Cornet Band in this photo. (Margaret Bates photo)

1887: Charles Cobb and Jacob Hersey received the first diplomas at Patten Academy. If you're wondering if it really did take them 39 years to get through the curriculum at the Academy, read more about this in Chapter Ten!

A "receiving tomb" was built at the Patten Cemetery.

Joseph Bodwell died shortly after becoming the governor of Maine. He was replaced by Sebastian Marble, who served as governor until 1889.

1888: A grammar school was established in the Patten Academy building. For several years, the teacher of the grammar school students also served as the assistant to the principal of the Academy.

The Quincy, Cooper, and Rowe building was built by Charles Quincy, Henry Rowe, and Ira Cooper on the site where Katahdin Trust Company is now located.

The Great White Hurricane, an east coast cyclonic blizzard, dropped up to fifty inches of snow in places, killed 400 people, and caused many shipwrecks.

This picture postcard dates from 1889. The Cooper, Quincy, and Rowe building is on the far right, and further up the street you can see the front of the Patten House. On the left is the Ira B. Gardner store. You can see the spire of the Baptist Church as you continue up the west side of the street. You can also see from the photo that, whether by design or coincidence, Patten had a very wide Main Street. The charm of the village was enhanced by the elm trees gracing both sides of Main Street as you travel north. Below that is another postcard looking right at the Patten House. You can see Huston Clothing on the left and the Cooper, Quincy, and Rowe building on the right.

Author's Note:

At the ends of Chapters Three through Eight, you will see information I gleaned from the *Maine Register.* Each year's edition of the register listed all the businesses in each community in Maine

The registers in the earliest years were arranged by type of business, so I had to read practically the whole register. But from around 1860 on, they were arranged by county, with the towns in each county arranged in alphabetical order. Therefore, out of a five-inch thick book, I only had to read two or three pages!

I made my research a little easier in two ways: First, I did not read the registers for every single year. Therefore, it is possible that I may have missed a business which was in operation for only one or two years. That said, I do think I read enough publications that I missed very few businesses.

Second, rather than creating a separate list for each calendar year, I grouped the information by the eras I used as my chapter titles. For example, the lists at the end of this chapter include all the services, merchants, and manufacturers I found listed in registers published between 1866 and 1899. A particular business may have been established before or after 1866, may have only been in existence for a brief time between 1866 and 1899, or may have been in existence before and after 1899 (and thus would be included as well in the listings at the end of Chapter Four. I realize my readers might wish to know the specific years when a particular business was in operation. If you really want more specific information, go online, go to the library in Patten, or travel to the library in Houlton and do the research yourself!

You might also notice that a name might be repeated within the list beside a bullet. For example, in the bullet for *blacksmith* under *manufacturing*, you will see John Bragg, Bragg & Perry, and Bragg & Bradley. That might mean one of three things:
1. Mr. Bragg worked on his own, then in partnership with Mr. Perry, then in partnership with Mr. Bradley.
2. Mr. Bragg is the same person in two of the businesses and a different Bragg was involved in the third business.
3. There were three Mr. Braggs involved in the three different businesses.

The *Maine Registers* published between 1866 and 1889 yielded this information:

Services:

- Barbers: P.W. Frye, Fred E. Arnold
- Dentist: Martin B. Smiley. Don't you think that's a great name for a dentist? He established his practice after 1885 but before 1891.
- Doctors: Jesse Howe, ? Fisher, ? Sanford, H. A. Bascom, E.W. Perry, Frederick Bigelow, O.F.Best, Hubert Best, Benjamin C. Woodbury, Benjamin Woodbury, G. Frank Woodbury, and William T. Merrill. [Dr. Best also owned Patten Drug Company from 1891-1900. Dr. Benjamin C. Woodbury established a practice in 1870, and his sons Dr. Benjamin Woodbury and Dr. G. Frank Woodbury later joined his practice. The first Woodbury doctored until 1905, and G. Frank practiced medicine in Patten for almost fifty years.]
- Hotels: The Patten House (C.L. and/or Lucius Hackett),The Shin Pond House (Charles Sibley, then Lewis Cooper), Frye's Inn (Jacob Frye), a public house owned by Paul Peavey. The Bradfords owned and operated the Bradford Inn in Moro at this time.
- Justices: S. E. Benjamin, John Scott, Bertram Smith, Daniel Scribner, Horace Miles, Ira B. Gardner, Rives Mitchell, and Hiram B. Hersey
- Lawyers: S.E. Benjamin, John Scott, Bertram Smith
- Postmasters: Calvin & Mary (Stetson) Bradford, Daniel Scribner, Stanley Wescott, and William Scott Kellogg

Merchants:

- Agricultural implements and fertilizer: C.W. Wescott, L.M. Carver
- Confectionary store: Mrs. William Howes (Mount Chase)
- Dressmakers: Mrs. Mabel Crommett, Miss Elsie Miles, Miss Mary Mitchell, Mrs. Mary Merrill
- Dry and fancy goods: Miss Minerva L. True
- Furniture: J.W. Leslie
- General stores: John Gardner, A.T. Coburn, Gardner and Coburn, Laroy Miles, Ira B. Gardner & Sons, Charles R. Brown, Calvin Bradford, Bradford and Merrill, R. Mitchell, George T. Merrill
- Groceries and meat: C.H. Quincy
- Jewelers: S. P. Hussey, J.K. Osgood, Abial Huntley, Smiley & Maddocks
- Millinery: Mrs. F. C. Moody, Miss Minerva L. True, Mrs. Cora Wescott

Manufacturers:

- Blacksmiths: John Bragg, G. Smith, Bragg & Perry, Robbins & Burho, C.W. Cramp, G. Brown, S.W. Robbins, Bragg & Bradley, A.P. Ryder, Esty & Twitchell   Note: By the 1880's, John Halbert Twitchell, who came to Patten in the early days, was joined in the blacksmith business by his son, John Elmer Twitchell.
- Carding and grist mills: C.A. Gifford, B.T. Gifford
- Caskets and coffins: Jerome Frye, Huston Brothers
- Furniture and woodwork: F.C. Coffin, Gilman & Kimball, Gilman & Carlisle
- Harnesses: O. Cobb & Son, William Smallwood
- Lumber: Samuel Harvey (Mount Chase), William R. Gifford
- Shingles, clapboards, grist mill: John and Ira Gardner
- Shoes and boots: Horace Miles, G.W. Cooper
- Starch: Patten Starch Company (owned by John and Ira Gardner)
- Tinware: C. Bradford, G.T. Merrill
- Wheelrights: Charles Allerton, Hugh Anderson

The map on the next page shows the layout of Patten around 1875. The map I used wasn't dated, but I didn't see John and Ira Gardner's starch factory, built in 1879, at the foot of Mill Hill, and I did see the Methodist Church, built in 1871. I also found a very similar map for Mount Chase which was dated 1875. Please note the names of the streets:

Aroostook Road: now Main Street
School Street: now Founders Street
Mechanic Street: now Katahdin Street
Parsonage Street: now Houlton Street
Fish Lane: now Dearborn Street

The map shows the Baptist, Congregational, and Methodist churches; the school on School Street and Patten Academy; and the location of Dr. Luther Rogers's and Dr. Bascom's doctor's offices. The map also shows properties owned by Ira Fish, Eli Kellogg, Samuel Wiggins, and E.G. Stetson. The site marked J. Goodwin is now known as the Bradford House.

These businesses were marked on the map: Jacob Frye's steam mill and his cheese factory, Minerva True's millinery shop, The Gardner and Coburn store, Calvin Bradford's post office, The Patten House, another Gardner store, Oliver Cobb's harness shop, Samuel Benjamin's Law Office, Horace Miles's cordwainer shop, and Ichabod Morrill's blacksmith shop. (There were two sites owned by Mr. Morrill—one on Main Street and one on Mill Street. I was surprised, however, that there was no property listed for J.H. Twitchell, who also had a blacksmith shop. Twitchell's shop was at one point located on the same site on Main Street that is marked for Ichabod Morrill. Either Twitchell's was located elsewhere around 1875 or it was located on the lot owned by Morrill at the time this map was made.) I'm almost positive that the lot marked P. Peary should be Paul Peavey.

I redrew the map of Patten on page 55 and the map of Mount Chase on page 56. The map on page 57 is a scan of a map of the Waters Road, Frenchville, and the Happy Corner Road that I thought was legible enough to leave as is.

The last page of this chapter shows some typical U.S. census entries. This information came from the 1870 census report for Mount Chase.

PATTEN, MAINE AROUND 1875

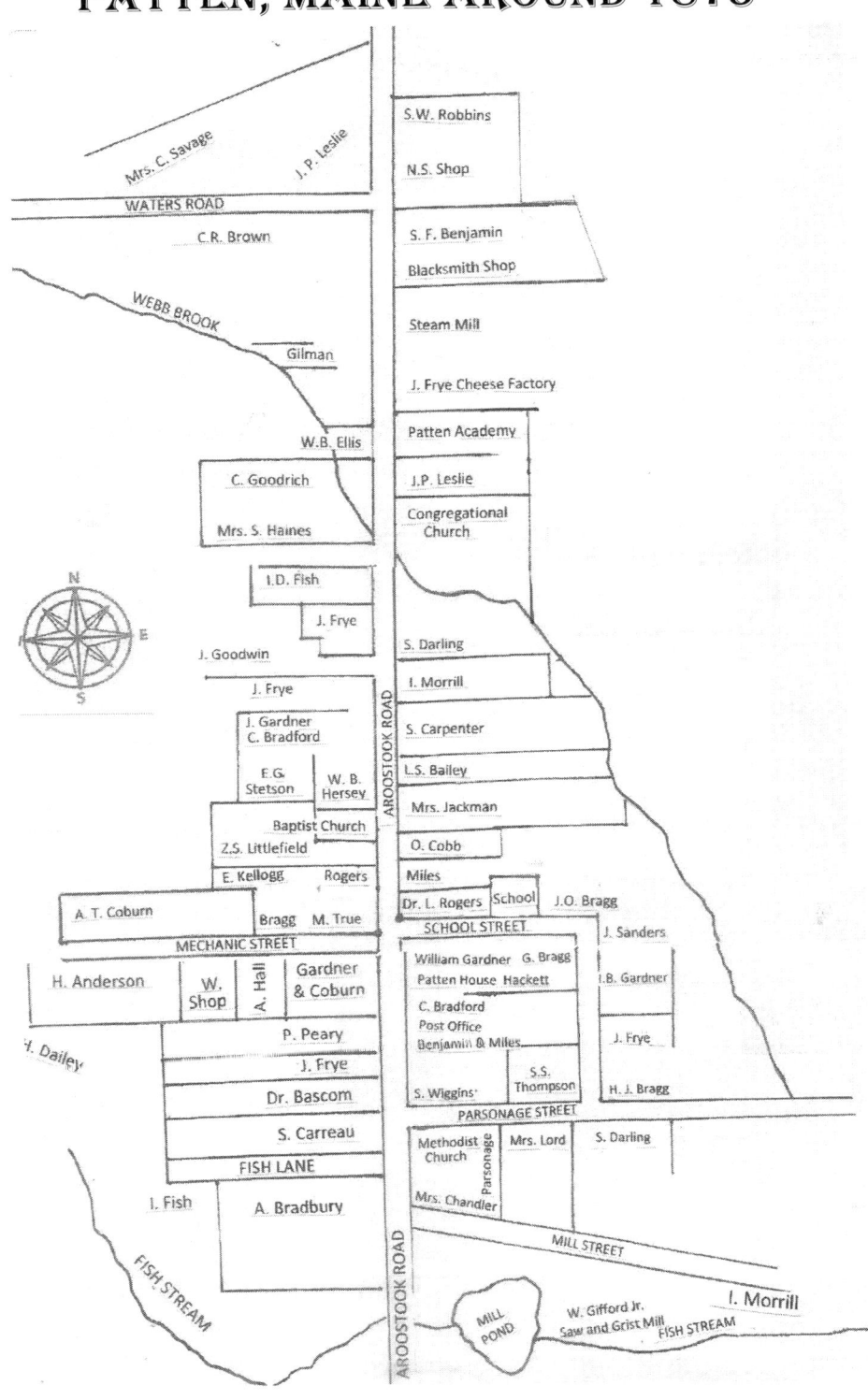

MOUNT CHASE, MAINE AROUND 1875

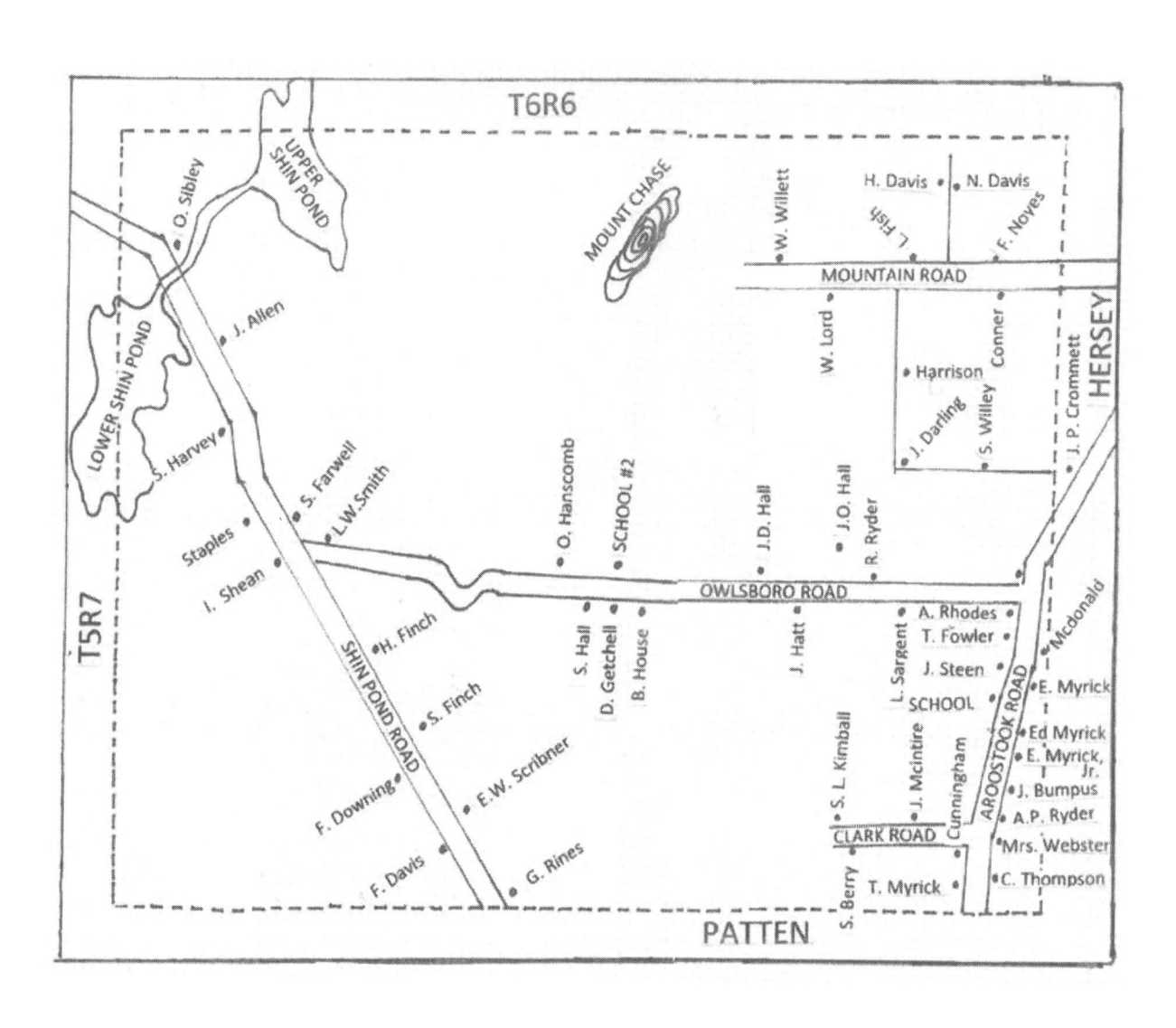

THE ROADS AROUND PATTEN AROUND 1875

Census Report of 1870: These people all lived at the Myrick residence:

MYRICK	Ezra, 68, Farmer, b. Burnham, ME
	Elizabeth, 63, Keeping house, b. Bucksport, ME
	Edwin P., 22, Farmer, b. Mt. Chase, ME
	Mary, 23, Keeping house, b. Bowdoin, ME
CUNDY	Ida M., 12, b. Mt. Chase, ME
	Lucy M., 7, b. Mt. Chase, ME
MYRICK	Uriah, 34, Farmer, b. Greenbush, ME
	Elvira, 22, Keeping house, b. New Brunswick
	Willis, 1, b. Mt. Chase, ME
LLOYD	John, 33, Farm Laborer, b. England
CROMMETT	William, 35, Farm Laborer, b. New Brunswick

Census Report of 1870: These people lived at the Rines residence:

RINES	George, 69, Farmer, b. Waterville, ME
	Margaret, 60, Keeping house, b. New Brunswick
	Frank E., 20, b. Athens, ME
KNIGHT	Jane, 47, Domestic, b. New Brunswick
GRANT	Hubbard J., 8, born Mt. Chase ME

I noticed these things about the census reports:

- There were more farmers than any other occupation in Mount Chase in 1870.
- Several households included children with a different last name.
- Several households included three generations.
- Several households had a hired domestic and/or farm laborer.
- There were a lot of Mount Chase residents who had been born in Canada.
- The largest number of children in one family was seven.
- David and Mary Bumpus, who had lost two children in 1853, were still living in Mount Chase. Their last name was spelled *Bumpas* on the report.
- Men who worked in lumber camps were included in the census for the town in which the camp was located.

CHRISTOPHER COLUMBUS COBURN

Christopher Columbus Coburn was born 1848 in Crystal. He was the son of Silas and Laura Coburn. After his death in 1919, Christopher's son, Ferdinand Rupert Coburn, transcribed Mr. Coburn's diary, which told the story of Mr. Coburn's life from 1871 until his death at the age of 71. Following is a brief synopsis of that diary.

In 1871, Mr. Coburn was 23 years old. Over the next few years, he worked for a variety of people in Patten, Mount Chase, and Sherman doing a variety of jobs, including woods work, mill work, and farm work. Among others, he worked for W. H. Coffin, America T. Coburn, Leonard W. Ordway, Hiram B. Hersey, Roscoe Ordway, R.D. Royal, the Widow Wescott, J.P. Leslie, George Finch, Joshua Goodwin, Ezra Blake, James Parker, Anderson Darling, and Jacob Frye. He mentioned trading horses with Samuel Wiggins.

By 1875, Mr. Coburn had his own farm and planted potatoes, among other crops. Throughout this part of his life, he tended the farm as well as working out for others. He married Nancy J. Moore in August of 1875, and his first child, Lucy, was born July 30, 1876. His Sept. 25, 1976 entry read: *My little girl died. Did not work.* His first son, Henry, was born in 1877.

In 1878, Mr. Coburn wrote that he corked (caulked) his shoes in preparation for working on the drive for Martin Main. He would continue to work on the spring log drives throughout the years, including working for Ira B. Gardner, Kelso, Webster, Joy & Dudley, Parks, Coolidge White, Mr. Palmer, and Con Murphy.

In 1878, he moved to his father's farm on the Cow Team Road and mentions picking cranberries in the big bog.

Mr. Coburn's son Henry died in 1880 of black diphtheria, after which Mr. Coburn himself contracted the disease. In September, he moved his wife to her parents' home, and he moved himself to William Mitchell's. He later moved his wife to George McKenney's. During this time period, he worked for Dr. Benjamin Woodbury and Warren & Coffin.

Mr. Coburn wrote that it snowed all day on October 7 of 1885, and he finished digging his potatoes the next day. In December, he took on a cruising job for Coolidge White.

From 1886 on, Mr. Coburn did not do as much farming. He seemed to be seeking out life further away from civilization. He built a camp and worked in the woods, and, in 1887, he began doing some guiding. In 1889, he trapped with John Francis, a Penobscot Native American from Old Town. He also mentioned working at Mitchell & Leslie's Bowlin Falls lumber camp. He celebrated Thanksgiving with his wife at her parents' home.

In 1890, he was not home much as he continued working in the woods and trapping on the East Branch. In 1891, he and his brother-in-law, Elmer Moore, began making snowshoes to sell. His father died that spring. During the summer he raised a few potatoes and got in the hay, but by winter he back in the woods.

In 1892, his wife's brother-in-law, William Scribner, joined the snowshoe-making business. Mr. Coburn spent most of the spring trapping. That fall, he guided for a sporting camp at Katahdin Lake.

In 1893, his mother died. His son Ferdinand was mentioned as helping him with cutting wood for telegraph poles. That summer, the Coburns got a divorce and Nancy was granted custody of their youngest son, Arthur.

Around 1895, he started up a new business, cutting hoop poles. He also took a "tramp trip" through Aroostook County with his son Ferdinand. After that, he returned to his life of working in the woods, guiding, trapping, and making snowshoes. He was often accompanied by his sons Ferdinand, Oren, and Allard. At times, his youngest son Arthur also joined him.

In 1900, Mr. Coburn's "stomping grounds" seemed to have moved north to Oxbow and Masardis and even further north to Caribou. His life continued to involve woods work and guiding. In 1903, he learned to ride a bike; unfortunately a short time later he fell from his bike and broke his hip, leaving him with a permanent limp.

Mr. Coburn continued his nomadic life, although he did mention seeing his sons from time to time. His sons had married and had homes of their own by 1912. In his later years, Mr. Coburn got into the business of ice-cutting. He visited friends and relatives in between odd jobs. He also spent much more time at his sons' home, helping them with farming, carpentry, and other chores. He even mentioned taking his granddaughter to the movies. It was during an afternoon of hand mowing in his son Ferdinand's hay field in 1919 that Mr. Coburn died unexpectedly. He was found by other workers sitting by a stump with a smile on his face. A few days later, his four sons carried his coffin to its last resting place in the Moro Cemetery.

Author's note: Christopher Columbus Coburn did not accomplish any deeds during his life that should have earned him a page in a history book. But he does represent the men who lived in the Patten and Mount Chase area in the late 1800's and early 1900's. It seems that there were very few days when he did not have some type of work to do. He was strong, enterprising, and knowledgeable about many different kinds of work. His family life was in many ways typical of that era as well; women were often left alone with the children for long periods of time while the head of the household was off working somewhere to support the family. It was unusual that Mr. and Mrs. Coburn got a divorce, but it does not appear that he by any means deserted his family. He was rather stoic about the hard times in his life; of the death of his daughter, he just said, "My little girl died." But I felt that his choice of wording showed a strong connection to the child. He was that odd mixture of family man and woodsman, a nomad who devoted a lot of time to being with others. In the 19th and 20th centuries, there were a lot of men like Mr. Coburn living in Mount Chase and Patten. In 21st century, there are very few men like Mr. Coburn around anywhere.

CHAPTER FOUR: THE TOWNS FROM 1890 TO 1917

You may be wondering why I decided to end Chapter Three in 1889 rather than finish out the Nineteenth Century and start the Twentieth Century in Chapter Four. My reason is this: 1890 marked the beginning of the technology revolution in Patten! Modern inventions were changing the way people communicated, the way they worked, the way they travelled, and even the way they went to the bathroom. Life would never be the same for Patten citizens!

Note: Please refer to Chapters Ten through Sixteen for more detailed information on schools, the library, healthcare, emergency services, community organizations, lumbering, farming, and the area's sporting camps from this era.

1890: The Patten Telephone Company was organized by John and Ira Gardner, Charles Dudley, and B.L. Smith. The first line out of town was connected to the Bangor and Aroostook Railroad Station in Crystal. In 1897, the first phone was installed in Patten. The first telephone office was located in the Bailey & Evans store, but in 1907 was moved to the Huston and Morse store. The citizens of Patten and Mount Chase no doubt marveled at this amazing invention! What would they think of today's phones that can tell you the time, take pictures, type messages, and connect you to almost any type of information you'd ever want to know?

The J. K. Osgood store was built next to the lot on the south corner of Main and Founders Streets.

Abial Huntley secured the patent on an invention. It was a cord or twine holder to use to wrap packages in a store.

The population of Patten was 936, and Mount Chase's count was 284.

By the 1890s, steam tractors were being manufactured, but they were expensive and difficult to maintain.

The Johnstone, Pennsylvania, flood killed over 2,000 people. It happened when a dam broke after several days of heavy rain.

1890, cont.: Benjamin Harrison served as the U.S. president from 1889-1893. Edwin Burleigh was Maine's governor from 1889-1893.

1891: The Huston and Morse Clothing Store was built. It was located on the east side of Main Street. At some point it was also called Huston Clothing.

The first part of Patten Drug Company was built on the corner of Katahdin and Main Streets. Dr. O.F. Best was the pharmacist.

1891-1892: Calvin Bradford of Patten served in the Maine House of Representatives.

1893: The second part of Patten Drug Company (photo above) was built. In later years, a single roof was built over the two sections of the building. The Drug Store operated in the north half of the building and other businesses operated in the south side of the building until 1970 when the drug store expanded into the south side. The second story of the building(s) had apartments for rent. This photo from Eleanor Sargent Hunter shows the drug store, the Hall House, the house that is now Calculations, and the library. The man in the center of the photo is riding a bike.

Joshua Goodwin sold his buildings and property to Ezekiel Bradford. Ezekiel was the son of Calvin and Kesiah Bradford, who had moved to Moro in 1836 and operated an inn there. (Ezekiel was a brother to Calvin Bradford who was a politician, a Patten postmaster, and owner of a tinware shop.) The property in Patten remained in the Bradford family for the next 105 years and was a working farm for many of those years.

1893, cont.: Lawyer John Scott of Patten finished a stint as principal of Patten Academy before serving in the Maine House of Representatives in 1893-1894. During this time, Calvin Bradford of Patten (see previous entry) served in the Maine Senate. Henry Cleaves was Maine's governor and Grover Cleveland was the U.S. president from 1893-1897.

The 1893 Patten Town Report states that W. W. Woodbury was paid $17.00 for painting the hearse. The report published the names of those receiving assistance. The town maintained a farm which generated some income for the town. The reports included names of citizens appointed to fill the positions of *sealers of weights and measures*(who verified that scales measured accurately) and *surveyors of wood, bark, and lumber* (scalers).

The Cheniere Caminada hurricane in Louisianna killed 2,000 people. Its impact was compounded by two recent intense storms.

The Sea Islands Hurricane killed 2,000 people near Savannah, Georgia.

Charles and Frank Duryea founded the first American automobile manufacturing company. Within a decade, Oldsmobile, Rambler, Cadillac, Winn, and Ford were also producing cars.

1894: The citizens of Patten voted to pay Bangor and Aroostook $15,000 for the laying of tracks between Patten and Sherman and building a railroad station. The station was completed in 1895.

1896: Thanks to lawyer Bertram Smith, a problem with the funding of the railroad was taken care of successfully in a court case. The railroad tracks were finished on September 1st, and the first Bangor and Aroostook Railroad train came into town shortly thereafter. A trip from Patten to Mattawamkeag by horse team took ten hours, while a trip by rail took four hours. This event marked a tremendous change in the way businesses in the area could operate, as it became much easier to import and export goods. The train also meant that people could travel to other communities much more easily.

1896, cont.: The Patten Town Reports of this era listed names with marriage, birth, and death records. The 1896 report listed 10 marriages, 35 births, and 15 deaths. Of the deaths, nine were children under the age of eight. Diphtheria and whooping cough were prevalent throughout the year.

1897: W. L. Bonney, principal of Patten Academy expressed the need for a new Academy building in his report to the town of Patten. Irene Olsen quoted him on pages 39-40 in her *History of Patten Academy*: "The condition and surroundings of our building are a physical and moral menace to every pupil…Not to furnish the best teaching force, the best appliances, the best buildings is worse than poor economy. It is an outrage on those to whom we owe a most sacred duty…It is hoped that the good business sense and the common sense of the citizens of Patten will take hold of this matter at no distant day and give us a school building, the crying need of which there can be no question." One of the biggest problems with the building was keeping it warm. Mr. Bonney and the citizens of Patten had no way of knowing that the decision to build or not build a new Academy would very shortly be taken from their hands. On the morning of November 9, 1897, Patten Academy burned to the ground. As it burned, the janitor remarked, "Well they can't complain about her being too cold this morning, anyway." The High School and Grammar School students finished out the school year in the newly built Oddfellows hall.

A giant snowstorm dumped six feet of snow over the area in March. Men desperately shoveled roads to reach logging camps where horses were lodged, but a number of horses starved to death before they could get food to them. When I shared this story with my husband, he told me a story about his grandfather (Tellis Coolong), a fellow from Patten named Henry Rowe, and a big snowstorm (maybe even the 1897 storm). Tellis and Henry had been staying in a woods camp some miles west of Shin Pond and became snowbound as a result of a storm which left the roads impassable. The men had good shelter and enough food to last them until the roads got plowed or the snow melted in the spring, whichever happened first. Tellis was content to wait it out, but Henry got impatient and decided to walk to Patten. He borrowed Tellis's snowshoes and struck out. Through sheer determination, Henry made it home. You will read more about Henry and his life in Patten in Chapter Five.

1897, cont.: William McKinley served as the U.S. president and Llewellyn Powers as Maine's governor from 1897-1901.

1897-1904: Bertram Smith of Patten served as the county attorney. He had previously served in the Maine House of Representatives, and later was appointed the first Justice of the Superior Court for Penobscot County.

1898: Patten published a newspaper called *The Light*. An issue from 1898 included articles about a teachers' convention, a Sunday School rally, a concert by students from Patten Academy, and game killed during hunting season. Sherman news included these two items: *The wife of Rev. I. C. Bumpus has been poorly this fall. W.T. Sleeper appears to be on the gain from his attack of biliousness.* Lest you think Sherman was a dull place compared to Patten, there was also an article about the renovation of the church in Sherman. Note: I read odds and ends about Patten's newspapers here and there, but did not work out a timeline. At various times, these papers were published in Patten: *The Voice, The Tribune, The Katahdin Kalendar, The Light, The Patten Banner, The Mimeograph,* and *the Katahdin Valley Times.*

The Second Patten Academy, shown in the post card picture at right, was built on the site where Patten Academy Alumni Park now exists. Jacob Frye's cheese factory was torn down to make space for the new Academy. The Grammar School was also housed in the Academy building.

1898, cont.: Herbert Nelson Gardner of Patten (photo at left; *History of Patten Academy*) was the first principal of the new school building. He was a graduate of P.A. and the son of Ira B. and Helen Gardner. He was married to Winnifred Wescott, daughter of Cora and Charles Wescott.

Eight Patten and Mount Chase men served their country during the Spanish-American War. One of these, Roland Sampson Scribner, son of Daniel and Tenie Scribner of Patten, died while serving. He had been a sophomore at the University of Maine when he enlisted and was assigned to Co. B, 1st Maine Regiment Infantry, Maine Volunteers. He contracted typhoid fever at Chickamauga and died at a hospital in Portland, Maine. The photo shows his headstone in the Patten Cemetery. Roland was the 4th generation of Scribners to serve during an American war. You can read more about the Scribners at the end of this chapter.

1899: The Patten Town Report proved that Patten people look out for each other. In the interest of an elderly man and his wife, the town decided to build them a small house to live in until they passed away. The report states, *"We can, when the present occupants are done with it (which in the course of human events must be within a few years as both Mr. Goodwin and his wife are upward of 75 years of age and in poor health) sell the house for all that it cost or rent it at a good percent, so that although we had no appropriation or vote of the town for this purpose, we have done that which was in the interest of economy and humanity in building it."*

Jacob Hersey was the postmaster of Patten.

1899-1902: Halbert P. Gardner of Patten served in the Maine House of Representatives. He was a graduate of P.A. and the son of Ira and Helen Gardner.

1900: George and Edwin Merrill bought the lumber mill and named it Merrill Mill Company (photo at right).

The town had installed gasoline street lights by this time.

Patten's population was 1,172, and Mount Chase's population was 299.

Dr. Elmer J. Farnham took over ownership of Patten Drug Company. Mrs. Finch included in her history a story about a particular house call Dr. Farnham made. He got word that a logger at a remote lumber camp needed medical attention. He traveled with a horse and pung (a small cart) to Crommett's (just beyond Shin Pond), on horseback to Sebois, on foot wearing hip boots through water to the Sebois River, by canoe across the river, and on snowshoes through the woods to the lumber camp. Miraculously, the man was still alive. Dr. Farnham treated him successfully, but the story had an even happier ending when the man paid his bill!

Dr. G. Frank Woodbury also practiced medicine in Patten during this time period.

The Great Galveston Hurricane killed as many as 12,000 people. It was the deadliest hurricane in US history. It was accompanied by an 8-15 foot storm surge and 145 mile per hour winds.

Early 1900s: An important technological advance around this time was the flush toilet. What a relief it must have been during a cold Maine winter to use an indoor toilet rather than the traditional outhouse! (I was always befuddled by my grandmother's insistence on keeping her outhouse well into the 1950's. Even good changes are sometimes hard to make!)

Early 1900s, cont.: Patten's mode of transportation was changing as well. The photo at the right shows the first car dealership in Patten. It was owned by Dr. E.J. Farnham and was connected with Grant's Garage and was located on the north side of Founders Street. (Maybe Dr. Farnham thought it would be easier to make house calls in a car than it had been by horse and wagon.)

1901: Alvin O. Lombard of Waterville invented the Lombard Log Hauler. The use of this machine marked the beginning of the use of machines instead of horses in the logging industry.

William McKinley had just started his second term as U.S. president when he was assassinated. Theodore Roosevelt served as president from 1901-1909. John Fremont Hill served as Maine's governor from 1901-1905.

1902: Huston Brothers built a dam by the Merrill Mill and opened an electric light plant, and Patten installed electric street lights.

The town had a fire engine and a building to store it in.

The Mount Chase Town Report stated that H.R. and D. Butterfield were manufacturing shovel handles.

1903: The Carding Mill, which manufactured furniture, was built.

Paul Gagnon built a race track, fairgrounds, and ball field just across the town line in Crystal. The Patten Academy baseball and football teams used the field for practice and home games, as there was no athletic field in town. Patten's team of racing horses was called *The Rogers.* Note: Another resource puts this event as occurring in 1913.

1903-1906: Halbert P. Gardner served in the Maine Senate.

1904: Merrill Mill bought out the Huston Brothers light plant.

Plans were being made to install sewer lines. Evidently the idea of indoor toilets was catching on in Patten.

Long distance telephone lines connected Patten with the rest of the world when Patten, Island Falls, Smyrna Mills, and Sherman Mills formed the Katahdin Farmer's Telephone Company. Edna Rowe was an operator during this period.

In 1904, Mount Chase's valuation was $64,371.00 and Patten's was $546,858.00.

Gladys George (photo at left) was born in Patten while her parents were in town with a touring group of Shakespearean actors. George went on to have a successful career as an actress in film and on Broadway.

1905: Patten Primary School was built.

The second Patten House and the Cooper-Ryder store were built. The Patten House had 35 rooms. Proprietors during this time period were George Russell and the Nevers brothers. The photo at right shows Huston Clothing (built in 1891), the Patten House, and Aaron Smith Clothing (built after 1906). The next two buildings, not shown in this photo, were the Quincy, Cooper, and Rowe building (built in 1888; probably the site of the Cooper-Ryder store) and the Evans and Bailey Store and Express Office. These buildings were located on the east side of Main Street. (Margaret Bates collection)

1905, cont.: The Patten Town Report included ads for businesses, including O. Cobb & Son (harnesses and horse supplies), Bettel & Baston (repairing and painting of wagons—the painting to be done by a first-class painter), L.A. Savage (clothing and dry goods), Sylvanus P. Hussey (practical watch maker and optician), J.E. Nevers (groceries), Ira B. Gardner (general store), and the Palmer House.

P.W. Frye's ad listed the following items: lunch room, confectionery, fruit, tobacco and cigars, soda, small beer, ice cream, oysters in season, Victor and Edison talking machines, barbers' supplies, and a first class barber shop. P.W. was Preston, son of Jerome Frye.

In this general time period (1905-1915), Patten Academy's yearbook, *The Mirror*, was a treasure trove of advertisements—many of them quite comical— for Patten businesses. This ad for Atwood Ryder was in the 1915 issue: When you are in need of a B & A Mileage at 3 cents or have chapped Hands or Sore Throat or your Horse has Scratches and Galls of any kind, why, just call at the home of Instant Relief Cough Syrup where you can get a remedy for a lot of ills of life. Toothache stopped in three minutes if anything but cold steel will stop it. Here you will find a fine line of Groceries at Bottom Prices for Cash. Cigars, Tobacco, and Pipes. Also School Supplies. Cash Paid for Old Rubbers.

Also in this general time period, *The Mirror* ran this ad for the Chase Opera House: Moving Pictures and Illustrated Songs. A good place to spend an evening with your friends. No pictures will be shown that will offend the most refined tastes. Main and Raymond, Proprietors. Mr. Main was Henry Main, and perhaps Mr. Raymond was N.O. Raymond, the undertaker. As far as I can tell, this establishment was situated on Katahdin Street and also housed a harness shop owned by Mr. Main and Arden Brittain. The Chase Opera House was mentioned by Mrs. Bradford as the site of graduation exercises from time to time; *The Mirror* reported that the 1911 graduation ceremonies were held there. The alumni notes in the editions of *The Mirror* around this time reported that Beryl Palmer of Patten was providing the musical accompaniment for the moving picture shows.

The Mount Chase Town Report also included ads, but they were all for Millinocket or Bangor businesses. One of the ads was for the annual Eastern Maine State Fair, which promised to be spectacular for an admission cost was 50 cents. The town received a reimbursement of $1,012.11 from the state for the care of E. Bumpus at the Maine Insane Hospital. The town had been paying for the care of this individual at the hospital for several years. The town had also paid for the legal services related to the Bumpus case in 1905, which leads one to believe that the town had pressured the state for this reimbursement.

1905, cont.: William Cobb was Maine's governor from 1905-1909.

1906: The first machine-dug well was drilled at the house on the south corner of Heald and Gardner Streets, now owned by Letha Tucker.

Patten had built a jail with two cells.

The San Francisco Earthquake killed 3,000 people and destroyed 80% of the city.

This picture shows one of the first cars to drive up Main Street. Shown in the picture are Frank Jarvis (the driver), Mabel Porter, Ethel Anderson, and Thersa Steen (the little girl). In the background you can see the two parts of Patten Drug Company, built in 1891 and 1893. (Patten Heritage Calendar)

1907: Paul Peavey operated a stage coach. This photo shows the coach making a stop in front of the Patten House.

Patten had a pest house. This was a place where people who had a serious infectious disease could be quarantined. And, yes, it was openly called the pest house!

While diseases were the most common reason children died in this era, accidents also took young lives. Around this time in Patten, a little boy named Harley Cunningham was killed when he was caught in the wheel of his father's wagon. He was a brother to Wesley "Jim", Ralph, and Bill Cunningham.

1907, cont.: The Palmer House (photo at left) and their horse stables burned.

The McKenney Brothers opened a jewelry/watch/repair store. The name of this business was later *McKenney the Jeweler*. You can read a little tidbit on Mr. McKenney on page 84.

The photo below right shows Patten Academy's 1907 baseball team.

Front Row: Guy Palmer, Clifford Wescott, Kempton Coady
Middle Row: I. Finch, Leo Coady, Philip Hussey, Principal L. G. Paine, Hazen Rogers
Top Row: K. Parker, Carl Twitchell, Earl Finch, Hal Patterson

Boys' football and girls' and boys' basketball were introduced at Patten Academy for both boys and girls. Track was also being offered as an extracurricular sport.

Bertram Smith of Patten served in the Maine House of Representatives.

1907-1908: The Mount Chase Town Report stated that William Howes was the Myrick Postmaster and Ted Crommett was the Shin Pond postmaster. (In those days, the Route 11 part of Mount Chase was the Myrick district.) Ted Crommett was now operating the Shin Pond House, and Mrs. William Howes still had her confectionery shop.

1908: Mannie Peavey bought Peasley Dam; it has since become known as the Peavey Dam. Peasley Brook kept its name, but at this location it is also called Peavey Brook. It was a popular swimming hole in the 1900's, even though it was full of leeches!

Dr. June B. Robinson was a dentist in Patten around this time.

1908, cont.: Annie L. Rogers Smith, daughter of Luther and Mary Rogers, launched a successful career as a cartoonist. She had initially tried submitting cartoons using her first name Annie, but had better success using the name "Lou" Rogers, whom the public would assume was a man.

Between 1908 and 1940: The Sears Roebuck Company sold 70,000 homes. Customers could order their home from a catalog, choosing from 370 different designs ranging in price from $191.00 for a 3-room house (16 feet X 20 feet, with a kitchen, living room, and bedroom) to $5,972.00 for a two story colonial. The materials were shipped by rail and could be bought pre-cut. Although fairly simple to assemble, the houses were sturdy and can still be found throughout the United States, including Ken and Beth Bates's home in Patten. Their house was built by a Quint and has been occupied by at least 6 different households over the years.

The Patten Town Report started publishing the names of those people who hadn't paid their taxes. The town had a building to house the hearse.

1909-1910: Verdi Ludgate of Patten served in the Maine House of Representatives. Bert Fernald was governor of Maine from 1909-1911, and William Howard Taft was the U.S. president from 1909-1913.

1909-1912: Winfield Scott Kellogg of Patten served in the Maine Senate.

1909: The Patten Hardware was opened by Chester Richardson, Sr. The store was located on the site that is now Richardson's Farm Supply. Note in the photo at the right that there are cows as well as gas pumps on Main Street.

1909, cont.: Another view of the hardware store (in the photo at the left from the 1991 Patten Heritage Calendar) shows a restaurant and barber shop beside the store. Some other businesses/proprietors around this time included Ira F. Cooper, Mrs. Cora Wescott, Mrs. Bettel, Mrs. I.E. Leslie, Abraham Savage, Huston Clothing, Aaron Smith, Howard M. Tozier, Irving Bragg, Bailey & Drew, R.H. or H.R. Grant, Edward Ambrose, H.G. Bither, Ira B. Gardner & Sons, Hodgman Realty (Halbert Gardner), and Watson & Company, which might have been my great-grandparents Henry and Melvina (Dow) Watson or M.J. Watson (who showed up in the business listings at the end of the next chapter). Or maybe M. J. was Melvina! I tell you, it gets gnarly trying to figure these people out!

1910: The Baptist Church closed.

Hal Gardner, son of Ira and Helen Gardner, built his home (photo at right courtesy of Vicki Richardson) on Houlton Street. You can read more about this amazing structure in Chapter Eleven.

The population of Patten was 1,406. Mount Chase had 227 residents.

In its four years of existence, the Patten Academy girls' basketball team had never lost a game. In 1910, they won the State Preparatory School Champion-ship. Left to right in the photo are Annie Carpenter, Daffa Morrill, Grace Coady, Lota Boynton (my great-aunt), and Eva Smallwood.

-75-

1911: Dr. Lore Rogers (son of Luther and Mary Rogers and brother of Annie Lou Rogers) was appointed as the Representative from the United States to the International Dairyman's Congress in Stockholm, Sweden. Rogers was a noted bacteriologist who made several important discoveries about maintaining and using dairy products. You can read more about the Rogers family at the end of this chapter.

The Great Fire of 1911 destroyed most of Bangor's downtown area. A fire at the Triangle Shirtwaist Factory in New York City led to the deaths of 146 workers who couldn't escape from the burning building because they were locked in.

Frederick Plaisted was Maine's governor from 1911-1913.

1911-1912: The Shin Pond House burned in 1911. It was rebuilt the next year by Zenas Littlefield Harvey. He also built cabins to accommodate clients. Shin Pond had a post office across the street from the hotel. It was operated by Lula Hatt, Harvey's sister-in-law.

1912: J. E. Twitchell, son of blacksmith J.H. Twitchell, had also become a blacksmith. The photo at the right shows his shop on Main Street near Webb Brook. At various points during the time Twitchell was a blacksmith, he joined up with other men in partnerships. Mr. Twitchell was considered to be highly skilled in working with metal.

The Mount Chase Town Report listed motor boats, logs, and lumber as well as livestock under personal property. Money was spent by the road commissioner, Electus Oakes, for 12 ½ pounds of dynamite and 100 feet of fuse. Sounds like major road construction was in the works!

The Patten Town Report stated that the population of Patten was 1,407 people, with 497 of them between the ages of 5 and 21. There were 49 births, 22 marriages, and 20 deaths (7 of which were children) that year. The town had a rock crusher. Money was appropriated for a sinking fund.

1912, cont.: Speaking of sinking, 1912 was the year that the Titanic sank after hitting an iceberg in the North Atlantic Ocean. More than 1,500 people drowned because there were not enough life boats for everyone, even though the Titanic had been advertised as the most amazing vessel ever built. There were 710 survivors.

Still speaking of sinking, I had a sinking feeling when I discovered that the governor of Maine in 1912 (Frederick Plaisted) authorized the illegal take-over of the island of Malaga off the coast of Maine. With motives of economics (the possibility of turning Malaga into a tourist destination), eugenics (wiping out "undesirables" by sterilization or other means), racism (the residents were black, white, native, or mixed races), and snobbery (some felt this island was a blight on Maine), about 45 residents of Malaga were forced to leave their homes. The residents, who were poor to begin with, fared poorly elsewhere. Eight residents were incarcerated at the Pineland Home for the Feebleminded, including six who were in no way mentally incapacitated. Even the remains in 17 graves were dug up and put into five coffins and buried at Pineland. In 2010, Governor Baldacci apologized to the descendants of these unfortunate souls.

1913: The Great Lakes Big Blow (also called the White Hurricane) was a cyclonic blizzard that struck the area in November, a typical month for severe storms around the Great Lakes. This particular storm was the deadliest and most destructive disaster in Great Lakes history. The city of Cleveland, Ohio, was paralyzed under two feet of snow and ice. The storm killed 250 people and destroyed 19 ships.

Bertram Smith of Patten served in the Maine House of Representatives from 1913-1914. William Haines was Maine's governor from 1913-1915, and Woodrow Wilson was the U.S. president from 1913-1921.

1914: Mannie and Tad Peavey cut ice from Peasley Brook and delivered it around town with a wagon.

Halbert P. Gardner of Patten ran for Governor of Maine as a member of the Progressive Party.

1914, cont.: The Patten Town Report indicated that there was a town hall and a public dump, but there no longer was a town farm. The new town hall had been built at the corner of what are now Founders and Gardner Streets. It had electricity and plumbing and was heated with coal. There was, however, one disappointment for the town: basketball was not allowed in the gym for fear it would be too destructive. A compromise was reached before the next basketball season by putting nets over the lights and bars over the windows. C.E. Merrill earned $1000.00 a year as principal for Patten Academy.

1915: A Patten dentist, Dr. Justin N. Rogers, and his wife, Maud McLeod (a graduate of Patten Academy in 1913), were killed in a car accident at a railroad crossing near Farmington. They were on their honeymoon.

Dr. Manson D. Brown opened a dentist's office, which was located at one time on the 2nd floor of the Rowe Building. He filled cavities and pulled teeth until the 1940's and was also the owner of Brown's funeral home.

Oakley Curtis was Maine's governor from 1915-1917.

The Patten Town Report informs us that the town had a truant officer, five constables, two winter and four summer road machines, a rock crusher, and a building in which to store the machinery. Some interesting expenditures are listed in the town report. Two men were reimbursed by the town for sheep that had been killed by dogs, and the University of Maine was paid for analyzing beer. Horses were hired for the assessors to use. Assistance to the poor included money given to tramps. (This was a common occurrence.) Dr. E.J. Farnham was reimbursed for disinfecting material.

Alumni updates in the *Mirror* reported that Ralph Miles was clerking at Quincy & Rowe and was also chauffeur for Q & R; Dr. Ben Woodbury Jr. was doctoring in Portsmouth, N.H.; Earl Finch cooked and clerked at F.W. Peavey's establishment, Clifford Wescott worked at the Creamery, Raymond Hagar was clerking at the Drug Store, Mabel Rowe was a phone operator, Dove Soule (Chapman) was playing the piano for movies in Bangor, and Beryl Palmer did the same in Patten.

This photo shows Main Street looking north in 1915. On the west side of Main Street you can see the bandstand, Ira B. Gardner & Sons, Patten Drug Co., two houses, and the Baptist Church. On the east side of Main Street are Quincy, Cooper & Rowe, Bradford's Tin Shop, Aaron Smith Clothing, Patten House, and the J. K. Osgood store.

1916: Francis Peavey built the Peavey Block. This building still stands. For many years, it housed a hotel and restaurant. In more recent years, various stores, including the present day Richardson's Hardware, have occupied the building. At one point during these years, there was a pool hall in the back of the restaurant. Dr. G. Frank Woodbury had his doctor's office upstairs.

This photo of Patten's east side is from Eleanor Sargent Hunter. The sign over the auto is for the A.L. Pinette store.

Saint Paul's Roman Catholic Church was built by Paul Gagnon. It is located at the corner of Katahdin and High Street.

1917-1918: World War I had started in 1914 as a conflict between several European countries. The United States stayed neutral for the first three years of the war, although it provided various means of support to the Allied Forces. On April 6, 1917, the United States declared war on the German empire and subsequently sent four million personnel (nicknamed doughboys) to Europe over the course of its involvement in the war. Eighty-six young men and three nurses from the Patten and Mount Chase area enlisted in the military.

1917-1918, cont.: Tom and Minnie's Walker's son Private 1st Class Raymond Walker (born in Hersey in 1895, photo at right) was the only local resident killed in action. He first served with Co. K, 2nd Rgt. Infantry, Maine National Guard. As a member of Co. K, 103rd Infantry Regiment, 26th Division, he died in Xivary, France in June, 1918 at age 22. He was buried in Plot C, Row 29, Grave 13 at the St. Mihiel American Cemetery in Thiaucourt, France.

His brother Fred, who later lived at Matagamon, was severely wounded in the same battle. The American Legion Post in Patten was named after Raymond Walker. Also wounded in battle were Eddie Mitchell and Louis Deschane, who was awarded the French Croix de Guerre.

Included in the 110,000 deaths of Americans who died in Europe were the 43,000 who lost their lives in an influenza pandemic. Private Harold "John" Daley (born in 1894 in Mount Chase, photo at left) was the son of Edgar (Edward?) and Lucia Daley and brother of Ada Johnson. He was a member of the 103rd Infantry Regiment, 26th Division. He died one month after arriving in Europe of pneumonia in Oct., 1917, and is buried in Plot A, Row 31, Grave 28, at Meuse-Argonne American Cemetery, Romagne, France. Private John Coote (born in Patten in 1887) photo at right) was the son of Mitchell and Nellie Coote and the brother of William, John, and Luella Coote. He died of pneumonia while serving with the 24th Co. 20th Engineers.

Jessie Mariner (born in 1887 in Mount Chase) was the daughter of Madrid and Clara (Steen) Mariner and the sister of Margery Ann and Julia Louise Mariner. Her grandparents were John and Marjorie (Fish) Steen of Mount Chase and her uncle was the Mount Chase Ira Fish. Jessie died of flu in October 1918 just two months after enlisting as a Red Cross nurse while stationed in Georgia. She is buried with her mother and grandparents in the Route 11 Mount Chase cemetery.

1917: Carl E. Milliken of Island Falls served as Maine's governor from 1917-1921.

Patten was publishing a newspaper called *The Katahdin Herald.* An issue from 1917 included articles about Francis Peavey's restaurant, the local men who had enlisted to fight in World War I, who was visiting whom around the area, and the need for a bank.

In one devastating fire, the east side of Main Street burned flat. The fire, which started in wall partitions near a chimney, burned a residence on School Street (now Founders) and these businesses: the J.K. Osgood store, the Patten House (with an annex, barns, and stable), the Huston-Rowe clothing store, Calvin Bradford's tin shop, the Aaron L. Smith clothing store, the Howard Tozier grocery store and an upstairs apartment, the Quincy and Rowe general store and telephone office, William Coote's restaurant, and Fred Bailey's furniture store and express office along with an upstairs apartment. Four families were left homeless. The proprietors of the Patten House at this time were Archie and Donald Nevers. This photo taken the day after the fire shows the west side of Main Street: the Ira B. Gardner & Sons store, the bandstand, the Peavey block (which included Francis Peavey's restaurant), Patten Hardware, Bowers Gas Station, and a house.

The year 1917 seemed to be a logical place to end this chapter. It was in many ways the end of an era in Patten history. The years ahead would be a time of transition as World War I vets returned to their families, towns, and jobs, and Patten would be trying to rebuild its Main Street. There was a popular consensus at the time that World War I had been the war to end all wars; sadly, we know that wasn't true. Patten residents probably thought that the worst possible thing could have happened to their town. Sadly, we know that the area would face many more challenges in the years to come.

The *Maine Registers* from 1890 to 1917 and other resources yielded this information:

Services:

- Barbers: C.H. Quincy, P.W. Frye, Fred E. Arnold, Henry Rith, Francis Peavey, Anthony Sousa, E.E. Finch (barber shop and restaurant)
- Carpenters: H.A. Crommett, J.H. Palmer, Batchelder H. Huston, Fred Huston, Frank Bates, John Grant and Son, Frank Crommett
- Dentists: M. B. Smiley, June B. Robinson, Justin Rogers, Manson D. Brown
- Doctors: Benjamin C. Woodbury, W. T. Merrill, G. Frank Woodbury, O.F. Best, Elmer J. Farnharm
- Electricity: Huston Brothers, Merrill Mill
- Employment and ticket office: A.L. Pinnette
- Express office, misc.: Fred Bailey (whose mother Adaline was Eli Kellogg's daughter)
- Furniture repair: H. R. Grant
- Garage: Charles Ellis, Grant's Garage (F.A. Grant; auto repair and painting)
- Hides, skins, furs, tanning, taxidermy: Barnard Savage, Abraham Smith, David Armstrong
- Hotels: Patten Exchange (Simeon Pomeroy), Patten House (George Russell, Carpenter & Quincy, Nevers Brothers), Shin Pond House (Lewis Cooper, Zenas Harvey), Ted Crommett
- Insurance and Real Estate: Winfield Kellogg, Howard Tozier, Ira Carpenter, Hodgman Realty (Halbert Robinson)
- Justices: Bertram Smith, Hiram Hersey, Daniel Scribner, Ira B. Gardner, Loring B. Huston, Charles Wescott, Sylvester L. Huston, Raymond Gardner
- Lawyers: Bertram Smith, John Scott, Verdi Ludgate (Mr. Ludgate was also an accomplished musician and worked with Patten Academy students who were competing in public speaking events.)
- Livery stables: Fred Roberts, Nevers Brothers
- Music teachers: Mrs. Henry C. (Alice) Rowe, Miss Emma Lane
- Photography: Albert Klein, E.M. Sipprelle
- Plumber: George F. Burleigh
- Postmasters: Winfield S. Kellogg, Daniel Scribner, Jacob Hersey
- Restaurants: I.H. Bragg, Francis Peavey, William Coote, The Lunch Cart (Howard Ambrose), E.E. Finch
- Surveyors: C.E.Cobb, H.G. Robinson
- Telephone Service: Patten Telephone Co., Katahdin Farmers Telephone
- Undertaker: N.A. Raymond
- Water: Patten Water Company (Ira B. Gardner, President)

Merchants:

- Agricultural implements: L. M. Carver, Charles W. Wescott
- Automobiles: E.J. Farnham
- Clothing and footwear: L. A. Savage, Huston Clothing, Aaron Smith, H. A. Scribner Shoe Co., A.L. Pinnette, Nathan Arbo (Mount Chase)
- Confectionaries: Mrs. William Howes (Mount Chase)
- Dressmakers, milliners, ladies accessories, dry goods: Mrs. Mabel Crommett, Miss Elsie Miles, Miss Mary Mitchell, Mrs. Mary Merrill, Mrs. W.H. (Rubie) McKenney, Mrs. H.D. Miles, Mrs. W.W. Pond, Mrs. C.W. Clark, Mrs. Charles Killam (whose daughter was married to William Coote), Mrs. F. C. Moody, Mrs. Cora Wescott, Mrs. Ilbert Leslie Co. (Fanny Wheaton; her ad read: Brickety Brackety, Hoo Rah Rack, Call on us for whatever you lack.), Patten Dry Goods (Anna Morse and Bertha Huston; they sold McCall's Patterns), Mrs. E.G. Bettell
- Furniture: J. W. Leslie, Huston Brothers, Bailey and Drew, Patten Furniture and Harness Co.
- General stores: Gardner & Coburn, Bradford & Merrill, R. Mitchell, I.F. Cooper, Ira B. Gardner & Sons, George T. Merrill, Leroy Miles, Quincy & Rowe, J. F. Hersey, the Grange Store (manager James Sprague)
- Groceries/meat: C. H. Quincy, Howard Tozier, Atwood Ryder, The Bell Grocery, Huston and Morse, Patten Bakery (H.M. White), The Little Store (J. F. Shean), I.H. Bragg (fruit, confectioneries, soda, pipes, cigars, tobacco)
- Hardware stores: Patten Hardware (C.G. Richardson)
- Horses: H.W. Brown, Ira D. Carpenter
- Jewelers, watch and eyeglass repair, clocks, china, silverware, etc.: Abial Huntley, S. P. Hussey, W.A. McKenney, McKenney Brothers, C. S. Grindal
- Pharmacy: Patten Drug Company: Dr. O.F. Best, Dr. Elmer J. Farnham
- Potatoes and fertilizer: Quincy & Rowe, E.J. Parker, Patten Produce Co., F.G. Huston

Note: Mrs. Rubie Ella (Wotton) McKenney (1853-1936) was married to William H. McKenney (1845-1917) and had two children, Ira and Lena (Brown). She was also married to William A. McKenney (1845-1906, the jeweler) at some point during her life. W.A. worked as a jeweler in Boston. The 1920 edition of *The Jewelers' Circle* reported that W. A. McKenney had made a recent trip north to Patten for a short visit, and Abial Huntley had driven south in his automobile to visit Boston.

A Huston Clothing ad from this era announced that Parcel Post service was now available, and Huston Clothing would pay the postage to deliver your order.

Manufacturers/Farmers:

- Blacksmiths: Bragg & Perry, Robbins & Burho, C.W. Cramp, Frank McGraw, Burton Bettel, F.W. Edwards, Amos Curran, ? Parker, Twitchell & McGraw, Bragg & Bradley, A.P. Ryder, J.E. Twitchell & H.G. Robinson
- Boots and shoes: Horatio Miles, G. W. Cooper
- Carding and grist mill: C. A. Gifford
- Caskets and coffins: Jerome Frye, Huston Brothers, P.W. Frye
- Furniture and woodwork: Gilman & Carlisle, Gilman & Merrill, Huston Bros.
- Harnesses: Oliver Cobb & Sons, William Smallwood, L.W. Harris
- Logging operations: See Chapter Thirteen
- Lumber and spools: Merrill Mill (G.T. and E. L. Merrill)
- Lumber: William Gifford, Jerry Foote (Mr. Gifford's son-in-law)
- Milk: O.J. Parsons
- Patten Bottling Company (Irving Bragg)
- Patten Planing Company (L.B. Huston, Manager)
- Shingles, clapboards, grist mill: John and Ira Gardner
- Starch: Patten Starch Company (John & Ira Gardner, T.H. Phair, J.T. Piper)
- Tinware: C. Bradford, G.T. Merrill, G.F. Burleigh
- Wheelrights: Huston & Blake, A.P. Ryder, John O. Soule, N.W. Finch, Herbert Crommett, Charles Allerton

The history of Patten's businesses was confusing at times.   One reason is that some of my sources relied on oral history, and facts might have gotten changed over the years. Another reason was that any one man could be involved in several different business ventures at a time. A third reason was that often fathers and sons had the same name, and often there were brothers who were businessmen at the same time. (I had an awful time with J. Frye—was that Jerome the undertaker or Jacob the cheesemaker?)   But the biggest reason for the confusion was the constant changing of business partners. For example, John Gardner had these businesses at one time or another: the Gardner and Stetson Store, the Gardner and Coburn Store, the John Gardner Store, and the John and Ira B. Gardner mill. So if mistakes have been made, it might be my fault, or it might not be!

To help keep myself straight on some of the families of several generations who lived in Patten and Mount Chase through the years, I started making charts. The family charts on the final pages for this chapter might help you keep a few of the families straight. Or they may not. (If a name is underlined, that means there is more information below.)

BRADFORD: Calvin Bradford (1793 to 1875) was born in Turner, Maine and moved to Moro in 1836. He was married to Kesiah Keen, and they had at least three sons, <u>Ezekiel</u> and two of whom were named <u>Calvin</u>; the first died in 1835 at the age of 14. The Bradford family owned the Bradford Inn in Moro until 1893.

- Calvin Bradford was born in Moro in 1840. He married Mary Stetson, the daughter of Elbridge Stetson, for whom the Stetson Memorial United Methodist Church was named. Calvin and Mary were postmasters in Patten for a time. He was a town leader and represented the area in the 1891 state legislature. He had a tinware shop.
- Ezekiel Bradford (1828-1913) married Helen Bathsheba Bradford (1837-1893). When she became seriously ill in 1893, Ezekiel purchased Joshua Goodwin's property and home on Main Street in Patten because of her need to be closer to medical attention. Sadly, she passed before the move was completed. Ezekiel maintained Goodwin's farming business, producing milk and crops for sale. Ezekiel and Helen had three children: <u>Freeman</u>, Jennie (1871-1925), and Annie (1865-1941). The two girls never married.
  - ➢ Freeman Bradford was born in Moro in 1875. He was a farmer and town leader and was a staunch supporter of Patten Academy. His first wife, Marcia Weeks Bradford, was a teacher in Limestone and then at Patten Academy. After she died, he married Irene Olsen, who was born in 1914 in Hollis Center, Maine. Her family moved to Patten in 1930 so that Irene and her brother Dudley could attend Patten Academy. In 1937, she joined the faculty at Patten Academy. After Freeman died in 1958, Irene ran the farm for several years. She was a town leader, a devoted Methodist, the unofficial town historian, and the author of an excellent book about the history of Patten Academy. Irene died in 1996.

Note: Irene's brother Dudley Olsen became a local businessman after graduating from Patten Academy. He married Marguerite Hatt of Patten. They had two children, Janine Olsen Bertone and Kristin Olsen.

SCRIBNER: Daniel Scribner (#1, 1718-1802) served in the Revolutionary War as a captain. He was married to Elizabeth Taylor and they had at least nine children: Lydia (Pitts), Abigail (Coffin), Hannah (Whitham), Joseph, Daniel, Susan (Kimball), Nathaniel, and Betsey (Cates).

- Daniel Scribner (#2; 1776-1862 or 1872) was born in Waterboro, Maine and moved to Crystal in 1842. He and his first wife, Hannah Kneeland, had two children: Sally (married Hiram Willard, had at least ten children) and Aaron. Daniel and his second wife, Hannah Sampson, had at least eleven children: Asenath (Cole), Nathaniel (married Mary Peasely), Diana, William, Reuben (married Elizabeth Sterling), Mary Ann (King), Hannah Cole, Jemima S., Miles Sampson, and Daniel Sampson. They had also had another child named Daniel Sampson who died at the age of three.
- Aaron Scribner (1800-1865) was married to Diadoma Stevens (1806-1865). They had at least twelve children: Thomas, Ruth, Gideon, Lucy, Aaron, Hanson, Ruth, Sarah, Elizabeth, Abner, and Daniel. Aaron died as a result of burns from a fire that killed two of his children, Abner and possibly Daniel. There were two Ruths: the first one died in 1840 and the second one was born in 1842. Aaron and Diadoma also had a son named Francis who was wounded in the Civil War. Francis married Eliza Ann Hayden Scribner, who was previously married to his cousin Miles Sampson Scribner (see below).
- Hannah Cole Scribner married John Troop of Patten, who was killed in action in the battle of Cold Harbor during the Civil War.
- Jemima S. Scribner married Lorenzo Wadlin of Patten. They had at least two children. Loammi Hooper Wadlin was killed in action in 1864 in the battle of Cold Harbor along with his uncle John Troop. Another son, Ira Fish Wadlin died of disease in 1864 in New Orleans.
- Miles Sampson Scribner (1810-1892) first married Lavinia (Lovena) Partridge McPheeters (McPheeters; 1810-1852) with whom he had a son, Miles Sampson Scribner, born in 1834. Miles and his son Miles served together in the Civil War in the 8th Regiment Infantry, Maine Volunteers. Miles, Jr. died in Washington, D.C. in 1864. He was married to Eliza Ann Hayden and they had two children: Charles Ransom (b. 1859) and Lovina Marie Allen (1862-@1894). Miles Sr.

(Scribner family continued on next page)

later married Louise (Lovisa) Fish (Fisk) Harmon (1834-1870; born the same year as Miles, Jr.!).

- Daniel Sampson Scribner (#3; 1834-1913) married Tenie A. Warren in 1845. During the Civil War, he reached the rank of Sergeant and served with the 1^{4th} Maine Regiment, Volunteer Infantry. He fought in the Mississippi River campaigns and in Baton Rouge, LA, and was captured by the Southern army during a battle in Winchester, VA. He was held at Libby and Belle Isle Prisons before being discharged. He returned home to Patten where he was a successful farmer and merchant. He was active in town and church affairs, was in the Masons, and served as postmaster for a time. Daniel and Tenie had at least four children: Loammi Wadlin (named for his uncle who died in 1864), Roland Sampson (who died during the Spanish American War), Rosalie (died in infancy), and Caleb Warren.
  - Caleb Warren Scribner (1882-1968) was the son of Daniel and Tenie (Warren) Scribner. He was born in Patten and was a 1901 graduate of Patten Academy. He was a farmer and served as the Inland Fish and Game Warden Supervisor for the state of Maine. He and Lore Rogers were responsible for the creation of the Lumberman's Museum. He was a good friend of Maine Governor Percival P. Baxter and was an organizer of the caribou replacement project. At his funeral in 1968, Scribner was referred to as Mr. Patten and even as Mr. Northern Maine. In 1904, Caleb married his first wife, Margaret Emma Main, the daughter of Martin Van Buren and Lucy Main and sister of Henry Main. Caleb and Margaret had at least five children: Archer, Archer's twin Hugh (who died at around age one), Faustina, Daniel, and Elizabeth (Chadbourne Largay). In 1941, Caleb married Laura Green (also referred to as Laura Pedder); she was a well-respected teacher at Patten Academy. In 1961, Caleb married Althea Bemis.
    - Archer (1911-1967) served as Patten's first town manager in 1940. He married Yvonne Pinnette and they had seven children: Daniel, Warren, Wade, Paul, Peter, Barbara, and Joanne.
    - Faustina Warren Scribner was born in 1906 in Patten and married Frederick L. Quint. They had five children: Pauline Arbo Foster, Melvena McNally Hathaway, Margaret Laurosonis, Winnifred Bradstreet, and Frederick Quint (married Betty Desmond).

Several Scribner descendants of Pauline, Melvena, and Frederick still live in the Patten and Mount Chase area.

LESLIE: William Leslie (b. 1766) married Mary Chase and had at least three children: Elizabeth, George, and Samuel. He also married Sarah and had at least two children, William and Mary Ann. Samuel Chase Leslie (1791-1845) was an experienced millwright who had built mills in Massachusetts, Lincoln, Bangor, Dixmont, and Exeter before moving to Patten. Samuel was married to Elizabeth Thomas (1793-1846) and they had at least eight children: William (b. 1818, married Sarah Kneeland), David (1819-1847), Esther (b. 1820, married Luther Blackwell, James Ballock (b. 1823, Married Cynthia Kneeland), Samuel Chase (b. 1826, married Mary Ann Dolber), John Putnam, Sylvester J. (b. 1831, married Isabelle Huston of Hersey), and Mary Eliza (1835-1858, married Levi Blake). John Putnam (J.P., 1828-1888) married Sarah Cary and had at least three children: Lena (1868-1885, m. W.T. Cobb), Ilbert (I.E., b. 1863, m. Fanny Wheaton), and Cora (born 1879, m. Charles Wescott). J.P. also married Julia Butters Phillips and had a daughter Elizabeth. Note: I also came across the names Sylvanus Leslie and J.W. Leslie. Sylvanus's name appears on the special 1837 census list for Patten, living alone and over the age of 21. J.W. Leslie appears as a Patten merchant during the time period 1890-1917.

WESCOTT: Samuel Wescott married Mary Jane. They had a son James Warren Wescott, who married Mary Gove (died 1853). James and Mary had at least four children: William (drowned at Matagamon), John (died of Civil War wounds), Daniel (died of disease in Louisiana during the Civil War), and Harrison. James Wescott married again, to Mae Elvira Giles, and they had at least four children: Mary, Edith, James (born 1859), and Charles (b. 1855). Charles married Cora Leslie.

CHARLES AND CORA (LESLIE) WESCOTT: Charles W. Wescott was a lumberman, photographer, farmer, and merchant (selling agricultural implements) at various times and held the town positions of auditor, trial justice, and deputy sheriff at various times. He was also involved in horse breeding and racing along with his son Stanley. Cora attended Patten Academy and studied music in Boston; she was a milliner and dressmaker. Charles and Cora had at least six children: Lena Mae (1883-1885), Thurman (1887), Stanley (1889), Clifford (1891), Chester (1893-1895), and Winnifred (married Herbert Nelson Gardner: see Gardner family history). The surviving children all attended Patten Academy and various colleges. Stanley served as Patten's postmaster at one time.

ROGERS: Caleb Rogers (1772-1847) was born and died in Newbery, MA. He was married to Elizabeth Ordway, and they had at least two children, <u>Luther</u> and David.
- Dr. Luther Rogers (1800-1877) was born in Newbury, Massachusetts. He attended the Medical School of Maine and in 1827 graduated from Dartmouth College with a medical degree. After practicing medicine in Massachusetts and southern Maine, he moved his family and practice to Patten around 1842, becoming Patten's first doctor. Dr. Rogers helped found the Congregational Church and was a founding trustee of Patten Academy. He was married to Hannah Bailey and they had four children: Sarah (1837-1920, married Charles Fish, 1832-1915), <u>Luther Bailey</u>, Edwin Searle (died in the Civil War), and Lucasta.
  - Colonel Luther Bailey Rogers (1840-1927) was the son of Luther and Hannah (Bailey) Rogers. As a teen, he was active in the Patten Rifle Company and enlisted to fight in the Civil War. He fought in the same battle that killed his brother Edwin and was later wounded in battle. He returned home and became a successful farmer, lumberman, and businessman. He married Mary Hersey, who died 15 days after giving birth to their daughter Matilda. He then married Mary Barker, and they had several children: Edwin, <u>Lore,</u> Mary, Annie Lou (who became a well-known cartoonist), David, Ruth(married Angus MacLean; more on them in Chapter Twelve), and Luther. Colonel L.B. (as he was known) built camps at Shin Pond and at Lunksoos on the East Branch of the Penobscot and often invited groups of Patten Academy students to enjoy the camps.
    - Dr. Lore Alford Rogers (1875-1975) was the son of Luther and Mary Rogers and a Patten Academy graduate. He was a well-known bacteriologist who made important discoveries about maintaining and using dairy products. He represented the U.S. at the International Dairyman's Congress in Sweden in 1911. After retirement, he returned to Patten, operated Katahdin Creamery for several years, and helped establish the Lumberman's Museum. He was married to Beatrice Oberly and they had a son John Oberly Rogers (who was a lawyer in Patten for many years and was married to Caroline Averill). After Beatrice's death, Dr. Rogers married Katherine Keiper Sherman, the librarian and the widow of a friend.

GARDNER: John Gardner (1812-1902) was born in Buckfield, Maine, the youngest of eleven children of Jonathan and Sarah Gardner. He left home to fend for himself around 1831, working first in the boat canals in southern Maine before opening a country store in Paris, Maine. In 1838, he married Mary A. Colburn (1818-1894, daughter of Samuel and Harriet Colburn of Sumner), and they moved to Patten in 1841. He immediately opened a "country store" and became active in town affairs, including serving as postmaster, selectman, town clerk, town treasurer, and for eight years deputy sheriff. His initial business prospered and he established others, including a starch factory and a lumber mill. He served as a member of the Maine House of Representatives in 1846 and was part of the committee which enacted a temperance law. In 1868-1869 he served in the Maine Senate, where he was instrumental in passing legislation to build and maintain rural roads. He was a good friend of Hannibal Hamlin, who said John was one of the best men he ever knew. John was generous and gave freely to various charities. His wife Mary was a woman of strong faith. She and John were happily married for 56 years. They had four children: Ira Bernard Gardner, Ida Rosalie Robinson, Eva Alberta Lurvey, and Almy Evelyn Webster Kellogg.

- Almy Gardner married Alphonso Webster, then married Winfield Scott Kellogg in 1886. He was the son of Eli and Fanny Kellogg, two of Patten's earliest settlers. Winfield was previously married to Emma Jewell of Monticello. Almy and Winfield had one child, Gemma, who died in infancy.
- Colonel Ira Bernard Gardner was born in 1843 in Patten. As a teenager, he joined the Patten Rifle Company (the local militia). In 1861, he joined Co. I, 14th Maine Infantry Regiment, and left to fight in the Civil War. In 1863, he returned to Maine to retrieve some new recruits and to make a quick trip home to Patten to see his sweetheart, Helen Darling. Along the way, he was involved in a steamboat collision and saved several soldiers from drowning. Upon arriving in Portland, while waiting for a horse and cart, Ira visited a Portland tavern, where he was accosted by a group of Copperheads who were angry about the draft. He escaped with his life, thanks to a friend who happened to be in the tavern at the same time. Upon arriving in Patten, he discovered Helen was off visiting friends in another town.

(Gardner family continued on next page)

They finally met up three days later, just in time for Helen to accompany him partway on his trip back to the war. In March, 1864, he returned home again long enough to marry Helen. (Her family chart is below.) In September, 1864, he lost his right arm at the Battle of Opequan Creek, near Winchester. He had been promoted rapidly through the ranks due to great leadership skills and bravery in battle; he achieved the rank of Brevet Lieutenant Colonel. After the war, he was a Patten businessman and town leader. He owned stores, mills, and logging operations. He wrote a book about his war experiences called *Personal Recollections of a Boy Volunteer.*

DARLING: Jonathan Darling (1741-1828) married to Hannah Holt (1741-1826). They had at least one child, Samuel Darling (1781-1859), who moved to Patten in the 1830's. His first wife, Hannah Osgood, was born in 1785 and died while giving birth to their son Anson Darling in 1806. Anson was lost at sea in 1844. Samuel and his second wife, Polly (Mary) Jellison (1792-1871) had at least 7 children: Hannah (married a Bradbury), Horatio, Samuel Jr. (married Mary Fairfield), Sarah, Louisa, Mary Dean, and Isabel (married Thomas Haynes). Three of the sisters—Sarah, Louisa, and Mary Dean—married three brothers: Augustus, Offin, and James Palmer, respectively, and their brother Horatio married Harriet Palmer. They were the children of Jonathan Palmer, one of Patten's first settlers.

- Horatio Nelson Darling (1813-1897) was elected as a selectman at Patten's first town meeting in 1841. He married Harriet Palmer (1816-1904) and they had at least one child, Helen M. Darling.
  - Helen M. Darling was born in 1842. Helen was a teacher in Patten and Island Falls. She organized the Chautauqua Circle and belonged to the 20th Century Club. Her 1924 obituary commented that her husband, Ira B. Gardner, was the wealthiest men in Northern Maine.

(Gardner family continued on next page)

THE CHILDREN OF IRA B. AND HELEN (DARLING) GARDNER

- Halbert Paine Gardner (1867-1952) was named after a general that his father Ira had served under during the Civil War. Hal Gardner completed Patten Academy at the age of 16 and worked as a bookkeeper for his father. He also was a Patten businessman and was involved in Huston Clothing Company and Hodgman Realty & Manufacturing Company. He served in the Maine House of Representatives from 1899-1902 and in the Maine Senate from 1903-1906, and he ran for governor as a member of the Progressive Party in 1914. He was not elected, but continued to remain active in politics throughout his life. He married Adelaide Darling of Ashland in 1893, and they had two daughters, Helen P. and Dorothy. In 1910, he built the home that later became Resthaven Nursing Home. (You can read more about this remarkable house in Chapter Eleven.) The family moved to Portland at some point after 1910. Halbert was regarded by his colleagues and constituents as a remarkable speaker and was viewed not only as a man of wealth and power but as a wise and philanthropic citizen.
- Raymond D. Gardner (1868-1945) became a prominent businessman in Patten. He married Georgie Kelsey (1874-1901, daughter of G. Edward and Harriet Kelsey), and they had five children: Everett Kelsey, John R., Ira B. (died at age 39 in 1944), Halbert Paine, and George Edward. Everett was married to Clara Hall (1895-1977). He survived military service during World War I only to die while serving in the South Pacific during World War II. John R. married Eva Coolong, daughter of Tellis and Mathilda (Campbell) Coolong (see also pages 96-97). Their son John T. Gardner told me he was delivered in their home on Houlton Street by Dr. Frank Woodbury, who suggested his middle name, *Tertius*, which is Latin for *third*. John T. had a sister Georgie who was named after her grandmother.
- Mary Ida Gardner (1871-1921) married Sylvester L. Huston (see page 94).
- Herbert Nelson Gardner (1877-1941) graduated from Bowdoin College and the University of Maine Law School. He served as principal at Patten Academy and at Dexter High School before opening a law office in Portland. He married Winnifred Wescott, daughter of Charles and Cora (Leslie) Wescott of Patten (see page 89).
- An unnamed infant son, died in 1885.

HUSTON (pronounced HYOO-stun): Samuel Huston (1805-1893) was born in Plymouth, Maine, the son of James and Nancy Huston, and died in Patten. He married Harriet Pushor, (1810-1904) who was born in Fairfield, Maine. Samuel and Harriet moved to Hersey. Mr. Huston was a carpenter, served as a justice, and owned a grocery store. They had at least one child: <u>Batchelder Hussey Huston</u>.

- Batchelder Hussey Huston (1833-1912) was born in Pittsfield and died in Patten. In 1861, he married Lucetta Drew (1843-1923). They had at least seven children: Annie (1862-1938, married Edwin E. Morse, 1858-1931), <u>Loren</u>, <u>Sylvester</u>, <u>Ferdinand</u>, Mabel (1877-1962, married George Mayo), Frank (1882-1965, married Agnes Ambrose of Sherman), and <u>Frederick</u>.
    - Loren Batchelder Huston (1865-1943) was born in Hersey and died in Patten. He married Bertha Finch in Patten in 1893. L.B. Huston owned a grocery store, was the manager of the Patten Planing Company, served as a justice, and was active in the Patten Brass Band.
    - Sylvester Leslie Huston (1871-1922) was born in Hersey and died in Patten. He married Mary Ida Gardner (1871-1921, daughter of Ira and Helen Gardner) in 1895. Sylvester was active in town affairs and was the leader of the Patten Brass Band at one point.
    - Ferdinand Gilman Huston (1875-1950) was born in Hersey and died in Patten. In 1898 he married Effie McManus Hackett (1874-1970), who was from Oxbow. Ferd was a potato and fertilizer dealer, ran an insurance company, sold automobiles, and was on the first board of directors for Katahdin Trust Company. Ferd and Effie had two children: Robert (1906-1912) and Cecil Batchelder Huston (1900-1975). Cecil married Alberta Richert and they had three sons: John, Albert, and Kay.
    - Frederick Samuel Huston (1884-1974) married Lettie Mary Corliss in 1910 and Vella Porter (born 1889 in Patten) in 1921. Fred and Vella had two children: Sylvester and Waldon. Fred was a carpenter in Patten for many years.

MYRICK: Thomas Myrick (1777-1885) was probably born in southern Maine. He and Harston Weeks were the first residents of Mount Chase when they moved here in 1837. Thomas was married to Eunice Bethel (1777-1850, from Burnham, Maine. They had at least three children: Ezra, Thomas, and Emily. Emily married Henry Pike Buzzell, Jr.; theirs was the first marriage in Patten.

- Ezra Myrick (1802-1882) was born in Burnham, Maine and moved to Mount Chase shortly after his father did. He and his wife Elizabeth (1807-1885, from Bucksport) had at least nine children: Sarah and Temperance (1829, twins; Temperance m. Levi Caldwell), Orthelia (1832), Uriah, Sylvanah (1837), Ezra (1839, m. Octavia), Richard (1841), Electa, and Edwin (1847, m. Mary Carr).
  - Uriah Myrick (b. 1832 or 1836 in Greenbush) married Elvira Hatt. They had at least nine children, including Alonzo, Harold, Lester, James, Raymond, Authelia, Ira, Willis, and Irving. Uriah died in 1905 and is buried in the Mount Chase Cemetery.
    - Willis Myrick (1869-1956) married Lucast Howes (1872-1945, born in Mount Chase). They had at least five children: Ira, Amy, Lilla, Henry, and Earl. Ira married Beatrice Curry and was a business owner in Patten, including a gas station and general store. They had a daughter Margaret, who married Dale Bates and had three children: Kenneth, Claudia, and David. Amy Myrick married Lloyd Morse and had five children: Philip, Paul, Judy, Becky, and Ann. The Morse family owned and operated a gas station on the corner of the Shin Pond Road for many years.
    - Irving Myrick (1875-1940) married Margaret Doan. They had at least two children, Ira (who died as an infant) and Vaughn (1901-1961). Irving owned and operated sporting camps, first the Trout Brook Hotel and then Myrick's Sporting Camps at Grand Lake, Matagamon.
  - Electa Myrick (1845) married John Hatt. They had seven children, including Lucy, who married William Howes.
- Thomas Myrick (1815-1885) married Louisa Kimball (or Soper, 1815 or 1818 - 1906). They had at least one child, Melville.
  - Melville Myrick (1862-1934) married Eva Bither (1864-1944). She was a teacher and a superintendent at Mount Chase Schools. They had at least three children: Burleigh (1896-1967, married Lillian), Freddie (born in 1905), and Opal (1893-1956). Opal also taught school in Mount Chase.

CAMPBELL FAMILY (Pronounced Camp-bell): Norman Campbell was born in Fort Kent around 1820-1830, the son of Rufus and Susan (Jackman) Campbell. He married Matilda Wiles from Andover, Maine. They had at least twelve children, Fred, Susanne (Mitchell), Augusta (Perkins), Sarah, Isreal (married Celease Belanger), Norman, Mathilda, Lucinda, Charles, Mary Adelaide (married Burton Howe; parents of Dyke Howe and Virginia Fifield), Rufus (married Margaret Crandall; they are responsible for Millinocket area Campbells), and Julia. (Notes: The spelling of *Isreal* was used consistently in most resources. Mathilda is also spelled Matilda. This genealogy focuses on the Campbells who lived in Patten and Mount Chase.)

- Fred Campbell (1854-1910) married Mary Dechane (1851-1936). They had at least seven children: Joseph, Isreal, Norman, Mary (Boynton), Roscoe (married Rosella), Charlotte (Wing), and Jessie (Finch).
    - Joseph Campbell (1877-1936) married Julia Michaud (1882). Their son Eugene (1906-1974) married Alice Peavey (1907-1997). Their son Donald is the gentleman who provided me with a great deal of information and many photos for this history. He is married to Madeline Rose Bishop and they live in Patten. Joseph and Julia's son Ronald (1907-1970) married Winnifred Shorette (1913-2002) and they had at least six children: Helen (Ballard), Pauline (Bates, Withee), Louise (Marr, Jones), Ronald Jr., Edmund, and Carole Ann (Cole).
    - Isreal Campbell (1881-1948) married Sarah "Sadie" Haye. They had at least seven children: Mary Eleanor (1910-1972, m. Jesse Chaloux), Lenna (1911-1955, m. Tad Howard), Annie (1911-2010, m. Spurgeon Somers), Mary, Gilbert "Mike," (1912-1988, m. Mabel Shorette), and Rufus (died at age twelve in a logging accident). Sadie also had a daughter named Mae.
    - Norman Campbell (1883-1936) married Katherine Violette. They had Cyrus, Ruel, Walter, Winnie, Gilbert, Mabel, and Esther. Cyrus Campbell married Alexina Pinette. They had five daughters: Geraldine (Little), Margaret (Palmer), Esther "Connie" (McHugh), Irene (m. Ken Lord), and Norma "Butchie" (m. Bruce Campbell).

(Campbell family continued on next page)

- Norman Campbell (1862-1924) was born in Fort Kent but at some point moved to Baker Lake (Lac Baker), New Brunswick, where he married Hannah Fitzgerald (1863-1936), who was the daughter of George and Ann (Coro) Fitzgerald (originally from Ireland). Norman and Hannah had at least ten children. The first child, Mary Mame, was born in Baker Lake in 1888, but the other children were born in Patten: Daniel (1890), Henry (1890), Mathilda (1891), Joseph (1896), John (1901), Effie (1904), Phyllis (1904), Burt, and Clara. Norman and Hannah are both buried in Patten.
    - Effie Campbell (1904) married Peter Baker and they had at least eleven children: Charles (1928-2009), Ethel (Blake), Phyllis (m. Roland Wilkins), Mary (m. John Dickinson), Virginia (m. Roy Anderson), Tellis (died at age 2), Winnifred (Jandreau), Arthur (m. Marcia), Albert (m. Donna Barker), Marguerite (m. Kent Michaud), Peter, and Clarence (m. Ardis Blakely).
    - Clara Campbell married Merle Noonan, Sr. and they had four children: Merle, Jr., Pauline, Jean, and Linda.
    - Mathilda Campbell (1891-1934) married Telesphore Coulombe (Tellis Coolong) in 1907 in Patten. Tellis (@1879-1949) was the son of Joseph and Idella (or Adele) Pelkey (or Pelletier) of Baker Lake, N.B. He had two brothers, Joseph and Felix, and a sister Lena (m. Fred Cyr, had son Francis Cyr). Mathilda (in photo) and Tellis had at least twelve children, seven of whom died in infancy. The surviving children were Eva (m. John Gardner), Earl, Henry (m. Elsa), Hadley (m. Patricia Cunningham), and Chester (married Barbara Sargent). After Matilda's death, Tellis married Lena, and they had one son, James (m. Peggy MacArthur).
- Charles Campbell (1870-1934) married Christine Landry (1871-1933). They had at least seven children who died in infancy, including Charles, Earl, and Iva. Their surviving children were Alfred, Harold (m. Hester Wilkinson), James, Lena (m. George Carter), Melvin (m. Helena Wilkinson), Walter, Freeman (m. Ruth Waite), Clifford (m. Eleanor Gordon), and Mary "Carrie" (m. Harold Wilson).

(Campbell family continued on next page)

- Alfred "Fred" Campbell (1892-1975) married Pearl Young (1892-1975). Their children were Fred Clayton (m. Harriet Dwyer), Arlene (m. Carleton Huntley), Neal (m. Muriel Main), Christine (m. Leroy O'Hara), and Jean (m. Charles "Curley" Tarr). Pearl was also married at an earlier date to Guy Sibley and had a son Charles Sibley.
- James Campbell (1900-1978) m. Lottie Cairns (1909) and they had at least five children: Iva Christine (m. Laurel Johnson), James, Jr., Helen (m. Danny Baker), Charles, and Charles's twin, who died at birth.
- Walter Campbell (1906-1992) married Agnes Torrey (1916-2003). They had five children: Milton, Betty (Higgins), Walter, Vernon, and Melvin.

(There are many Campbell descendents still living in the Patten and Mount Chase area. If you would like a more complete Campbell family history, please contact me.)

I got a little surprise when I did some research on Ira Dearborn Fish. I discovered a whole 'nother Ira Fish family living in Mount Chase! Let me give you a little info about both families.

PATTEN'S IRA FISH: Ira Dearborn Fish (1790-1872) married Abra Ann Hayes (1795-1879). Ira established a residence in Patten after he did the initial survey of T4R6 for Amos Patten but does not seem to have immediately moved his family to Patten. Ira and Abra had three children: Ira D. (1822-1890), Charles (1832-1915), and Louise (1836-1841).
- Charles Fish attended Patten Academy, Colby College, Harvard, and Bowdoin College, then returned to Patten to serve as the principal at Patten Academy. He married Sarah Louise Rogers (1837-1920), daughter of Dr. and Mrs. Luther Rogers. They had four sons and two daughters, including a daughter Mary Lucasta (1863-1938).

(Mount Chase Ira Fish on next page)

MOUNT CHASE'S IRA FISH: John Fish (1794-1877) was from Vermont, and his wife Elizabeth (1798-1876) was from New Brunswick. They both died in Mount Chase. They had at least seven children, all born in New Brunswick and some of whom died in Mount Chase: David, John (1819-1897), Louise (1821-1877, married a Hatt), Ira, Amos, Mary Ann, and Marjorie (or Margery).

- Ira Fish (1825-1879) married Hannah Taylor and they had at least three children: Augustus (1865), William (1867), and Edward (1869).
- Marjorie Jane Fish was born in 1835 and married John Steen (1830-1892). They had at least five children, all born in Mount Chase: Wilbur, James, Joseph, Percy, and Clara.
    - Wilbur Steen (1864 or 1865) married Annie West. They had at least three children: John (1894, married Burdice Downing), Archie (1896, married Thersa Mitchell, had daughter Pauline Nott), and Dale (1900-1953, married Laurie Downing).
    - James Wellington Steen (1867-1915) married Stella Reed (1873, from Winn). They had at least three children: Geneva (1896, m. Lawrence Robinson), Verna (1900), and Marjorie (1904). Stella was a Superintendent of Schools in Mount Chase at one time.
    - Joseph Steen (1872-1944) married Ella Comfort Philpot.
    - Percy Steen (1875) married Gertrude Porter (1877-1963) from Ohio. They had at least seven children, all born in Mount Chase: Amos (1899-1975, married Flora, 1901-1975), Carroll Howard "Pat" (1902 or 1903-1965, married Mildred Killam), Herschel (1904-1991, married Lyda Gifford, had Herschel and Robert), Maurice (1908), Jessie (1913-1996, married Stanley Giles and Hadley McDonald), Elizabeth (1923), and an infant. (You can read more about four of the Steen brothers on page 421.)
    - Clara Steen (1879) married Madrid Mariner; they had at least three children: Margery Ann, Jessie Belle, and Julia Louise Mariner. Jessie died of influenza while serving as a Red Cross nurse in Georgia during World War I.

There now, doesn't that help you keep everybody straight? Patten/Mount Chase is like any typical small community where everybody seems to be related in some way to everyone else. I don't know if every family is like this, but a common topic of conversation in our family is trying to figure out how *so and so* is related to *what's his face* or *you know who I mean*. I guess it's the small town version of tracing your lineage back to the Mayflower.

CHAPTER FIVE: THE TOWNS FROM 1918-1945

The fire that burned the whole east side of Main Street in 1917 was devastating. Almost a century of development, from a wilderness to a busy Main Street, disappeared in one day. But the men and women who called Patten home picked themselves up, dusted the ashes off their clothes, and began rebuilding. The next quarter of a century saw great growth in the dual community of Patten and Mount Chase.

Please refer to Chapters Ten, Eleven, and Twelve for more detailed information on schools, the library, healthcare, emergency services, and community organizations. Chapters Fourteen, Fifteen, and Sixteen provide more information on lumbering, farming, and sporting camps from this era.

1918: The Katahdin Trust Company was founded by a group of local men. The first Board of Directors included Henry C. Rowe (president), Eugene Brown (vice-president), Charles Byram (clerk and treasurer), George Goodrich (assistant treasurer), Raymond Gardner, Charles Quincy, George Merrill, Edray Parker, Burton Howe, Ferdinand Huston, and Verdi Ludgate. The KTCo building rose from the ashes on the east side of Main Street on a lot purchased from Charles Quincy and Henry C. Rowe. The photo below shows a crowd gathered for the bank's first day in operation.

1918, cont.: Henry C. Rowe served as the president of Katahdin Trust for 25 years, from 1918 until 1943. His grandfather Simeon was from Harrison, Maine, and moved to Patten some time after the birth of his son Alfred H. in 1845. Alfred served in the Maine Infantry during the Civil War. He and his first wife Lucy (Leslie) had three sons: Alfred (born around 1865), Henry C. (born in 1867), and Charles (born in 1870). Alfred and his second wife Mary (Stinson) had a daughter Edna (born in 1878). Henry's grandfather Simeon died in 1891 and his father Alfred died in 1905; both were buried in the Patten Cemetery. Henry held a variety of jobs besides being KTCo's president, including woods worker and store owner. Henry and his wife Alice, who was a music teacher, lived in the house later owned by Frank and Sally Landry. Alice died in 1948, and Henry died in 1957 at the age of 90. They are buried in the Patten Cemetery; their gravestone includes the words *Au Revoir*.

A flu epidemic hit town, causing school to be closed for five weeks.

The Great Train Wreck in Nashville, Tennessee, left 101 people dead. It was the deadliest rail accident in US history.

Around this time: A stage was being run between Patten and Matagamon. At one point in the history of this stage route, Erastus Harvey of Patten was the driver. He was married to Hannah Lonergan of Portage.

Patten men must have liked those Lonergan girls, as Hannah's sister Laura married Archie Nevers and her sister Emma married Herbert Brown. Archie Nevers was the proprietor of the Patten House when it burned in 1917. He became a prosperous farmer and was the owner of Half-Way House, twenty miles from Patten (although I don't know what it was halfway between).

Herbert Brown (husband of Emma Lonergan) was a farmer, lumberer, and truckman whose parents Gilbert (1818-1896) and Lovina had moved to the Patten area from southern Maine. Gilbert worked as a blacksmith, teamster, and truckman in Patten. Herbert's brother Eugene had married Lottie Parsons and owned a large factory in Patten in the early 1900s. (And I bet you thought we had all those family histories taken care of.)

1919: The Henry Rowe building was erected on the east side of Main Street. A variety of businesses occupied the building over the years, including grocery stores on the first floor and Patten Insurance Agency and doctors' offices on the second floor. The building was later owned by the Harrington family.

A tank containing 2.3 million gallons of molasses exploded in Boston, killing 21 and injuring 150 people, killing numerous horses, and destroying buildings.

1919-1920: H. Merritt Cunningham of Patten served in the Maine House of Representatives.

1920: Linwood Palmer and Ray Gardner built a creamery. It was located on the corner of Rogers Lane and Dearborn Street.

The building which later housed Ken Lord's grocery store was built on the east side of Main Street.

Miss Main from Crystal had a harness shop and post office on the site behind Ira Gardner's store. She was most likely related to Henry and Ethel (Webster) Main of Crystal—perhaps may have even been their daughter Myrtle, who was born in 1903. This also may have been the site of the Chase Opera House, owned by Main and Raymond, and a harness shop owned by Main and Brittain. In 1930, Miss Main turned her harness shop/post office into a boxing and wrestling ring, and in 1939, Ira and Shinny Howes opened a movie hall there called the New Theater.

The Red Saw Mill was built at the bottom of Finch Hill on the southwest side of the bridge.

Dr. M.P. Hanson opened a doctor's office in Patten.

This photo from Eleanor Sargent Hunter's collection shows the shoveled sidewalk in front of Katahdin Trust Company.

1920, cont.: Burton W. Howe of Patten was the delegate from Maine to the Republican National Convention.

The Mount Chase Town Report included the announcement of the marriages on September 13, 1920, of Henry Pelkey of Mount Chase and Dorah Shorett of Patten and Lesley Pelkey of Mount Chase and Mina Shorett of Patten. The town had fixed its roads and paid the state $492.00 for a patrolman.

J.C. Sprague and A.G. Johnston were granted a patent for a log loader. The introduction to their application read, "Be it be known that we, J.C. Sprague and A.G. Johnston, citizens of the United States, and residents of Patten, have invented certain new and useful improvements in log-loaders....This invention relates to a device for facilitating the loading and handling of logs, and is especially designed for the handling of four-foot pulp logs and ties."

The population of Patten was 1,498, and the population of Mount Chase was 239.

American women were granted the right to vote through the ratification of the 19th Amendment.

Commercial radio broadcasting began in the 1920's.

Also during the 1920s, improvements had been made to gasoline–powered tractors so that they were practical for use on farms. Farming was becoming a more important part of the area's economy, but logging was still big business as well. In his book *Campfires Rekindled* (p. 106), George Kephart wrote: "In the 1920s, the annual log drives were still the most exciting, the most dangerous, and certainly the best publicized phase of Maine logging operations...It was the assurance that the supply of logs—the lifeblood of dependent mills and communities—was being replenished."

1921: Joe Ambrose operated a restaurant.

The creamery was bought by Hoods but closed after a few months.

The Island Falls branch of Katahdin Trust Company opened.

Mount Chase now had a town hall; it was the former McKenney School.

Around this time, Irving B. Myrick, was operating Myrick's Sporting Camps at Grand Lake, Matagamon. He had previously owned the Trout Brook Hotel.

1921, cont.: Frederick Parkhurst died after serving as governor of Maine for only 26 days. He was succeeded by Percival P. Baxter, who served until 1925. The US president from 1921 to 1923 was Warren G. Harding.

1922: Verdi Ludgate was a lawyer and judge in Patten. He also must have had a fine singing voice, as he was asked to sing at Ruth Rogers's wedding around this time.

You could buy a car from one of five different automobile dealers: Elmer J. Farnham, Charles S. Grindal, Ferdinand G. Huston (photo at left), Francis W. Peavey, or James C. Sprague. Chester G. Richardson also sold cars at some point during this era. As more and more people bought automobiles, the need for repair work and gas led to the establishment of many garages throughout the rest of the century. One of the first garages was the Grant Garage on School Street (now Founders Street), owned by Frank A. Grant. Dudley Olsen and Forrest Smith also had garages on this site. At one time, there was a huge ramp which allowed vehicles to be driven up to the top floor of the garage.

In Mount Chase, Mrs. Howes still owned her confectionery shop, and Nathan Arbo was now selling groceries along with clothes.

1923-1924: Verdi Ludgate served in the Maine House of Representatives. The US president, Warren G. Harding, served two years of his term as president before dying in 1923; he was succeeded by Calvin Coolidge, who served until 1929.

1924: Fire destroyed the Merrill Mill. It was rebuilt, but it was not successful and closed down. Since the Mill also produced the town's electricity, the town was left without power for a time.

This photo postcard was post-marked 1924 and shows the Oddfellows' Hall on the right and the Masons' Hall on the left on Houlton Street.

1924-1927: The 1924-1925 Mount Chase Town Report indicated that the town had been divided into six districts for the purpose of actions taken on the town roads. In 1926, the report stated that work had been done on the Aroostook Road, the Owlsboro Road, the Shin Pond Road, the Shin Pond Bridge, the Mountain Road, a Third Class Road, and State Aid Road No. 1. The 1926-1927 report added State Aid Road No. 2. I was unable to match numbered districts with names of roads.

1925: Ralph Brewster served as Maine's governor from 1925-1929.

During this time period: The Patten and Mount Chase Town Reports included the amount of money paid out as bear bounties. The bear bounty, as well as porcupine and hedgehog bounties, continued to be offered at times throughout the century. The towns also paid residents who had livestock which had been killed by bears, but the state fully reimbursed the towns.

1926: A fish hatchery (called a fish-feeding station at the time) was established on the Owlsboro Road in Mount Chase. It had seven rearing pools and handled 50,000 trout, which stocked local ponds. (Eleanor Sargent Hunter photo)

1927: In November, a flood took out all three bridges in Patten. The photo at right shows the bridge at the foot of Mill Hill. The flood was caused by the remnants of a hurricane; the tropical storm affected all of New England. Eighty four people died in Vermont as a result of the storm.

Five Patten Academy boys drowned in Shin Pond during the storm. They were crossing Upper Shin Pond in a canoe, on their way to a hunting camp. They were Roy and Arthur Shean, Keith Ingerson, Robert Finch, and Ken McKenney. The town held a special memorial service for the boys, whose bodies were recovered throughout the days following the accident. A poem called *Fifty Years Hence (or The Tragedy of Shin Pond)* told the sad story of the drowning; you can read this poem at the end of this chapter.

1927, cont.: Colonel Luther B. Rogers passed away. He had been a prominent figure in town affairs, including serving as a trustee for Patten Academy, for many years. He had loved Patten's young people and sponsored many Shin Pond outings at his camps for them. To honor Mr. Rogers, the entire P.A. student body attended his funeral and marched to the cemetery for his burial.

My grandparents, Leo and Damaris (Stewart) Boynton were married in 1927. She was a graduate of Patten Academy and had been working as a bookkeeper at Patten Drug Company.

Believe it or not, analog computers had been invented by 1927. Another sign of the future was the bombing of a school in Bath Township, Michigan. Forty-five students and faculty died as Andrew Kehoe sought revenge for his difficulties as a local politician.

1927-1928: Howard Wood of Patten served in the Maine House of Representatives.

1928: The David Jones family emigrated from Wales to Patten. Mr. Jones opened a barber shop on the corner of Founders and Main Streets.

Howard Ambrose opened a restaurant beside Mr. Jones's barber shop. This photo shows both businesses.

The Congregational Church (later the Grange Hall) closed.

In Mount Chase between March 1927 and March 1928, five people died. Four of these were infants. While reading town reports, it was astounding how many children died in infancy in these years; the rate in 1900 was 10-35 deaths per hundred children born; by 1950, it dropped to below five deaths per hundred. In 2016, the rate was less than one per hundred births. There are several reasons for this positive change, including improvements in hygiene, quality standards for milk, improved living conditions, be tter prenatal care and nutrition, and more available defenses against illnesses. (These statistics are for the United States.)

1928, cont.: The Patten Town Report listed 40 radios, 89 musical instruments, and 202 automobiles as taxable property. There was street lighting and a picture booth.

The library, called Patten Memorial Library, moved into the now closed Baptist Church. The WCTU Reading Room had 2,950 books to get the library started.

The Mount Chase Town Reports for 1928 and 1929 indicated that the citizens voted to reimburse R.D. Gardner the sum of $50.00 as payment for repairing the road leading to Upper Shin Pond. The road had been damaged by heavy and excessive travel in November 1927 when the five boys drowned. They also voted to keep the Myrick, Owlsboro, and Shin Pond Schools open. (Whenever enrollment dropped below eight students at a school, the townspeople had to vote to keep it open.) They appropriated money for the public health nurse and a new bookkeeping system.

The last long log drive on the West Branch of the Penobscot River took place.

The Okeechobee Hurricane was second deadliest hurricane in US history. It killed over 5,500 people in Puerto Rico and Florida.

1929: The Stock Market crashed, beginning the era known as The Great Depression. Patten citizens may have been better off than city folks as they were more self-sufficient, but they were definitely impacted by the depression. The town reports during this time period were very sad to read. The list of the town poor was much longer than it ever had been. The Red Cross donated flour, and local businesses such as the A & P and the First National donated other food. The flour came in cloth bags that could be used as fabric for making clothing, another way to save money during the lean years. An anonymous donor paid for shoes and clothing for those in need. One Patten business that did not survive the depression was Chester G. Richardson's Patten Hardware store. Mr. Richardson was owed thousands of dollars that he was unable to collect from local logging operations. You can read about the effects of the depression on local schools in Chapter Ten.

1929, cont.: The Fire Department had a new pumping unit and some hand grenades. A water reservoir had been established on land owned by C.G. Richardson. It was made from reinforced concrete and held 7,500 gallons of water.

Boyd Harrington of Patten served in the Maine House of Representatives from 1929-1932. William Tudor Gardner was Maine's governor and Herbert Hoover was the U.S. president from 1929-1933.

1930: Miss Main's harness shop and post office was turned into a boxing and wrestling ring.

The population of Patten was 1,278, and Mount Chase's population was 210.

1931: The Pentecostal Church was built.

Dr. Lore Rogers reopened the creamery. He named it the Katahdin Creamery (photo at right).

Governor Percival Baxter bought land between 1931 and 1962 in the area around Mt. Katahdin. Baxter then donated this land to create Baxter State Park.

A stage was running three times a week from Patten to Matagamon. In Mount Chase, G.L. Root owned Birch Point Camps and Forman Smith owned Lower Shin Pond Camps. Both catered to hunters and fishermen.

This fantastic photo of the east side of Patten's Main Street was taken on August 11, 1931, during an American Legion parade. (Photo by Zocalli, courtesy of Paper Talks 2017 Northern Penobscot County Edition.)

In the background (the top part of the picture), you can see the Patten Town Hall and a two-story garage on Founders Street; the garage had a long ramp that was used to drive a car up to the second story. The Myrick home is across the street from the town hall.

Starting at the right of the photo and moving left are a building supply lot, Katahdin Trust Company, the U.S. Post Office, Patten Lion's Club, the Atlantic and Pacific grocery store, and the small convenience store that was later operated by Ira Myrick, then Earl Giggey, then Ken Lau.

1931, cont.: Now let's take a look at the other side of Main Street around this time.

Starting on the left side of the photo, you can see a barber pole and a sign which says Peavey Inn Café, both of which were owned by Francis Peavey. Next is Cunningham's First National Store, then Charlie Smallwood's buffet and lunch (with a Coca Cola sign). The big building is the Ira B. Gardner store. Next, beyond the Katahdin Street entrance, is Patten Drug Company. The tower at the right is part of the Hall house.

This photo shows Main Street looking south from the drug store.

-109-

1932: The Patten Juvenile Band had been created.

1933: As the newly elected president, Franklin D. Roosevelt created the Works Progress Administration and the Civilian Conservation Corps as part of his New Deal, which was designed to help America recover from the Great Depression. Operating out of camps all over the United States, the CCC recruited over three million young men. The CCC had two goals: to provide jobs for young men and to engage in projects which would protect or improve the environment. The projects included erecting fire towers, building fire roads, fighting fires, planting trees, controlling erosion, protecting wildlife habitats, and improving waterways. The workers were paid about $30.00 a month. The CCC has also been credited with saving businesses in communities where camps were located, as they purchased locally supplies for the camps and the projects.

Patten was the site for CCC Camp 159 (near Spruce Street, photo at right). Hay Lake and Shin Pond were also CCC sites. A town report from this decade states that if it weren't for the WPA, the town would have been forced to turn the affairs of the town over to the state. Instead, the number of paupers was actually reduced. In the Patten area, much necessary road and bridge repair work was done. Some cottages were moved from Hay Lake to Patten for people to live in (a move which provided some income for the town as well in the form of rent money).

1933, cont.: The CCC also built the road from Shin Pond to Matagamon. This photo shows the bridge over the East Branch of the Penobscot at Matagamon. (Photo courtesy of Laurie Johnson Libby.)

1933: Hubert Nevers of Patten served in the Maine House of Representatives from 1933-1934. Louis Brann was Maine's governor from 1933-1937.

The last long log drive on the Penobscot River took place.

1935: Hubert Nevers (photo at left) became the postman. He held that job until 1970. At that time, the Post Office was located next to Katahdin Trust Company on the east side of Main Street.

Patten and Mount Chase worked on building tourism by increasing the amount of advertising for the area's natural advantages and attractions. In 1936, Maine first started issuing license plates with a logo. The design on the plate was meant to raise awareness that Maine was a great tourist destination.

1935, cont.: Dr. G. Frank Woodbury and Manley Woodbury Kilgore, both of Patten, edited and compiled *Personal Recollections of English and American Poets* by Edward Everett Hale. I stumbled upon this interesting bit of information as I was doing some online research. Edward Everett Hale (1822-1909) was a famous author, historian, and minister from Massachusetts; he wrote *The Brick Moon* and *The Man Without a Country*, which later was made into a movie. The following quote is attributed to Hale: "I am only one, but I am one. I cannot do everything, but I can do something. And because I cannot do everything, I will not refuse to do the something that I can do."

I know I have gotten a little off track here, but I felt that this quote puts into words an attitude which was and is held by most Patten and Mount Chase residents.

Patten town reports in the 1930s mentioned Mother's Aid and Soldier's Aid as part of the town's assistance to the poor. Mount Chase Town Reports did not list these. Both towns showed a large increase in the number of "town poor" and the number of individuals with unpaid taxes. Both towns also had accounts with overdrafts.

1936: The American Thread company was in operation at the foot of Mill Hill. The photo at left shows Lloyd Morse delivering a load of pulpwood to the mill. The wood was used to make wooden spools for thread.

1936, cont.: Mount Chase was reorganized as a plantation, most likely as a solution to financial problems caused by the depression.

The Patten Town Report mentions a new doctor in town: Dr. George Hoekzema.

1937: This photo from 1937 shows buildings on the east side of Main Street. You can see a gas station, an A & P store (bought by Ken Lord nine years later), the Post Office, Katahdin Trust Company, and the Rowe building which later housed a grocery store and the Patten Insurance Agency. Beyond the Rowe building is a small store which has been over the years Gillie Brown's grocery store, Laura Scribner and Melvena Hathaway's clothing store, and the State Liquor Store.

George Francis "Kid" Peavey (photo at left) won the state Lightweight Golden Glove boxing championship and went on to compete at Boston Garden where he won his first bout but lost his second.

Delmont Bates of Patten served in the Maine House of Representatives from 1937-1940. Lewis Barrows was Maine's governor from 1937-1941.

Nine-year-old Roger Violette, son of Alfred and Jeanne Violette of Mount Chase, died when he was kicked in the head by a horse. Roger had been born in 1928 and had siblings George, Jeannette, Paul, Pauline, and Alice at the time of his death. After Roger's death, the Violettes added to the family with Vernon, Fred, Larry, and Norman. The family lived in the farm house just north of the Shin Pond Cemetery on the west side of the Shin Pond Road.

1937, cont.: Al Brady and Clarence Shaffer were killed by FBI agents on Central Street in Bangor after trying to buy guns and ammunition at Dakin's Sporting Goods. Brady was the leader of a gang which was wanted by the FBI for armed robbery, murder, and escaping from jail. A large crowd, which had gathered on the streets to celebrate Columbus Day, witnessed the shoot-out.

The Hindenburg, a German zeppelin airship, crashed as it attempted to land in Manchester County, New Jersey, killing 36 people.

1938: This photo shows Finch Hill after it had been shoveled out by hand by the local CCC crew.

Two-year-old Tellis Baker, son of Peter and Effie Baker, died when he fell on a knife which he had managed to retrieve from the top of a kitchen cabinet. He was discovered lying in the garden by his mother. Tellis's siblings were Charlie, Clarence, Arthur, and Peter Baker, Ethel Blake, Mary Dickinson, Phyllis Wilkins, Virginia Anderson, Winnie Jandreau, and Marguerite Michaud. Tellis was named after Effie Baker's brother-in-law, Tellis Coolong.

1939: Ira and Sherwood (Shinny) Howes opened the movie hall where Miss Main's boxing room had been located on Katahdin Street. Their establishment was called "The New Theater."

1939, cont.: Sam Antworth bought the Merrill Mill and converted it from a lumber mill to a plywood mill. Several French families from Northern Maine who were familiar with the manufacture of plywood moved here to work at the mill. They included the Corriveau, Bishop, Roy, Rossignol, Skidgell, and Bossie families.

Mt. Katahdin became famous when twelve-year-old Donn Fendler got separated from his family and got lost coming down off the mountain. Donn spent nine days alone in the wilderness without food or adequate clothing before reaching a camp at Lunksoos on the East Branch of the Penobscot more than 35 miles from where he had gotten lost. Note: Mr. Fendler passed away in October, 2016 at the age of ninety. He had devoted his senior years to sharing his remarkable story with students throughout Maine.

A tornado destroyed farm buildings on Ash Hill. The photo to the right shows Durwood Glidden's farm.

The Patten Town Report for 1938-1939 contained a letter from the selectmen outlining ways the town was going to try to pull itself slowly but surely out of debt and pay all of its bills.

1940: Vivian Grant became a judge. He held that title until 1962.

The Town Hall and Forrest Smith's garage on School Street (now Founders Street) burned.

-115-

1940, cont.: Lloyd Morse opened a garage on the corner of the entrance to the Shin Pond Road. It had previously been owned by Hal Patterson then Ira Myrick.

Chet Richardson, Jr. (photo at right) was crowned the state boxing champion. Other boxers from Patten from that era were Arthur Peavey, Rollie and Rex Asher, and Vaughn White.

The Patten Town Report that came out in 1940 included the text of a new town ordinance which had been designed to decrease the loss of property due to fire. It included regulations for building or placing hearths, chimneys, boilers, furnaces, ranges, and stoves; for disposing of ashes; and for electrical wiring. It warned citizens against leaving debris in public roadways. The plans for new buildings had to be approved before a building permit would be granted. No explosives would be allowed other than on the Fourth of July. Other town ordinances dealt with traffic flow, stop signs, and reasonable speed on local streets and roads. It also stated that the selectmen would designate certain streets to be closed during the winter months so the children could slide on them. Willow Street (called Kenney Hill by sliders, photo) was one of these streets.

The population of Patten was 1,548. This was the largest population of the community ever recorded by the Census Bureau. The 1940 Census named Maple Street as the residences for Pauline Howes and Herman and Emilie Rowe; perhaps the south end of Pleasant Street was called Maple Street. Many of the other streets in town and roads outside of town still did not go by their current names. The population of Mount Chase was 198, dropping below 200 for the first time since the town was incorporated.

1940, cont.: The 1939-1940 Mount Chase Plantation Town Report included articles in the warrant pertaining to keeping the roads open during the winter for delivery of mail, preparing the road for Patrol Maintenance, building a new town office, supporting the Patten Memorial Library, contributing to the Maine Publicity Bureau, paying off debt, membership in the Maine Municipal Association, and buying snow fence.

In those days, snow fence was commonly used as a way to keep snow from blowing and drifting into roadways. It took quite a bit of work to put the fencing up, and it had to be checked and repaired annually. This photo from Laurie Johnson Libby shows a typical winter scene with snow fence in place.

1940s: Dr. George Banton began a career in dentistry. He had offices in Patten over Stratton's and in Island Falls, where he lived. Florence Sargent was his assistant for many years. She had gone back to school to learn how to do her new job.

Black and white television broadcasting began. Digital computers came into use. However, they didn't really become household items until the 1980s.

1941: The second town hall was built. Mrs. Priscilla Allen Newcomb suggested it be named "Founders Memorial Hall" in honor of the pioneers who founded the town. The building was dedicated in August. The Patten Academy Alumni Association played a large part in getting the new building built so quickly, as they did a very successful appeal to former Academy students for donations. The town offered the lot where the old building had stood, and $2,000.00 was received from the insurance on the building.

Leslie A. Dickinson became the pharmacist at Patten Drug.

The Patten Town Report for 1940-41 includes the name of Patten's first town manager, Archer Scribner. Funds were allocated for the celebration of the town's centennial anniversary. More area people were employed, and the town's debts were being paid off. Most of Patten's streets were being called by their current names.

1941-1945: President Roosevelt had spent his first four years in office dealing with the problems created by the Great Depression. Things were finally looking up for the United States when the Japanese bombed Pearl Harbor on December 7, 1941, leading President Roosevelt to declare war on Germany and Japan. Immediately, millions of American men—and some women as well—enlisted or were drafted to serve in the military during World War II. A large number of Patten and Mount Chase men and women—around 250—fought in World War II. Many families had more than one son or daughter serving in the military. Boyd and Ida Harrington sent off three sons and a daughter, and the Mulligan family had four sons serving at one time. Seven families from Patten had three sons and/or daughters serving. There were 26 pairs of brothers from Patten who served during WWII.

These Patten residents were part of a group of people who kept an eye to the sky during World War II, looking for war planes. Pictured are Boyd and Ida Harrington; Eleanor, Kay, and Ruth Hunter; and Mildred and Christine Grant. Local citizens also served as wardens who patrolled the area making sure residents were observing blackout regulations.

The nearby town of Houlton was the site of one of several prisoner-of-war camps established in Maine during the war. As many as 3,700 German prisoners at the Houlton camp worked on farms and in the woods, a great help since so many workers had gone off to fight in the war. The Germans were treated well by the Americans; some of the German soldiers actually felt guilty because they were better off than their families back in Germany. There was only one prison break. In early March of 1945, three young prisoners filled their shirts with food and headed out into the snowy Maine wilderness. After they were captured and return to the camp, they confessed they had only tried to escape because one of the American guards had dared them to and because they couldn't stand the thought of facing the Maine blackfly season.

1941, cont.: A new dam was built to replace a timber crib dam (built in the 1880's) at Matagamon. The new structure was 218 feet long and 30 feet high. The photo of the dam at the right is from the Matagamon Lake Association, which currently manages the dam.

Sumner Sewall was Maine's governor from 1941-1945.

1942: Henry Rowe retired as president of Katahdin Trust Company.

Roy Dudley, well-known as the ranger at Chimney Pond, died after being run over by a log truck as he was tending his traps in Stacyville.

1943: Zenas L. Harvey served as the president of Katahdin Trust Company from 1943 to 1952.

Wesley Porter, a skilled Maine woods guide from Patten, was killed at Webster Lake by Alfred Maurence. You can read more about this event in Chapter Sixteen.

1942-43: Guy Ordway ran the Birdseye Pea Vine Factory. It was located on the corner of Gardner and Founders Streets opposite the Founders Memorial Hall.

1943-44: The Patten Town Report for 1943-1944 was dedicated to Everett Kelsey Gardner, who died in 1943 while serving in the South Pacific. It also included a list of all the area men and women serving in the armed forces. It also provided this information:
- The new town manager was E. H. Shute.
- Patten farmers sold about 750 railroad carloads of potatoes. The school pupils were to be highly commended for helping farmers get the potato crop harvested. (There was a shortage of workers because there were so many young men serving in the military.)
- Taxable livestock and poultry included 147 horses and mules, 241 cows, 11 pigs, and 448 poultry.

Patten Town Report of 1943-44, cont.:

- Portable mills, logs, 20 gas pumps, 58 musical instruments, 238 radios, and 41 electric refrigerators were considered taxable personal property.
- The two biggest consumers of local tax dollars were the school department (26%) and the Highways and Roads Department (17%).
- About 200 men were employed at the veneer mill.
- An article in the warrant dealt with the sale of the CCC buildings.
- Over 10% of the town's population was serving in the armed forces, and another 10% was employed in defense plants in other cities and towns.

1944: Atlas Plywood bought the plywood mill. Atlas also had mills in Houlton and Greenville, but the Patten mill was the most successful.

The 1944-1945 Mount Chase Plantation town report was dedicated to Frank Lester Johnson, "who gave his life for his country." Nineteen men from Mount Chase served in the Armed Forces during World War II.

Mount Chase Plantation was paying Eastern Corporation and John A. McDonald for snow removal.

Robert Adams opened the Patten Hardware Store.

From this time period: Clive Hatt's sister Eunice Drake had 21 children. And she's smiling in this picture—probably glad she's too old to have any more! No, seriously, she looks like a lovely lady and probably had many grandchildren that she loved to spoil.

A military C-54 plane crashed into Fort Mountain in Baxter State Park, killing all seven men aboard.

During this time period, two beautiful homes sat at the top of Mill Hill. The top photo shows the Hathaway House, which was located where Ellis Family Market now has a parking lot. It was torn down to make room for a Chevron gas station. The bottom photo (courtesy of Kenny Bates) is of the D.L. Smith residence. This house still stands at the south corner of Main and Dearborn Streets, although it is vacant at this time.

1945: One-man chainsaws came into use in Maine logging operations.

Following an epic snowstorm, Eastern Fine Paper shipped by train a "super snowplow." The plow had a sixteen-foot high blade and traveled two miles per hour. It did a tremendous job until it got to Crommett Field, above Shin Pond. There it buried itself in snow, and there it remained. The next spring, road crews built the road around it. The Patten Town Report mentioned that it had been a costly winter for erecting snow fence and plowing the roads.

Horace Hildreth was Maine's governor from 1945-1949, and Harry S. Truman was the US president from 1945-1953.

All the church bells and school bells in Patten rang out on May 7 when Germany surrendered, ending the war in Europe. On August 6 and August 9, the US dropped atomic bombs on Japan. On September 2, Japan formally surrendered, and World War II was over.

Six Patten or Mount Chase natives lost their lives in the war:

- Private 1st Class Frank Johnson was the son of Fred and Ada Johnson of Mount Chase. He served with the 12th Infantry 4th Infantry Division of the Army. He died June 15, 1944, in England after being wounded on Normandy Beach. He was buried in the Normandy American Cemetery in France.

- Samuel Smith was the son of Charlie Smith of Patten. He died of injuries after falling off a truck.

- Aviation Ordnanceman 3rd Class (Navy) Wallace Blackwell Grant was the son of Lester and Ida Grant of Patten. He was declared Missing In Action June 22, 1945 while serving in the Pacific on a mission as an aerial navigator at sea. His name was included on the Honolulu Memorial in Hawaii.

- Boatswain Mate 2nd Class Everett Gardner (1898-1943) was the son of Ray and Georgie Gardner and the husband of Clara (Hall) Gardner of Patten. He was lost at sea in the Pacific on a Navy Seabees mission. He was also a World War I veteran. His name also appears on the memorial in Honolulu.

The VFW post in Patten was subsequently named the Grant-Gardner Post in honor of Everett Gardner and Wallace Grant.

- Private First Class Philip Smallwood was the son of George and Susie Smallwood of Patten. He served in the 209th Infantry and the 75th Infantry Division in the Army. He died in the Battle of the Bulge in Belgium on Jan. 20, 1945 and is buried in the Patten Cemetery. He was awarded the Purple Heart posthumously.

- Private First Class Paul Peavey was the son of Charles "Tad" and Marian Peavey of Patten. He served with the 145 Infantry 37th Infantry Division of the Army. He was killed in action Feb. 20, 1945 in the last battle in Manila in the Philippines.

The following is a letter to Paul's mother Marian dated March 20, 1945.

Co. C. 145 Infantry
Dear Mrs. Peavey
It is with the deepest regret that I must inform you of the death of your son, Pvt. First Class Paul D. Peavey on the 20th of February 1945 in the City of Manila, Luzon, P.I. Your son's platoon occupied a building during a battle. The enemy placed mortar fire on the building and your son received a fatal wound and died in the Bn. Aid Station. Everything possible was done to save your son's life. He received the best medical aid possible. Your son was a soldier of the highest caliber. He was loved and respected by all who knew him. His death was a great shock and loss to us all. He was buried in the Army Cemetery at Grace Park, Manila, with full military honors. If there is any information you would desire, or a picture of his grave, please request it. I place myself at your service.
Very truly yours,
Raymond C. Spalsbury

(After the war was over, the Peaveys moved Paul's body to the Patten Cemetery.)

★★

PFC Kenneth Lord, from Patten, Maine, served with the Fifth Army on the Italian Front during World War II. The photo at the right is a picture of Ken in Verona, Italy. In December of 1943, Sir Winston Churchill conceived a plan to drive back the German and Italian armies in Anzio and Nettuno and claim Italy for the Allies. Fighting began in January of 1944 and continued until June 2, when the British and American forces claimed victory by taking over Rome. The cost of the victory was high: 7,000 soldiers were killed and 36,000 were wounded or missing in action. As with all war experiences, the survivors were left to deal with the horrors they had seen in battle. Ken dealt with his memories in part by writing the following poem in December, 1944, as a way to honor and remember his fallen comrades.

A TRIBUTE TO THE ANZIO DOUGHBOY

Dear God! The battle is over, and they've been laid to rest,
But please let us not forget those boys who did their best.

Yes, the fight is over and quiet are the grounds
Where several hundred crosses mark the beachhead mounds.

Let each and every soldier who fought by his buddy's side
Kneel down in perfect tribute to those who bravely died.

We'll all remember Anzio, have seen the bloody sight
Of wounded dying comrades crying in the night.

Yes, gruesome are the pages that tell the story well,
Of gallant fighting doughboys who fought and killed and fell.

So, God, this is my tribute to those boys lying there:
Lift up their war torn bodies to Thy castle in the air.

And when this war is over, let all the credit go
To all those gallant doughboys who rest at Anzio.

Maine Registers for the years 1918-1945 and other resources provide the following information:

Services:

- Bangor & Aroostook Railroad Agent: J. F. Price
- Bank: Katahdin Trust Company
- Barbers: Henry Rith, Edward Ambrose, A.E. Dunlap, Francis Peavey, J. H. Patterson, Frank Sibley, Anthony Sousa (Sousa also did laundering and pressing)
- Blacksmiths: Frank McGraw, Bert Bettel, Twitchell & Robinson, James King, Amos Curran, King and Curran
- Boxing and wrestling ring: Miss Main
- Carpenters and painters: Frank Bates, H.A. Crommett, J.H. Palmer, L.B. Huston, Fred Huston, Frank Crommett, D.C. Craig, L. V. Stevens, Pearl Joy, Emmett Birmingham, Frank Andrews, E.L. Miles
- Dentists: H. J. Rogers, Mrs. June Robinson, M.D. Brown
- Doctors: E.J. Farnham, G.F. Woodbury, Millard P. Hanson, George Hoekzema, Bernard Gagnon
- Electricity: Merrill Mill (G.T. Merrill, B.W. Howe, H.M. Cunningham)
- Employment and Ticket Office: A.L. Pinette, John Mahaney, Peavey & Dunlap, F.W. Peavey
- Engineer: Charles Cobb
- Express Office: Fred Bailey
- Freight, taxi: Crommett Transit Co., John Giberson, J.S. Mitchell
- Garages: Smith Motor Co., Berry & Benn, E.L. Harvey, Katahdin Garage, Frank A. Grant, Black and White Service Station, Huntley's Service Station, Drake's Garage (E.B. Drake), Smith Battery Service
- Hides and skins: Bernard Savage
- Hotels: Patten Exchange (Simeon, then Nathaniel Pomeroy), Patten House (Brown Brothers), Peavey Inn/The Inn (Francis Peavey), Shin Pond House (Zenas Harvey), Crommett House/Lumberman's Hotel (L.J. Crommett)
- Ice: Charles Peavey
- Insurance: W.S. Kellogg, Howard Tozier, H.M. Cunningham, F.G. Huston, George W. Goodrich
- Justices: Verdi Ludgate, Daniel Scribner, Raymond Gardner, Loring B. Huston, Bertram Smith, Fred Bailey, Charles Wescott, George W. Goodrich, Charles E. Cobb
- Lawyers: Bertram Smith, Verdi Ludgate
- Livery Stables: Fred Roberts, Erastus L. Harvey
- Lodging: Mrs. J.O. Soule, Mrs. E.R. Woodbury, Mrs. Henry Knowles, Mrs. Bert Hamm, John Giberson
- Music teachers: Mrs. H.C. Rowe, Miss Emma Lane, Mrs. Dove Chapman

(list of services continues on next page)

- Photographers: Albert Klein, Sipprelle's Studio (E. M. Sipprelle) (Note: Mr. Siprelle was married to Velmont Soule, who was a sister to Dove, who married Charles Vaughn Chapman, who were the parents of Helen, who married Willie Garton.)
- Plumbers: George Burleigh, Frank Allen
- Pool rooms: Frye's Pool Room, F.W. Peavey, Edward Ambrose
- Postmasters: Jacob Hersey, Stanley Wescott, Mrs. Theresa Tozier, Hubert Nevers
- Real Estate: Hodgman Realty &Manufacturing Co. (Halbert Gardner), H.M. Cunningham, A.F. Patterson
- Restaurants: Maverick Lunch (George Smallwood, F.R. Smallwood—in Peavey Block), I.H. Bragg, Harold Palmer, Francis Peavey, George Smallwood, William Coote, Frank McElroy, The Lunch Cart (Howard Ambrose), Patten Lunch/The Luncheonette (J.H. Ambrose)
- Surveyors: C.E. Cobb, H.G. Robinson, E. O. Grant
- Telephone service: Katahdin Farmers Telephone Company (Operators M. J. Watson, Mrs. Nora West, Helen Darling)
- Theater: Chase Opera House, Henry Main, Ira and Sherwood Howes (The New Theater)
- Town managers: Archer Scribner, Eldon Shute
- Undertaker: N.O. Raymond
- Water: Patten Water Company (Ira B. Gardner, R.D. Gardner, presidents)

Merchants:

- Automobiles: E.J. Farnham, F.G. Huston, C.G. Richardson, C.S. Grindal, F.W. Peavey, J.C. Sprague
- Bakery: H.M. White
- Clothing, footwear, sporting goods: L.A. Savage, Aaron Smith, Huston Clothing, A.L. Pinette (whose store was next to the bank), N. Roy
- Dressmakers, milliners, ladies furnishings and accessories, dry goods: Mrs. Mabel Crommett, Miss Mary Mitchell, Mrs. Mary Merrill, Mrs. W. H. McKenney, Mrs. Charles Killam, Mrs. W.W. Pond, Miss Elsie Miles, Cora Wescott, I.E. Leslie, Patten Dry Goods
- Farm implements: C.W. Wescott, A.P Ryder, C.G. Richardson, Boyd Harrington
- Fertilizer: Bertram Birmingham
- Flour, grain, feed, seed: Patten Grange
- Furniture, wall hangings, woodwork: Bailey & Drew, Patten Furniture Co. (Fred Bailey)
- General stores: I.F. Cooper, Ira B. Gardner & Sons, Quincy & Rowe, Grange Store, W.T. Cobb, Henry Rowe, Alice Myrick (Mount Chase)
- Groceries and meat: M.J. Watson, Howard Tozier, Atwood Ryder, Frank Grant, E.R. Woodbury, C.E. Merrill, The Grub List (L.B. Huston), Archie Nevers, First National Store (Walter Cunningham) , J.F. Price, Nathan Arbo (Mount Chase)
- Hardware and tools: Chester G. Richardson, Sr.

(list of merchants continues on next page)

- Harnesses, blankets, and ropes: L.W. Harris, Miss Main, Bailey & Richardson, Samuel Gee, Patten Harness Company, Main & Brittain (Henry Main and Arden Brittain, whose father Thomas had a tannery in Island Falls; the Brittains also manufactured moccasins)
- Horses: H.W. Brown, Ira D. Carpenter, G.B. Ordway
- Jewelers: McKenney Brothers, Clifford Grindal (who sold class rings and pins)
- Pharmacy: Patten Drug Company: Dr. Elmer J. Farnham, Leslie A. Dickinson
- Potatoes and fertilizer: Quincy & Rowe, E.J. Parker, Patten Produce Co., F.G. Huston, Boyd N. Harrington, C.G. Richardson

Manufacturers/farmers
- Creamery: Patten Grange Creamery, Patten Creamery (sold cream to Eureka Ice Cream, owned by S.C. Spratt and J.E. Webb of Island Falls)
- Coffins and caskets: P.W. Frye, N. Raymond
- Long and short lumber, spool bars: Merrill Mill
- Logging operations: See Chapter Fourteen
- Lumber: David Monteith (Hersey)
- Milk: Albert Chase
- Patten Planing Mill (Managers L.B. Huston, F.G. Huston)
- Poultry: I.H. Lidstrom
- Starch: T.H. Phair, J.T. Piper, C.E. Clark
- Tinware: G.F. Burleigh, H.R. Grant

Another group of men that should be recognized in this history were the road crews who made it possible for Patten and Mount Chase residents to shop, get to work, go to school, have fun, worship, and visit each other. It's hard enough to keep our rural roads in good repair and well-plowed nowadays, but in times past much back-breaking labor was required to get the job done. Merle Mitchell had this photo of some Patten men loading the sand truck with shovels and muscles. And to get the sand on the roads, they rode on the back of the truck and strewed the sand with shovels. Left to right are Bob Gogan, Chet Birmingham, Frank Landry, Clayton Alward, Frank Giles, and Ernest Mitchell. So thank you, road crews past and present. You keep us going!

THE TRAGEDY OF UPPER SHIN POND
By Tilson Palmer and Harry Patterson

Fifty years from now, men that are boys today
Will tell their boys a story at the end of a playful day,
Gathered 'round a fireside, thinking of them that's gone,
Discussing the destiny of men and the mysterious beyond.
Your mother and I, said the father, when in our early teens,
Were classmates with two brothers by the name of Shean.
Ingerson was in the group, McKenney was there, and Finch.
The brooks we fished around the town, we knew them all by inch.
In memory's dusty chambers I recall some fifty years ago,
Of the tragic end of these boys where the Shin Pond waters flow.
In 1927, the fourth day of November,
The weather record of that day we older ones well remember,
The boys in health and vigor left their homes at noon.
Little did they think when leaving that their times would come so soon.
The angry winds had whipped the Shin Pond waters to a foam,
And claimed five boys as victims less than two hours from their homes.
The aim of the lads, who had lived in years around a score,
Was a hunting trip across the pond, a sport they did adore.
And five of them with dunnage in a seventeen-foot canoe
Undertook to cross the pond with all the danger in view.
But their empty craft found drifted ashore told the awful tale
And supplied evidence beyond a doubt they were lost in a gale.
The news was heralded in the surrounding towns of the calamity at the Pond
And to the parents of the homes from which the boys had gone.
From nearby towns came food and help from many a volunteer
In search of the bodies of the youths that mothers held so dear.
Eager fathers grappled with neighbors by their side
As anxious mothers waited and wept for the boys they knew had died.
Prayers went out for those mothers who since have gone above.
No one else can feels the pangs of pain just like a mother's love.

For ten long days they labored, before they found the last.
One thousand people gathered to help and watch them at their task.
Five funerals were held in Patten and all the village grieved
As the narrow confines of the tomb the remains of the boys received.
And in the cemetery on the hill underneath a mound
Sleeps today five boys who fifty years ago were drowned.
The pond is calm today. The deer are on the ridge.
The rabbit beats a crooked path across the frozen bridge.
The shy old bear and the monarch moose, the pride of a hunter's prey,
The porcupine roams and the red fox cruise at the end of a November day.
The saplings around the pond, the children of the trees,
Have grown to sturdy maples that whisper in the breeze.
They whisper to their children as I whisper to you
Of the boys and how they perished from a capsized canoe.
This, my children, happened many years before your time,
And one of those boys was your uncle, and he was a brother of mine.
And I'm thinking tonite how they struggled with no one there to save
As one by one they disappeared beneath the angry wave.
Let's place a wreath to the grave of Keith, this was the Ingerson boy.
Let's put flowers green on the mound of the Sheans, Arthur and Roy.
Let's spread fully as many on Kenneth McKenney as symbols of love.
Let's cover the grave of Robert Finch and pray that their souls are up above.
Let's sprinkle a few on the mothers' graves, too, that lie beside their boys,
For they were the prides of their fathers' hearts and their mothers' only joys.

Robert Finch (left) and Keith Ingerson (right)

Pictures from Facebook Page
So You Think You Know Maine

A CIVILIAN CONSERVATION CORPS TRIBUTE

The following item came from a website which consisted of tributes to men who served in CCC camps in Maine in the 1930s. This tribute was written by Elizabeth Williams Martin of Canaan, Maine, in honor of her father, Malcolm Earl Williams. Although Mr. Williams was not from Patten, he did serve with the Patten camp and worked on the construction of the road from Shin Pond to Matagamon. On October 16, 1936, Mac was assigned to the 159th Company at Patten and into Hay Lake Camp. Mrs. Martins says, "Very remote and rugged, these wooded, mountainous forests were where work began on building the road south towards Mount Katahdin, a project which was to ultimately intersect with the Greenville Camp's roadwork. In Patten, Mac progressed from doing hardrock drilling, making holes for the dynamite in the solid rockface, to dynamite engineer as they blasted through the Horse Mountain rockface enroute to Baxter State Park. But first, they had to cut down the huge trees along the route, 25 feet along either side of the center and 20 feet beyond, clearing the underbrush. It was arduous work. Weeks turned into months…"

"Fast forward to 2004: In October, at my brother Mike's suggestion, he and I and our father took a trip to the old CCC territory up north. It was a beautiful fall day, with a bit of a chill in the air, and as we rode along, dad recalled the different places he remembered…..After miles of riding, it seemed, we easily found the bridge built by his group nearly seventy years before, over the East Branch of the Penobscot River at Grand Lake, Mattagamon Township 6, Range 8. We drove right over it, turned around and went back over it! Then we parked and got out. In a moment, he was down the bank, checking out the underpinnings of the bridge! All the original work still stood, and dad was very proud and pleased that it was still standing and in such good shape….As we passed Horse Mountain we expressed amazement at the sheer steepness and difficulty of the terrain. We wondered aloud how a crew of young kids could have been so successful in blasting and moving all the heavy rock away to make that long road, many miles in to the park. It was a difficult enough job for mature men, let alone teenagers. In those years he and the others grew to be men the hard way."

You can go to this website to read more of this tribute and other tributes to CCC workers: http://www.state.me.us/sos/arc/ccc/tributes.shtml

CHAPTER SIX: THE TOWNS FROM 1946 TO 1968

The end of World War II brought many changes to life in the United States. The baby boom which occurred in the post-war years also contributed to a growth in the population of Patten and Mount Chase. The towns prospered with an economy based on logging (including mills), farming, and tourism/sporting camps. Since these businesses were so important in the towns' histories, I will address them further in Chapters Fourteen, Fifteen, and Sixteen. Also, please refer to Chapters Ten, Eleven, and Twelve for more detailed information on schools, the library, healthcare, emergency services, and community organizations.

1946: World War II hero Dr. David S. Ascher opened a doctor's office in Patten.

The Patten Women's Club was established. This club is a service organization which has accomplished many projects for the betterment of the community.

Gillie Brown had a grocery store at the site that is now Ellis Family Market. Gillie's wife was Lois Philpot Brown, a teacher at Patten Primary School.

World War II veteran Ken Lord opened his Atlantic & Pacific store on the east side of Main Street. Ken was married to Irene Campbell and they had three children: Jeff, Kathy (Howes), and Elizabeth. On the right side of the photo you can see the post office; not shown on the south side of the Post Office was Katahdin Trust Company. The space between the A & P and the post office was used by a variety of businesses, including a feed store owned by Gus Lord and a plumbing shop owned by Russell Arbo.

WW II veteran Dudley Olsen returned to Patten and opened up a garage on Founders Street. He married Marguerite Hatt, daughter of Curtis and Flora Hatt.

1946-1948: During this time, Mount Chase Plantation was doing well, reporting it had an unappropriated surplus of $2706.78.

1946-1948, cont.: The Patten Town Reports contained some very good news for the town. The state had designated Route 11 as a state highway, meaning that the town of Patten no longer had to be responsible for (and pay for) the plowing of that road. The town invested in some new equipment to keep the village streets plowed well and even began trucking snow away from Main Street. The Town Reports also said that Joseph McGillicuddy had replaced Elden Shute as the town manager. The wooden bridge over Fish Stream had been replaced by a concrete bridge, with the state providing funds under the State of Maine Bridge Act. Each year at town meeting, the citizens had to vote whether or not they wanted to have Daylight Savings time.

Businesses on Main Street reflected the changing times. Beauty shops came into being, and Phyllis, Charlene, Catherine, and Mad offered cold waves and zoto and machine perms. (Men still had several choices of barber shops, where you could also swap the latest news.) On the weekend, you could catch a movie at The New Movie Theater or get a new treat called a dairy cream at a new type of restaurant called a drive-in. Grocery store chains in Patten included the First National and the A & P. Walter Cunningham operated the Economy Cash Market, which was advertised as a self-service grocery. Somebody named Titus sold fresh fish. You could get Curtis, Boss, or Chippewa footwear at Huston Clothing. Del McLellan was selling dry goods and notions in Sherman Station before he opened a clothing store in the south half of the Drug Store building. Larry Madison handled jewelry, cameras, radios, stationery, watch repair, sewing machine supplies, and coal. Hardware stores sold milking equipment, radios, record players, and appliances. Patten had a Western Auto Store. Patten Insurance Agency was owned by several investors before it eventually was owned by Edgar Harrington. Forrest Smith was an International Harvester Company tractor and implement dealer, including bean sprayers and bean dusters. Phil Nightingale also sold farming equipment. Brand names at garages included Amoco, Cities Service, and Tydol. Lloyd Morse sold Studebakers, Dudley Olsen sold Fords, and Joseph Nash sold Chevrolets. If you didn't have your own car, you could call the Nash-Ordway Taxi Service. And if you couldn't get there on the ground, you could charter a plane ride from Elmer Wilson, Arthur Augustine, or Ray Porter!

Telephones were fairly common household items by the 1940s. In those days, you couldn't do much on your phone without calling the operator—the only people you could call directly were those one or two households who shared a party line with you. There were some common etiquette rules for sharing a party line:

- Before ringing the operator to make a call, always listen to make sure someone on your line isn't already using the phone.
- If someone on your line was holding a long, drawn-out conversation with someone, you could say politely that you would like to use the phone now.
- Don't rubber. (That means listen to someone else's conversation.)

But most of your calls went through the operator. You would give your phone a good crank and the operator would ask you what number you wanted to call. There were no phone directories in those days, so if you didn't know the number, the operator would look it up for you. Then she would connect you with the person you were trying to reach. Patten and Mount Chase shared the same phone office and had several very capable operators who manned the switchboard at the Patten telephone office on the north corner of Founders and Gardner Streets. One of those operators was Letha Tucker, who gave me a list of operators during this time period and told me a couple of anecdotes about her experiences as an operator. Eva Hulbert was the supervisor over the Patten operators. She was well-respected by the women who worked under her, and she was supportive of them when they had a cranky customer. Some of the operators were Erlene Bishop, Deanna Morse, Helen Palmer, Emma Porter, Sally Flannery, Carolyn Ryan, and Vera Finch. Janet Hardy and Nadine Kennedy of Oakfield also worked in the Patten Office at one point. These ladies probably knew more about what was going on in the area than anyone else, but of course anything they heard was considered confidential information. Telephone operators had to handle emergencies and notify firemen as to where the fire was. They kept a list of people (and their blood types) who were willing to be blood donors and could be instrumental in matching a donor with a needy recipient in an emergency. I didn't use the phone much when I was growing up, but I knew if there was an emergency, the operator could help me out. Letha also told me they had their share of nuisance calls, including calls in the middle of the night from drunks wanting to know if the beer parlor was still open. (They didn't consider that an emergency.)

1947: This photo from the 1991 Patten Heritage Calendar shows Main Street in 1947. The building on the left with the upstairs bay windows was the Peavey block. It housed the Patten Inn (which had rooms upstairs), a coffee shop, and a store owned by an Ordway. The next building was Charlie Smallwood's convenience store. Beyond the telephone pole you can see the Ira B. Gardner building and Patten Drug.

Patten Academy's boys' basketball team had a very successful year, including a win in Boston in a regional tournament. Patten Academy had 88 students and Boston Latin had 1800 students and was an all-boys school. The Patten Academy Eagles coach was Willis Phair, and the players were Lloyd Wilson, Carroll Hatt, Gilman Rossignol, Kenneth McCourt, Thurston Townsend, Hollis Bates, Harley Dow, Lynn Vickery, and Sonny Cunningham. The cheerleaders were Delores Kilgore, Pat Harvey, Geraldine McElroy, Winnifred Quint, and Joyce Hall. This photo shows the team upon their triumphant return from Boston. The team was inducted in the Maine Sports Hall of Fame in 2016.

If you want to learn more about this event, check out Irene Olsen Bradford's *History of Patten Academy* or the 1947 Patten Academy yearbook (both available at the library). There is also quite a bit of information online about Patten Academy's Dream Team.

1947, cont.: The *Grandcamp,* a French ship carrying a load of fertilizer, exploded in Galveston Bay, killing at least 581 people, including 25 of the 26 Texas City Fire Volunteer firefighters. That explosion caused a second ship, the *Highflyer*, to explode as well. It remains the deadliest industrial accident in U.S. history.

A coastal forest fire destroyed 1,000 homes, leveled seven communities, and destroyed 17,000 acres of land in Acadia National Park.

1948: Dick Ordway operated a Gulf Service Station on Main Street on the lot that is now owned by Steve Anderson. This photo shows a Labor Day parade in front of the garage.

C.G. Richardson, Sr. and his son Chet opened Richardson's Hardware. It was located in the Peavey Block, where the north side of Richardson's now exists. Chet Jr. was married to Virginia Bates Richardson, and they had two children: Steven and Lois (Main).

The Patten Town Report in 1948 had a special section on the logistics of replacing Patten's water system. The town was not meeting the minimum fire safety requirements for water pressure and pipe diameter, and the system also needed to reach more parts of the town and be able to protect the plywood mill and the potato houses in case of fire. Forty fire hydrants would be installed, as well as a standpipe and reservoir.

Zenas Harvey of Shin Pond (Mount Chase) was a Maine delegate to the Democratic National Convention.

1949: Patten Grammar School was built. This postcard photo shows the grammar school on the left and Patten Academy on the right.

The Shin Pond House burned. You can read more about the history of the Shin Pond House in Chapter Sixteen.

The 1949 Patten Town Report said that Founders' Memorial Hall had new bleachers and the town had a new fire truck. Furniture with a value over $500.00 was taxed as personal property. Katahdin Farmers Telephone Company, Farm Home Electric Co-op, and Maine Public Service Company provided utility services.

Frederick Payne was Maine's governor from 1949-1952.

1950s: Forrest Smith ran a tractor garage behind his house (photo at right) two lots north of the library. This building has now been converted to apartments and Sheldon Anderson keeps construction equipment and has storage units in the back of the lot.

John O. Rogers practiced law in Patten.

Television sets became common household items in the 1950's.

1950: The Patten Lion's Club had been established.

The Patten Town Report for 1950-51 named T.R. Bartlett as the town manager. The town had established a curfew of 9:00 for children under the age of sixteen.

1950, cont.: The population of Patten was 1,536, and Mount Chase's population was 250.

The Korean War began. Patten sent off 75 men and women to serve in the Armed Forces throughout the conflict. This war officially began on June 25, 1950, but like all wars, there were other events which led up to the war. Before and during World War II, Korea was ruled by Japan. After Japan surrendered in 1945, the Soviet Union (a U.S. ally during WWII) claimed North Korea, and the U.S. established a military presence in South Korea. However, by 1948, the relationship between the U.S. and the Soviet Union had disintegrated and the "cold war" was in full swing. The Korean War began when the North Korean and Soviet forces (with support from China) invaded South Korea. The United Nations responded by calling for a ceasefire. When that request was ignored by the Soviet Union, the UN forces (military units from 21 countries, with the U.S. military accounting for 88% of the total UN forces) started fighting back. The war continued until an armistice was signed on July 27, 1953. A demilitarized zone was created between North and South Korea, P.O.W.'s on both sides were released, and military actions ceased. However, no peace treaty was ever signed, leaving an uneasy relationship between North and South Korea. Even today, Korea continues to be a place that the United States keeps a close eye on.

Ensley Wheaton, Jr., son of Ensley and Lillian Wheaton of Patten and Mineola, New York, was killed at the age of 19 while serving on the oil tanker Esso Greensboro in the Gulf of Mexico. The Greensboro was traveling west with a full load of crude oil when it collided with the Esso Suez, traveling east in dense fog. The Greensboro immediately exploded, killing 37 crew members, including Mr. Wheaton and the captain of the ship. Mr. Wheaton was also survived by his brothers Ross and Lee and sister Trudy, who were living in New York at that time.

The town of Flagstaff, Maine disappeared under the waters of Flagstaff Lake when the Log Falls Dam was built on Dead River by Central Maine Power Company.

1951-52: The Patten Town Report for 1951-52 was dedicated to Boyd Harrington. Besides being a leader in town affairs for many years, Mr. Harrington had also served as County Commissioner from 1930 until his death in 1951. The town report also stated that the town manager was Stanley E. Johnson. The Patten Aero Club and a local Boy Scout troop had been established. Evidently it had been another tough winter with snow-blocked roads, as one town debit was reimbursement to farmers for milk they had to dump because the milk truck couldn't get to them.

Frederick Payne resigned as governor of Maine in order to become a US senator. Burton Cross finished his term and was then elected to serve as governor from 1953-1955.

1952: Walter Cunningham opened an IGA grocery store in the south side of the drug store.

Willard McIntire became the president of Katahdin Trust Company, a position he held for 29 years until 1981. Mr. McIntire was a local potato farmer, and his wife Violet was a teacher at Patten Grammar School for many years. They were both loved and respected by the community. They were the parents of Judy Smallwood, Glennys Heath, and Burtt and James McIntire.

Phil Cunningham of Patten Academy became the school's highest scorer ever with a total of 1,446 points.

1953: Joe and Florence Hall took over the Patten Inn and continued to run it as a restaurant and hotel until 1966.

The east side of Main Street included Ken Lord's A & P, Quint's Clothing Store, the Post Office, Katahdin Trust Company, Rowe's General Store, and F.R. Bailey, who did shoe repair, acted as a railway freight agent, and sold unfinished furniture and various notions.

Stanley Johnson, Town Manager, started off the Patten Town Report for 1952-53 with a letter announcing that, for the first time in many years, the town had ended the fiscal year with a surplus rather than a deficit. All the schoolhouse notes had been paid off, and a new school bus and a new town truck and plow were paid for. A single parking fine of $1.00 contributed to the town coffers, but the town was forced to give Asa Glidden a tax abatement of $3.60 because he had been taxed for a cow he didn't own. Taxable personal property now included "electrical and other modern appliances." A fund was established for the care and maintenance of the shade trees which lined Main Street.

The town report also stated that the citizens had voted to appropriate $10,000.00 to enlarge Founders Memorial Hall and $15,000.00 to build a town garage and a fire house. The Patten Planning Board was established. This committee would oversee projects having to do with school buildings, roads and sidewalks, the town water supply, and sewerage and would also search out opportunities to attract new industry to Patten.

The Korean War ended. 2nd Lt. Frank Kilgore, grandson of Lionel and Mary Kilgore of Patten, lost his life in Korea. He was killed in action at Chorwon Area, Outpost Harry, as a member of the 15th Infantry Regiment of the Army. He was 23 years old.

Dwight D. Eisenhower served as the US president from 1953-1961.

WABI made its first television broadcast from Bangor, Maine. You could view it on Channel 5. It was briefly an NBC affiliate, but has been a CBS affiliate since then. It was owned by Horace Hildreth, former governor of Maine. It is still owned by the Hildreth family, making it the oldest station in the United States to be owned by one family.

1954: Fire destroyed the Stan Johnson and Eltha Mitchell homes and the Beehive. The Beehive was a boarding house owned by Edna Rigby which was located where Ricky and Linda Lyons now live. Three families were living in the boarding house at the time.

Glendon Larkin was a lawyer in Patten.

Patten was presented an award of merit for achievement of noteworthy projects during 1953 by the State of Maine Publicity Bureau.

George and Rose Merrow took over management of the general store in the Ira B. Gardner building. It had been previously under the management of Dick Aucoin and was part of a chain called Stratton's. These stores were originally called *five-and-dime stores* because, at that time, you could buy a lot of things in the stores for five or ten cents. However, inflation caused them to later be called *five-cent to a dollar stores*.

Items in the 1953-54 Patten Town Report are listed below.

- Town manager Robert Anderson announced that a new fire station had been built on Dearborn Street (photo at right), a new town garage had been built on Katahdin Street, and an addition had enlarged the Founders Memorial Hall.
- A tractor with a gravel scoop and a snow scoop had been purchased.
- Carver, Cedar, and School streets had been tarred, and the fire pond on Crystal Street had been completed.
- Work was being done on the Shin Pond Road fire pond.
- Bleachers had been erected at the ball diamond.
- Mr. Sylvio Raymond, a tree surgeon and owner of Chadwick's Florist in Houlton, had begun pruning the trees on Main Street.

1954, cont.: It was a sign of the times that forty horses and mules and 539 milk cows (along with various other livestock) were taxed. The number of horses and mules in town was declining (it had been 256 in 1932) while the number of milk cows was increasing. Cars, trucks, skidders, and tractors were supplying the horse power instead of horses, and modern machinery meant that dairy farmers could care for larger herds.

November 11 became known as Veterans Day, a time to honor American veterans of all wars. Patten and Mount Chase certainly had their share of veterans to honor. The red poppy symbolized the death of a person in the armed forces.

WLBZ TV (Channel 2) began broadcasting television shows from Bangor. It was briefly a CBS affiliate, but has been an NBC affiliate since then. It was owned by Murray Carpenter and the Rines Family.

1955: Robert L. Anderson was Patten's town manager. In his 1954-55 letter, he stated that it had been a difficult year weatherwise, with almost continual snowfall or rainfall, including two hurricanes. Hurricane Edna caused $3,673.53 worth of damages to culverts and roads; thankfully the State and Civil Defense Administration reimbursed the town almost $3500.00 towards these expenses. Mr. Anderson reminded citizens to not deposit snow from their driveways into the roads and warned they could be fined up to $10.00 if they did so. A new truck with hydraulic equipment and a new one-way snowplow were purchased.

The town turned over ownership of Founders Memorial Hall to the school department for financial reasons.

A rather strange article in the warrant for the 1955 town meeting read: *To see if the town will vote to authorize and direct the Selectmen to work for the enactment of a bill in the current legislature to move the town of Patten from Penobscot County to Aroostook County.* I think that would have made a lot of sense, but it evidently got shot down quickly, since it never happened!

The town appropriated money every year for swimming lessons throughout the 1950s and 1960s. These were held at Shin Pond and were taught by Red Cross certified instructors.

1955, cont.: The Patten Town Reports also provided this information:

- Chester Coolong made a new map of Patten, and houses were numbered. New street signs were erected and paving of town streets began. At this time, Cedar Street became Gardner Street.
- Because of improvements in fire safety, insurance premiums for properties within a three mile radius of the fire station were reduced by 30%.
- No town poor names were published in the report; the town helped out children through Aid to Dependent Children (ADC) and the elderly through Old Age Assistance (OAA).
- Personal property tax was paid on 483 cows, 34 horses and mules, and 480 domestic fowl.
- The fire pond at the corner of Route 11 and the Shin Pond Road was completed and was open during the winter for ice skating.
- A new jail had been installed.
- The local citizens no longer voted annually to observe or not observe Daylight Savings Time. However, it wasn't until 1966 that the United States passed an act that all parts of the U.S., with a few exceptions, would set their clocks ahead an hour in the spring and back an hour in the fall.
- Sliding on Willow Street was discontinued during these years.

Edmund Muskie served as Maine's governor from 1955-1959.

Around this time: Del McLellan opened a clothing store in the south half of the Patten Drug Company building.

1956: Leo Dickinson opened a barber shop on Katahdin Street. At one point in time, there was a pool hall behind the barber shop.

1956, cont.: Lore Rogers and Caleb Scribner began collecting artifacts and photos which became the basis of the Lumberman's Museum. Rogers and Scribner also built displays and models which accurately depict lumbering operations. They used the rear part of the library to house their collection.

Lore Rogers   Caleb Scribner

WAGM TV (Channel 8) began broadcasting from Presque Isle. It has been primarily a CBS affiliate, although in its early days, it broadcast shows from all three of the major networks. It was originally owned by Harold Glidden, Aroostook Broadcasting Corporations, and WAGM radio. In 1957, it was sold to Horace Hildreth, who owned WABI TV in Bangor.

1957: Pearl "P.C." Clark was killed in a car accident on Peavey Corner. Also in the car were Maynard Robinson and Arnold Hafford. Investigating officers were Herbert Joy, Bert Coffin, and Russell Arbo.

A First National grocery store opened in the Rowe building. It was managed by Alfred (Mickey) McCafferty (photos left and right). Mickey and his wife Bertha (Glidden) had four children: Brent, Mellissa Madden, Susan DeNobile, and Jane Ross.

1957-1958: The Patten Town Report was dedicated to Henry Rowe who had recently passed away. Mr. Rowe had been a town leader in many capacities throughout his life.

The town now had an official police force, with Russell Arbo serving as the first chief of police. The town continued to employ several constables as well. Mr. Arbo had the authority to make arrests, jail serious offenders, and levy fines. Most of the offenses had to do with cars and/or alcohol, although he did investigate and assist in an arrest in a manslaughter case.

1957-1958, cont.: A fire at the town garage caused about $2,000.00 worth of damage. The Patten Development Corporation was established.

The Mount Chase Plantation Report stated that the Plantation would enter into a contract with the Town of Patten whereby Patten would provide fire protection for Mount Chase for an annual sum of $300.00. Voters authorized the appointing of a school committee to study the benefits of school consolidation.

1957-1962: Ida M. (Gagnon) Harrington of Patten served in the Maine House of Representatives. She was the daughter of Paul Gagnon, wife of Boyd Harrington, and mother of Boyd, Jr., Edgar, and Joseph Harrington and Mary Pauline Woodside.

1958: The Patten Little League Team won the Maine Championship.

The Katahdin Creamery closed.

Some of the movies shown at the Patten Theater included *The Pajama Game, Man of a Thousand Faces, Band of Angels, Decision at Sundown,* and *An Affair to Remember.*

1958-59: The Patten Town Report was dedicated to Freeman Bradford, who had been killed in a motor vehicle accident in Presque Isle in November of 1958. Mr. Bradford had been a local potato farmer who was very active in town affairs and had served many years as a trustee of Patten Academy and a trustee of Patten Memorial Library. He was predeceased by his first wife Marcia Weeks Bradford and survived by his second wife Irene Olsen Bradford.

The report published the names of the town poor (except for veterans, the elderly, and children), but this was the last time it did so. The 1958-1959 Patten Town Report listed the tax rates since 1950. It went from a high of 108 mils in 1950 to a low of 78 mils in '58 and '59. The town was doing well economically through these years.

1959: Dead River Oil Company opened.

Atlas Plywood was sold to Joe Sewall and J.M. Huber. (Sewall sold out to Huber in 1962.) J. M. Huber had its beginnings in Munich, Germany in the late 1800s, where Joseph Maria Huber had an ink factory. In 1883, Huber began developing markets in the United States for his ink. He opened his first dry color plant in Brooklyn, New York, in 1891. In 1916, the Huber family opened a plant in Bayonne, New Jersey, and in 1920 they set up shop in Swartz, Louisiana. For the rest of the 20th century, their business expanded and diversified. They became involved in oil and gas exploration, chemical research, the production of silica and other plastics, and the production of oriented strand board (OSB) and plywood. They now have their headquarters in Edison, New Jersey, and are the largest family-owned business in the United States. Although Huber hasn't operated the mill in Patten since 1980, the company still manages landholdings in the Patten and Mount Chase area. (Laurie Johnson Libby photo)

Four different men occupied the governor's office during 1959. Edmund Muskie resigned in January just before the end of his term, and Robert Haskell was acting governor for five days until Clinton Clauson began his term. However, Clauson died suddenly on December 29th, and John Reed was elected to finish Clauson's term. Reed, a potato farmer from Fort Fairfield, Maine, was re-elected in 1963 to serve a second term. After his term ended in 1967, Reed was appointed as the United States ambassador to Sri Lanka and the Maldives.

1960: The population of Patten was 1,312. The population of Mount Chase was 179, its lowest census count.

Henry and Mary Schmidt opened Mount Chase Lodge on Upper Shin Pond.

1960, cont.: Three-year-old Mark Arbo was killed on Main Street in front of his home when he dashed out in front of a pulpwood truck. His parents were Russell and Pauline (Quint) Arbo, and his brothers and sisters were Margo (Sartory), Mike, Mari (Mimi Birmingham), Marty, Matthew, Malcolm, Maxfred, and Martha (Tremblay).

All of the Mount Chase schools had been closed except for the Myrick School on the north road. In the 1959 Mount Chase Plantation Report, Superintendent of Schools Thomas Burdin, Jr., urged Mount Chase residents to appropriate money for new toilet facilities at Myrick.

Color television sets showed up in Patten during the 1960s. CB radios also became popular, particularly with farmers and truckers. Woodsmen started using skidders to move logs in the woods.

The Great Chilean Earthquake was the strongest earthquake ever recorded. It measured 9.6 magnitude on the Richter scale and created a tsunami that hit Hawaii. Six thousand people were killed as a result of the earthquake and tsunami.

1960-1961: Televisions became taxable personal property, although furniture and other appliances were removed from the taxable property list in the 1960-61 Patten Town Report. James MacArthur was now the town manager. There was another unusual article in the warrant for town meeting. It read: *To see if the town will vote to authorize the Overseers of the Poor to require those receiving financial assistance from the town to refrain from operating motor vehicles.* I don't know how that one turned out, although it is no longer a town ordinance if it did get enacted.

1961: In his book *Yankee Loggers,* which was published in 1961, Stewart H. Holbrook commented on Maine's annual spring river drives. Holbrook says on page 75, "The river driving era did not come to an end with a bang….almost before one realized what was going on, the transportation of logs from woods to mills had been taken over by the internal combustion engine."

1961, cont.: John F. Kennedy served as the United States President from 1961-1963. At that time, the United States was still actively trying to suppress the spread of Communism. During his first year in office, Kennedy authorized the invasion of Cuba at a site called the Bay of Pigs. The goal of the operation was to overthrow the Communist government of Fidel Castro, but the American forces were defeated by Castro's military.

1962: The Hall house on the north side of Patten Drug Company was torn down to make space for the new post office building to be built at its present location. Katahdin Trust Company later expanded into the old post office space. The building on the right side of the photo was owned by Russell and Pauline Arbo and is now the site of Calculations.

The Patten Town Manager, James MacArthur, died suddenly in March and was replaced by Robert Anderson.

The Lumberman's Museum was moved to its present site. The building in the photo at the right was the reception area at that time and also housed many artifacts and remarkable models of logging camp buildings and equipment.

Traditionally all Maine towns and cities charged a poll tax. The poll tax was originally established as a way to prevent poor people and particularly African Americans from voting. The poll tax in Maine towns and cities was $2.00 at first, and then was raised to $3.00. In 1962, The United States Congress proposed the 24th amendment to the Constitution. The amendment stated that payment of one's poll tax could no longer be used as a condition of being allowed to vote in federal elections. The next steps were for the amendment to be enacted into law and for a majority of states to ratify the amendment in their own governments.

1962, cont.: In the Patten Town Report, televisions and musical instruments were listed as taxable personal property. A new tractor and backhoe had been purchased, as well as a new fire truck which cost $8,792.00. The Patten Highway Department was established. The town began issuing a snowplowing contract, which in the winter of 1961-62 was awarded to Lloyd Morse. The town was receiving Surplus Commodities which could be distributed to local citizens.

There were two interesting articles in the warrant for the annual town meeting:

Article 13: To see if the town will vote to elect a committee of five whose duty it will be to carry out the plans of erecting a medical center under the direction and assistance of the Sears Roebuck Community Medical Assistance plan.

Article 23: To see if the town will vote to allow business establishments not exempted by law to keep open for business on the Lord's Day, Memorial Day, July 4th, November 11th, and Thanksgiving Day.

The town of Mount Chase established a municipal dump.

Many of my readers probably remember a news clip from 1960 showing the leader of the Soviet Union, Nikita Khruschev, pounding his shoe on a table in anger during a meeting of the United Nations General Assembly. (As it turned out, no such image was ever recorded; it was one of the first successful uses of Photoshopping. However, most historians—and Khruschev himself— agree that the incident happened. To add chaos to the shoe-pounding, the United Nations Assembly President broke his gavel trying to restore order to the meeting.) Theatrics aside, relations between the Soviet Union and the U.S. deteriorated to all-time low in 1962, bringing the two countries to the edge of a full-scale nuclear war. The U.S., under President Kennedy, had deployed missiles to Italy and Turkey, and Khruschev had started moving missiles into Cuba, which was governed by his cohort Fidel Castro.

1962, cont.: An American spyplane spotted the ballistic missiles being brought in to Cuba, and the U.S. immediately demanded that they be removed. After a period of extreme tension between the two nations, an agreement was reached. The Soviet Union agreed to dismantle and withdraw the missiles from Cuba, and the United States would do likewise in Italy and Turkey. Additionally, the United States agreed to never invade Cuba again without direct provocation. Everyone took a deep breath of relief as the threat of war subsided. The Soviet Union, embarrassed by Khruschev's antics and his leadership, ousted him from office in 1964.

1963: James Hannigan was now the town manager. The Board of Trade published a brochure advertising local sporting camps. The Civil Defense Committee was disbanded after at least twenty years of existence. The state was planning a major construction job on Finch Hill and Patten's Main Street.

One of the town reports from this time period was dedicated to Dudley Olsen (1916-1963) who had been a prominent businessman and town leader throughout his adult life. He was still working in his garage on Founders Street on the day he died. He was survived by his wife Marguerite (Hatt) and children Janine Olsen Bertone and Kristin Olsen.

The Maine School Administrative District #25 was formed in March of 1963; it was made up of Patten, Mount Chase, Stacyville, and Sherman.

1963: Ranger Ralph Heath of Sherman died in October while trying to rescue a woman who was stranded after leaving the Knife Edge Trail on Mount Katahdin. As Ranger Heath began a search and rescue operation, the remnants of Hurricane Ginny slammed into Mount Katahdin, dropping eighteen inches of snow and causing white-out conditions. Mrs. Margaret Ivusic died of exposure and blood loss from an injury, and Ranger Heath (photo at left) died of exposure. Their bodies, encased in ice, were recovered the following May.

1963-1964: The town submitted applications for two federal projects: a watershed flood control project (which would deal with flooding and erosion problems along Fish Stream) and a new sewer system. Both projects would include pollution controls.

Ida Harrington of Patten served in the Maine Senate.

The nation was stunned when President John F. Kennedy was shot and killed while riding in a motorcade parade in Dallas, Texas on November 22, 1963. In the car with him were his wife Jaqueline and the governor of Texas John Connally and his wife Nellie. A police officer, Patrolman J.D. Tippit, was shot as he pursued the assassin, Lee Harvey Oswald. However, Oswald was captured shortly thereafter. Ironically, before Oswald had to stand trial, he himself was shot and killed by Jack Ruby. There was much discussion as to the motive behind the assassination, including a popular theory that Oswald did not act alone and that the murder was actually part of a conspiracy.

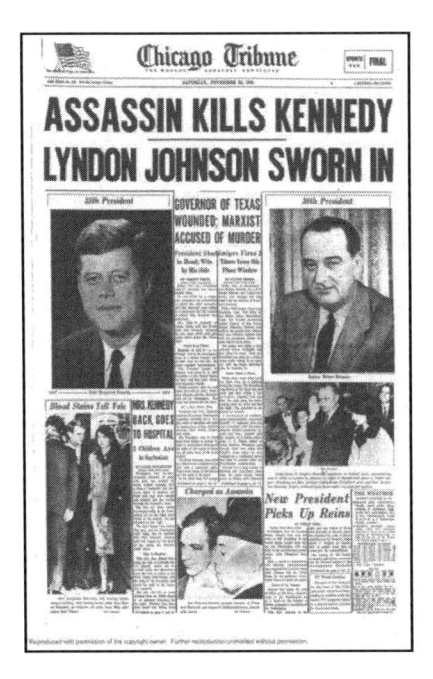

President Kennedy was a popular president who had been injured in the line of duty while serving his country during World War II. He is remembered for the popular quote: *And so, my fellow Americans, ask not what your country can do for you, but what you can do for your country.*

After Kennedy's death, Vice-President Lyndon Baines Johnson was immediately sworn into office. Johnson finished Kennedy's term and then was elected to serve from 1965-1969.

1964: The Willigar family's barn burned.

Dean and Frances McKenney opened McKenney's Clothing store, located in the south half of the Patten Drug Company building. They remained in business at that site until 1967, when they moved across the street to the north corner of Main and Founders Street.

1964, cont.: Maine's Congress ratified the 24th amendment to the Constitution. (See 1962 above.) The amendment was passed. However, that did not mean the poll tax was done away with immediately, as there was no law against having a poll tax unless it was tied to voting privileges for federal elections.

1965: The United States became involved in the Vietnam War from 1965 to 1973. The war started as North Vietnam, which was a communist country, tried to take over South Vietnam. The US and several other countries fought alongside South Vietnam to prevent the spread of communism. A strong protest movement against US involvement in Vietnam divided our country and was partially responsible for public disrespect for the American soldiers. Eighty-two local men enlisted or were drafted.

John Bernard "Bernie" Brawn died by drowning in Snowshoe Lake while on a fishing trip with friends over Memorial Day weekend. He was the son of Joe and Edna Brawn, who had a farm on the corner of the Shin Pond and Barleyville Roads.

The Patten Memorial Library was renamed Veterans Memorial Library.

WVII TV (Channel 7) began broadcasting from Bangor. It was owned by a group of businessmen and has always been an ABC affiliate.

1965-1966: The Patten Town Report stated that Firth Smallwood was now the town manager. Telephone service was now through the Maine State Telephone Company. The Town Poor included cases labeled *Aid for Exceptional Children*. The town report was dedicated to the memory of Vinal Heath, who had served the citizens of Patten as a selectman for 12 years and a school bus driver.

Arthur and Eugenia Sharpe operated Sharpe's Tourist Home on Main Street. They had previously owned Katahdin Hunting Lodge and Camps several miles north of Patten.

1966, cont.: Esther Lord opened a greenhouse. Theodore Main also operated a greenhouse in the area.

Jim and Melvena Hathaway took over the Patten Inn and continued to run it as a restaurant and hotel until 1968.

Forrest Anderson, son of Earl and Frances (Noyes) Anderson, died after being struck by a pickup truck. The accident occurred right in front of the Anderson home on the Shin Pond Road. Forrest had just celebrated his twelfth birthday two days previously. Forrest was survived by nine siblings: Filena, Fleetwood, Fulton, Fonda, Dwight, Dwinal, Sheldon, Steve, and Stacy Anderson.

1967: John Brown Septic Tank Services took on a job that few want to do, but many need to have done.

On Main Street, McKenny's Clothing moved from the south part of the Patten Drug company building to the site across the street on the north corner of Founders and Main Streets. Subsequently the Drug Store expanded inot the souh half of the building. Mickey and Louise Fogg bought Bine's Drive-In, and Bob Adams sold Patten Hardware Store to Royce Smallwood.

The Green Valley Association was established. This program provided housing and programs for mentally challenged adults.

In 1967, the last class graduated from Patten Academy. The following year, Patten and Sherman high school students attended the newly constructed Katahdin High School. The Grade Seven students joined the Grade Eight students in the Academy building.

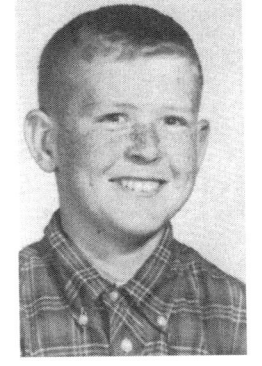

Ronald Libby of Patten (photo at left) had barely begun his senior year of high school when he was killed in a traffic accident just north of the cemetery. He was the son of Harley and Dorothy Libby and the brother of Harley, Kenneth, and David Libby and Gayle Glidden, Jeannie Schenk, and Brenda Rodgerson.

1967, cont.: The Mount Chase Plantation Report included livestock, furniture, fixtures, television sets, and watercraft as personal property and was still charging a poll tax. Mount Chase paid Patten $300.00 for fire protection and appropriated money for the Katahdin Valley Development Authority. The term *town* poor was replaced by *public assistance*. The residents rarely voted in favor of publishing names of those who received assistance. An article in the warrant for town meeting read: *to see what action, if any, the plantation will take in regard to disposing of the Myrick School House.* The article was passed over at town meeting.

Charlie Marr of Patten died in Baxter State Park. He was guiding two sportsmen and accidentally drowned at Trout Brook.

In Patten, the fiscal year for town business was changed from March-February to January-December. The Patten Town Report for 1967 said that Firth Smallwood was still the town manager, but Lloyd McKenney had replaced Russell Arbo as chief of police. Maine had passed a law to remove all sewage from streams and rivers by October 1, 1976, so Patten began making plans for a new sewer system. The project to tear up and replace Main Street was begun. All of the beautiful elm trees that lined the east side of Main Street had to be cut down because of the new street project, and many of the trees on the west side were cut down because they were dying of Dutch elm disease.

Interstate 95 was completed to Houlton, once again changing the lives of Patten and Mount Chase citizens. While opportunities for health care, recreation and entertainment, and shopping expanded, it also meant that people were less dependent on Patten's businesses. The Interstate, with exits at Sherman and Island Falls, bypassed Patten and continued as far as the Canadian Border west of Houlton. Thankfully, for the sake of the towns' economies, Patten and Mount Chase still remained the north entrance to Baxter State Park and the area still had its prime hunting grounds and fishing holes.

1967, cont.: The Patten Water District was enlarged and now had 166 customers. New pipes and hydrants would be installed when the new streets were constructed.

Margaret Chase Smith of Maine was in the middle of her years as a respected politician. She had already been active in Maine politics when she was elected to fill the U.S. House of Representatives seat vacated when her husband, Clyde Smith, died while in office. Mrs. Smith was then reelected several times. She was the first woman from Maine to serve in the U.S. Senate and the first woman in the nation to serve in both houses of Congress. She served as Maine's senator until 1973. In 1964, Smith became the first woman to be nominated for the presidency by a major political party. She lost in the Republican primaries, but continued to campaign for the Republican candidate, Barry Goldwater.

Kenneth Curtis served as Maine's governor from 1967-1975.

1968: The Patten Town Report was dedicated to Caleb Scribner, who had recently passed away. Scribner had been actaive in town affairs since 1917 and had served with the Maine Warden Service as a game warden and warden supervisor. He was also the co-founder of the Lumberman's Museum, helping preserve the area's logging heritage for generations to come.

Walter Phillips built a home and plumbing business on the South Patten Road where the Katahdin Valley Health Center Administration building now stands.

Bruce and Norma Campbell took over the Patten Inn. They ran it as a restaurant, and they also had a chain saw shop and a NAPA store there.

The first class graduated from Katahdin High School in 1968.

1968, cont.: The Patten Town Report for 1967 (which was published in March 1968) was dedicated to Second Lieutenant Leslie A. Dickinson, who had been killed in Vietnam. He had been born on February 1, 1945, and died on February 3, 1968. At the time of his enlistment in 1966, Dickie was a student at Colby College in Waterville, Maine. He served with G Company, 2nd Battalion, 7th Marines, First Marine Division FMF. At the time of his death, Dickie's parents, Leslie "Dick" and Dorothy Dickinson, owned and operated Patten Drug Company. Dickie was also survived by his sister Shasta. At the end of this chapter, you can read an article about Dickie which appeared in the Colby College campus newspaper after his death.

Reverend Martin Luther King, Jr., a civil rights activist, was assassinated in April by James Earl Ray. Dr. King was remarkable in that he called for non-violent action to achieve equal rights and respectful treatment for African-American people. Dr. King's best-remembered speech was his *I have a dream* message, but there were many other thought-provoking words spoken by him. A quote that seems as relevant in 2016 as it was in the 1960s reads:

Darkness cannot drive out darkness; only light can do that.
Hate cannot drive out hate; only love can do that.

1968, cont.: Just two months after the death of Dr. Martin Luther King, Senator Robert F. Kennedy of Massachusetts, himself a strong supporter of civil rights, was assassinated by Sirhan Sirhan because Kennedy was sympathetic to the nation of Israel. The world was shocked by the deaths of these two men who had only the best interests of humanity at heart. Robert Kennedy's brother Ted remembered his brother with these words:

My brother need not be idealized, or enlarged in death beyond what he was in life; to be remembered simply as a good and decent man, who saw wrong and tried to right it, saw suffering and tried to heal it, saw war and tried to stop it. Those of us who loved him and who take him to his rest today, pray that what he was to us and what he wished for others will someday come to pass for all the world.

Once again, we reach the end of an era. It is remarkable to think about how much Patten and Mount Chase changed during the years from 1946 to 1968, especially Main Street in Patten. Farming—especially potato farming—had become a much larger part of the area's economic base, and sporting camps were numerous, especially in Mount Chase. Every available space on Main Street was occupied by a wide variety of businesses which very adequately served the needs of the residents. There were four active churches, and consolidation had been accomplished fairly smoothly. The town reports were full of reports from many different committees which were contributing to the vitality of the town. In spite of the tragedies (local, national, and worldwide) which had occurred recently and the war which continued in Vietnam, it seemed like the towns of Patten and Mount Chase were headed for a remarkable finish to the 20th century.

Maine Registers from 1946-1968 and other resources include this information.

Services:

- Airplane Chartering: Arthur Augustine, Elmer Wilson, Ray Porter, Scotty Skinner
- Banking: Katahdin Trust Company
- Barbers: J. Hal Patterson, Howard Birmingham, Leo Dickinson, F.W. Peavey, Kip's Barber Shop, St. John's Barber Shop
- Beauticians: Phyllis Beauty Shop, Leavitt's Beauty Shop, Deanna's Beauty Shop, Judy's Beauty Shop, Pat's Beauty Shop, Catherine Foss, Charlene's Beauty Parlor, Mad's Beauty Shop
- Blacksmith: James King, Dearborn's Blacksmith Shop
- Carpenters, painters, and decorators: Curtis Hatt, Carl Grant, Cyrus Nason, Chester McManus, Lawrence Violette, Henry Rigby, Robert Rogers, Wesley Giles, Robert Smallwood, Frank Violette, Victor Michaud, Ensley Wheaton, George Smallwood, Alonzo Albert, John's Painting and Decorating
- Chiefs of Police: Manley Brown, Lloyd McKenney, Russell Arbo, Ken Garnett
- Civil Engineer: Halbert G. Robinson
- Clothing care: New York Tailoring Co. and Dry Cleaning (Ira Myrick)
- Delivery: Cole's Express from Houlton, George Howes, The Bangor and Aroostook Railroad (Fred Bailey, freight agent)
- Dentist: Dr. George Banton
- Doctors: Dr. G. Frank Woodbury, Dr. David Ascher, Dr. John Dennison, Dr. Joseph Herson, Dr. William Daniels in Sherman, Dr. Clyde Swett in Island Falls, Dr. Maniuchehr Mozaheney
- Electricity: Farm-Home Electric Co-op (later Eastern Maine Electric Co-op) and Maine Public Service Company
- Garages/service stations, oil: Roland Huntley, Joseph Nash (Cities Service), Nash-Ordway, Leland Webster, Harold Marr, Staples Motor Company, Arthur Augustine, Lawler Brothers, Dudley Olsen (Amoco), Morse's Service (Tydol), Cities Service Company, Ira Myrick (Tydol), Porter Brothers Flying A Service, Harvey's Gulf Service, Cities Service (Eugene Ballard), Ballard's Filling Station, Elmer Wilson Flying A Service, Myrick's Esso, Myrick & Bates Esso, Patten Filling Station, Giggey's

(services continued on next page)

- Hotels and lodging: Shin Pond House (Arthur Augustine, then Dale and Margaret Bates, then Richard and Teddy Schmidt), Peavey Inn, Ham's Motel, Kermit Howes, Patten Inn, the Patten House (Joe and Florence Hall, then Jim and Melvena Hathaway, then Bruce and Norma Campbell), Cunningham's Tourist Home, Hamm's Lodging, Smallwood's Rooms and Bath
- Insurance and real estate: Patten Insurance Agency (Robert Adams, John Elliott, George S. Ordway, Boyd,Sr., Boyd Jr., and Edgar Harrington
- Justices: Fred Bailey, Laura White, John Rogers, Caroline Rogers, Robert Anderson, Vivian Grant, Ida Harrington, James Hannigan, Robert Adams.
- Lawyers: John O. Rogers, Glendon Larkin
- Movie Theater: The New Theater, the Patten Theater (Ira & Shinny Howes, projectionist Herschel Cole
- Nursing care: Resthaven Nursing Home
- Plumbing: Russell Arbo, Robert Smallwood, Humpy Gould
- Postmaster: Hubert Nevers
- Restaurants: Howard Ambrose, Standard Café, Patten Inn and Coffee Shop (H.H. Hatt, Jr.), Cis's Grill, Chester McElroy, Cottage Restaurant, George Ketch, The Country Kitchen, Star Restaurant, Hall's Restaurant, Mac's Restaurant, Boynton's, Ava Dean Clam Shop, The Patten House, Bine's Drive-In, Fogg's Drive-In, La Romano Pizzeria (owned by Charlotte and George Rigby), Charlie Smallwood
- Sporting Camps: Shin Pond House (Zenas Harvey), Camp Fairview, Point of Pines, Shin Pond Camps, Camp Wapiti (Roger J. Bail, Prop.), Bowlan [sic] Camps, Jerry Pond Camps, Pleasant Lake Camps, Mattagamon [sic] Camps, Augustine's, Katahdin Lodge, Birch Point Camps, Lower Shin Pond Camps (Forman Smith), Foster's Wilderness Camps
- Surveyors: Halbert G. Robinson, Joseph Stickland
- Taxi: Nash-Ordway
- Telephone service: Katahdin Farmers' Telephone Company (later Katahdin Telephone Company, then Maine State Telephone Company)
- Town Managers: Elden Shute, Joseph McGillicuddy, Theodore Bartlett, Stanley Johnson, Robert Anderson, James MacArthur, James Hannigan, Firth Smallwood

(services continued on next page)

- Undertakers: Brown Funeral Home, Bowers Funeral Home
- Upholstery: Bill (Willie) Garton
- Water: Patten Water Company(later Patten Water District)
- Welding and brazing: Patten Welding Company, Lloyd Morse, Raymond Porter, Leonard Gould, Lawler Brothers, Dudley Olsen, Roland Huntley, Morse's Service Station, Harvey's Gulf.

Merchants:
- Agricultural implements: Forrest Smith, Willard McIntire, Philip Nightingale
- Autos and Automotive Supplies: Western Auto (Ira Myrick, Nash-Ordway), A.L. Rogers (Lloyd Morse, agent), Ordway Motor Company, Cameron Ford Sales, Cameron's Auto Sales
- Chainsaws: Howes's Chain Saws, Ballard's Filling Station, Morse's Service Station (Lombard)
- Corsetiere: Linnie Smallwood
- Department Stores and Clothing: Stratton's 5c to $1.00 Store (managers George and Rose Merrow), Huston Clothing, Rowe's General Store, Quint's, Mila Bailey, Scribner's (Laura Scribner) and later McNally's (Melvena Quint McNally Hathaway), McLellan's (Del McLellan from Sherman) and later McKenney's (Dean McKenney), Ira Myrick and later Earl Giggey, the Lantern Shop, Fred Bailey
- Fabric: the Fabric Shop
- Fertilizer: Fred Quint, Charles Cunningham, Patten Hardware, Arthur Crouse, Bradford and Elliott, Harrington Farms
- Furniture: Patten Trading Post: Charlie Smallwood, Allan Noyes
- Grain: Eastern States Farmers Exchange, Charles Cunningham, Linwood Lord, Ken's Nationwide
- Groceries and convenience or variety stores: Patten Grocery Company, William Cameron, Arthur Augustine, Earl Anderson, Daigle's Place, Marley Wheaton, Annie McDonald, McLaughlin's Store (Ola and Emma McLaughlin at Shin Pond), Wild Land Grocery (Fifields), Economy Market (Walter Cunningham), Titus Fresh Fish, Ken Lord's A & P and later Ken's Nationwide, Charles Smallwood, First National Stores (Mickey McCafferty), Bob Cunningham's IGA and later Bud & Geri Bell's IGA, North End Market, Ira Myrick and later Earl Giggey, Anderson's Variety

(merchants continued on next page)

- Hardware and appliances: Richard T. Ordway, Patten Hardware (Lowell Barter & Bob Adams), Richardson's Hardware, Russell Arbo's Sales and Service
- Ice: George Peavey
- Jewelry, watch repair, etc.: Larry Madison, G.J. Nichols
- Oil: Putnam Brothers (from Houlton), Cities Service Co., Myrick's Esso, Myrick's Tydol, T.A. Stephenson, Earl Armstrong, Myrick and Bates, Dead River Oil Co.
- Pharmacy: Patten Drug Company: Leslie A. Dickinson, Alfred "Turk" Schurman
- Sporting Goods: Ira Myrick, Huston's Clothing, Richardson's Hardware, Arbo's Sales and Service

Manufacturers and farmers:
- Atlas Plywood, then J.M. Huber Corp. (plywood, hardwood logs, pulp)
- Creamery: Katahdin Creamery (Dr. Lore Rogers)
- Dairy Farms: Perley and Rodney Harris, Ivory and Robert Guptill
- Eastern Pine Sales Corp. (lumber)
- Katahdin Creamery (butter, cheese paste)
- Logging companies: Farrell Lumber Company, Chamberlain Logging Company, Katahdin Logging Company, Arnold Shorey, Hollis Shorey, Hollis Ordway, Clifton Webster
- Ordway and Son (sawmill)
- Potato shippers and farmers: Ralph Robinson, Fred Quint, Bradford and Elliott, W.F. Edwards and Son, C.E. Cunningham and Sons, John Hanson, Robert Anderson, Wendell Kennedy, Merritt Everett, Ora Beattie, Harrington Farms, Crouse & McIntire, Philip Nightingale, Robert McNally, Perley and Rodney Harris, Webb Farms, Arthur Crouse, Willard McIntire, O.J. McLaughlin, Lester and Thurston Townsend
- Sawmill: Chester McManus

REMEMBERING DICKIE DICKINSON

In 1968, 2nd Lt. Leslie A. Dickinson of Patten lost his life in Vietnam. Dickie (as he was known to hometown friends) had graduated from Patten Academy in 1963, where he had been active in sports, yearbook staff, public speaking, and dramatics. He had been a member of the National Honor Society and represented Patten Academy at Maine Boys' State. At the time of his enlistment in early 1966, Dickie was a third-year student at Colby College where he was majoring in American Civilization and was interested in writing. He decided to join the military because he felt that he was living in an artificial environment and needed to gain a new perspective in order to write about real life.

Dickie was remembered by a fraternity brother as "an unlikely Marine," but just as he had always been, he continued to be a high achiever in boot camp and officer training. He was commissioned a second lieutenant and was given the orders he had requested to serve in Vietnam. He arrived in country on December 17, 1967 and was stationed in Da Nang as an infantry platoon leader in the 2nd Batallion, 1st Marine Division.

A month and a half later, the situation was heating up in the days prior to the Vietnamese New Year's holiday called Tet, which fell on January 31st. On the first day of Tet, Dickie's unit was out on patrol when it engaged with a North Vietnamese unit which was setting a traffic ambush. Two Vietnamese civilians were killed, and two were wounded, along with five marines in Dickie's unit. He was one of the wounded. He was transported to a hospital off the coast of Vietnam, but he died of multiple shrapnel wounds on Feb. 3, 1968.

As would be expected, Dickie's death was a shock to the community of Patten and to the Colby Campus. He was one of 58,156 war fatalities, the first of four Colby students to die in Vietnam, and the sole Vietnam fatality from Patten, although there were a number of area residents who did a tour in Vietnam.

Robert M. Lloyd remembered Dickie in an article entitled *Who Has Not Heard Them?* which appeared in the May, 2000, issue of *Colby Magazine*. He wrote about the Colby response to the news of Dickie's death.

> **Les Dickinson's death was marked by an outpouring of emotion on campus. The Colby Echo of February 16, 1968, contained a full page on his loss. A combined chorus of Colby students attended and sang at memorial services held in Patten on Wednesday, February 14. On the day that the Echo told of his death, 2nd Lt. Leslie A. Dickinson, Jr., was buried with full military honors at Arlington National Cemetery. His grave is located on the hill below the Tomb of the Unknown Soldiers**

Lloyd quoted the words of Archibald MacLeish:

> *The young soldiers do not speak. Nevertheless, they are heard in the still houses; who has not heard them? They have a silence that speaks for them at night and when the clock counts. They say: We were young. We have died. Remember us.*

Lloyd finished by writing about the four Colby lives lost:

> *Their four lives and our remembrances of them should cause reflection on the enormity of the war and what it took from us.*

[Note: The article also contains biographies of three other Colby students who died in Vietnam. This article is available online at http://www.colby.edu/colby.mag/issues/fall00/vietnam/]

REMEMBERING OUR VETERANS

Vietnam veterans were not always honored in the United States as they should have been. However, this wasn't the first time in the history of our country that war veterans were dishonored. I came across a book called *Eastern Maine and the Rebellion* by R. H. Stanley and Geo. O. Hall which included some surprising information about Maine's support—or lack of support—for President Lincoln and the Union Army. Even in those times there some bitter divisions between the political parties, and there were men throughout Maine who supported states' rights and therefore the right of the Southern States to secede from the Union. The Copperheads in particular tried to stir up dissent and went so far as to attack men in uniform, including Colonel Ira B. Gardner of Patten. When the war ended in 1865, towns across Maine celebrated the Union victory and proudly displayed the Stars and Stripes...except for a few businessmen who refused to put out the flag in front of their businesses. One such Bangor "secesh" (supporter of the right to secede) just happened to be named Amos Patten. In the heat of a confrontation with other locals, Mr. Patten actually torn down the flag and burned it. Later that day, a lynch mob formed and went out hunting for him, but he could not be found. He did issue an apology, explaining that he meant no disrespect for the flag but was driven by his rage at being coerced to fly it. The charges were eventually dropped, but Mr. Patten was never forgiven by the community of Bangor. [Note: Patten was located along a popular route (the Aroostook Road) taken by deserters fleeing to Canada. Jim Leslie was arrested in Patten for disloyalty to the Union after it was discovered he had been helping soldiers get "over the line." He was taken to Portland, where he had to be let go because of a technicality in the law. There were soldiers from the area who deserted during the war.]

However, in general, Maine has always remembered its war veterans well. There are monuments in almost every town—including Patten— which remember not only those who were lost in battle, but also those who fought. There are three specific programs that I want to recognize here. The first is the Walking Stick program established by Galen Cole of Bangor, himself a WWII veteran. These walking sticks, manufactured in Maine by the Peavey Manufacturing Company, are available to any veteran of any war.

Honor Flight Maine is an organization that was formed to provide Maine veterans with the opportunity to visit war memorials in Washington, D.C. Donald Campbell of Patten was part of an Honor Flight group of veterans who probably would not otherwise have been able to make such a trip. These trips are also another way to honor these veterans' service to our country. The photo above shows Donnie during the Korean War, and the photo at the left was taken when he visited the Korean War Memorial during his trip to Washington, D.C.

A third program which honors our veterans is the Wreaths Across America event. Now a national program, WAA had its beginnings at the Morrill Worcester wreath company in Harrington, Maine. In 1992, Morrill and his wife Karen donated a number of wreaths to be laid on veterans' graves at Arlington National Cemetery in Washington, D.C. In 2007, the project was officially named Wreaths Across America. Since then, convoys of trucks have transported wreaths to Arlington and many other veterans' cemeteries across the U.S. My brother, Scott Harris of Patten, has been one of those truckers who make the yearly December trip to honor those who sacrificed their lives for our country. He uses his own truck, but a specially designed trailer has been designed to be used in the convoy. The trailer has a picture of Scott's son, Dustin, on it. Dustin lost his life while serving in Iraq in 2006. Scott and his wife Lorna visit local organizations to increase awareness of the Wreaths Across America mission: **Remember our fallen U.S. Veterans, Honor those who serve, Teach your children the value of freedom.**

-165-

A COMPARISON OF PRESIDENT ABRAHAM LINCOLN AND PRESIDENT JOHN F. KENNEDY

The information below, which appeared after President Kennedy's death, notes a number of similarities between Kennedy and President Lincoln.

LINCOLN	KENNEDY
Lincoln was elected to Congress in 1846.	Kennedy was elected to Congress in 1946.
He was elected President in 1860.	He was elected President in 1960.
His wife lost a child while living in the White House.	His wife lost a child while living in the White House.
He was directly concerned with Civil Rights.	He was directly concerned with Civil Rights.
He was shot in the back of his head in the presence of his wife.	He was shot in the back of his head in the presence of his wife.
Lincoln was shot in the Ford Theater.	Kennedy was shot in a Lincoln car, made by Ford.
He was shot on a Friday.	He was shot on a Friday.
The assassin, John Wilkes Booth, was known by three names, comprised of 15 letters.	The assassin, Lee Harvey Oswald, was known by three names, comprised of 15 letters.
Booth was killed before being brought to trial.	Oswald was killed before being brought to trial.
There were theories that Booth was part of a greater conspiracy.	There were theories that Oswald was part of a greater conspiracy.
Lincoln's successor was Andrew Johnson, born in 1808.	Kennedy's successor was Lyndon Johnson, born in 1908.
Andrew Johnson died 10 years after Lincoln was shot.	Lyndon Johnson died 10 years after Kennedy was shot.

www.school-for-champions.com › History

CHAPTER SEVEN: THE TOWNS FROM 1969-1999

Although we finished Chapter Six on a positive note, the years from 1969 to 1999 saw changes in Patten and Mount Chase that were not all positive. These were tough years economically for the area. Patten's population declined from 1,368 in 1980 to 1,111 in the year 2000. But there were some important new businesses established during these years, and Patten and Mount Chase residents have always been tough enough to face life's struggles.

As I read town reports from this era, it was ironic that even though the populations of Mount Chase and Patten were getting smaller, the town reports were getting bigger. In the early days, a Maine town was pretty much a self-contained community, taking care of its own business with its own tax money. However, as time went on, and particularly in the last half of the 20th century, the state and federal governments became increasingly involved in community affairs, including education, sewer systems, public dump sites, roads and streets, welfare, the environment, work safety, law enforcement, and court systems. Communities received government funds or assistance through revenue sharing, grants, reimbursements, and services, but the citizens often had to come up with additional tax dollars to pay for whatever needed to be done to meet mandates the government had established. Financial spreadsheets became increasingly complicated as money was transferred here and there, in and out of accounts. It just compounded the situation when the government developed a love affair with acronyms and was also constantly changing titles of programs and committees and organizations and initiatives and whatever. Sometimes the communities felt the government was interfering; other times they were appreciative of the assistance they got from state and federal governments.

Note: Please refer to Chapters 10-16 for more detailed information on schools, the library, healthcare, emergency services, community organizations, lumbering, farming, and tourism/sports camps.

Another note: I'm going to begin Chapter Seven with descriptions of two Community Assistance Programs that were greatly appreciated by many residents of Patten and Mount Chase. Following those descriptions is the chronological list of events from these years.

PENQUIS CAP

In 1969, the Penquis Community Action Program was established in Patten. It provided many services to low-income residents of Patten and Mount Chase but also benefited the communities as a whole. Penquis CAP used the empty Grange Hall (renamed Katahdin Community Center) as its headquarters until 1981, when it was moved to the rear part of Merrow's Department Store. The outreach of this program was divided into five areas: Community Organization, Family Planning, Headstart, Donated Foods, and Operation Mainstream. Naomi White, Kay Violette, and Rubenia Botting were very instrumental in making this a successful program. The services of Penquis CAP over the years included something for everyone.

Children	Headstart, recreation center in basement of Katahdin Community Center, health clinics, Girl Scouts, swimming lessons, Patten Youth Club, dental services at the Chester Dental Clinic, immunizations
Senior citizens, disabled or ill people	Ceramics classes, chartered bus trips, meetings, volunteer drivers, home care nursing, homemaker services, RSVP (Retired Senior Volunteer Program), REAP (Rural Elderly Assistance Project), Meals for Me, Katahdin View Senior Citizens
General public	Donated foods (serving over 200 families in the area), family planning, cooking classes, nutrition information, sewing classes, beautification projects, a clothing bank, mental health counseling, winterizing homes, HEAP (energy assistance), a co-op shop where people could sell items they had made

In the late 1980s, Penquis also sponsored the Emergency Crisis Intervention Program; the Preventive Health Program; the Early and Periodic Screening, Diagnostic, and Treatment program; a housing program known as Section 8; and Project Ride. New programs in the 1990s included Dial-a-Ride, the Medicare/Medicaid Assistance Program, and the One Day Care Program.

By 2000, the Penquis CAP office in Patten had been phased out, but the organization was still helping Patten and Mount Chase residents. Both towns still contribute money to Penquis CAP annually.

CETA and THE PENOBSCOT CONSORTIUM TRAINING AND EMPLOYMENT PROGRAM

The Comprehensive Employment and Training Act (CETA) was a federal law that provided opportunities for unemployed people to get job training and assistance in finding jobs. An offshoot of this was the Penobscot Consortium Training and Employment Program, which came to Patten and Mount Chase around the same time as Penquis CAP. The consortium offered on-the-job training, classroom training, public service employment, youth work programs, and work experience for the purpose of building a good resume,. It was also a sponsor for the Migrant Seasonal Farmworkers Program, JTPA (Job Training Partnership Act), HEP (High School Equivalency Program), SYEP (Summer Youth Employment Program), and Job Corps. Its office in Patten was capably run by Norma Pond. At a time when the Patten and Mount Chase area was designated as an economically depressed area, this organization helped many individuals and families. It was renamed the Training and Development Corps in 1984, and was also known as the Office of Training and Employment. The Patten office was closed in 1988, but Mrs. Pond still did Public Relations and took applications, after which she referred clients to offices in Houlton or Millinocket. Until she retired in 2001, she also continued to work with Katahdin High School to help area residents get high school diplomas.

* * * * *

A partial list of some other social and health service agencies which have assisted Patten and Mount Chase residents includes Eastern Area Agency on Aging, UVEC Food Pantry, Agape Food Pantry, American Red Cross, the Salvation Army, Toys for Tots, Public Health Nurses, Hospice Care, Visiting Nurses, Home Care Agencies, Farmers Home Administration, and Southern Aroostook Soil and Water.

Late 1960s: Mrs. Mary Hafford, wife of Herb Hafford, was killed when a log truck left the road and crashed into her house.

1969: The steeple on the Methodist Church was dedicated to Second Lt. Leslie A. Dickinson, who had been killed in Vietnam.

Leon Roy was killed in a hunting accident. At the time, Leon was employed as a guide for Harold Schmidt at Camp Wapiti. The accident occurred as Leon was helping a client from Connecticut with his target practicing.

Patten lost a dedicated public servant when Russell Arbo died suddenly. He had been a local businessman for many years, but had more recently served capably as Patten's chief of police from 1962-64 and 1966-68.

The last train rolled through Patten.

The Kingdom Hall of Jehovah's Witnesses church was built on Houlton Street.

A new Patten ordinance for parking on Main Street was enacted. Vehicles would angle park on the east side of the street and parallel park on the west side of the street. There were some additional areas designated for parking. Plans were made to plant some new trees along Main Street. The Patten Planning Board came up with a Community Development Plan.

Mount Chase stopped charging a poll tax.

Patten and Mount Chase have been served well by their public works employees. Patten's Bruce Campbell, Barry Tower, Cecil Gallagher, and Kevin Noyes and Mount Chase's Randy McKenney and Hadley McKenney have kept things running smoothly. They are often overlooked but deserve thanks from residents of both communities!

1969, con't.: Neil Armstrong and Buzz Aldrin became the first humans to walk on the moon.

Richard Nixon served as the U.S. president from 1969-1974.

An Aquarian Explosion: Three Days of Peace and Music, better known as Woodstock, took place in up-state New York. As many as 400,000 people (mostly between the ages of 18 and 30) gathered to listen to 32 musical performances by some of the most successful rock bands of the era. There were a few logistical problems, but amazingly there was no violence. Peace, brother.

1970: Marian Guptill was appointed Officer-in-Charge of the Patten Post Office. She was appointed Postmaster the following year, a position she held until 1981.

The town manager of Patten was Firth Smallwood and the chief of police was Manley Brown. Mr. Brown was assisted by the presence of a state trooper in the area. No household items were considered personal property. Livestock was still taxed as personal property, however, and there was still a poll tax. Mount Chase paid Patten $600.00 for fire protection. Lloyd Morse had the Mount Chase snow plowing contract.

Stratton's 5 cents to $1.00 became Merrow's Department Store. George and Rose Merrow sold just about anything you would ever want: clothing, fabric and sewing needs, shoes and boots, craft supplies, yarn, home decorating items, rugs, towels, bedding, curtains and rods, greeting cards, stationery, Christmas decorations, and toys!!!

Katherine Hurlbert, known affectionately as Dolly, was killed in a hit-and-run accident on Feb. 7, 1970. She had been born in Patten in 1947 as part of one of the area's larger families. Her brother Charlie still lives in Patten.

The population of Patten was 1,266, and Mount Chase's population was 197.

As the Vietnam War continued to take the lives of American soldiers, U.S. citizens, especially college students, staged anti-war protests. At a protest at Kent State University in Ohio, four students were killed when National Guard Soldiers fired into the crowd.

1971: Patten was designated as an economically depressed area and could qualify for assistance with town projects under the Public Works and Economic Development Act of 1965.

The last pulp drive on the West Branch of the Penobscot River was conducted.

Open burning at public dumps was no longer allowed. Towns had to have a sanitary land fill, which would be a great expense to the community. Patten also needed a new sewer system, but all the initial plans called for systems that were considered too expensive for area residents to pay for.

This was the last year a poll tax was collected in Patten.

The Northern Maine Regional Planning Commission was established. Patten appropriated funds annually for the commission.

A tennis and basketball court was set up on the east side of Main Street on the former Patten Academy lot.

Fred Smallwood had the Mount Chase snowplow contract for the winter of 1971-1972.

1972: The movie hall closed. It had been owned by Ira and Shinny Howes since 1939 and had provided many hours of entertainment for area folks.

The Patten Town Report stated that the Patten Town Dump had been moved away from Fish Stream, a temporary fix at best. After ten years of studies and planning, the Fish Stream Watershed project was voted down by the town's citizens. Frank Landry and Sons held the contract for snow removal. The State of Maine was now the Sealer of Weights and Measures. This was the last year money was appropriated for the Maine Publicity Bureau.

Frank Landry also had the Mount Chase snowplow contract for the winter of 1972-1973.

I went to the town office in Patten and Kemp went to the town clerk's home in Mount Chase to get our marriage licenses! (Just had to throw that in!)

1973: Scotty Skinner established Scotty's Flying Service, and Raymond Sommers established Sommers Electric.

The town received funds from the government in the form of revenue sharing.

1973, cont.: The Mount Chase Plantation Report was dedicated to George Rigby, who had recently passed away. He had been born in 1909 in Hersey, the son of Judson and Estella (Lord) Rigby. George had been active in town and state government, was a plumber and woods worker, and was the owner of La Romano Pizzeria in Patten along with his wife Charlotte.

William Cohen served in the U.S. House of Representatives and then the U.S. Senate from 1973-1997. He then was appointed as the Secretary of Defense from 1997-2001.

1974: Kathleen "Cassie" Rogers was the town manager. In the town report, she thanked Clive Hatt for his dedicated work at the cemetery and George Dunn for his work in his part in establishing the ambulance service.

Katahdin Valley Health Center was established. Their first office was in the back of Merrow's store.

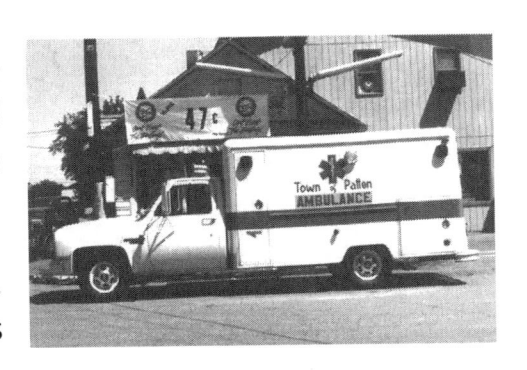

The library underwent a major renovation by removing the wall between a back room and the main room of the library. Sadly, the librarian, Kathleen K.S. Rogers, passed away in 1974. Christine Shorey became the librarian.

Fire destroyed several buildings owned by John and Filena (Anderson) Desaulniers in the vicinity of the Shin Pond House, which the Desaulniers had owned since 1972. Destroyed were a grocery store (operated by Ola and Emma McLaughlin) with an upstairs apartment, a barn/garage, and a laundromat. A sporting goods store owned by E. Richard Schmidt also burned.

The Mount Chase Plantation Report did not tax livestock for the first time. The town paid Sherman, Stacyville, and Island Falls $1,322.50 for their assistance in fighting the fire at Shin Pond. Patten also assisted in that fire.

1974-1975: Junior High students from Patten and Sherman began attending the newly consolidated Katahdin Junior High School, housed in the former Katahdin High School. A new school was built on the opposite side of Route 11 to accommodate Katahdin High School students.

Marilyn Somers, Craig Sponseller, Deanna Morse, and Karen Hall (left to right in photo) formed a gospel singing group called The Good News Singers. They traveled to Providence, RI, to make an album in 1978 and disbanded in 1980.

Charlotte Rigby, who made the best pizza in Northern Maine, was murdered in her home in 1975. She had been born in 1914, the daughter of Cora Seavey Stuart. In 1936 she married George Rigby. She was survived by two daughters, Brenda and Judie.

The Mount Chase Fire Department was established with Craig Hill as its first chief, a position he has held since then. The town bought a fire truck and equipment with money received from Federal Revenue Sharing. The residents still appropriated $600.00 for fire protection, but doesn't seem to have given Patten the lump sum of the money from 1975-1977.

Mount Chase appropriated money to pay Patten so that Mount Chase residents could use the Patten dump.

Around this time, Phil Howes was the owner of a laundromat and opened a tailoring and dry cleaning store in Millinocket. Mr. Howes was also a piano tuner.

Richard Nixon resigned from the office of U.S. president rather than risk being impeached and removed from office. The charges against Nixon and other involved Republicans had to do with illegal gathering of information (wiretapping and burglary), sabotage of the Democratic Party, tax evasion, improper use of government agencies, illegal acceptance of gifts (bribery), and lying to the investigators and the American people. Nixon's vice-president, Gerald Ford, served as president until 1977.

1975: The Patten Town Report was dedicated to Lore Rogers and Hubert Nevers. Donald Grant was the town manager, a position he held until 1982. The report reminded citizens that a 10:30 p.m. to 6:00 a.m. curfew had been put into effect in response to vandalism, noise disturbances, and delinquency. Extensions had been granted on the sewer system and the dump/sanitary landfill projects. The town no longer listed welfare as "town poor" but referred to it as "general assistance."

The *S.S. Edmund Fitzgerald* sank in Lake Superior in a "November gale." All twenty-nine crew members aboard drowned. The accident remains a mystery in that no distress call was made. The *Fitzgerald* was the largest cargo ship operating in the Great Lakes at the time. Canadian singer Gordon Lightfoot memorialized the event in his song *The Wreck of the Edmund Fitzgerald.*

James B. Longley was the first popularly elected independent governor in the United States. He served as Maine's governor from 1975-1979.

1976: Patten celebrated the U.S. bicentennial with special events and fireworks.

Meadowbrook Manor opened. Deanna Morse remains the manager of this senior citizens housing organization.

The Oakfield branch of Katahdin Trust Company was opened.

Wendall Hall died suddenly in an accident on the Shin Pond Road. He was the husband of Karen Hall and the father of Paige (Cunningham), Carter, and Jill Hall.

The Mount Chase Plantation Report published the rules for using the municipal dump. John Brown was the landfill sanitation engineer. Frank Landry had the snowplow contract. Town meetings were held at the Myrick School House on Route 11.

1976, cont.: The Patten Town Report for 1976 was dedicated to Arthur Crouse. Mr. Crouse was a successful potato farmer and had taught the agricultural program at Patten Academy for several years. He was survived by his wife Glenna and four children: Arthur, Jr., Geraldine (Giles), Phyllis, and Steven. The Patten Water District was transferred to the town.

Jim Hathaway built a motel on the north corner of Dearborn and Main Streets. A house last owned by Mr. and Mrs. Frank Hunter was torn down in the process. Mrs. Hunter was previously Mrs. Roy. The motel later became Hathaway's Apartments.

Rick and Sara Hill assumed ownership of Mount Chase Lodge.

The photo below dates from sometime shortly after 1976. On the left, the long building is Hathaway's Motel, and the tall building behind it at the far left is the movie theater. The roofs behind the motel are Richardson's and Merrow's. On the right side of the photo, you can see the Methodist Church and in the background, you can see the Patten Town Hall. On the east side of Main Street, you can see a Texaco garage, the Scribner building which at some point housed the State Liquor Store, the Rowe building with a grocery store on the first floor and Patten Insurance Agency on the second floor, Katahdin Trust Company, Ken Lord's grocery store, and Earl Giggey's gas station and general store.

1976, cont.: A law was passed in the Maine legislature banning pulp and log drives due to environmental concerns. The drives had pretty much become a thing of the past anyway, since trucks had become the most common mode of transporting wood to the mills.

1977: Patten Academy was torn down.

The Rockabema Snow Rangers snowmobile club was formed. This club has greatly enhanced the winter tourist industry in the Patten and Shin Pond areas by maintaining many miles of beautifully groomed trails. The clubhouse was also approved to be rented out for public or private gatherings.

The Patten Town Report stated that much work had been done on the town water system, including redrilling the existing well and drilling a new well on the Patten Grammar School lot. SAD #25 turned Founders Memorial Gym back over to the town; voters now had to decide if they wanted to renovate the building or sell the building and lot. The town office was moved to the Grammar School. The dump was becoming a big problem with the new law banning open burning. The town was now required to compact and cover the garbage every other day. The town could either buy a bulldozer and hire a worker to deal with the garbage or contract the bulldozer work out.

In Guyana, South America, Jim Jones persuaded 918 people to kill their children and themselves by drinking poison. Jones was the leader of the People's Temple cult which originated in the United States but was relocated to Guyana, at some point before this incident.

James Earl "Jimmy" Carter served as the U.S. president from 1977-1981. As a president, he received mixed ratings, but no one can deny that Jimmy Carter accomplished some great things after his term was over. He was awarded the Nobel Peace Prize for establishing the Carter Center in 1982, an organization for advancing human rights. He has been instrumental in conducting peace negotiations and advancing disease prevention. In recent years, he has been a public figure as he has worked with the Habitat for Humanity project. First Lady Rosalynn Carter was active in White House political doings and was also an advocate for establishing better mental health care and erasing stigmas against mental illness.

1978: Fred and Harriette Parker set up beehives and began selling honey.

Ervin Tower built Crystal Lumber Company, which he owned until 1986, when it became Ward Clapboard.

Donald Grant announced bad news in the 1978 Patten Town Report. He said that as a result of double digit inflation, the taxpayers were facing a 31% tax increase.

I was the plantation clerk and Kemp was an assessor (selectman) for the plantation of Mount Chase. In those days, the town clerk worked from home and was responsible for selling hunting and fishing licenses and for recording births, marriages, and deaths. People went to the tax collector's house to pay their taxes. We paid our excise taxes in Mount Chase but registered our vehicles in Patten. The town office was used for meetings and voting.

The Mount Chase Fire Department had built another truck and purchased more fire equipment, but paid Patten $1,000 for fire assistance. The Patten Ambulance Service was charging $5.00 per capita for residents in its member towns. An article in the warrant to close the Mount Chase dump (sorry...landfill) was passed over—Mt. Chase was in the same boat that Patten was. They needed their dump, but it wasn't meeting sanitation codes.

The Great Lakes Blizzard killed 23 people in New York and Ontario, Canada.

1979: Norman and Erlene Bishop opened Pa's Pizza. It had been previously owned by George and Charlotte Rigby (La Romano Pizzeria) and Reggie and Sharon Porter. After the deaths of Norman and Erlene, their daughter Christe Crouse managed the business.

The Shin Pond House, owned by John and Filena Desaulniers, burned. This was the third time fire had destroyed a hotel at that site. Fire officials determined arson had caused this fire.

1979, cont.: Glenn Somers, son of Bobby and Marilyn Somers, drowned in Shin Pond. He was seventeen years old and had just graduated from Katahdin High School four days earlier. The tragedy was compounded when his father, Robert Somers, died suddenly two months later. Mr. Somers was an active member of the Patten Fire Department. Surviving members of the Somers family were Mr. Somers's mother, Annie Somers, his wife Marilyn, and his son Barry. Barry passed away suddenly in 1997.

The Patten Town Report announced the good news that the Peavey Corner/Peasley Brook project had been completed and three out of four of the town's fire ponds had been dredged and enlarged. The bad news was that the dump was quickly filling up since it could no longer be burned. The town report urged people to sort out their garbage as required.

The Getty Mining company began the Mount Chase Mining Project and found a massive-sulfide deposit. (*Massive* in this context does not mean large.) Mount Chase is of volcanic origin. Everyone was hoping for another Gold Rush (the economy of the area could have used a boost) but the project never got beyond the testing phase.

Mount Chase went back to being a town. The Mount Chase **Town** Report listed nine members of the Fire Department, which responded to eight fires in 1979. New tax maps had been prepared and reevaluation was in process. The ambulance per capita rate went to $8.65.

Joseph E. Brennan was Maine's governor from 1979-1987.

1980: The J. M. Huber Plywood Mill burned, putting 100 people out of work.

Michael Arbo became the pharmacist and owner at Patten Drug Company.

The Oddfellows Hall on Houlton Street was torn down.

The Patten Ambulance Service Advisory Committee was established, with a member of the ambulance crew as Director. Patten had five representatives, Stacyville had three, and Mount Chase, Crystal, and Hersey/Moro each had one.

1980, cont.: George Bates of Patten was seriously injured when his small plane crashed and caught on fire after take-off from Caribou Pond north of Baxter State Park. George was able to get out of the plane, but not before he was burned over 60% of his body. Scott Skinner, who had taken off just before George, turned back and discovered what had happened. He managed to load George into his plane by using George's belt as a handle. George was not expected to live, but after spending many months in recovery and therapy, he was able to return to his normal activities. George's wife Liz assisted greatly in the healing process. George had previously crashed another plane in 1975. Ironically, his granddaughter Lisa Bates was a passenger in a helicopter that crashed in the Maine woods in 2013.

Philip "Mickey" Mulligan was killed in a truck accident. Philip was the son of Claude and Marion Mulligan, the husband of Vonnie (Chaloux) Mulligan, and the father of Michelle and Brad Mulligan. (1971 yearbook photo at right)

The Mount Chase Planning Board had been busy and had finalized the town's Comprehensive Plan and Zoning Ordinance. However, when the document was put to the vote, it was defeated, not once, but twice (by a narrow margin both times) by the residents. One of the details in the plan/ordinance that was in contention was what to do about deer yards within town limits. The defeat of the plan meant that Mount Chase was once again under the authority of LURC.

The Mount Chase Town Report was full of good news. Louise Ellis, chairman of the board of selectmen, stated that the town books had been straightened out and thanked MMA (Maine Municipal Association), the Bureau of Taxation, and LURC (Land Use and Regulation Commission) for their assistance in this matter. The town now had a surplus account. There were ten members of the Fire Department, which responded to 9 calls, including two fires in Patten. Mount Chase appropriated $1,000 for fire protection, but only paid Patten $636.00. Donis Carver of Mount Chase had the snow removal contract. Plans were being made to improve the Shin Pond Cemetery and the Owlsboro Road from the Fish Hatchery west.

1980, cont.: However, the Patten Town report was mostly doom and gloom. It had been a difficult year financially for the town, with high energy costs and lots of unexpected expenses. The dump was a growing problem as the piles of garbage kept growing. The streets and roads were deteriorating and the water system was barely adequate for the town's needs.

The town of Patten town had helped some local businessmen establish Patten Veneer Products using a $50,000 government grant. They were able to use a new steam chest that fortunately had not destroyed when the Huber mill burned. Unfortunately, the mill was not successful and soon closed.

The population of Patten was 1,368. Mount Chase had 233 residents.

The Indian Land Claims agreement granted land in various parts of Maine back to Native Americans of Maine. This land included areas around Matagamon Lake west of Patten and Mount Chase.

George Mitchell served as a U.S. senator from 1980-1995, as Senate Majority Leader from 1989-1995, as U.S. Special Envoy for Northern Ireland from 1995-2001, and for U.S. Special Envoy for Middle East Peace from 2009-2011. He then left the political arena and became a businessman, serving at various times as director for Walt Disney, Fed Ex, Staples, the Boston Red Sox, and other organizations.

Mount Saint Helens in Washington erupted after several previous warning signs. The eruption killed 57 people and was the most disastrous volcanic eruption in U.S. history. The eruption reduced the height of the mountain by 1,280 feet.

A massive heat wave killed at least 1,700 people as temperatures across much of the United States topped 90° almost every day from June to September.

1981: Katahdin Valley Health Center opened its clinic on the site where the Oddfellows Hall had been located.

1981, cont.: Edgar Harrington served as president of Katahdin Trust Company from 1981 to 1992 with the exception of a period of time when Ray Prescott was president.

Bruce and Norma Campbell closed their NAPA store. Richardson's Hardware expanded into the south side of the Peavey Block.

Craig and Terry Hill opened Shin Pond Village at the site where the Shin Pond House had stood. The village included a restaurant, store, public showers and bathrooms, a laundromat, and a room for public events. (Photo courtesy Terry Thurston Hill)

A large addition was built on to the Patten Pentecostal Church. The addition, which was dedicated in May, 1981, was paid for entirely by donations.

In the Town Report, Manager Donald Grant reported that the sewer system, septic waste disposal, and road repairs were ongoing issues. He publicly came to the defense of the selectmen, saying that they had a tough job trying to deal with all the town's problems and should not be treated as public whipping targets.

Lynn Olsen Brown established a pre-school program called the Country Village Nursery School at her home.

Ronald Reagan served as U.S. president from 1981-1989.

1982: Calvary Christian Academy School opened on the South Patten Road near the Ash Hill lookout. It closed in 1995.

Harriet V. Campbell was appointed as Patten's Postmaster.

The fire department was kept busy with fires at the Ken Cheeseman home and Ray Porter's paddle shop (both on the Shin Pond Road), the Parson's home (beside the library), and a fire at County Forest Products (on the Crystal Road).

1982, cont.: Donald Grant resigned as he had accepted a job as Searsport's town manager, and Rhonda Harvey took over as Patten's town manager. She reported that the town had sold seven pieces of property and three pieces of equipment. Some of the streets in town had been hot-topped. An extension to Katahdin Street had been constructed and Valley Street was reconstructed. A zoning ordinance was being discussed. A big concern for the town was the high cost of street lighting.

1983: The first Patten Pioneer Days celebration was held. It still is celebrated on the second weekend in August, which coincides with the date of the Lumberman's Museum annual bean-hole bean dinner.

Jerry Michaud opened the Four Seasons Restaurant in the building on the south side of Richardson's Hardware.

John Tower, Jr., of Patten, age 41, was murdered in Mount Chase by Jay Thibodeau, age 18, of Connecticut and recently of Patten. The motive for the murder remains unclear. Tower's body was found three days after the murder by hunters on the Gardner Point Road in Shin Pond. He had died from a gunshot wound to the back of the head.

Al and Lou Ellis opened Ellis Family IGA in the Rowe Building on the east side of Main Street. This photo shows the Rowe Building and the Scribner building, which housed the State Liquor Store in the 1980's.

Dr. Martin Hrynick joined the staff at Katahdin Valley Health Center. He later opened up a private practice with an office in the Milliken Memorial Hospital building in Island Falls. (The hospital had closed in 1974.) His practice is now located in Sherman and is called Northwoods General Practice. Dr. Hrynick also has a regular shift in the emergency room at Houlton Regional Hospital.

Katahdin High School was recognized twice for the high quality education it was providing for area students.

1983, cont.: The Patten Town Report reported the demise of the sewer system project that had been worked on for quite some time. However, the sewer system problem was not going away, as the permits to dump sewerage into streams would expire in 1984 and would most likely not be renewed again. The town was now working with the Department of Environmental Protection to establish the "Small Community Program." This program provided individual sewer systems, with the state furnishing 90% of the costs and the recipient furnishing 10% of the costs.

Mount Chase's town government was now managed by three selectmen and an Administrative Assistant who replaced the former positions of town clerk and tax collector. Annie Lord was the first to hold this position. Mount Chase also had a practically new town hall; Charles Rogers and Stan Sinclair, with help from Danny Coolong, Craig Hill, and other residents, had given the old school house a complete makeover. The town appointed Randy McKenney as Public Works director. He was in charge of keeping roads plowed in the winter and he did a great deal of work on the Owlsboro Road in the summer.

A forest fire near Chesuncook and Telos Lakes burned 400 acres of forest. The fire was most likely the result of a lightning strike.

The U.S. Embassy in Beirut was bombed by Islamic militants, killing 63 people, 17 of whom were Americans.

Mr. Yuri Andropov, who held the highest political office in the Soviet Union, invited Samantha Smith to visit him to discuss a letter she had recently written to him. Miss Smith, who was born in Houlton in 1972, wrote the letter to urge Mr. Andropov to work to encourage world peace. He assured her that he would do so. Tragically, Samantha died just two years later along with her father in a Bar Harbor Airlines plane crash.

1984: The new town office opened on Katahdin Street.

This photo from 1984, shows the annual Halloween parade and the cost of pork chops at Ellis Family IGA.

The 1984 Patten Town Report stated that nine individual sewer systems had been installed under the DEP's Small Community Program. The town also officially removed itself from the existing sewer system and would claim no responsibility "in any way, shape, or manner" for any problems with it. The system was currently being used by only a few homes and businesses on Main Street. In other town developments, a twelve-payment plan had been established for taxpayers. This worked well for many residents of Patten, and was a boon to the town as well as it provided tax revenue throughout the year. There was a big increase in dump costs due to new DEP regulations.

In Mount Chase, Susan Bates was appointed as Administrative Assistant, a position she held until 1990.

Joan Benoit Samuelson of Maine won a gold medal at the US Olympics in the marathon event.

1985: Avon and Lizzie Willett celebrated their 77th wedding anniversary. At that time, they had been married longer than any other couple in the state of Maine.

Louise and Scott Skinner opened the Wilderness Variety Store.

Eighteen-month old Christina Beebe died at Eastern Maine Medical Center after falling into an abandoned milk cooler which was partially filled with water. The accident took place at a potato house in which her parents, Jeffrey and Sarah Beebe, were living while they waited for a nearby house to become available for them to move into.

1985, cont.: Stanley Sinclair, age 72, of Shin Pond, was killed in a snowsled accident near Nesowadnehunk Lake in T4R10, part of Baxter State Park.

Dawn Bragdon was killed when her vehicle veered into the path of an oncoming log truck. The accident occurred on Ash Hill.

George A. Violette was killed in an ATV accident on the Clark Road. He was the son of George and Kay Violette of Patten and brother of Jerry, Mike, Alice (Beaulieu), and Loretta (White). George had graduated from Katahdin High School in 1982 and from Eastern Maine Vocational Technical Institute in 1984. (photo courtesy of Jerry Violette.)

Calley and Currier Co., Inc., of New Hampshire, bought the plywood mill. They began manufacturing veneer.

The Patten dump was no longer a dump; it was now a sanitary landfill. But the name change did nothing to solve any problems. An article in the warrant for the annual town meeting asked the voters to see if the town would enter into a Regional Dump Agreement with area towns to create a regional landfill. The town's chief of police, Orrie Hunt, resigned, marking the end of a local police force. On the plus side, thirty-three sewer systems for single households had been installed through the Small Community Sewer Program and many renovations had been done on the municipal buildings.

Eleanor Sargent Hunter, daughter of Carroll and Florence Sargent, joined the Feed the Children organization as a Certified Registered Nurse Anesthetist. She traveled throughout the United States and to other countries. She received several awards for her work with women and children, including Husson College's Outstanding Nurse of the Year award and the University of Maine's Mary Ann Hartman award.

A McDonald's in San Diego, CA, was the scene of the shooting of 22 people.

1986, cont.: Resthaven Nursing Home was sold to Central Maine Health Care Corporation. Rachel Alward continued to be the manager of the home.

Sandra J. McNally was appointed as Patten's Postmaster. Physicians' Assistant David Caron was hired by Katahdin Valley Health Center.

A 100-year-old house and barn on the North Road burned, killing 38 cows which were in the barn at the time. The farm was owned by Judson Cunningham and his sister Doris, whose father Charles had farmed there in the early- to mid-1900s. The Cunninghams and an elderly aunt who lived there with them were left homeless.

A forest fired burned almost 300 acres of land near the East Branch of the Penobscot.

Billy Davis, formerly of Rhode Island, bought the Walter Phillips home and shop on the South Patten Road. Davis and his sister Nancy opened North Country Discount Supply in the former shop. The business was later turned over to Nancy and her husband Dan Coolong. The home later burned and the store building was used by the Headstart Program. This building was torn down in 2016 when Katahdin Valley Health Center opened an administration building on the site.

Mount Chase was working on its rural roads. Hadley McKenney was appointed as Road Commissioner, a position he held until 1997. He worked tirelessly plowing snow in the winter and keeping roads in tip-top condition year-round.

Patten was also working on its rural roads, many of which were repaired and paved in 1986, thanks to the Patten's Public Works man, Cecil Gallagher. A water department project restored water pressure to Main Street. More sewer systems were being installed through the Small Community program. The regional landfill organization was checking out facts and figures for establishing a landfill that would serve the local communities. The town received $30,000 in Federal Revenue Sharing. This money had come in handy in years past for funding important town projects, but was not a guaranteed source of income in the years to come.

The Space Shuttle Challenger exploded 73 seconds after lift-off, killing all seven crew members, including Christa McAuliffe, a teacher from New Hampshire.

1986, cont.: The Edmund, Oklahoma, Post Office was the scene of a murder spree that left 15 people dead.

1987: Patten Academy Alumni Park was created by the Patten Women's Club. The bell from the former Academy building is the centerpiece of the park. Several flower beds are planted by local groups, families, or individuals. The park is an integral part of Patten Pioneer Days and has also been site of ecumenical church services, musical presentations, and memorial activities. The park is beautifully maintained, and in 2012 the bell tower was repaired.

Ray Porter set up a Quonset building on the Shin Pond Road to house his paddle shop.

Fred Smallwood opened a full-service garage and gas station on the crest of Finch Hill.

Phil and Marge Heath were operating a Christmas tree farm on the Waters Road.

The Robert and Pat Morrarty home in Patten burned. In Mount Chase, an old house and a trailer burned, but a new house owned by Al DeGregario was saved.

The Scribner building on the south side of Ellis's IGA (last occupied by the Maine State Liquor Store) and a gas station on the corner of Main Street and Houlton Street were bought by Al and Lou Ellis and torn down.

A noise control ordinance was established in Patten. Under discussion were the closing of Patten's landfill, the construction of a salt-sand storage facility, establishing the Katahdin Valley airport, building a bio-mass plant in the Patten/Crystal area, and capital improvements.

Manley Brown of Mount Chase, a long-time Shin Pond bus driver, passed away. He had also been a Patten constable and was active in Mount Chase town government. He was survived by his wife Mildred, his daughters Frances (McKenney) and Lela (Long) and his sons Dana and John.

1987, cont.: The Houlton branch of Katahdin Trust Company opened.

John R. (Jock) McKernon served as Maine's governor from 1987-1995.

1988: Al and Lou Ellis built a new grocery store on the site of the former Scribner building.

George Landry, age 34, died as the result of an accident involving a bulldozer. George was the owner and operator of George Landry and Sons Contractors and worked in the lumbering industry. He was married to Barbara Stevens Landry and had four children: Paul, Bobbie Jo, Michael, and John. He was the son of Frank and Sally Landry.

In the Patten Town Report, town manager Rhonda Harvey stated that the town had tried to keep the water system functioning using only money received from user fees, but had been forced to invest other town funds into some major repairs to well houses, pumps, and pumping stations. More updates would have to be done in the future. The town could now register boats, snowmobiles, ATV's, and trailers. It was announced that the planning board would be reorganized and hopefully could meet the demands of the various issues the town was facing. Patten had endorsed legislation and efforts to achieve comprehensive property tax reform.

In Mount Chase, the warrant for town meeting included articles about businesses obtaining liquor licenses and Sunday sales of liquor. The voters approved an article to use surplus money to build a town garage. Some of the snowplowing was contracted out, but the town also maintained its own plowing equipment. The town was going through a reevaluation process.

1988, cont.: D.A.R.E. (Drug Abuse Resistance Education) was introduced to Patten and Sherman fifth-graders. The program was an effort by law enforcement officers across the U.S. to reduce the number of youths who got involved in drugs, gangs, and violent behavior.

The ABC Nursery School was opened at Stetson Memorial United Methodist Church. Teachers who managed the preschool from 1988-2006, when it closed, included Eve Rice, Kristy Mitchell, Lela Long, and Leanne Anderson.

Mrs. Karen Wood of Hermon was killed in a tragic hunting accident. Mrs. Wood stepped out into her backyard and was shot by hunter Donald Rogerson, who mistook her for a deer. The event sparked heated discussions as people across Maine argued about liability in the incident.

1989: The Grange Hall was torn down.

Tina Mari Birmingham was killed in an ATV accident. She was the daughter of John and Mari (Mimi) Birmingham, the sister of John and Chester Birmingham, and the granddaughter of Russell and Pauline Arbo and Chester and Winona Birmingham.

George and Rose Merrow closed Merrow's Department Store. They had been in business for thirty-five years.

Patten's Town Report stated that the sewer project application had been submitted to the Department of Environmental Protection (DEP) and that construction would begin in May of 1990. A study of the water system had been completed, and an application for financing the project had been submitted. Voter approval was still needed. Patten was exploring the extremely controversial and expensive issue of solid waste disposal with the Northern Penobscot Regional Solid Waste Association. Gregg Smallwood was given a three-year contract for snow removal.

1989, cont.: The Mount Chase Fire Department held its first chicken barbecue and fireworks celebration in conjunction with Patten Pioneer Days.

The Berlin Wall was torn down, reuniting East and West Germany for the first time since 1961.

George H.W. Bush served as U.S. president from 1989 to 1993.

1990: The population of Patten was 1,256, and Mount Chase's population was 254.

In the Patten Town Report, the new town manager, Margaret (Peggy) Daigle reported that a design for the new sewer system had been chosen, a Federal Housing Administration (FHA) grant/loan had been secured, and additional funds were coming from the Environmental Protection Agency (EPA) and DEP. However, it was discovered that some of the recently installed sewer systems were not properly hooked up and were still discharging waste in Webb Brook and Fish Stream. FHA had approved funding for improvements to the water system, including construction of a 400,000 gallon reservoir and new water main distribution lines.

Two local men who were serving in the 112th Med Evac Company of the National Guard were deployed to Iraq or Germany during the first Gulf War, called Desert Storm. Ed Noyes, a Patten Ambulance E.M.T., served in Iraq, and Kemp Coolong, a Mount Chase selectman, served in Germany.

The Northern Katahdin Valley Regional Chamber of Commerce was established to discuss ways to bring more tourists into the area.

Susan Sheehan took over the Mount Chase Administrative Assistant job. She held that position until 2001. A bathroom was added to the Mount Chase Town Office.

Home computers came into common use in the 1990s.

1991: Dana Cole built a motel/restaurant called Millstream Lodging on the site where the Grange Hall had stood. It burned in 1997.

1991, cont.: The Presque Isle branch of Katahdin Trust Company opened. Since then, fourteen more branches have been opened, as far north as Fort Kent and as far south as Scarborough.

Steve and Cheryl Anderson opened the Downtown Deli at the site where The Red Moose Trading Post now exists. They later moved the business to the north corner of Main and Founders Street.

Patten Town Manager Paul Beattie reported that both the water system and the sewer system projects were being paid for with grants and low-interest loans. The water system project design had been completed and put out to bid.

The Northern Katahdin Valley Solid Waste Committee was formed with Patten, Mount Chase, and nine other towns to tackle the project of creating a landfill to deal with solid waste.

The Northern Katahdin Valley Regional Chamber of Commerce, with a membership of 54 businesses, had compiled a directory for the chamber areas and was printing a snowmobile map.

Patten had a year-long celebration of its sesquicentennial anniversary of becoming a town.

The Soviet Union fell, officially ending the Cold War which had begun in 1947. The fall came when fifteen Republics separated themselves from the Soviet Union and became independent countries/states.

George Hennard, an angry and bitter man who hated women and ethnic minorities, killed 24 diners at a Luby's restaurant in Killeen, Texas. Some of the people were killed when he drove his truck into the restaurant and others were shot by Hennard.

1992: Steve Richardson served as president of Katahdin Trust Company from 1992-1998.

1992-1993: The sewer collection and treatment system was installed and households had been hooked up. Owen Murphy was hired to oversee the sewer system operation as well as the water system. Phase I of the water system project was done. There were now twelve operational fire hydrants and a 400,000 gallon reservoir. The fire insurance category was reduced, allowing a 14.3% savings on fire insurance premiums for those households that used the town's water system.

The town received a $700,000 Community Development Block Grant, which was used for upgrading recreational facilities, reconstructing downtown streets, installing storm drains, and revitalizing the business district.

The town of Patten was in good shape financially. There were unexpended balances in many accounts and the mil rate increased only .05 in spite of a substantial increase in the MSAD#25 budget.

The closure plan for the Patten landfill was approved by the DEP and the dump was closed in December of 1993.

The Northern Katahdin Valley Solid Waste Committee changed "Committee" to "Disposal District" in its name. A piece of land in Dyer Brook was purchased to be the site of the new landfill.

1993: Thomas Sheehan served as the Northern Katahdin Valley Solid Waste Disposal District member from Mount Chase from 1993 to 2001. He was an active member who worked hard to help the organization get up and running.

"The Storm of the Century" was a natural disaster experienced by 40% of United States citizens. As it raged from Cuba to Canada along the east coast, it killed 318 people with its high winds, record cold temperatures, and up to 44 inches of snow in areas where snow rarely fell.

The Waco Siege in Texas left 168 members of a cult led by David Koresh dead when a fire of unknown origins was set in one of the buildings on the compound.

1993, cont.: Al-Qaeda terrorists were responsible for the explosion of a bomb in the basement of the World Trade Center, killing six people and injuring 1,042 others.

Bill Clinton served as U.S. president from 1993-2001. Clinton narrowly escaped being ousted from office when impeachment charges were brought against him in 1998. Clinton was accused of perjury and obstruction of justice, both of which occurred when he was testifying in court concerning an extra-marital affair with a White House intern and a sexual harassment charge. The impeachment charges were brought by the Senate but failed in the House.

1994: Ray Porter sold his paddle shop business to Jim Carson.

The town erected a new veterans memorial honoring veterans of conflicts from 1941-1994. It stands alongside the World War I monument in front of the library. This photo shows Ken Lord leading the dedication service for the new memorial. Later, names of veterans of conflicts from 1994 to 2001 were added.

Phases II and III of the water project were completed except for some landscaping and the renovations of the two pump houses.

Mount Chase bought a computer for the Town Office.

The Mount Chase Landfill was closed. The town entered into a contract with White Knight Solid Waste for curbside pickup of garbage. The town appropriated resident tax money to pay for the service; as a result, individual residents did not have to pay for the service.

1995: Dr. Richard Engroff opened his own dentistry office on the Shin Pond Road.

Steve and Cheryl Anderson bought the former McKenney's Clothing Store and moved their deli to that location.

Anti-government militant Timothy McVeigh drove a truck up to front of the Alfred P. Murrah Federal Building in Oklahoma City, Oklahoma, and then used a remote control to set off a bomb he and his cohort Terry Nichols had placed in the truck. 168 people—including 15 children—died and 680 people were injured. Six children in the building's day care area survived but were left with serious, life-changing injuries. An iconic photo taken that day shows a fireman cradling the lifeless body of Baylee Almon, who had celebrated her first birthday the previous day. McVeigh was executed in 2001 and Nichols is serving life in prison.

Angus King served as Maine's governor from 1995-2003. He was the second popularly elected independent governor in the United States. Olympia Snowe served as a U.S. Senator from 1995-2013.

1996: Town manager Paul Caruso reported that the Maine Department of Transportation had finished its Houlton Street Project. The town was in good financial condition except for the new sewer system, which was in dire straits.

Ambulance and fire calls were going to a dispatcher at the Penobscot County Sheriff's Department, which allowed for much quicker response time.

Patten lost its well-loved teacher, farmer, author, historian, mentor, and friend to all, Irene Olsen Bradford. She was buried in the Patten Cemetery.

Joel Fitzpatrick became the pharmacist and owner of Patten Drug Company.

1997: Peter Ellis opened the Al-E-Oop Restaurant formerly Jerry Michaud's Four Seasons Restaurant. This building was torn down in 1998 and is now the site of Richardson's Farm Supply and McNally Farm Produce.

1997 cont.: Ken Lord's grocery store was closed after 51 years of being in business. Ken was a well-loved Main Street businessman with a heart of gold for his customers. In the last several years, Ken's son Jeff had worked with his father.

Peter and Jon Ellis assumed ownership of Ellis Family IGA.

The town of Mount Chase was awarded a DEP Block Grant in the amount of $4,537.00 to be used for septic disposal. Tremblay's E-Z Hauling now had the contract for garbage pick-up.

Susan Collins of Caribou served as a U.S. senator from 1997-2013. She became well-known as a bipartison senator and for never missing a vote.

1997-1998: In a two-step process, Patten Primary and Patten Grammar Schools consolidated with Sherman and Stacyville Elementary Schools. They moved into the former Katahdin Junior High School building (now called Katahdin Elementary School), and the junior high students moved into the high school building (now called Katahdin Middle and High School). It was a difficult time as the last school buildings within each of the communities closed their doors, but the Katahdin Schools continued to provide a quality education for their students. And just as important, all of the employees in the schools—bus drivers, cooks, custodians, teaching staff, and administration—were and still are committed to the total well-being of each and every student.

Bonnie Nettles and Marshall Applewhite convinced 39 members of the Heaven's Gate cult to commit suicide so that they could start a new life on another planet by boarding a spaceship which supposedly was traveling in the tail of the comet Hale-Bopp.

1998: In January, the North American ice storm became Maine's worst natural disaster. Patten and Mount Chase were not as directly affected by the devastation as more southern parts of the state were. Some areas in Maine and Quebec lost power for up to 45 days, and damages totaled in the millions of dollars. Thirty-five people lost their lives as a result of the storm. This photo is not from Patten, but it does show the effect the storm had on power lines. It is amazing that these poles are still standing.

Rhonda Harvey replaced Paul Caruso as Patten's town manager, and Kevin Noyes replaced Cecil Gallagher as Public Works Director. This position now included the title of *Code Enforcement Officer*. Mr. Noyes was the go-to guy for anything you might need to know about regulations for Shoreland Zoning Ordinances, Land Use Ordinances, or Building Ordinances. There was a 7% reduction in the mil rate. Patten Primary School and Patten Grammar School were given back to the town by SAD #25. No plans had been made about what to do with the buildings.

Northern Katahdin Valley Waste Disposal District established a "Pay as You Throw" policy as a way to reduce costs to the member towns.

The Homestead Exemption program reduced property taxes for qualifying Patten and Mount Chase citizens.

Patten and Mount Chase joined the Upper Valley Economic Council (UVEC) along with Stacyville and Sherman. The goal of this organization was to promote the area and hopefully revitalize the towns.

1998, cont.: Bobby and Brenda Raymond bought the clam shop.

The town of Mount Chase contracted all its snowplowing out. Phil Morse plowed the town's roads from 1998 until 2008.

Jon Prescott served as the president of Katahdin Trust Company from 1998 to the present.

1999: Patten's fire house was enlarged with an addition. Volunteer labor did most of the work.

Morse's Garage closed and was torn down. It had the distinction of being the garage that had stayed open for the longest period of time in Patten. It had even remained within the same family for almost sixty years. The fire pond behind the garage was filled in as the lot was cleared, marking the end of an era in Patten history in several regards.

A chickadee replaced the lobster on Maine license plates.

UVEC (to which both Patten and Mount Chase belonged) held a dog sled race, assisted business development by applying for and getting grants, preserved jobs for local businesses, set up its website, and established an interactive distance learning program at the high school. The last accomplishment made it easier for area citizens to take college courses without having to travel long distances.

The Northern Maine Development Commission did a study of the Patten and Mount Chase area—its strengths, weaknesses, economic assets, work force statistics, etc.

1999, cont.: Eric Harris and Dylan Klebold killed 15 students and teachers at Columbine School in Littleton, Colorado.

The Sherman V.F.W. sponsored the visit of the Vietnam Veterans Moving Wall Memorial to the Sherman and Patten area. The Moving Wall is a small scale replica of the actual Vietnam Veterans Memorial in Washington, D.C. It travels throughout the United States, giving people who cannot travel to Washington the opportunity to pay tribute to Vietnam veterans and honor fallen soldiers. In the photo below, Loren Ritchie is speaking at the opening ceremonies.

In the photo to the right, Dot Dickinson is looking at the etching of the name of her son, Second Lt. Leslie A. Dickinson, Jr.

The citizens of Patten and Mount Chase had never dishonored any war veterans, including Vietnam veterans, but it was greatly appreciated by all veterans that their sacrifices were being honored publicly.

Events such as the moving wall ceremonies have a way of bringing people closer together. But people from Patten and Mount Chase had always showed how much they cared for each other, especially when someone was having a particularly tough time. Food was toted into homes regularly, helping hands were offered, benefit dinners helped others financially, prayer chains were active, and funerals were well-attended. No matter how tough times got, these small town residents kept reaching out to others. They were *community* members in every sense of the word.

Maine Registers from 1969-1999 and other resources include this information:

Services:

- Accountants: Robert Adams, Vaughn Chapman, Deanna Morse
- Airplane Chartering: Arthur Augustine, Elmer Wilson, Ray Porter, Scotty's Flying Service (Scott Skinner), Virgil Lynch
- Architect: Kenny Phillips
- Bail commissioner: Robert Adams
- Banking: Katahdin Trust Company
- Barbers: Leo Dickinson, F.W. Peavey, Mike Barnett
- Beauticians: Phyllis Madison, Patty Violette, Frances McKenney, Mrs. Kent Smallwood, Theresa's Headquarters (Theresa Patterson Schmidt), Codgie's Hairport (Colleen Martin), Magic Scissors (Bethann Carver), Viv's Hair We Are (Vivian Brownlee), Trendsetter's Hair Studio (Danielle Cole)
- Building Contractors, Carpenters, Painters: Henry Rigby, Robert Rogers, Wesley Giles, Robert Smallwood, Frank Violette, Victor Michaud, Alonzo Albert, John's Painting and Decorating, Royce Smallwood, Walter Phillips, Bruce McNally, Kenny Phillips, Kenneth Cheeseman, Dana Cole, Wendell Harvey, Kevin Higgins
- Burglar and Fire Alarm Systems: Automatic Alarm Company
- Chiefs of Police: Manley Brown, Lloyd McKenney, Russell Arbo, Ken Garnett, Frank Violette, Orrie Hunt
- Delivery: Cole's Express from Houlton, George Howes, The Bangor and Aroostook Railroad, United Parcel Service, James Gray
- Dentists: Dr. George Banton in Island Falls, Dr. Richard Engroff
- Doctors and Physician Assistants: Dr. William Daniels in Sherman, Dr. Clyde Swett in Island Falls, Gus Konturas, Craig Sponseller, Ronald Blum, Ted Pettengill, James Guanci, Martin Hrynick, James Ryan, David Caron
- Electricians: Russell Arbo, Robert Smallwood, Sommers Electric (Raymond Sommers), John's Electric (John Flannery), Melvin Electric (Wayne Melvin), Charles Electric
- Electricity: Eastern Maine Electric Co-op, Maine Public Service Company
- Electronics/Satellite Service: Valley Street Satellite Sales (Ola Wayne and Diana Tucker)

(services continued on next page)

- Excavating/Grading/Landscaping Contractors: Lester Conklin, Leroy Giles and Son, Frank Landry and Sons, Jacar Inc. Landscaping, Cole's Lawn Care
- Fuel Oil: Dead River Oil Co., Gallagher's Heating Oil, Hank Green Heating Oil
- Garages/service stations: Morse's Service/Morse's Exxon/Morse's Irving (Lloyd, Phil, and Paul Morse), Harvey's Gulf Service (Bob Harvey), Ballard's Filling Station (Cooche Ballard), Patten Filling Station, Giggey's/Giggey's Esso (Earl Giggey), Cameron's Mobil Station (Billy and Ricky Cameron), Carver's Chevron (Donnie Carver), George Bates & Sons, Robert O. Keim, Main Street Auto Body (Al David), Patten Auto Body (Claude Ouellette), Gallagher's Auto Parts and Gallagher's Chevron (Chris Gallagher), Smallwood's Garage (Fred Smallwood), CAS Auto Sales
- Health Clinic: Katahdin Valley Health Center
- Hides, Skins, and Furs: Maine Wilderness Fur
- Hotels and motels: Shin Pond House (Augustine, Bates, Schmidt, Desaulniers), Patten House/Campbell's Inn (Hall, Hathaway, Campbell), Cunningham's Tourist Home, Hathaway's Motel, Sharpe's, Millstream Lodging (Dana Cole), Bartlett's Lodge (Steve and Laurie Bartlett)
- Insurance: Patten Insurance Agency (Edgar Harrington)
- Jeweler: Larry Madison
- Justices: Robert Anderson, Robert Adams, Firth Smallwood, Carroll Sargent, Filena Desaulniers, Deanna Morse, Carole Nash, Eileen Moore, Karen Hall, William Davis Jr., Jeanette Gallagher
- Laundromat: Wash Tub
- Nurseries: Esther Lord's Greenhouse, Backyard Greenhouse, Patten Floral
- Nursing care: Resthaven Nursing Home/Mountain Heights Health Care Facility, Friendship Manor
- Patten Theater: Ira and Shinny Howes
- Postmasters: Hubert Nevers, Marian Guptill, Philip Wyman, Harriet Campbell, Dianne London, Sandra McNally
- Real estate: Patten Insurance Agency, Francis Dunn, Royce Smallwood, Katahdin Valley Real Estate (Dunn & Smallwood), Nevers Real Estate, United National Real Estate
- Recycling and Redemption: Patten Redemption Center, MRN Redemption

(services continued on next page)

- Restaurants: Clam Shop (Ava-Dean, Hugh Cunningham, Justin Glidden, Geraldine Craig, Vivian Brownlee, Bobby & Brenda Raymond), The Patten House, Drive-In (Bine Whitehouse, Mickey & Louise Fogg, Ken & Monica Lau), La Romano Pizzeria (Charlotte & George Rigby, Reggie & Sharon Porter)/Pa's Pizza & Subs (Norman & Erlene Bishop), Eager Beaver, Campbell's Drive-In, Four Seasons Restaurant (Jerry Michaud)/Al-E-Oop Restaurant (Peter Ellis), Shin Ponderosa (Ricky Cameron), Downtown Deli and Pizza (Steve & Cheryl Anderson), Shin Pond Pub, Bartlett's Lodge
- Sign Painters: John Noyes, Stacy Bishop Carter
- Sporting Camps and Campgrounds: Birch Point Camps, Lower Shin Pond Camps, Mount Chase Lodge (Henry Schmidt, Rick & Sara Hill), Point of Pines, Shin Pond Camps, Camp Wapiti, Bowlin Camps (Jon and Betty Smallwood), Jerry Pond Camps (Vernald & Freda Stubbs), Pleasant Lake Camps, Shin Pond House, Foster's Wilderness Camps (Chub & Fran Foster), Katahdin Lodge and Camps (Arthur & Eugenia Sharpe, Finley & Marty Clark), Eager Beaver Lodge, Bear Mountain Lodge (Carroll & Deanna Gerow), Lyman's Hillside Lodge (Lyman Botting), Shin Pond Lodge, Bradford Camps (Dave Youland), Driftwood (Harold Schmidt), Matagamon Wilderness Campground (Don & Diana Dudley), Patten Hunting Lodge, Conklin's Wilderness Camps (Lester & Marie Conklin), North Country Lodge (Goodman family), Bear Facts Lodge, Shin Pond Village & Campground (Craig & Terry Hill)
- Surveyors: Francis Dunn, Keith McElroy, James Perz
- Taxidermy: Michael DeRespino, Gene Bahr, Myrna McDonald
- Telephone service: Maine State Telephone Company (later Continental Telephone Company, Contel of Maine, GTE of Maine, Northland Telephone Company)
- Town Managers: Kathleen Rogers, Donald Grant, Rhonda Harvey, Margaret Daigle, Paul Beattie, Paul Caruso, Rhonda Harvey (returned)
- Undertaker: Bowers Funeral Home
- Upholstery: Willie Garton
- Water: Patten Water Company, later Patten Water District
- Welding and brazing: Morse's Garage (Lloyd Morse), Bob Harvey's Gulf, Roland Huntley, Dick Hall & Sons, Katahdin Welding and Steel (Steve Crouse)

Merchants:
- Agricultural implements: Willigar's
- Autos and Automotive Supplies: Patten Auto Parts, Carver's Auto Parts, Cameron Ford Sales, CAS Auto Sales
- Bait: Charles McLaughlin, Scott Skinner
- Chainsaws: Kermit Howes, Ballard's Filling Station, Morse's Service Station, Coolong's Small Engines (Hadley and Kemp Coolong)
- Crafts and Hobby Shop: Carol Ann Crafts
- Department Stores, Variety Stores, and Clothing: Stratton's 5c to $1.00 Store/Merrow's Department Store(George and Rose Merrow)), McKenney's Clothing (Dean and Frances McKenney), Earl Giggey, Shin Pond Country Store, Amber's Klassy Klos (Amber Craig), Patten General Store (Ken Lau), Wilderness Variety (Scott and Louise Skinner), Patten Trading Post, North Country Discount (Billy Davis, Dan and Nancy Coolong), North Gate Sports Shop
- Fertilizer: Charles Cunningham, Arthur Crouse, Harrington Farms
- Furniture: Allan Noyes
- Gift Shops: Maine Card Co., Viv and Lisa's (Brownlee) Gift Boutique
- Grain: Ken's Nationwide/Ken & Jeff's Market
- Groceries: William Cameron, McLaughlin's Store (Ola and Emma McLaughlin at Shin Pond), Ken's Nationwide/Ken & Jeff's Market (Ken and Jeff Lord), Bell's IGA (Bud and Gerry Bell), Earl Giggey's, Anderson's Grocery, Plantation Trading Post (Fulton and Vicki Anderson/Victor and Gloria Glantz), Ellis Family IGA
- Hardware and appliances: Patten Hardware (Bob Adams), Richardson's Hardware, Western Auto
- Oil: Putnam Brothers (from Houlton), Cities Service Co., Myrick & Bates, Earl Armstrong, Dead River Oil Company, Carver's Chevron, Carver's Fuel
- Pharmacy: Patten Drug Company: Michael Arbo, Joel Fitzpatrick
- Snowmobiles: Patterson and Schmidt
- Sporting Goods: Richardson's Hardware, Patten Hardware, Earl Giggey's, Western Auto, Northgate Sports Shop
- Video Equipment and Rentals: Bates Video, Pa's Pizza 'n' Subs, Ken and Jeff's Market

Manufacturers:
- Bear Paw Wood Shop
- Calley and Currier Company (Veneer Mill)
- Country Forest Products (Bobby Porter)
- Crystal Lumber Company (Ervin Tower)
- Grant's Dairy
- Katahdin Creamery (butter, cheese paste)
- J.M. Huber Corp. (plywood, hardwood logs, pulp)
- Lord's Double A Sawmill/Double A and CG (Austin Lord, Dwinal Anderson, Carl Guptill)
- Northland Mill and Lumber Company, Inc.
- Parker's Honey (Fred and Harriet Parker)
- Patten Veneer Products
- Porter's Wood Working
- Porter's Paddle Shop/JMC Corp.
- Shaw and Shaw
- Ward Clapboard (owned by Holly Ward, managed by Cecil Gallagher and others)

Foresters:
- Dave Brooks
- Francis Dunn
- Adelbert "Skeet" Noyes
- James Perz
- Donald Shorey

Logging Operations:
- Michael Craig
- George Landry and Sons
- Perkins and Porter
- Arnold Porter and Son
- Arnold Shorey

Potato Farming and Shipping:
- Joe Brawn
- Arthur Crouse
- Harrington Farms
- Harris Farms
- Heath Brothers
- Qualey Farms
- Fred Quint & Son
- Thurston Townsend
- Webb Farms

Dairy Farming: Robert Guptill, Don Slauenwhite

Trucking:
- Dan Baker
- Fred Brownlee
- Ronald Campbell
- David Chaloux
- Michael Detour
- David Gardner & Sons
- Brian L. Glidden
- Chester Glidden, Jr.
- Scott Harris
- Carroll Heath
- Dana Landry
- Frank Landry
- Pitt Landry
- Richard Landry
- George Landry & Sons
- John Marr
- Craig Morse
- Rick Morse & Sons
- Gregg Smallwood
- Graydon Watson

Christmas Tree Farm: Phillip Heath

THOUGHTS ABOUT OUR PLACE IN THE WORLD

In 1973, I was asked by an "outsider" if we people from northern Maine were able to keep up on the national news. I guess this person thought that because she was staying in a camp without electricity and running water, that was the way we natives lived as well. (She had already told me that she knew we got around on snowmobiles in the winter.) I will grant that in the past, we were somewhat isolated from the outside world, but by the 1960's, that was no longer the case. Modern technology was connecting even the most remote places on earth—like Patten and Mount Chase—to everywhere else on earth. Newspaper headlines and television news broadcasts kept us informed daily of what was happening around the world.

You may have noticed that many of the events that I included in this history of Patten and Mount Chase did not occur in either of the two communities, and sometimes did not even happen in Maine. But what was happening outside our communities did have a strong impact on our day-to-day lives. For example, most of us remember in vivid detail what we were doing when we heard that President Kennedy had been shot. (My husband was serving an after-school detention at Patten Academy.) Local teens screamed along with thousands of other fans when the British invasion (the Beatles, for you younger readers) appeared on the Ed Sullivan show. For the first time, we watched our soldiers fighting a war in a jungle across the ocean. We were shocked to see the actual footage of National Guard troops firing into the throng of students at Kent State as they protested that war. In 2001, we watched with horror—moments after it happened— as hijacked planes flew into the World Trade Center and the Pentagon and crashed into a field in Pennsylvania. We have gotten to know our politicians better than we know some of our own relatives (and better than we really want to, in some cases). We have watched the World Series and the Super Bowl and the tournament games in Bangor in real-time.

Yes, we surely know what is going on around the world on a day-to-day basis. In fact, we even know what is going on beyond earth's atmosphere. We were awed when we saw the photos of Alexei Leonov floating in space in 1965, and we gloated when Neil Armstrong and Buzz Aldrin walked on the moon in 1969, before the Russians got there. And we have marveled at the photos of distant planets.

And because we conquered space, we can't hide in our own back woods anymore. Satellite images show our town, our house, and even our pickup truck parked in the dooryard. (That's actually a satellite photo of my house and my pickup truck! The photo must have been taken in late April or early May—you can see the remains of the snow banks at the edge of the woods.) And because we—well, some of us, anyway— mastered the technology of the computer and the internet, the details of our lives are public information.

Change is happening in our world faster than ever before in history. We only need to look at the histories of Patten and Mount Chase to know that. Some of us are excited about the changes we can expect in the future, while others yearn for the simplicity of days gone by. There is no doubt that most of the changes have been a benefit to humanity: immunizations and improved health care, ease of communication and information at our fingertips, modern appliances and flush toilets and automobiles. But we now worry about our involvement in the wars of other countries, about the appalling conditions that some people around the world and even in our nation have to live in, about drugs and gangs, about terrorist attacks and school shootings, about global warming and pollution, about the morality and capabilities of our elected officials. Are we going to hell in a handbasket, or are we headed for grand new adventures? There is one thing we do know: whatever happens down the road, the residents of Patten and Mount Chase will be part of it.

CHAPTER EIGHT: THE TOWNS FROM 2000-2016

There was great concern as the clocks turned from the 20th century to the 21st century. Would our modern technology fail drastically if it couldn't cope with the new date? How would we survive without electricity, phones, computers, appliances, hot running water? Would we even be able to gas up our cars? Sometimes it makes you wonder what we've done to ourselves! Life was so much simpler in the old days, wasn't it? It's understandable why there are some people who now live *off the grid* or why they take vacations that let them enjoy the great outdoors and get back to basics.

But most of us really appreciate being able to watch television, make a quick trip to Bangor, and use our indoor toilets. Patten and Mount Chase residents sort of have the best of both worlds. We can live in homes and even camps with all the modern amenities, but we're surrounded by the best Mother Nature has to offer. The wilderness is right around the corner!

So now that Y2K is no longer a threat to life as we know it, let's get back to the history of Patten and Mount Chase. This was what was happening in our neck of the woods and in the outside world from 2000 to 2016.

2000: The Patten Town Report stated that Patten had a new animal control ordinance to deal with the problems of dogs running loose and barking noisily. It also enforced immunization of dogs, particularly against rabies. In other town goings-on, the Patten Ambulance Service got a new ambulance and upgraded equipment. Patten formed a road committee to develop a long-range plan for maintaining town roads and to come up with ways to fund road projects. The site Patten had selected for a new salt/sand facility was approved by the DEP. New *Welcome to Patten* signs had been painted by Mr. McQuarrie. Sadly, one of these beautiful signs was stolen almost immediately.

Patten's population was 1,111, and Mount Chase's population was 247.

2001: Christina Morgan Gray (age 24) was murdered by her estranged husband, Harold Gray (age 68), outside Pitt Landry's garage. Tragically, the same bullet that killed Christina also killed her sister, Vicki Morgan (age 19). Mr. Gray then killed himself.

Arrick Hood of Mount Chase died unexpectedly. He grew up on the Owlsboro Road as the son of Preston Hood and Annaliese Jakimides and brother of Tanek and Tamara Hood. He graduated from Katahdin High School in 1998 and was a former Marine. He was 21 years old at the time of his death.

It was a sign of the times that the communities were having a hard time finding people to fill positions, especially to find enough people to serve as volunteer firefighters. The population of the area was decreasing steadily as young people had to settle in other places to find work. Patten's population in 2000 was 1,111, and Mount Chase had 247 souls. The downward trend was especially noticeable when reading the town clerk's report in the annual town reports for the last ten years or so: consistently, there were more deaths than births. The towns were slowly turning into Senior Citizen communities. But these trends did not spell *dying* communities by a long shot. One of the more positive trends of the 21st century was the availability of grants (federally, state, and privately funded) to help small communities pay for their projects. The towns in the area also actively pursued ways to revitalize their communities and provide employment for more people. Maine's State Department of Economic Development had assisted local businesses in retaining employees, and UVEC had helped open several new businesses, including a restaurant, a garbage collection business, a tree and wreath business, an alpaca farm, and an internet business. It was working on signage for the International Appalachian Trail and the Katahdin Trail. UVEC had also assisted existing businesses and was advertising the area by having a booth at trade shows.

The Patten Cemetery had been enlarged by buying an adjacent piece of property from Bob Smallwood, and the Patten Fire Department had purchased a new pumper. Boyd/Pine Tree had the Mount Chase trash pick-up contract. The town hall was refurbished, and a new computer system was installed.

2001, cont.: Christine Shorey retired from her position as town librarian. She had run the library very capably for twenty-seven years. She promoted use of the library by setting up story time for pre-schoolers, by inviting school classes to visit the library regularly, by setting up computers, and by filling shelf after shelf with books, magazines, and videos that appealed to every possible age group and interest. Christine was replaced by Susan Hess.

9-1-1 became an important number in the lives of Patten and Mount Chase citizens for two reasons. First, they could now use this simple number to call the Ambulance Service, the Fire Department, or a law enforcement agency. The towns had spent several years working on assigning numbers to houses and businesses throughout the whole area, thereby giving each site within the towns a physical address.

The second reason 9-1-1 became important was the horrific events that took place on September 11th, 2001. The two towers of the World Trade Center in New York and parts of the Pentagon in Washington, D.C. were destroyed by terrorist attacks which involved flying three passenger planes (with passengers aboard) into the buildings. Terrorists also hijacked a fourth plane, which crashed in Pennsylvania. Subsequently, the United States military forces became involved in hostilities in Afghanistan.

George W. Bush served as U.S. president from 2001-2009.

2001-2002: Sally Landry of Patten served in the Maine House of Representatives.

2002: The Henry Rowe building was torn down. The property had previously been jointly purchased by Al and Lou Ellis and Katahdin Trust Company. Since then, Katahdin Trust Company has expanded to the south and Ellis Family Market has expanded to the north.

The fire tower on the top of Mount Chase was moved by helicopter to the Lumberman's Museum, where it was restored. It was estimated to be about sixty years old and had been last used in the 1960's. (1982 photo courtesy of Laurie Johnson Libby)

2002, cont.: In Mount Chase, Rhoda Houtz became the Administrative Assistant, a position she held until 2008. Pine Tree Waste Disposal Service was picking up Mount Chase garbage and continued to do so through the writing of this book.

Patten's town manager Rhonda Harvey stated in the annual town report that the town needed to develop a comprehensive plan in order to receive grants from the state. The Planning Board had sent out a survey to the general population, but response was scarce. Ms. Harvey asked for more community support to accomplish this important task. On a more positive note, the library was able to get a $10,000.00 New Century Grant that would be used to catalogue the books into an automated system. Both the Fire Department and the Ambulance Service had also received grants in 2002. While the Fire Department and the Ambulance Service both needed more warm bodies, they were well-equipped and well-trained and were performing vital services to the communities in the upper Katahdin Valley area. Surprisingly, budgets in all the towns' departments were in good shape. The Ambulance Service was practically paying for itself with the numerous transfers for other towns they were being called upon to make.

The deadliest traffic accident in Maine history occurred when a van fell off John's Bridge into the Allagash River in northwestern Maine. The van was carrying fifteen Hispanic migrant workers to a logging site. Only one worker survived the accident.

2003: The Upper Valley Economic Council (UVEC) was continuing to promote the area at trade shows.

Patten received a Community Development Block Grant for $113,000 to connect Meadowbrook Manor to the town's sewer system. Another CDB grant of $400,000 was used to replace failing wells and septic systems for individual households in town. MDOT awarded Patten with a $10,000 grant which was used for lighting, fencing, and improvements at Patten Academy Alumni Park.

2003, cont.: Other financial news in the town report stated that Patten's town government was being paid to oversee governmental services for Hersey and Moro Plantation. Patten and Mount Chase had worked with ten other towns to organize a cooperative to purchase fuel at a much better rate than they would have been able to get as individual communities. It was not an easy feat during such tough economic times, but the town of Patten actually managed to decrease the mil rate from $19.15 to $19.10.

In Mount Chase, a flagpole was erected at the Town Office site, beautiful new *Welcome to Mount Chase* signs were placed on the North Road and Shin Pond roads, and the cemetery on the North Road had some landscaping work done.

Doris DeRespino replaced Susan Hess as the librarian, a position she still holds as of the writing of this book.

John "Jack" McPhee, formerly of Patten and a pilot with the Maine Warden Service, died when his Super Cub plane crashed in the Maine woods. He was the son of Malcom and Dorothy McPhee and had previously been married to Sharon Howes, herself the daughter of a game warden.

The United States became involved in hostilities in Iraq.

After a successful space mission, the space shuttle Columbia disintegrated as it reentered earth's atmosphere, killing all seven crew members aboard. The problem was traced back to damage done to the shuttle during take-off and was related to the shuttle's thermal protection system.

John Baldacci served as Maine's governor from 2003-1011.

2004: Beth Bates opened Chickadee Realty on Main Street, and Dr. Ronald Blum opened an office on Founders Street. Both of them restored older homes in the process.

Patten Grammar School was burned by the town. After the building had been returned to the town from MSAD#25, the town had explored a variety of options for using the building, but none of these ideas made it past the thinking stage.

2004, cont.: Ervin and Dawn (Hotham) Tower donated a house on Main Street to house the Patten Historical Society. Immediately, historical items and photos were donated to the society to create a wonderful museum of Patten's History.

A 9.1 magnitude undersea earthquake near Sumaka, Indonesia, created a tsunami which traveled over 5,000 miles to South Africa. The earthquake was strong enough to vibrate the entire planet. But the real damage was done by the tsunami, which killed 230,000 people directly or indirectly.

2005: EastMill Credit Union opened.

The Calley & Currier veneer mill closed. It was subsequently sold to Anderson Hardwood Flooring and was renamed Appalachian Katahdin, LLC. Town manager Harvey worked with the new owners to renovate and reopen the mill in 2006, thus saving around thirty jobs .

Craig Hartsgrove bought the clam shop.

Higher than normal rainfall did a great deal of road damage, particularly to the Barleyville, Frenchville, and Happy Corner Roads.

Patten started a reserve account with $250,000 for the purpose of building a new municipal building.

Wesley "Junior" Porter (age 81) drowned in Mattawamkeag Lake in Island Falls when the boat he was fishing from capsized. Clair Sides of Sherman also drowned, but Porter's brother-in-law, Charlie Hurlbert, managed to reach shore. Mr. Porter was the son of the Wesley Porter who was shot and killed by a Canadian draft-dodger in 1943.

2006, cont.: Hurricane Katrina killed 1,836 people in Louisiana and other Gulf Coast states. It remains the most expensive disaster in United States history.

2006: Lights were installed on the Patten Ball Field. The photo at the right shows one of the lights high above the ground behind the Patten Academy Alumni Park.

There were almost overwhelming changes going on at the Patten Town Office. Rhonda Harvey had resigned in November, 2005. In January, Ruth Peters took over the job, but she resigned in June. In July, Deborah Bivighouse became the town manager. At the same time as all the expected chaos of changing leadership was occurring, the town was implementing a new computer system, requiring all data to be entered and extensively checked. Town clerk Terri Gantnier Conklin and temporary assistant Carolyn Hartin Roy managed to hold down the fort capably. The situation was eased somewhat by the office being closed to the public two afternoons a week while record-keeping was tackled.

Around 2006, General Assistance was still appropriated yearly, but the town was reimbursed for what it spent. General assistance was provided in voucher form only and solely for emergency expenses such as food or medical attention. By the late 1990's, there was no longer a Penquis employee working in a Penquis office in town, but annual requests for money were still received from the agency through 2015. Another organization that hadn't been mentioned in town reports recently was UVEC. Upon doing a little online research, I discovered that at some point all the communities pulled out of UVEC with the exception of Sherman and Stacyville. The organization continues to pursue ways to improve the economy of the area and also operates a food bank in Sherman.

2006, cont.: Specialist Dustin J. Harris was killed by a roadside bomb during the war in Iraq. Dustin was assigned to the 172nd Brigade Support Battalion, 172nd Stryker Brigade Combat Team, Fort Wainwright, Alaska. Dustin had developed the desire to enlist after the events of September 11, 2001. He loved the military and was just days away from being promoted to Sergeant. Dustin was the son of Scott and Lorna Harris of Patten, the brother of Dylan Harris, and the grandson of Rodney and Esther Harris of Patten and James and Sandra Troutt of Sherman. Spec. Harris was buried in the Patten Cemetery. A bench in his memory was later placed in the cemetery.

"Dustin's Act of Heroism was that he chose to always be the Gunner, due to his concern for others. He was well aware of the risk of [serving as] Turret Gunner on any mounted patrol. He always volunteered to assume that risk, because he recognized that the rest of the vehicles and fellow soldiers in the patrol depended on his mental alertness, judgment and skill. He also volunteered because of his love of family, his band of brothers, and not wanting those who were married or had children take on that risk."

Lorna Harris, AGSM National Flag Guard, Proud Gold Star Mother, Spc. Dustin J Harris, KIA 4/06/06, Bayji, Iraq.

In the days following Dustin's death, Marty Arbo used his own money to place American flags on poles up and down Main Street in Patten. When people realized what he had done, donations poured in, and Arbo was able to place seven flags in the Patten Cemetery: the U.S. flag, the prisoner-of-war flag, the Maine flag, and the Army, Air Force, Navy, Marines, and Coast Guard flags. Since then, Arbo has maintained the Main Street Flag Fund through donations.

2006, cont.: Five young girls were shot at an Amish school in Lancaster, Pennsylvania, by Charles Roberts. One of the most astonishing facets of the tragedy was the complete forgiveness offered to Roberts' widow, parents, and children by the Amish community.

2007: Jeanne (Townsend) and Craig Morse opened Hangar Pizza on the north road. Morse had built an airport on the site which could be used by small planes and kit planes.

Mount Chase erected a Quonset building to be used as a salt/sand shed.

Deborah Bivighouse served as Patten's town manager from January to August, and Terri Conklin finished out the year. She continued to serve as the Patten Town Manager until 2015.

Steve Anderson opened Cutting Edge Lawn Care.

Kevin Noyes, Patten's Public Works go-to guy, received the Maine Rural and Water 2007 Award for Outstanding Operations in Water and Sewer Departments. Only two such awards were given in the state. The same year, Doris DeRespino was featured on the cover of the December 2007 issue of *Country Magazine* as the Number One Country Librarian.

Gas prices went over $3.00 a gallon for regular gas.

As a result of mental health problems, Seung-Hui Cho shot 33 students at the Virginia Polytechnic Insitute in Blacksburg, Virginia. The incident remains the second deadliest shooting by a single gunman in U.S. history.

2008: The building on Main Street which had housed Merrow's Department Store burned down. The structure was built by Ira Gardner in 1885, making it 123 years old. The building had been owned in more recent times by Edgar Harrington and Fred Smallwood.

Tabitha and Stephen King made a donation through the Stephen King Foundation to the library. The money was used to build new steps and a ramp.

2008, cont.: Steve and Cheryl Anderson opened the Magic Wand Car Wash in the building between Hathaway's Apartments and Richardson's Hardware. At a later date, they opened the Main Street Outback Garage—you guessed it—out back of the car wash.

Rhonda Brophy of Mount Chase became the owner of the building and vacant lot on the north side of Richardson's Hardware. The site now houses the Red Moose Trading Post, a laundromat, apartment rentals, and a small building which was leased to Wally Drew for her Daisy Boutique, which opened in 2009.

Carroll Gerow of Moro was killed when the bulldozer he was operating ran over him as he worked on his property at Bear Mountain Lodge. He was the husband of Deanna (Merrill) Gerow; the brother of Carlton, Carolyn (Latour), and Peter; and father of Toni and Todd Gerow.

A heavy rain storm in April washed away roads in the Patten and Mount Chase area. FEMA provided help to get these roads back to an acceptable state.

Gregg Smallwood received the contract for snowplowing Mount Chase roads.

Gas prices went over $4.00 a gallon for regular gas.

Barack Obama became the first African-American president of the United States. He was reelected in 2013 to serve a second term.

2009: The building which had housed Ken Lord's grocery store was torn down.

The Primary School burned, leaving the Will family homeless.

Kingdom Hall of Jehovah's Witnesses closed.

The Patten Town Report stated that the town was appropriating money for the Eastern Area on Aging, the Red Cross, Patten Little League, the Lumberman's Museum, the Historical Society, Patten Senior Citizens, and the Agape Food Pantry. Mount Chase also supported these or similar organizations.

2010: Ken Lau's gas station (Patten General Store), the Dairy Cream, and the former Dead River Oil building were torn down. Dead River had moved into an office in the north side of the Bartlett's Lodge building a year or so prior to 2010.) The DEP assisted with the removal of four underground fuel tanks. DEP also assisted the town with the replacement of thirty residential oil tanks within the town's wellhead protection area.

The town acquired the old garage which stood between the Deli and the Rec Center. It was torn down to make a parking area for the Deli and the Rec Center. The town truck was replaced.

Jon and Peter Ellis greatly expanded the size of their grocery store, now called Ellis Family Market.

The Appalachian Katahdin veneer mill closed.

Stephanie Berry was appointed Officer-in-Charge of the Patten Post Office.

The population of Patten was 1,017. This was the lowest census count since the 1890 census. The population of Mount Chase was 201. Although Mount Chase's lowest census count was 179 in 1960, this was still lower than when Mount Chase became a town in 1864, when it had 250 residents.

Jutta Beyer was appointed as Administrative Assistant in Mount Chase, a position she held until 2013. Renovations were made on the Mount Chase Town Office.

2011: The Appalachian Katahdin buildings and contents were sold or auctioned off.

2011, cont.: Patricia Adams, 67, died in an automobile accident on Oct. 28. She was the daughter of Bob and Minnie Adams and the sister of Richard and Donald Adams and Roberta Moore.

Patten town manager Terri Conklin reported that the town office had chosen some new computer programs to use in handling the town's finances. The DEP replaced 62 residential heating oil tanks within the town's wellhead protection area. Public works director Kevin Noyes reported that Hall Street and Spruce Street had been paved and there was a plan in place to replace a bridge on Waters road. The town backhoe had been replaced. Mr. Noyes had this to say about the waste water treatment facility: *"The waste water department struggles to keep its head above water. Believe me, this is not a good position to be in, in this business."* He went on to make a fervent plea to those homeowners hooked into the facility to not run sump pumps into the system and to NOT FLUSH DISPOSABLE WIPES! Mr. Noyes made this plea year after year, but people didn't just didn't get it. The wipes clogged the system, requiring equipment to be dismantled, cleaned, and reassembled frequently, at considerable expense to the taxpayers.

Paul LePage was elected to serve as Maine's governor from 2011-2015. In 2015, he was reelected e a second term.

The 2011-Super Outbreak was a series of 362 tornadoes which struck central and southern states over a three day period.

A tsunami was created by a 9.0 magnitude undersea earthquake which was strong enough to shift Earth on its axis and move Honshu Island eight feet to the east. The tsunami killed 18,000 people and caused 235 billion dollars worth of damage when it struck the coastal area around Tohoku, Japan.

Balancing the town's budget in those tough economic times was difficult to say the least. The problem was compounded in 2012 because the town was going to lose more than $106,000 in revenues from the state because of Governor LePage's determination to balance the state budget. Another problem each year was that the school budget was not finalized before town meeting.

2012: Three young men from Patten and Mount Chase died from injuries. Nick Hall (photo at right), a climbing ranger in Mount Rainier National Park in Washington State and son of Carter and Mary Hall of Patten, died at the age of 33 as he was attempting to rescue climbers stranded on Mount Rainier. Ryan Bates (photo at left), son of Carroll Bates of Mount Chase and Susan York of Island Falls and father of Bryce and Hayson Bates, died at the age of 36 in a car accident on Route 11 in Mount Chase. Mark Arthurs (son of Patricia Adams of Patten) died in a biking accident at the foot of Mill Hill in Patten.

John M. Jamo was appointed as Patten Postmaster.

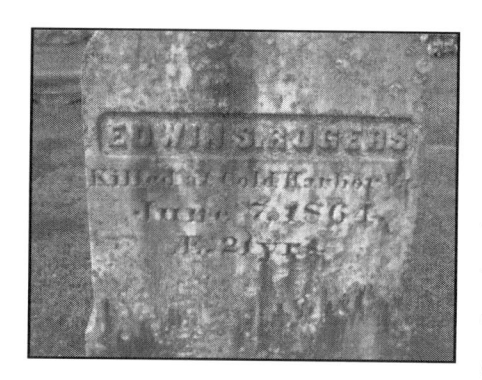

In an effort to make some progress on getting a comprehensive plan written, the town began paying members of the planning board $15.00 per meeting. In other town news, it was reported that the roof on the town garage had collapsed, thus forcing the town to make a decision about whether or not to build a new facility and whether or not to relocate it to a different site. The town decided that the most economically feasible option was to build a new garage at the same location. In the meantime, some of the town's equipment was stored in the fire house. A project at the cemetery to repair crumbling and fallen stones was started.

Vicki Hashey-Nanni, proprietor of the Shin Pond Pub, held her first annual Shin Pond Pub Cancer Walk. Each year the walk raises thousands of dollars which directly benefit local cancer patients.

Hurricane Sandy struck Haiti and the U.S. east coast, killing 200 people.

2012, cont.: The deadliest school shooting in U.S. history occurred when Adam Lanza shot his mother and then went to Sandy Hook Elementary School in Newtown, Connecticut, where he shot and killed 20 children and six staff members before killing himself. His disturbed mental state had been worsened by his obsession with weapons and violent video games.

2013: Richardson's Hardware opened two greenhouses on the corner of Main and Founders Street.

A blow to the town was the closing of the Parks and Recreation building due to "potential major structural defects." Rec Director Michele Roshto was able to relocate some of the activities to the Katahdin Schools and the athletic field, but the townspeople missed the other activities the Rec had been offering.

In the Patten Town Report, Kevin Noyes stated that the new town garage was finished, and he was very pleased to be able to park his equipment on a cement floor (rather than a dirt floor, as was the case in the former garage) in a brightly lit area. He reported that Scribner Street had been repaired to solve a water drainage problem. Town manager Terri Conklin reported that the stone repairs at the cemetery were continuing. She also thanked Diane Peck and Carol Plecs for planting flowers in the garden in front of the town office and the Green Valley residents for tending the flowers there and on Main Street all summer.

Lisa Bates, formerly of Patten, was involved in a helicopter crash near Waterville. Lisa, who is an Inland Fisheries and Wildlife Biologist, had been working on a bear-study through Unity College. On the day of the crash, Lisa and pilot Ed Friedman were tracking a bear which had been collared. After the plane crashed, Lisa pulled the seriously-injured Friedman to safety away from the plane. She then bushwhacked through dense forest to get to a road where she could summon help. Lisa has appeared on North Woods Law with games wardens as they locate, tranquilize if necessary, and put collars on bears. Lisa is the daughter of Jeff Bates and the granddaughter of George and Liz Bates.

2013, cont.: Lisa Sommers Fogg died during a fire which burned her home in Winn, Maine. Lisa was employed by the Challenger Learning Center in Bangor and lived in Winn with her husband Bobby Fogg. She was the daughter of Raymond and Glenda Sommers of Patten and the sister of David Sommers of Dyer Brook.

Lora Ryan was appointed as the Administrative Assistant of Mount Chase, a position she holds through the writing of this book.

In July, a Montreal, Maine & Atlantic Railway train transporting crude oil exploded in Lac Megantic, Quebec. The explosion occurred after the train's brakes failed and the train rolled unattended into the village center of Lac Megantic, where it derailed, caught on fire, and exploded. Forty-seven people were killed, 40 buildings (including businesses) were destroyed, 53 vehicles were demolished, and the Lac Megantic's downtown area was destroyed. The community's 2,000 residents had to be evacuated because of the toxic smoke from the fire.

2014: Project Graduation took over the annual chicken barbecue as part of Patten Pioneer Days. The Mount Chase Fire Department continued to put on an impressive fireworks display as part of the celebration.

Donald Campbell, a Korean War veteran, was part of a group of Maine veterans who were flown to Washington, D.C. to visit war memorials. Honor Flight Maine provided this opportunity to veterans who might not otherwise be able to make such a trip and also to honor their service to our country. (See page 165 for more about Honor Flight Maine and Donnie.)

Mount Chase celebrated its sesquicentennial anniversary of becoming a town with events held at the Mount Chase Town Office. The Mount Chase Fire House roof was repaired.

The town of Patten made a decision to make repairs to the Parks and Recreation Building. There was an article in the Town Report's warrant for funds to hire Northern Maine Development to assist the planning board with writing a comprehensive plan for the town. In public works news, Gardner Street had been paved and the Happy Corner/Frenchville road had been repaired.

2014, cont.: Work began on enlarging the Patten cemetery. In 2014, trees were cut down on the south side of the cemetery, and in 2015, the lot was cleared and leveled. In 2016, Steve Yates cleaned the headstones. Steve Anderson's Cutting Edge Lawncare crew kept the cemetery looking beautiful.

Six people were killed and dozens critically injured when Islamist terrorists Dzokhar and Tamerlan Tsarnev detonated two pressure cooker bombs near the finish line of the Boston Marathon. Police identified and tracked down the brothers two days later. Tamerlan died from bullet wounds he received during the apprehension and from injuries he sustained when his brother ran over him in order to get away from the police. Americans watched live television coverage as law enforcement officials conducted a manhunt in the streets of Boston before finally finding Dzokhar Tsarnev hiding in a boat in a residential area two days later.

2015: White supremacist Dylan Roofe shot and killed nine people who were conducting a prayer session at the Emanuel African Methodist Church in Charlestown, South Carolina.

2015, cont.: Captain Michael Davidson sailed the El Faro, a US cargo ship crewed by U.S. Merchant Marines, into the fury of Hurricane Joaquin in the Caribbean Sea. All 33 crew members drowned, including five with strong ties to Maine and Maine Maritime Academy. It was later determined that Captain Davidson bore some responsibility for the incident as he ignored warnings about the severe weather, possibly because he was under pressure to deliver his cargo on time.

2015-2016: It was another year of great changes in the town office. The town manager from January to October was Terri Conklin, and from November to December, it was Rose Bragdon, with Carolyn Roy holding down the fort during transition times. Early in 2016, Raymond Foss was appointed town manager. He stated in the town manager's letter for the 2015 Town Report that he wanted to increase the transparency of the town government.

The Patten Town Report announced that the Recreation Building renovations had been completed and the Rec Department was back to business as usual. The town had turned down the proposal to hire Northern Maine Development to assist the planning board in writing a comprehensive plan. Mr. Foss stressed again the importance of having this plan in place in order to be more eligible for grant money.

The R.S.U. 50 School Board put forth a proposal to close Katahdin Middle/High School and bus those students to the Southern Aroostook School in Dyer Brook. In response, a group of concerned citizens formed *Leading Our Communities' Access to Learning* (LOCAL) to address the challenges facing local schools.

Our Mission

The mission of L.O.C.A.L is to organize a collaborative effort to withdraw from Regional School Unit 50 and explore other K-12 school organizations, such as an Alternative Organizational Structure. At the forefront, this effort is to ensure that we, as communities, are doing our due diligence to provide the best educational experience for our children and aid in the economic prosperity of our region. It is our belief that keeping our local schools open is vital to the success of our students and communities!

2015-2016, cont.: The committee was representative of the towns of Patten, Mount Chase, Moro, Hersey, Sherman, and Stacyville. LOCAL was concerned that the distance from one end of RSU#50 to the other was just too great a distance to bus students to school and activities if the high schools were consolidated at Southern Aroostook. They also were frustrated at the board's inability to pass a budget that sustained and satisfied all the member towns.

LOCAL's first success was the part they played in convincing the school board to keep Katahdin Middle/High School open. At the time of this writing, the committee is exploring a withdrawal from the RSU and the formation of an Alternative Organizational Structure which would keep the Katahdin Schools open.

2016: Patten celebrated its 175th anniversary of becoming a town. Various events were held throughout the year.

Celebrating 175 YEARS

Haymart began selling wood pellets called *hotties*.
Haymart had bought the former veneer mill at the foot of Mill Hill in 2013. Haymart is also involved in organic farming and planted crops in the Patten area in 2016. They hope to begin manufacturing plant pellets at some point.

Landholdings acquired by Roxanne Quimby were turned over to the federal government to create Katahdin Woods and Waters National Monument. Reaction from the residents of Patten and Mount Chase (and outlying communities as well) ranged from "hate it" to "love it." Some residents saw the monument as detrimental to the logging industry. Some worried it would impact the number of people traveling to the area to enjoying hunting, fishing, and sports such as ATV and snowmobile riding. Others felt the monument would be beneficial to the economy of the area, with a fresh influx of tourists and outdoor lovers.

A blizzard that dropped up to 66 inches of snow in North Carolina before continuing up the east coast killed 55 people.

The death of fifty people at an Orlando, Florida nightclub became the deadliest shooting in U.S. history. Because the shooter, Omar Mateen, had ties to Muslim extremists, it was also the second deadliest terrorist attack in U.S. history.

2016, cont.: Businessman Donald Trump defeated Hillary Clinton in the 2016 presidential elections in one of the dirtiest campaigns in U.S. history. Many Americans went to the polls to vote for the candidate they found least objectionable. The election was unusual in that Mrs. Clinton won the popular vote, but Mr. Trump accumulated enough electoral college votes to win the contest. Mrs. Clinton, wife of former president Bill Clinton, was the first woman to be nominated for president by a major U.S. political party, and Mr. Trump is the first president who has never held a previous public office.

Strange as it sounds, global warming can sometimes cause colder and snowier weather than normal. On December 16, the Polar Vortex cause temperatures in Patten to plummet to -37°F, and one morning in January of 2017, Houlton, Maine, had the distinction of being the coldest place in the United States. The winter of 2016-2017 ended up being a great winter—at least for snowmobilers. I recorded about 120 inches of snowfall at my house between November 2016 and April 2017. A short January thaw and a longer February thaw helped compact the snow so snowsled trails were open into the month of April.

Main Street, circa 2016: the Ellis Family Market and Katahdin Trust Company.

I wonder what Patten and Mount Chase residents from years past would think if they walked down Main Street today. Would they approve or disapprove of the changes? Would they be overwhelmed by the number of items in the grocery store, or would they be disappointed they couldn't buy a new pair of pants? Would they appreciate the opportunity to be able to travel ten miles in ten minutes, or would they think life is too rushed in the 21st century? Would they be glad they lived here when they did, or would they be envious of how easy we have it in modern times?

Because change is inevitable, it is important to think about how we as a community will handle changes in our future. In the following excerpt from an early 2000's letter written to the towns which made up UVEC, Executive Director Charles Upton shared his thoughts on how small rural towns like Patten and Mount Chase should handle change. I think his comments could still be considered relevant.

You can't change the way the wind is blowing, so you have to adjust your sails and direction....I don't see another large employer coming to the area and putting dozens of people to work...Instead, I see a number of small businesses being formed or relocating to the area to take advantage of what we have to offer. We know how beautiful the area is and the small town feeling that nurtures us. That is something we have to offer newcomers... We need to keep an open mind about the changes that are taking place and work with them in order to maintain a workable and vibrant economy. All of this will take time and energy. Spending our energy on fighting changes we can't control will make us bitter...Working as a region will place us in a position where we can prosper, rather than decline...where we can see healthy and viable communities, rather than ones that "give up the ghost" and turn their futures over to the county and state.

And one more time, from the Maine Register for the years from 2000 to 2016... and other resources: (Note: **Bold** = still in operation at the end of 2016)

Services:

- Accountants: Deanna Morse, Hafford Accounting, **Calculations, Inc.**
- Airplane chartering: Scotty's Flying Service
- Architect: **Kenny Phillips**
- Bait: **Scott Skinner**
- Bank/Credit Union: **Katahdin Trust Company, Eastmill Federal Credit Union**
- Beauticians: Codgie's Hairport (Colleen Martin), Magic Scissors (Bethann Carver), Viv's Hair We Are (Vivian Brownlee), **Theresa's Headquarters (Theresa Patterson Schmidt), Carlene's Barbering and Family Hair Care (Carlene Conklin Duffy)**
- Bed and Breakfast: Bradford House (Filena Anderson Singer), **Mountain Glory Bed and Breakfast (Christina Shipps)**
- Building contractors: **Brownlee Builders (Robbie Brownlee)**, Ben Cullen, **Hunter Brothers (Peter, Tom, and John)**, Sheldon Anderson
- Communications: **Valley Satellite, Inc. (Ola Wayne and Diana Tucker, office moved to Hermon)**
- Dentist: **Dr. Richard Engroff**
- Doctors and Physicians Assistants: **KVHC, Martin Hrynick,** Ted Pettengill, **Dr. Ronald Blum, Dr. Robert La Morgese**
- Electricians: Sommers Electric (Raymond Sommers), **John's Electric (John Flannery)**, Wayne Melvin
- Electricity: **Eastern Maine Electric Coop**, Maine Public Service Co./**Emera Maine**
- Excavating, Grading, Snow Plowing, Landscaping, Lawn Contractors: Leroy Giles & Son, Frank Landry & Sons, **Gregg Smallwood, Raymond Landry**, Cole's Lawn Care Service (Greg Cole), **Cutting Edge Lawn Care (Steven Anderson), Sheldon Anderson**
- Garages/service stations: Patten Autobody, **Chris Gallagher's Auto Parts**, Morse's Irving**, Wayne Evan's Auto Service, Main Street Outback Garage and Magic Wand Car Wash (Steven Anderson), K & C Quikstop (Cole Lane), Lone Wolf Autobody (Jordan Ouellette), Savage Paint and Autobody (Casey Savage)**

(services continued on next page)

- Health Care: **Mountain Heights Health Care Facility, Katahdin Valley Health Center**
- Heating Oil: **Dead River Oil Company (office moved to Houlton), Bates Fuel (office in Stacyville)**
- Insurance: Patten Insurance Agency (Carter Hall)
- Plumbing: Patten Plumbing and Heating
- Postmasters/Officers-in-charge: Sandra McNally, Stephanie Berry, John Jamo, **Cody Pond**
- Real Estate: Chickadee Realty & Katahdin Appraisals (Beth Bates)
- Redemption Center: Moosehead Redemption, Nickelback Redemption, **Patten Redemption Center (Laurie Bartlett)**
- Restaurants: Pa's Pizza and Subs (Christe Bishop Crouse), Fogg's Drive-in (Mickey & Louise Fogg), Downtown Deli & Pizza (Steve & Cheryl Anderson)/**Debbie's Deli and Pizza (Debbie Birmingham)**, Raymond's Clam Shop, **Craig's Clam Shop (Craig Hartsgrove), Marie's Kitchen (Marie Conklin), Hangar Pizza (Jeanne Townsend Morse), Wilderness Variety (Louise & Scott Skinner), Shin Pond Village (Craig & Terry Hill)**
- Sporting Camps/Campgrounds: **Shin Pond Village and Campgrounds (Craig & Terry Hill and Blaine King), Mount Chase Lodge and Camps** (Rick & Sara Hill, **Mike & Lindsay Hill Downing**), **Matagamon Wilderness Campground** (Don & Diana Dudley, **the Christianson family), Bowlin Camps, Camp Wapiti (Travis Libby), Conklin's Lodge and Camps (Lester & Marie Conklin), Driftwood (Paul & Tracy Reed)**, Lyman's Hillside Lodge, Sportsman's Edge, **Patten Hunting Lodge (Bill Finney)**, Dri-Ki Lodge (Bob, Carrie, & Ricky Keim), **North Country Lodge (Goodman family)**, Bear Mountain Lodge (Carroll & Deanna Gerow), **Katahdin Hunting Lodge (Chuck & Chris Loucka)**
- Storage: **R & L Storage, Katahdin View Storage, Sheldon Anderson storage**
- Tavern: **Shin Pond Pub (Vicki Hashey-Nanni, manager)**
- Taxidermist: Myrna McDonald
- Telephone service: Northland Telephone Co. of Maine, **Fairpoint**
- Town Managers: Rhonda Harvey, Ruth Peters, Deborah Bivighouse, Terri Conklin, Rose Bragdon, **Raymond Foss**
- Waste/Septic Disposal: **John Brown, John Marr**
- Welding: **Katahdin Welding and Steel (Steve Crouse), Tommy Craig**

Merchants:
- Cars: CAS Auto Sales
- General/Misc. Stores: Merrow's Department Store, Patten General Store, Patten Trading Post, **Wilderness Variety (Scott and Louise Skinner), Shin Pond Village (Craig & Terri Hill and Blaine King)**, Maine Card Co, Viv and Lisa's Gift Boutique, **Daisy Boutique (Wally Drew), Red Moose Trading Post (Rhonda Brophy)**
- Greenhouse: **Richardson's Greenhouses (Nathan Richardson)**
- Groceries: **Ellis Family IGA**
- Hardware Store: **Richardson's Hardware (Nathan Richardson)**
- Pharmacy: **Patten Drug Company (Joel Fitzpatrick)**
- Sporting Goods: **Theriault Flies (Alvin Theriault)**

Manufacturers:

- Calley & Currier Co., Anderson Flooring, Appalachian Katahdin
- **Dri-Ki Woodworking (Ricky & Bobbie Keim)**
- **Haymart: Wood Pellets**
- **Parker's Honey (Fred & Harriette Parker)**
- Porter's Woodworking
- **Ward Clapboard (Rob Brownlee, owner; Cecil Gallagher, manager)**

Farming:

- Thurston Townsend
- **McNally Farm Produce (Kerry & Karen McNally)**
- **Drew's Cabbage Patch (Chris & Wally Drew)**
- **Qualey Farms**
- **Steve Crouse**
- Robert Guptill
- Don Slauenwhite

Christmas Trees: Phil Heath, **Ervin Tower**

Logging operations (business names not given):
- Carver, Dana and Jimmy
- Craig, Michael
- **Craig, Shawn**
- **McAvoy, Rick**
- McAvoy, Shawn
- **Ordway, Kent**
- Savage, Michael
- **Savage, Scott**

Trucking (business names not given):
- Baker, Dan
- **Brownlee, Fred**
- Brownlee, Travis
- **Campbell, Ronald Jr.**
- **Chaloux, David**
- **Gardner, David**
- **Gardner, David L.**
- **Gardner, Jodi**
- **Hanson, Mike (no longer lives in Patten)**
- **Harris, Scott**
- **Heath, Carroll**
- **Landry, Brendan**
- **Landry, Dana**
- **Landry, Paul**
- **Landry, Richard**
- Marr, John
- **McCarthy, Calvin**
- **Morse, Brett**
- **Morse, Craig**
- Probert, Randy
- **Raymond, Eric (no longer lives in Patten)**
- **Swallow, Kerry**
- **Willett, Scott Jr.**
- **Willett, Scott Sr.**

Top Row: A view down Main Street (left), the Patten Town Office, circa 2017 (right); Bottom Row: An aerial view of Shin Pond Village (left, courtesy Terry Thurston Hill) and a road-side view of Wilderness Variety & Weeze's Snack Bar (right).

CHAPTER NINE: UP AND DOWN MAIN STREET

As I was beginning to gather information about Patten and Mount Chase, I came across a wonderful map of Patten's Main Street showing who owned each lot. The map wasn't dated, but I decided that it must have been made around 1875, based on what was and wasn't included on the map. Then, as I was beginning to revise and edit this history, I got a phone call from Ray Foss at the Patten Town Office. He invited me to come in and look at a map of Main Street that had been given to the town by Rodney "Pat" Lord. This map was made by the Maine Department of Transportation in 1967 when they did extensive work on Main Street. It also showed who owned each lot. I have used these maps and other information to trace the ownership of the properties up and down Main Street (and a few nearby sites). This chapter will share that information with you. Please be aware that a particular property may have had other owners as well throughout the history of the site.

I have divided Main Street into five areas as listed below and made a numbered chart for each area. The charts give dates as I was able to determine them. The symbol @ means *about* or *estimated*; the actual date might be before and/or after the estimated date. The numbers are shown on the map on the next page. Any curves in the streets are not shown on the map, and the map is not drawn to scale.

AREA ONE: Shin Pond Road from Peavey Corner to Main Street and the west side of Main Street from Craig's Clam Shop to Patten Drug Company

AREA TWO: East side of Main Street from Patten Pentecostal Church to Deb's Deli

AREA THREE: Katahdin Street and the west side of Main Street between Katahdin Street and Dearborn Streets

AREA FOUR: Founders Street, the east side of Main Street between Founders Street and Houlton Street, and Houlton Street

AREA FIVE: Dearborn Street, Mill Hill, Mill Street, Spruce Street, Potato Row, and Finch Hill

Map

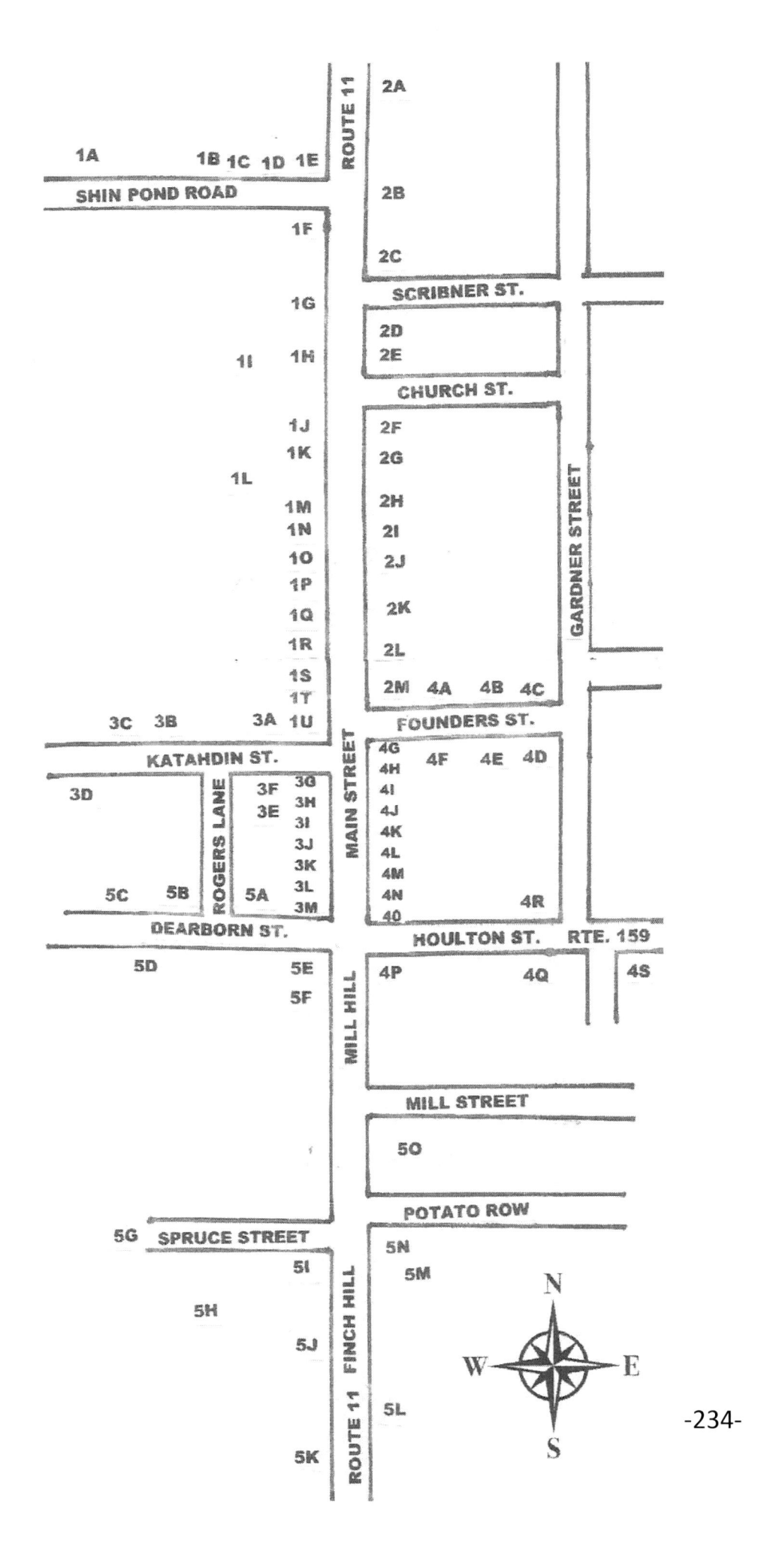

Streets and Roads:
- Route 11
- Shin Pond Road
- Scribner St.
- Church St.
- Gardner Street
- Founders St.
- Katahdin St.
- Rogers Lane
- Main Street
- Dearborn St.
- Houlton St. / Rte. 159
- Mill Hill
- Mill Street
- Potato Row
- Spruce Street
- Finch Hill / Route 11

Location Labels:

Block 1: 1A, 1B, 1C, 1D, 1E, 1F, 1G, 1H, 1I, 1J, 1K, 1L, 1M, 1N, 1O, 1P, 1Q, 1R, 1S, 1T, 1U

Block 2: 2A, 2B, 2C, 2D, 2E, 2F, 2G, 2H, 2I, 2J, 2K, 2L, 2M

Block 3: 3A, 3B, 3C, 3D, 3E, 3F, 3G, 3H, 3I, 3J, 3K, 3L, 3M

Block 4: 4A, 4B, 4C, 4D, 4E, 4F, 4G, 4H, 4I, 4J, 4K, 4L, 4M, 4N, 4O, 4P, 4Q, 4R, 4S

Block 5: 5A, 5B, 5C, 5D, 5E, 5F, 5G, 5H, 5I, 5J, 5K, 5L, 5M, 5N, 5O

Compass: N, S, E, W

-234-

AREA ONE: SHIN POND ROAD FROM PEAVEY CORNER TO MAIN STREET AND THE WEST SIDE OF MAIN STREET FROM CRAIG'S CLAM SHOP TO PATTEN DRUG

SITE	LOCATION	BUSINESSES AND OWNERS OR MANAGERS/ESTABLISHMENTS/HOMES
1A	Intersection of Waters Road and Shin Pond Road	Peasley Brook and Dam @ 1914: Peasley Brook and Peavey Dam: Manny & Tad Peavey Ice House, Manny Peavey home Jerry & Dorothy Peavey home, Peasley Brook, partial remains of dam
1B	@.75 mile west of intersection of Rte. 159 and Main Street	1962: Lumberman's Museum
1C	< one mile west of intersection of Rte. 159 and Main Street	Burton Betell's Blacksmith Shop Vic Michaud home Cooche Ballard home Mike and Amy Detour home ? home
1D	< one mile west of intersection of Rte. 159 and Main Street	Wesley Getchell—restaurant 1950: Raymond and Thelma Mitchell home Late 60's-early 70's: Leonard and Ruth Breidenstein Restaurant 1973-1980: Dick and Teddy Schmidt home 1982-1986: Scott and Amy Davis home 1986-2004: Dana and Bethann Carver home and beauty shop 2005: Craig and Jennifer Hartsgrove home

SITE	LOCATION	BUSINESSES AND OWNERS OR MANAGERS/ESTABLISHMENTS/HOMES
1E	North corner of intersection of Rte. 159 and Main Street	@1875: J.P. Leslie The Patten Exchange (a hotel run by Simeon, then Nathaniel Pomeroy) Lester and Hazel Glidden: Chicken House Ava Dean's Clam Shop (around 1958 or 1959) Hugh and Charlene Cunningham: clam shop Justin Glidden: clam shop Geraldine Craig: clamp shop Vivian Brownlee: clam shop @1987-2005: Bobby and Brenda Raymond: Raymond's Clam Shop 2005: Craig Hartsgrove: Craig's Clam Shop
1F	South corner of intersection of Rte.159 and Main Street	@1875: C.R. Brown Robert Finch home Before 1940: Hal Patterson garage, then lot owned by Ira Myrick 1940-1999: Morses's Garage: Lloyd Morse and sons Phil and Paul Empty lot (still owned by Morse family)
1G	Across the street from the intersection of Scribner Street and Main Street	Morse's Accounting home

SITE	LOCATION	BUSINESSES AND OWNERS OR MANAGERS/ESTABLISHMENTS/HOMES
1H	Across from north corner of Church St. and Main St.	@ 1875: W. B. Ellis @1900: F.W. Edwards Blacksmith Shop Fred and Amy Curtis: convenience store Velma and Alford Birmingham: convenience store Pat and Esther Lord: convenience store Tom Grass: convenience store Earl and Corris Giggey: convenience store George and Charlotte Rigby: pizza shop Reggie and Sharon Porter: pizza shop 1979-2001: Norman and Erlene Bishop: Pa's Pizza 2001-2006: Christe Bishop Crouse: Pa's Pizza Pa's Pizza (vacant, still owned by Christe Crouse)
1I	House behind Pa's Pizza	Frank Landry Billy Noyes Gloria Noyes
1J	House north of Dauphinee's Apartments	@1875: Ira D. Fish Humpy Merrill Frank and Patty Violette (home & beauty shop) Hank Green home Hank Green rental

SITE	LOCATION	BUSINESSES AND OWNERS OR MANAGERS/ESTABLISHMENTS/HOMES
1K	Dauphinee's Apartments	@1875: Jacob Frye John Rogers Law Office and home @1967: Everett McGraw Phil, Deanna, and Craig Morse (apartments) Gregg Smallwood (apartments) Dauphinee's Apartments
1L	Bradford House (listed in National Register of Historic Places as of 2003)	1833-?: David Haynes By 1840-41: Barn built (by Joshua Goodwin?) 1842: House built (by Joshua Goodwin?) ?-1867: Jacob Frye 1867-1893: Joshua Goodwin 1893-1998: Bradford family 1998: The Bradford House: Jack and Filena (Anderson) Singer
1M	Scribner House	1863: Jacob Frye; Jerome Frye built home Caleb Scribner House Dan and Verna Woodbury Other owners since around 1970
1N	Patten Historical Society	1840s: John Gardner built home Early 1900s: Halbert and Cora (Chapman) Robinson Mid-1900s: Charles Vaughn and Dove (Soule) Chapman Bill and Helen (Chapman) Garton Late 1900s: Ervin and Dawn (Hotham) Tower Patten Historical Society

SITE	LOCATION	BUSINESSES AND OWNERS OR MANAGERS/ESTABLISHMENTS/HOMES
1O	Anderson's Apartments	@1875: Calvin Bradford @ 1960s: Forest Smith's house and tractor garage Bud Patterson and Dick Schmidt snowmobile dealership Bob and Carrie Keim garage Sheldon Anderson's apartment building
1P	Lot between Anderson's and Veteran's Memorial Library	@1875: E.G. Stetson (back part), W.B. Hersey (next to street) Mitchell house @1967: Castine Pinkham Gerald and Ardeana Sheaff Bob and Nancy Black Parsons (burned in 1982) Sheldon Anderson Equipment/storage units
1Q	Veteran's Memorial Library	1845-1910: Baptist Church 1928: Veteran's Memorial Library (oldest public building in town)
1R	Calculations	@1875: Zenas Littlefield home Russell and Pauline Arbo home Mike and Dawn Arbo home Mike and Dawn Arbo: rented to Bryan and Julie Buhler Calculations: Melissa McAvoy Edwards
1S	Post Office	@1875: Zenas Littlefield home Hall family home 1962: Patten Post Office

SITE	LOCATION	BUSINESSES AND OWNERS OR MANAGERS/ESTABLISHMENTS/HOMES
1T	North corner of Kathadin and Main Streets; north half of Patten Drug Company	@1875: Eli Kellogg, Rogers E. H. Hall (burned in 1891) 1891: north half of Patten Drug built 1891-1900: Dr. O. F. Best 1900-1941: Dr. Elmer Farnham 1941-1967: Leslie Dickinson 1967-1980: Turk Schurman (building owned by others) 1980-1996: Michael Arbo 1996: Joel Fitzpatrick
1U	North corner of Kathadin and Main Streets; south half of Patten Drug Company	@1840: Minerva True Millinery 1893: south half of Patten Drug built, rented out for other businesses 1939: roof put over the two parts of the Drug Store @1952: Walter Cunningham IGA McLellan's Clothing (@1955-1964) 1964-1967: McKenney's Clothing Patten Drug

This photo from Eleanor Sargent Hunter's collection shows the Drug Store on the right, the Ira B. Gardner store in the center, and the Peavey Block on the left. The pennant signs are an advertisement for an upcoming Chataqua, which was a national movement that brought speakers, musicians, and other entertainment to communities throughout the United States.

-240-

AREA TWO: EAST SIDE OF MAIN STREET FROM PENTECOSTAL CHURCH TO DEB'S DELI

SITE	LOCATION	BUSINESSES AND OWNERS OR MANAGERS/ESTABLISHMENTS/HOMES
2A	< one mile north of intersection of Rte. 159 and Main St.	home 1931: Patten Pentecostal Church
2B	West of intersection of Rte. 159 and Main St.	@1875: S. E. Benjamin 1949-1998: Patten Grammar School (Town office located in school for a short time) 2004: building burned by town Patten Community Playground
2C	North corner of Scribner St. and Main St.	Amos Curran (or Curren) Blacksmith Shop 1855-1898: Jacob Frye's Cheese Factory 1870-1898: Jacob Frye's steam mill 1898-1967: Patten Academy 1967-1975: Patten Junior High 1977: torn down 1987: Patten Academy Alumni Park
2D	South corner of Scribner St. and Main St.	1847-1897: Patten Academy (burned) 1905-1998: Patten Primary School 2000-2004: David Alexander home 2004-2009: Richard Will home (burned) Empty Lot
2E	North corner of Church St. and Main St.	@1875: J. P. Leslie Before 1998: Charles Wescott home (burned) EastMill Federal Credit Union

SITE	LOCATION	BUSINESSES AND OWNERS OR MANAGERS/ESTABLISHMENTS/HOMES
2F	South corner of Church St. and Main St.	1865-1928: Congregational Church Before 1989: Grange Hall/Katahdin Community Center (torn down) 1991-1997: Millstream Lodging: Dana Cole (burned) David Cunha and Ray Porter Barbara Landry Bartlett's Lodge and Restaurant North side: Before 2005: EastMill Federal Credit Unit North side: 2005-2015: Dead River Oil Company Patten Redemption Center/Laurie Bartlett
2G	Empty lot across from Dauphinee's Apartments	@1837: Henry Blake's brick kiln @1875: Samuel Darling (possible site of furniture shop) Charles Brown Funeral Home Clifford and Eva (Brown) Grindal Jim and Mabel Doughty (trailer) @1967: Arthur and Eugenia Sharpe home Family from Massachusetts home (burned 2007) Empty lot/Gene Somers

SITE	LOCATION	BUSINESSES AND OWNERS OR MANAGERS/ESTABLISHMENTS/HOMES
2H	Craig Greenier	House built in 1864 @1875: Ichabod Morrill Blacksmith Shop J.H. Twitchell Twitchell & Robinson/J.E. Twitchell Blacksmith Shop @1967: Talmadge and Ella (Twitchell) Bishop home Robin Davis home Craig Greenier home
2I	Al and Cecily MacKinnon	1840: House built, Ira Fish owned lot @1875: S. Carpenter (Simeon or Seth) 1880: Laroy and Althea Miles @1919: Frank and Cecilia (Miles) Allen home @1950s: Frederick and Priscilla (Allen) Newcomb home Al and Cecily (Newcomb) MacKinnon home
2J	House between MacKinnon's and Marty Arbo	@1875: L. S. Bailey Fred and Mila Bailey home and clothing store @1967: Irving Bragg Bill Scribner home
2K	Marty Arbo	House built in 1846 @1875: Mrs. Jackman Frederick and Faustina Quint home Marty Arbo home

SITE	LOCATION	BUSINESSES AND OWNERS OR MANAGERS/ESTABLISHMENTS/HOMES
2L	Chickadee Realty	@1848: Oliver Cobb and Sons Harness Makers @1875: Oliver Cobb and also Horace Miles, cordwainer @1967: Archer Scribner Patten Insurance Agency: Carter Hall 1990-2015: Lakeview Appraisals & Chickadee Realty: Beth Bates Vacant building: Beth and Kenny Bates
2M	North corner of Founders and Main Streets	1841: Dr. Luther Rogers @1928: Jones's Barber Shop and Howard Ambrose's Restaurant Cities Service Ira Myrick gas station Billy Cameron garage Cooche Ballard garage (Ballard's Cities Service @around 1961) Arnold Porter garage 1967-1995: McKenney's Clothing 1995-2006: Downtown Deli and Pizza (Steve and Cheryl Anderson) 2006: Debbie's Deli 'n' Subs (Debbie Birmingham)

AREA THREE: KATAHDIN STREET AND WEST SIDE OF MAIN STREET BETWEEN KATAHDIN STREET AND DEARBORN STREETS

SITE	LOCATION	BUSINESSES AND OWNERS OR MANAGERS/ESTABLISHMENTS/HOMES
3A	Katahdin Street	Joseph Heath building @1875: Irving Bragg 1885: Patten Bottle Company: Irving Bragg Kerm Howes Leo Dickinson's Barber Shop Amber's Klassy Klothes (Amber Palmer Craig) Carlene's Barbering and Family Hair Care (Carlene Conklin Duffy)
3B	Katahdin Street	1984: Patten Town Office and Garage
3C	Katahdin Street	Codgie's Hairport and home Colleen Martin home
3D	Katahdin Street	1916: Saint Paul's Roman Catholic Church
3E	Katahdin Street	?-1954: Beehive—boarding house (Edna Rigby, burned) Ricky and Linda Lyons home
3F	Katahdin Street	@1875: A. Hall Prior to 1907: Palmer House (burned in 1907) @1914-1920: possible site of Main and Raymond (Chase Opera House, Moving Picture Theater), and Main and Brittain (harnesses) 1920-1930: Miss Main's Harness Shop and Post Office 1930-1939: Miss Main's Boxing and Wrestling Ring 1939-1972: The New Theater: Ira and Sherwood (Shinny) Howes (Larry Madison had a watch repair shop beside the theater) 1972-2008: Royce Smallwood and Francis Dunn storage; torn down Daisy Boutique: Wallace Drew

SITE	LOCATION	BUSINESSES AND OWNERS OR MANAGERS/ESTABLISHMENTS/HOMES
3G	West side of Main Street, corner of Katahdin and Main St.	@1875: Gardner and Coburn Store 1886-1954: Ira B. Gardner & Sons Store 1954-1970: Stratton's (manager Dick Aucoin, then George Merrow; building owned by Gardner family) 1970-1989: Merrow's (managed by George and Rose Merrow, building and property was owned by George and Rose Merrow, later Fred Smallwood) At various times, other businesses were housed in either the north half or the south half of the Stratton's/Merrow's store. These include: Bob Cunningham's IGA (north half) @1967: Bud and Geri Bell's IGA (north half) Kirby and Deanna Williams pawn shop & second hand shop (south half) 1974: Katahdin Valley Health Ctr. had a clinic in the back of the store 60's: Dr. Banton had a dentist's office upstairs Also apartments upstairs The building burned in 2008. There used to be a bandstand between the store and the next building. Now vacant lot owned by Rhonda Brophy
3H	West side of Main Street	Jacob Frye: Frye's Tavern and a hotel @1875: P. Peary (Peavey) 1930s: Charlie Smallwood Buffet and Lunch Allan Noyes's Trading Post/James Hathaway, owner @ 1967 Downtown Deli: Steve and Cheryl Anderson (1991-1995) Red Moose Gift Shop/Laundromat (Rhonda Brophy)

SITE	LOCATION	BUSINESSES AND OWNERS OR MANAGERS/ESTABLISHMENTS/HOMES
3I	West side of Main Street	@1875: P. Peavey 1916: Francis Peavey built the Peavey Block 1930s: Walter Cunningham's First National Store @ 1947: Ordway 1948-present: Richardson's Hardware: north half
3J	West side of Main Street	@1909: Restaurant and barber shop 1916: The Peavey Block built; Inn and Restaurant, barber shop 1947: Patten Inn (In this era, there was a restaurant and pool hall on the street floor and rooms and doctors' offices on the second floor.) 1953-1966: Joe and Florence Hall restaurant and hotel 1966-1968: Jim and Melvena Hathaway restaurant and hotel 1968-1981: Bruce and Norma Campbell restaurant, chain saws, NAPA After 1981: Richardson's Hardware: south half
3K	West side of Main Street	1909-1930s: C. G. Richardson, Sr.: Patten Hardware Also a barber shop and restaurant in the building 1944-1967: Bob Adam's Patten Hardware 1967-?: Royce Smallwood's Patten Hardware/Western Auto? Magic Scissors: Bethann Carver 1983-1997: Jerry Michaud: Four Seasons Restaurant 1997-1998: Peter Ellis: Al-E-Oop Restaurant, Washtub Laundromat Building torn down in 1998 2014: Richardson's Farm Supply/McNally's Farm Produce

SITE	LOCATION	BUSINESSES AND OWNERS OR MANAGERS/ESTABLISHMENTS/HOMES
3L	West side of Main Street	@1875: Dr. Bascom 1917: Bowers's Gas Station 1936: current building built; back part added in 1946 1948: Dick Ordway Bob and Tom Lawler (@1967 there was a Gulf Station here) Bob Harvey Dick Hall 1976: Main Street Auto Body (Al David) 2008: Main Street Outback Garage and Magic Wand Car Wash (Steve and Cheryl Anderson; they also own Cutting Edge Lawn Care)
3M	West side of Main Street, corner of Dearborn and Main St.	Gardner & Stetson store @1875: S. Carreau (not sure of spelling; could be Coro or Caro)) Jim King's Blacksmith Shop Frank and Kate Hunter, Frank and Julia (Roy) Hunter: home 1976: Hathaways' Motel; Hathaway's Apartments

This photo shows the Frank Hunter home before it was torn down to make space for Hathaway's Motel. (Eleanor Sargent Hunter photo.)

AREA FOUR: FOUNDERS STREET, THE EAST SIDE OF MAIN STREET BETWEEN FOUNDERS STREET AND HOULTON STREET, AND HOULTON STREET

SITE	LOCATION	BUSINESSES AND OWNERS OR MANAGERS/ESTABLISHMENTS/HOMES
4A	Empty lot between Deb's Deli and Patten Rec	@1875: school @1900: Dr. E.J. Farnham Ford Cars/Grant's Garage Smith Motor Co.: Forrest Smith garage (burned in 1940) @1945-1963: Dudley Olsen garage (property owned by someone from Houlton) Edgar Harrington storage Ken Lau storage Torn down—empty lot
4B	Patten Recreation Department	@1875: school and J.O. Bragg @1914-1940: Patten Town Hall (burned in 1940) 1941: Founders Memorial Hall (owned by town) 1955-1977: Founders Memorial Hall (owned by school department) 1979: Patten Parks and Recreation Building (owned by town)
4C	North corner of Gardner and Founders Street	@1875: J.O. Bragg Telephone office
4D	South corner of Gardner and Founders Street	1942-1943: Guy Ordway's Birdseye Pea Vine Factory Larry and Phyllis Madison home and her beauty shop Dr. Ron Blum's doctor's office
4E	Home across from Patten Rec	Gardner home Ira Myrick home

SITE	LOCATION	BUSINESSES AND OWNERS OR MANAGERS/ESTABLISHMENTS/HOMES
4F	Back of Richardson's Greenhouses on Founders Street	@1875: A.C. Bragg (possibly a blacksmith shop) Cyrus Campbell garage 1959-2005: Dead River Oil Company Redemption Center Building torn down in 2010 2013—Richardson's Greenhouses
4G	South corner of Founders and Main Streets: Richardson's Greenhouses, North building	1840: John Gardner store @1875: W. Gardner store (could be an error—possibly John Gardner) 1890-1917: J.K. Osgood Store Jerome Frye William Jackman (burned in 1891) 1891-1917: Huston & Morse Clothing (burned in 1917) Ira Myrick: gas station and general store Earl Giggey: gas station and general store Ken Lau: gas station and general store Torn down in 2010 2013: Richardson's Greenhouses
4H	Richardson's Greenhouses, South Building	1840: John Gardner store @1875—W. Gardner store (could be an error—possibly John Gardner) 1890-1917: J.K. Osgood Store 1891-1917: Huston & Morse Clothing (burned in 1917) Leonard Roy Shoe Shop (later moved to his home on Houlton Street) Bine's Dairy Cream (Bine Whitehouse, @1958-1959) Fogg's Dairy Cream (Mickey and Louise Fogg) Lau's Dairy Cream (Monica and Ken Lau) Torn down in 2010 2013: Richardson's Greenhouses

SITE	LOCATION	BUSINESSES AND OWNERS OR MANAGERS/ESTABLISHMENTS/HOMES
4I	Richardson's Greenhouses, Part Three	1842: the first Patten House (Lucius/C.L.Hackett, owner) 1885: the Patten House was enlarged to three stories 1905-1917: the second Patten House Building burned in 1917, owners Donald and Archie Nevers 1920: Quincy building built @1937: an A & P store 1946-1997: Ken Lord's grocery store (A & P, Nationwide, Ken & Jeff's) Apartments upstairs Torn down in 2009 2013: Richardson's Greenhouses
4J	Parking lot	1842: the first Patten House (Lucius/C.L. Hackett, owner) 1885: the Patten House was enlarged to three stories 1905-1917: the second Patten House Building burned in 1917, owners Donald and Archie Nevers 1920—Quincy building built A. L. Pinette Clothing Store Gus Lord Russell Arbo Bob Smallwood Laundromat (Wally McCourt) Torn down in 2009 Parking lot

SITE	LOCATION	BUSINESSES AND OWNERS OR MANAGERS/ESTABLISHMENTS/HOMES
4K	Katahdin Trust Company, North Half	@1875: Calvin Bradford, Post Office 1917: Aaron Smith Clothing and Calvin Bradford Tin Shop Building burned in 1917 ?-1962—Patten Post Office Katahdin Trust Company
4L	Katahdin Trust Company, South Half	Ephraim Fairfield store 1864-1892: Quincy Store (burned in 1892) 1888-1917: Quincy, Cooper, and Rowe building, telephone office @1900: Bung's Lunch (F.M. McElroy) @1900-1917: Evans and Bailey Express Burned in 1917: McElroy may have burned previously 1918: Katahdin Trust Company
4M	Ellis Family Market, North Half	@1841-after 1875: Horace Miles (cordwainer) and @1845-after 1875: Samuel Benjamin (lawyer) Burned in 1917 1919: Rowe Building built 1957: Mickey McCafferty's First National By 1967: building owned by Edgar Harrington Bud and Geri's Bell's IGA Upstairs: Patten Insurance Agency, doctors' offices Torn down in 2002 Katahdin Trust Company and Ellis Family Market

SITE	LOCATION	BUSINESSES AND OWNERS OR MANAGERS/ESTABLISHMENTS/HOMES
4N	Ellis Family Market, South Half	Gillie Brown Store
Laura Scribner store
Melvena McNally Hathaway store
State Liquor Store (owned by Melvena Hathaway); torn down in 1987
1988-1997: Ellis IGA (Al and Lou Ellis)
1997-present: Ellis Family Market (Peter and Jon)
4O	North corner of Houlton and Main Streets	@1838: Elbridge Stetson's cabin
@1875: Samuel Wiggins
Hathaway House/boarding house
Billy Cameron
(At one point this was a Chevron Station)
Cooche Ballard's garage (Ballard's Service, @1964-65)
Carver's Gas Station; torn down in 1987
1988: Ellis Family Market Parking Lot
On the adjacent lot, @1875: Patten Exchange (S.S. Thompson)
Agnes Howes home
4P	South corner of Houlton and Main Streets	1839: Ira Fish's sheep barn
1854: Methodist Parsonage built
1871: Stetson Memorial United Methodist Church built
4Q	South side of Houlton Street	Mason's Hall

SITE	LOCATION	BUSINESSES AND OWNERS OR MANAGERS/ESTABLISHMENTS/HOMES
4R	North side of Houlton Street	1898-1980: Oddfellows Hall 1981: Katahdin Valley Health Center
4S	South side of Houlton Street	1910-1916: Hal Gardner party home 1916-1947: Dick (or Dyke) Howe, then Burton Howe home 1947-1949: Clive Hatt boarding home 1949-1951: Joseph and Marjorie Nash 1951-1954: Rest Haven Health Care Facility (Bob and Opal Goodall) 1954: owner Mr. Sullivan, manager Justine Glidden Michaud Howard and Marian Parker Mountain Heights Health Care Facility and Baxter Apts: Dr. Steven Weisberger (owner) and managed by North Country Associates.

AREA FIVE: DEARBORN STREET, MILL HILL, MILL STREET, SPRUCE STREET, POTATO ROW, AND FINCH HILL

SITE	LOCATION	BUSINESSES AND OWNERS OR MANAGERS/ESTABLISHMENTS/HOMES
5A	North side of Dearborn Street	Patten Fire Department
5B	North side of Dearborn Street	1920-21: Patten Creamery 1931-1958: Katahdin Creamery Patten Water Company
5C	North side of Dearborn Street	Theresa's Headquarters (Theresa Patterson Schmidt)
5D	South side of Dearborn Street	1832: Ira Fish's Home Home: original Fish building with additions
5E	South corner of Dearborn and Main Streets	@1875: A. Bradbury Around 1945: D. L. Smith Humpy Gould Steve and Christe Crouse—vacant Note: The original house on this site may have been the first framed house in Patten, built by Jonathan Palmer in 1834. One source says this house stood until it was torn down by its last owner, Mabel Gould, almost a century later. Another source says it was later a hotel called *The Tavern*, run by Captain S.C. Leslie and it burned in 1929.
5F	Mill Hill	Possibly 1843: Samuel Darling's Furniture and Casket Shop Town Blacksmith Shop Murphy Garage Late 1940s: Billy Coote: shoe repair Herschel Cole home
5G	Spruce Street	Rhonda Harvey Accounting

SITE	LOCATION	BUSINESSES AND OWNERS OR MANAGERS/ESTABLISHMENTS/HOMES
5H	Near Spruce Street	1933-1937: CCC camps were established in this area
5I	South corner of intersection of Spruce Street and Rte. 11	Red Saw Mill
5J	Finch Hill	Donnie Carver garage Gallagher's Auto: Chris Gallagher
5K	Finch Hill	1987-1991: Fred Smallwood Garage (burned) 1999-2002: Pitt Landry garage and Kat's Pit Stop Dana and Jimmy Carver garage 2015: K & C Quik Stop (Cole Lane)
5L	Finch Hill	Perley and Sadie Harris farm 1984: John Brown Septic Tank Services, John and Faye Brown home
5M	Potato Row	John Marr Waste Removal
5LN	Potato Row	1989: Smallwood Construction, Inc.
5O	Mill Street	See Chapter Twelve for a complete listing of mills at this site

CHAPTER TEN: SCHOOLS AND LIBRARIES

We know that even before T4R6 and T5R6 became Patten and Mount Chase, the earliest citizens wanted good schools to provide a good education for their children and a good library to provide good books to read. Less than twenty years after the purchase of T4R6 was made, schools had been established, even including an academy for older students. Although Patten was at the far reaches of civilization, the local schools were comparable to those in the more settled areas of the state. Through cold and stormy winters, busy planting and harvesting seasons which required the help of young people, epidemics of illness, and teacher shortages, the Patten and Mount Chase residents kept their schools going.

SCHOOLS

Note: Most of this information about the schools in Patten and Mount Chase was gleaned from Patten and Mount Chase Town Reports, from yearly editions of the Patten Academy Yearbook (*The Mirror*), and from Irene Olsen Bradford's *History of Patten Academy*. Mrs. Bradford was a 1933 graduate of Patten Academy; her family had moved to Patten specifically so she and her brother could attend P.A. After college, she returned to Patten and taught at the Academy. I would recommend that you find a copy of Mrs. Bradford's book to read. It is very well-written, entertaining, and full of detailed information about Patten Academy from its inception until its 100-year anniversary. It also has many pictures of superintendents, principals, teachers, and students. I also recommend reading past issues of school yearbooks. They also are entertaining and full of information about people and the local businesses who bought advertising space from the seniors. While reading these yearbooks, I realized that teenagers today aren't that much different from teenagers of the past! Photos which were reproduced from Mrs. Bradford's book are indicated as "Bradford."

By 1838: There was a village school in T4R6. It was located where the cemetery now exists. The first teacher there was Miss Amanda (or May or Mary) Palmer, daughter of one of Patten's first settlers, Jonathan Palmer. Miss Palmer later married and moved away from Patten. Mr. A.G. Baker was the first teacher at the Happy Corner School, which was established a few years after the village school. Mr. Baker was a "veteran" of the Bloodless Aroostook War and was also a fine musician.

1847: in the mid-1840s, the citizens of Patten decided that they wanted a high school. In 1847, the Maine Legislature, under Governor John W. Dana, passed a bill which incorporated the Trustees of Patten Academy. The money needed to build the school was raised through donations and by selling land in neighboring T4R7, half of which had been granted to the town by the state. The picture at the right is the official seal of Patten Academy.

The Academy was built on a lot purchased from Joseph Heald on the south corner of what are now Main and Scribner Streets. The building had two stories, with dimensions of 42' X 32'. The outside work of the building was done by Edward Fairfield at a cost of $163.00, and the inside was finished by William Jackman for $140.00. The ground floor had one room, and the upper floor was divided up into classrooms. The only thing it lacked was a gymnasium, but in the early days this was not particularly important as organized sports programs were not offered to the students.

While the town did appropriate money yearly to support its operation, Patten Academy was somewhat financially independent from the town in that it charged tuition per student and was governed by a board of seventeen trustees. Among the early trustees of the academy were John Gardner, Ira Fish, James Mitchell, Samuel Benjamin, Dr. Luther Rogers, Samuel Darling, Alfred Cushman of Sherman, Levi Sewall of Island Falls, and Francis Weeks of Mount Chase. There were two terms: the fall term from September to November and the spring term from February or March until June. Tuition was set at $2.50 a term for Common Branch and $3.50 for Higher Branch. Some income was also generated by renting out the Academy for public use.

Mr. S. A. Eveleth was appointed as the first principal at Patten Academy, at a salary of $8.00 a week. This income was not enough to support a single man, let alone a family, so the principals in the early days of the Academy's existence had to find additional employment for those months when school was not in session. In its first fifty years, Patten Academy had forty different principals! The principal was responsible not only for administration, but also for the instruction of as many as sixty or more students ranging in age from ten to twenty-two. If he was lucky, he might have an assistant who was most likely a student at the Academy.

When Patten Academy officially opened its doors in the fall of 1848, there were 61 students (33 boys and 28 girls) enrolled. At least half of the students were from other communities such as Pittsfield, Enfield, Lincoln, Benedicta, Masardis, Belfast Plantation, and Golden Ridge Plantation (Sherman). These students paid $1.25 or $1.50 per week to board with families in town.

The Academy offered a well-rounded and rigorous curriculum, which was divided into two branches of learning. The Common Branch (the general course) included reading, writing, arithmetic, geography, and English grammar. The Higher Branch (for college-bound students) included Latin, Greek, French, history, botany, natural history, anatomy, physiology, philosophy, chemistry, algebra, and geometry. The Academy was one of the first schools in Maine to have a scientific laboratory, and students who attended P.A. were well-prepared for college. However, the school did not award diplomas until 1887. Prior to that, students tended to take the courses they wanted and left school when they (or their parents) thought they had had enough education.

One of the first success stories among Patten Academy students was that of Charles Fish, son of Ira and Abra Fish. Mr. Fish attended P.A. and went on to study at Waterville College (now Colby), Harvard University, and Bowdoin College. He then returned to Patten and served as the principal of P.A. from 1862 to 1866. He was an enthusiastic principal and teacher, even offering public lectures on chemistry and physics on Friday nights. He was largely responsible for Patten Academy's excellent laboratory. In 1866, he left Patten to become the principal and instructor at Washington Academy and later at Brunswick Academy. He had married Sarah Louise Rogers (daughter of Dr. Luther Rogers) of Patten in 1859, and they had four sons and two daughters. He is buried at the Riverside Cemetery in Brunswick.

Mid-to-late 1800s: Rural schools (as many as 17 at one point) began cropping up all over the Patten and Mount Chase area. Patten established schools on School (Founders) Street, on Finch Hill, in Frenchville and Barleyville, and on the Happy Corner, South Patten, North and Waters roads. Mount Chase schools included the Myrick School (North Road), the Mountain Road School, two Owlsboro Road Schools, the Willett School (which may have been one of Owlsboro schools), the McKenney School on the Shin Pond Road, the Harvey School at Shin Pond, and the Crommett School (beyond Shin Pond).

These were, of course, one-room schoolhouses, with one person teaching students from age five through the teens.   High school-age students generally attended Patten Academy. At times, school was closed during harvest and planting to allow students to help out at home. School might also be closed if the building couldn't be kept warm enough for the students' comfort or if the roads were impassable. Students got to school by horse and wagon. Sometimes these wagons even had a wood stove so the students could stay warm while traveling to and from school.

In the early days of settlement, the elementary schools were very loosely organized. Each school pretty much did its own thing, and the schools were not graded. Attendance was very spotty, as children were often needed to help out at home. In other cases, getting an education was not a priority for a family. As time went on, however, the schools became more organized and each town named a superintendent of schools. Eventually, Patten and Mount Chase jointly hired a superintendent who oversaw all their schools, and education became more standardized.

The rural school buildings were often used to hold community events, such as church services and town meetings. Adrian Carver tells the story of a town meeting held at the little red schoolhouse on the Owlsboro Road near the Fish Hatchery. A discussion got pretty heated up, and a fight ensued. Adrian's father, who was a very hairy man, got the worst of it when he tried to separate the combatants and one of them grabbed a fistful of Mr. Carver's chest hair. Now if that had happened while school was in session, the boys would have gotten a pretty stiff—and sore—punishment!

1873: Maine's state legislature passed the Free High School Act, which outlined the financial relationship between towns and academies. In Patten, this meant that local students did not have to pay tuition to attend Patten Academy; instead the town supported the school through an annual appropriation which was designated in the town report as "free high school and Patten Academy." The appropriation was paid to the trustees of Patten Academy. For the first few years, the appropriation for the Academy was $400.00. High school students from out-of-town had to pay tuition of $3.50 (lower branch) and $4.00 (higher branch) on an individual basis unless their own town picked up the tab. The money appropriated for the lower grade schools was handled by a school board.

1887: By this time, Patten Academy's curriculum had been organized and standards were set by which a student moved through the upper grades. A diploma was awarded when a student passed all the prescribed courses with a rank of at least 60% and fulfilled attendance requirements.

The first graduates of Patten Academy were Charles Cobb (on the left) and Jacob Hersey (on the right). They graduated from Patten Academy as well-educated men. Mr. Hersey became an assistant teacher at the Academy and served as Patten's postmaster for several years before moving to California. Mr. Cobb (who was the son of Oliver Cobb, the town's first harness maker) continued his education at the University of Maine, where he majored in civil engineering. He returned to Patten, taught for a time at Patten Academy, and then became the superintendent. He later served as the superintendent of schools in the Oakfield area.

1888: A grammar school was established, although it was housed in the Academy building. It included several grades preceding the Academy grades. The teacher of the grammar school was also an assistant to the Academy principal. The lower schools were also graded by this time.

1888, cont.: Burton L. Howe, Eleanor B. Bailey, Annie G. McCourt, and G. Frank Woodbury were the second graduating class at Patten Academy. Mr. Howe (photo at right from his obituary) had moved from Ashland to Patten in order to attend Patten Academy. He boarded with Horatio Darling and walked two miles to school every day. He graduated at the age of fifteen and went on to be a successful lumber businessman and a teacher. He was a good friend of Governor Percival Baxter and was one of the original group which climbed Mount Katahdin to study the feasibility of establishing a state park around the mountain. He served as a Maine delegate in the 1920 Republican National Convention. He was married to Mary Adelaide Campbell; they had two children: Dyke and Virginia (Fifield). Eleanor Bailey was the daughter of Adaline and Ephraim Bailey and the granddaughter of Eli and Fanny Kellogg. Her father Ephraim was a Civil War veteran and a harness maker. Eleanor's brother was Fred Bailey, who was a merchant and was active in town affairs throughout his life. Annie McCourt, who may have been called Goldie, was the daughter of Andrew and Martha McCourt and the sister of John and Mary. G. Frank Woodbury was the son of Dr. Benjamin Woodbury and followed in his father's footsteps; he practiced medicine in Patten for almost fifty years.

1889-1893: There were no graduating exercises at the academy because the school was experiencing a rapid turnover of teachers and the students weren't able to take the courses required for graduation. The principal of the academy, W.L. Bonney, urged the town citizens to dig into their pockets a little deeper so the school could pay better wages. He also denounced the idea of using high school students as teachers for the lower grades. In spite of the turmoil, Patten Academy was still turning out well-educated young people. Halbert Robinson earned a degree in Civil Engineering from the University of Maine, taught at UM for a few years, then oversaw the building of over forty bridges in Maine. Curtis Brown built a career with the railroad, and his brother Hadley had an important position at the Charlestown Navy Yard. Lore Rogers (son of Dr. and Mrs. Rogers) graduated from the University of Maine, got his doctorate degree, and went on to have a brilliant career in bacteriology before returning to Patten and establishing the Lumberman's Museum.

1894: Abigail Estrella Batchelder and Herbert Gardner graduated from Patten Academy. Although Miss Batchelder's family was from New Hampshire, she was the granddaughter of Horace Miles, Patten's cordwainer. It may very well be that Abby's parents sent her to Patten to get her education. She went onto have a life-long career in teaching, including teaching at a school in Tokyo, Japan. Mr. Gardner(son of Ira and Helen Gardner) served as the principal for Patten Academy from 1898 to 1902, after which he became a successful lawyer in Portland, Maine.

Note: Unfortunately, not everyone who attended Patten Academy was a model student. In the Patten Town Office vaults, I came across a list of several students' names and the fines (from $1.00 to as much as $5.00) that they owed the town for damaging school property. There were girls' as well as boys' names on the list.

1895: The Patten Town Report listed the elementary schools and the average number of students attending some of them. Attendance was not mandatory, but a student was automatically held back if he/she did not attend at least 40 days of school. The school year was extended to thirty-four weeks around this time.

Village schools:
  Primary School—30
  Intermediate School—30
  Grammar School—27

Rural Schools:
  Ordway District—20
  Hammond District—30
  Frenchville District—18
  Happy Corner District—30
  Purvis District—13

The Waters School (called the Adam Hill School) had been closed, but it reopened at some point before 1902. I believe the Ordway School may have been the South Patten School, and the Purvis School was most likely the Barleyville School. (On the map on page 57, a lot at the mouth of the Barleyville Road is labeled R. Purvis.)

1896: The Patten Town Report stated that because of the high cost of maintaining the rural schools, students who failed to attend at least 16 weeks of school were being charged a $25.00 penalty. Teachers were paid $6.33 per week. The Grammar School was accepting out of town students. Primary students in town went to the Mason's Hall for classes.

1897: The curriculum at Patten Academy was reorganized into five years of study at the Academy level and four years of study at the Grammar School level.

The first Patten Academy burned to the ground. Ironically, there had been discussion in the previous few years about building a new school, as the Academy building was in bad shape. The trustees had even broached the idea of buying Jacob Frye's lot (across the street, north of the existing Academy building) for the new school. However, the townspeople were hesitant to take on such a financial burden. As it turned out, they were left with no choice but to purchase the lot from Jacob Frye and build a new school.

1898: A new high school was immediately built and opened by 1898. (In the meantime, students attended classes in the Oddfellows Hall.) This new Academy was located on Jacob Frye's lot on the north corner of Scribner and Main Streets. It had classrooms and a large study hall room on the first floor, and the second floor was divided into classrooms. The grammar school occupied one floor and high school students the other; the first and second floors were open and airy, with lots of windows. The third floor contained a large tank connected to a windmill on the roof; these provided the school with a hot water heating system.

Financially, the town of Patten appropriated $4,000 towards construction costs, while the trustees of the Academy came up with an additional $1,000. Unfortunately, the total cost for the completed building was $9,309.53.

1900: Calvin Bradford had this to say about the price tag of the new high school in the Patten Town Report:

> *"We have of course heard much criticism of the cost of the building, of this we do not feel like saying much except that we, as a committee, took no important steps in the plans for the building or its appointments without consulting the tax payers as far as we could….we are sure you have got the worth of your money and in a few years, if not now, will be glad that you built it.*

The 1900 Patten Town Report also included this statement by the superintendent of schools, C.E. Cobb:

> *We have tried to aid our village teachers by closing their school buildings during the noon hour…This has saved us something in the way of cutting down the damage on building, school apparatus, and school books, as well as to lessen the trouble among the children who were in the habit of going to the school house two hours before school, to fight, plague the girls, and smash things until school time. Also the morals of our ninety pupils under eleven years of age can be looked after better…*

The report stated that 411 students had attended Patten and Mount Chase schools in 1899.

Around 1900, the United States passed compulsory education laws for the purpose of protecting child welfare. By 1918, all the states had passed some form of compulsory attendance law. However, enforcement of the law fell to individual communities, and the law was difficult to enforce even though fines could be levied on parents whose children were not attending school. In the Patten/Mount Chase area, attendance was often poor for any number of reasons, some of which were not the faults of the parents.

1901: The levels of each of the Patten village schools were as follows.

- Primary School included the 1st through 3rd years of school
- Intermediate School included the 4th through 6th years of school
- Grammar School included the 7th through 9th years of school
- Patten Academy included the 10th through 13th years of school.

The principal of the high school, Herbert N. Gardner, strongly recommended the addition of a business course in the high school. By 1904, bookkeeping, commercial law, and business arithmetic had been added to the curriculum. Earning a diploma was dependent on attendance (up to 20 points) and recitation (up to 80 points). If a student had an average of 90% or 80% along with perfect attendance, he or she did not have to take an examination to graduate. Graduates of the class of 1901 were Caleb Scribner, Allen Main, Mary Nelder, and Frank Allen.

1901-1902: Mount Chase's Town Report for 1901-1902 included a lengthy report from the Superintendent of Schools, Mrs. Eva Myrick. This chart shows some information about the five Mount Chase Schools.

District/Name of school	Teacher	Average Attendance	Sch. committee representative
1—Myrick(north road)	Mrs. Eva Myrick	26	Stella Steen
5—Mountain Road	Miss Avah Rigby	6	Alice Porter
2—Owlsboro Road	Mrs. Lucia Hannigan	19	Alice Porter
3—Crommett	Miss Rosa West	12	Luther W. Glidden
6—Shin Pond	Miss Edna Swaim Miss Ella Howes	10	Luther W. Glidden

I do not know what happened to District Four—evidently its school was closed at this time. Mrs. Myrick reported that she had visited each school *(including her own!)* one or two times each term (fall and spring). Her school started each term a week later than the other schools, giving her a chance to visit each school before starting her own work. She made mention of a particular teacher who wasn't able to do a good job because of being sick a lot and a lack of fuel to keep the school warm.

When I was doing research, I enjoyed reading the various reports which were included in the annual town reports, especially superintendent and principal's reports about the schools. Often, these reports were trying to straddle the divide between the taxpayers and the school committees. Usually they were well-crafted so that the appeals for money weren't blatant and the analysis of the education being offered by the schools was positive. But once in a while there was a report that was fairly blunt. As you might have guessed from Mrs. Myrick's comments about one of her teachers, she was one who wasn't afraid to be blunt. She had this to say about some of the critics of the way her schools were being taught:

> *The growlers still live; that class will always growl and find fault about this thing and that...There is no other one thing that will so discourage and cripple the earnest effort of the teacher more than the unkind remarks of parents in the presence of their children...I do not intend these remarks for the whole town... Trouble has entered simply in one district and that was simply out of jealousy and spite, not from any fault in the teacher whatever.*

1903-1904: Mrs. Myrick continued to tell it like it was in the next year's Mount Chase Town Report. She wrote:

> *The schools in our town for the past year have been exceptionally good and will rank with any of the rural schools in our vicinity, except in one case, which was not a satisfactory term to me, and we want to be very careful about hiring strangers and putting them into our schools without knowing something of their ability.*

Mrs. Myrick was not listed as a teacher in this report, but was listed as the Superintendent of Schools. The town paid $6.40 for Kelcy Parker's tuition for his attendance at Patten Academy. Mrs. Myrick noted that there were 131 children between the ages of four and 21 living in Mount Chase, but the average school attendance was 96 children. The town was receiving money from the state for free high school and for schooling state scholars.

It was difficult at times to track the Mount Chase schools and Patten's rural schools as they opened and closed frequently based on attendance, the conditions of the school buildings, and the cost of maintaining the schools. The rule of thumb was that if the number of eligible students at a school dropped below eight children, the school was closed **unless** the town residents voted at the annual town meeting to keep the school open. In my research, I found repeated instances that the townspeople voted to keep their schools open no matter how many children were attending. After sanitation laws went into effect, schools were at times closed due to failure to meet sanitation codes. Superintendents also weighed the cost of maintaining a school against the cost of transporting students to Patten's village schools.

The village schools were experiencing the opposite problem: too many students, not enough room, and not enough teachers. There were teachers who were teaching multiple grades with forty or fifty students in one room.

Finding good quality teachers was always a problem for rural schools throughout Maine for several reasons.

- Often rural schools could not or did not offer a competitive salary.
- There was a lack of trained teachers throughout the state.
- A qualified teacher might not want to teach in an overcrowded classroom.
- A qualified teacher might not want to teach multiple grade levels.
- A qualified teacher might not want to move to a rural environment.

Naturally, the superintendents wanted men or women who had attended normal school (a college for the training of teachers) or the University of Maine and who had some experience. However, at times, the district might have to hire a capable high-school student or local resident who had not attended college.

The townspeople began to discuss putting up another village school building to deal with the overcrowded buildings and overworked teachers. There were a lot of decisions to be made: Where would the school be located? How would the classrooms be laid out? What grades would it accommodate? How would they pay for it?

1904-1905: Mrs. Myrick's next report for the Mount Chase Town report was fairly mild. She noted that the fall term in three of the schools was cut short because of extremely cold weather.

1905: The taxpayers approved the building of the much-needed new school. It was located on the lot where the first Academy had stood. It was a one story building with a full basement. It may not have always been referred to as the Primary School and may not have always housed the lowest grades.

1906: The Patten village schools had been graded, creating eight distinct grades and a sub-primary. Students were expected to meet certain standards to move on to the next grade. William T. Merrill, who was serving as an interim superintendent of Patten schools, recommended that the number of classrooms a single teacher was expected to teach be reduced from three to two. There were four grades in the high school, and students were often referred to as Freshmen, Sophomores, Juniors, and Seniors.

Mr. Merrill formed a committee to look into the matter of creating a district of schools along with the towns of Millinocket, Sherman, and Stacyville and hiring a superintendent to manage all the schools (about 32 of them) within this district. This idea did not get beyond a discussion stage. A janitor had been hired to look after the village schools.

Around this time: There were many extracurricular activities offered at Patten Academy in the early 1900s, including debating, public speaking, one-act plays, glee club, band, winter carnivals, the Bonney Literary Society, Greek societies, Chautauqua, a German Club, a French Club, National Honor Society, Student Council, Future Farmers of America, and sports. A yearbook committee was also formed. The first yearbook was published in 1906 and was called *The Mirror*. Patten Academy's debating and public speaking teams competed successfully against other area schools.

The Bonney Literary Society at the Academy brought in guest speakers and held other entertainments to raise money for the school. An Upsilon Delta secret Greek society for boys had previously been formed, but was replaced by Nu Nu Pi in 1907. The Sigma Omega society was organized by the girls in 1907. In her book *History of Patten Academy*, Miss Olsen (Irene Bradford) stated that the goal of the boys' society was "to promote athletics, increase the intellect of its members, and abstain from evil doings." However, she said that the chief object of the girls' society seemed to be "to have a good time."

Patten Academy had also established sports programs. The P.A. teams were of excellent caliber. Track, baseball, football, tennis, and basketball were all offered at various times. The baseball, football, and track teams played at the Paul Gagnon fairgrounds and ball field on the Crystal Road until they created their own athletic field near the school in 1921. The photo at right (Bradford) shows the 1908 football team.

The 1908 girls' basketball team (photo at left; Bradford) included (left to right) Eva Smallwood, Winnifred Crommett, Grace Coady, Verna Carlisle, and Daffa Morrill. The girls also had a tennis team.

Basketball was a very popular sport, but for years the teams did not have a good place to practice or hold home games. The attic of the primary building, the Patten House hall, and the Grange Hall were used at various points, but of course, these were not ideal locations for sports. Even so, all of the school's activities were well supported by the public, both financially and by attendance at events. In almost all of the team pictures from this era, there was a boy or girl with the last name of Coady. Mona, Leo, Kempton, Grace, Conrad, Donald, and Hilda Coady were the children of James and Hattie Coady. James was the Chief Forestry Department Warden for the Trout Brook area. Several of the Coady offspring graduated from college and became teachers and/or school administrators. Kempton also worked with his father at Trout Brook for a time.

1908: The village grade schools received music classes from Miss Emma Bradford Lane. She was the daughter of Asa Hanson Lane (a teacher and photographer) and Anna Bradford (a teacher). Although Anna was not directly related to the Bradfords of Patten, she did have relatives living in Sherman. Emma attended the State Normal School at Lee, studied music in Boston, and graduated from New York University. While researching her family, I learned that her great-great-great-grandparents were killed by Indians in Massachusetts in 1756, but four children managed to escape.

1909-1910: The school in Shin Pond had been closed. Mrs. Stella Steen, Superintendent of Schools for Mount Chase, also recommended that the Mountain Road School be discontinued as only three children had regularly attended school during the fall term. She noted that the school year would have to be lengthened from twenty to twenty-six weeks due to a new law enacted by the legislature.

In Patten, the schools had already gone to a 34-week school year. The Hammond School on the North Road had closed. A telephone had been installed in the Primary School. The Primary School included grades Sub-Primary through six and had seven teachers, one of whom was also the principal. The Grammar School included grades seven to nine and had three teachers for the spring term and two teachers for the fall and winter terms. There were twelve teachers at the high school. The rural schools were Happy Corner, Purvis (probably Barleyville), Frenchville, and Ordway (possibly South Patten). It had been determined that it was cheaper to transport some rural students than keep a schoolhouse open. Eye and ear tests were given to all pupils above first grade, as mandated by a new state law. It was found that 36 students were defective in eyesight and 19 were defective in hearing. The girls' basketball team won the State Preparatory School Championship. They had not lost a game since the team had been organized four years earlier. (See page 75 for a photo of the team.)

1911: Patten Academy offered four courses of instruction. The Classical and Modern Languages courses were for college-bound students, and the English and Commercial courses were offered for the other students. Patten's seniors had a high percentage of students going on to further education. The Class of 1911 held their graduation exercises at Chase Opera House.

1912: Patten had seven school houses which served 78 rural students and 302 town students. W.M. Marr, Supervisor of Schools, submitted these comments to the Patten Town Report:

> *Parents, you should visit the schools at least once a term. Your presence will encourage the teachers and pupils to do their best work. Do not depend entirely on the rank card, but go and see for yourselves just what is being done. Last year, I told you that it is important that the home and the school unite their forces, that the devoted mother and the patient, toiling teacher intelligently cooperate for the awakening and enrichment of the mind and heart of the child. I still believe this is true.*

1913: Patten Academy's secret Greek societies were abolished in 1913 when the state passed a law forbidding their existence in high school.

A rather strange activity called *The Hare and Hound Chase* was organized in 1913. The Seniors, who were the hares, left paper trails for the hounds (the underclassmen) to follow on and off the school grounds to a destination where a campfire cookout was held. It was so popular that it continued into the 1940's. At times, some of the participants got carried away and some hazing actually occurred, although this was definitely not acceptable.

1913-1914: There were a lot of changes in the schools in Mount Chase. From this point forward, the superintendent of Patten Schools would also serve as superintendent of Mount Chase schools. William Marr was the current superintendent. The schools in 1913 for the spring term were Myrick, Willett, Mountain, Crommett, and Harvey, but Crommett School was not open for the fall term. Mr. Marr stated that all of the Mount Chase schools were to be closed at the end of the 1913 school year except for the Myrick School because of low attendance unless the townspeople voted at town meeting to keep them open. Evidently, they did so vote, since in 1914, the schools listed were Myrick, Willett, Mountain, and Crommett for spring term, and Harvey School (which was maintained for Zenas Harvey's children) was added for the fall term.

1913-1914, cont.: In the 1914 Patten Town Report, William Marr, the Superintendent of Schools, stated that they were spending too much money on transporting students and that the rural schools should be required to hold school 36 weeks a year.

Opal Myrick graduated from Patten Academy. She followed in her mother Eva's footsteps and became a teacher in Mount Chase. By 1930, she had moved to Millinocket, where she became such a well-respected teacher that an elementary school was named after her.

The Town Hall was built. However, the basketball teams were not allowed to use it because it was feared they might be too destructive. That problem was remedied the following year when nets were placed over the lights and bars were placed over the windows. From that point forward, the hall was the scene of many enjoyable activities within the community.

1916: The Mount Chase schools were Myrick, Mountain, Willett and Shin Pond; however Shin Pond School was not open for the fall term. The Harvey School was closed since Zenas Harvey's children had entered the higher grades. The Shin Pond students were conveyed to the Purvis School in Patten.

1917: The United States joined the Allied Forces in World War I. The Class of 1917 patriotically donated the $100.00 they had saved for their class trip to the American Red Cross. Some students from Patten Academy went even further to support the war effort by enlisting in the military.

A letter from the State Superintendent of Education stated that the record of students from Patten Academy was "of exceptional merit in all respects."

1918: The superintendent of schools, Arthur L. Todd, recommended that manual training and domestic science courses be offered to high school and upper grade level students. Patten schools had to be closed for five weeks during the fall term due to an influenza pandemic. The time was made up by going to school on Saturdays and shortening vacation time. (You can read more about this flu pandemic and the havoc it caused around the world in Chapter Eleven.)

1918-1919: The Mount Chase Town Report indicated that Mount Chase was now part of a school union with Benedicta, Hersey, Patten, and Stacyville. Superintendent Arthur Todd warned that the town needed to think about increasing the salaries of Mount Chase teachers as there was a state-wide shortage of teachers and Mount Chase would find it difficult to hire good teachers. In other trades and professions, salaries had increased over 100% in recent years, while teacher salaries had an increase of 12%.

As a teacher myself who taught through Whole Language, Maine's Learning Results, MAPs, LADs, MEAs, NECAPs, No Child Left Behind, and the beginnings of the Common Core Curriculum, I found this next piece of news interesting: Superintendent Todd said that the state was setting requirements for a course of study that all Maine schools were to follow. Mr. Todd was not just on the bandwagon, he was driving the horses, as he seems to have been deeply involved in the writing of the requirements.

1919-1920: A Parent-Teachers Association was organized in Patten, and an Academy playground was established.

1920-1921: In the Mount Chase Town Report, Superintendent Todd recommended that the children of the Owlsboro and Mountain Schools be conveyed to the Myrick School, and the children of the Shin Pond School be conveyed to the Barleyville School. By doing this, teachers' salaries could be raised and better teachers could be hired. From subsequent town reports, it appears that the Mountain Road School was closed, but the Shin Pond and Owlsboro Schools weren't.

Superintendent Todd also recommended that Mount Chase's school year go from around April 1st to mid-December. During the other months, road conditions were so bad it was difficult to convey students to school. He said this would allow the Patten teachers to work at the Mount Chase Schools during their summer vacation. Mount Chase would be getting some excellent experienced teachers at a salary within the means of Mount Chase taxpayers. I think his reasoning is somewhat flawed here, as the school sessions would definitely have had overlapped.

1921: In the Patten Town Report, the Superintendent of Schools, Lucy P. Leach, recommended extending the school year from 36 to 40 weeks and switching from a nine-grade system to an eight-grade system, not counting four years of high school. The Grammar School boys and girls had basketball teams, and plans were in the works for a boys' baseball team. She also informed Patten's citizens that a sanitation law for schools had been passed for the state of Maine, and neither the South Patten nor the Frenchville School met sanitation standards.

Leach's report in the 1921 Mount Chase Town Report urged the townspeople to appropriate enough money to clear up an ongoing overdraft. She said none of the Mount Chase schools met the requirements of a new sanitation law and that the citizens had two years to get the school buildings in proper shape. She also warned the citizens that the amount of money received from the state for school expenses would be reduced if attendance did not improve.

The courses of study at Patten Academy were English Scientific, College Preparatory, Commercial, and Agriculture. Classes were temporarily held in the Town Hall while a new steam heating system was installed in the Academy building.

1922-1923: The Mount Chase Town Report described the repairs made on the Owlsboro, Myrick, and Shin Pond Schools. The school year had been lengthened to 36 weeks. The new superintendent, Mr. M.R. Keyes, was disturbed because of the small class sizes (6-10 students per school), but he was impressed that the Myrick students had established a sewing class, had conducted a Modern Health Crusade (which led to an improvement in health habits), and had held two successful school parties which earned the school some money.

1923-1924: Twenty-three students were attending the South Patten School, 24 were attending the Happy Corner School, 21 were attending the Frenchville School, and 10 were attending the Barleyville School. The Barleyville School closed in 1924.

In 1924, the girls at Patten Academy organized the not-secret Nautahee Club, which had the admirable objective of visiting shut-ins.

1925: Colonel Luther B. Rogers had a flagpole installed on the Academy grounds.

1926: The Frenchville School closed.

1926-1927: The Mount Chase Town Report stated that a "new and modern" school house had been built on the Shin Pond Road and would open in the middle of the fall term. It seems that enrollment in the Mount Chase Schools was on the increase; in fact Mr. Keyes recommended that another teacher be hired for the Myrick School since the school would probably have 45 students ranging from Grade One through Grade Eight.

1927: Superintendent of Schools Charles S. Hulbert (photo at left; Bradford) stated that all the schools were greatly overcrowded: there were too many students per classroom and not enough classrooms. And besides that, new textbooks were needed.

For the first time, there was a report in the town report on Patten Academy's agriculture program. The Hammond School on the North Road was moved to the Academy Lot and became the agriculture building. The Aggie boys were studying concrete construction, learning how to keep farm business accounts, and assisting farmers in various ways.

Colonel Luther B. Rogers passed away. He had been a dominant figure in town affairs, including serving for many years as a trustee for Patten Academy. He had loved Patten's young people and sponsored many Shin Pond outings for them. To honor Mr. Rogers, the entire P.A. student body attended his funeral and marched to the cemetery for his burial.

1928: Superintendent Hulbert reported that Patten had 14 teachers and principals who were earning an average salary of $1,146.00. The teachers and principals (some people were both a teacher and a principal) were Floyd Abbott, Wallace Elliott, Madeline Miles, Annette Lane, Lois Springer, Doris Scott, Amy Curtis, Vera Lee, Helen Currier, Clare Cunningham, Marcia Bradford, Doris Kilgore, Lois Brown (Happy Corner School), and Laurel Cunningham (South Patten School). Four of these were graduates of the University of Maine, and the rest had attended normal school. Mrs. Curtis (photo at right, Bradford) was Amy Mitchell before marrying Fred Curtis, and Mrs. Brown was Lois Philpot before marrying Gilbert Brown. Marcia Bradford was Freeman Bradford's first wife. Clare Cunningham was a Patten native who married Donald Drew and had at least two children: Donald and Sally (our much beloved Shin Pond friend Sally Drew). Doris Kilgore was a Mount Chase and Patten native who married Dr. Bernard Gagnon, son of Paul Gagnon; they later lived in Houlton. Wallace Elliott and Laurel Cunningham were also from Patten. Vera Lee was a lodger with Mabel Philpot, and Helen Currier lodged with the Boyd Harrington family. Floyd Abbot also boarded with a Patten family. Madelyn Miles was from Newport.

The superintendent had this to say about the curriculum: *The schools have been supplied with a fuller, richer material for reading. Especial emphasis has been put on oral reading for expression and upon silent and intensive reading for understanding.*

The agricultural report for Patten Academy mentioned Aggie projects with cows, sheep, and potatoes. Patten Academy agricultural students had won a Potato Judging Contest at the University of Maine.

In his report for Mount Chase, Mr. Hulbert was pleased with the quality of the teachers, the attendance of the pupils, and two of the three school buildings. However, he had this warning about the Owlsboro School: if the town did not build a new Owlsboro school in the near future, the state would penalize the town because of its lack of sanitary toilets by withholding funding for the building of a new school.

1928-1929: Evidently, the townspeople took Mr. Hulbert's warning to heart, because the Mount Chase town report for 1928-1929 indicated that there were three new school buildings which the town could be proud of. Mr. Hulbert also noted that the school account ended the fiscal year with an overdraft which couldn't be helped because there had been an increase in the tuition charge to Patten Academy, Mount Chase had twice as many students attending Patten Academy, and conveyance costs had also risen quite a bit.

1929-1930: In the Mount Chase Town Report, Mr. Hulbert commented:

> *It is advisable to wainscot the walls of the coatroom of the Owlsboro and Shin Pond schoolhouses as the walls are not substantial enough to withhold the rough usage that usually comes from a poorly disciplined school. It is not my intention to retain very long the services of a teacher who has poor discipline… I recommend that they [the walls] be wainscoted.*

1930: The Future Farmers of America had been established, and the Aggie boys had done a project on potato diseases.

1931: In the Patten Town report, the Superintendent stated that several students from Patten Academy were doing extremely well at the University of Maine. Other good news was that the cost to the town for textbooks had been reduced and the state had donated a bus body to the schools. But that was about it for good news. The depression was taking its toll on education. Superintendent Hulbert reported that teachers' salaries had been reduced throughout the state by 12.5% and the state was going to reduce its allotment to Patten schools from $2,651.10 to about $2,000.00. He stated the dilemma clearly: "As parents we know the schools must be supported. As taxpayers we know that the tax burden must be reduced." He warned against using the school budget as a good place to slash appropriations, saying, "It is a decided injustice to every little boy and girl of Patten to continue to make drastic reductions in school appropriations without reducing other appropriations accordingly." There were 109 students enrolled at Patten Academy, of which 25 were tuition students. There were four courses of study: 23 students were in the agricultural course, 28 in the commercial course, 39 in the college preparatory course, and 19 in the general course.

Attendance had always been a problem for small town schools, as many of the students missed school in order to help with farm work. Students were expected to make up the work that they missed, but this was a difficult thing for students and teachers to accomplish. In 1933, the high school decided to have a potato harvest break of two weeks. It was considered a success; sixty one students (over half of the enrollment) worked in the harvest, including picking potatoes, driving truck, and working in the potato house. And no one had to make up any work, although some students also missed school before and after the allotted two weeks. (I was surprised to read in the 1940 town report that the harvest break had been discontinued, but it was later reinstated.)

1935: Teachers' retirement funds were being paid to the state.

The depression ground on throughout the 30s with no relief. The town of Mount Chase actually de-organized (went back to being a plantation) as a remedy to it financial woes, and the town of Patten also found itself in deep financial trouble and resorted to issuing town orders to pay its teachers. These orders were discounted 10-20% upon cashing, and it was difficult to find a place that was willing to cash them. Teachers' salaries were reduced again; one teacher had a 50% reduction in pay. It was very difficult to hire new teachers because of the low pay and the practically worthless town orders. Thankfully, by 1938-1939, the town orders had been done away with.

1940: Patten Academy was using a rotating system of classes. Donations of potatoes had paid for warm-up suits for the basketball players. Physical exams for the athletes were provided by Dr. Gagnon and Dr. Woodbury. Arthur Crouse was working hard to build up a strong agricultural program at the Academy. He had contacted some of the rural teens to encourage them to enroll at PA. He had obtained $200.00 worth of new tools, and the Future Farmers of America sponsored many enjoyable activities for Academy students.

The Patten Town Hall burned down in 1940, leaving the basketball teams with no place to practice or play their games. However, they still had teams and played their out-of-town games. Superintendent Hulbert broached the idea of building a gym for Patten Academy, but it never became a reality.

Early 1940's: The Mount Chase Plantation Report for 1940-1941 included a reminder from Superintendent Hulbert that the state's Equalization Fund was based on the amount the town appropriated for education. If the town reduced its appropriation for education, the amount received from the state was reduced. On the other hand, the Mount Chase schools were in good repair and well-supplied, so it didn't make sense to raise the appropriation unless the plantation wanted to buy new seats and desks at the Myrick School.

The United States became involved in World War II in 1941, and immediately local boys and girls dropped out of school to enlist or work. Superintendent Hulbert urged them to finish school before enlisting or going to work, offering them the option of completing the usual four years of high school in less time by taking extra courses each semester or going to summer school. Several courses were offered to benefit students who were planning to join the military.

The war also caused an extreme teacher shortage in Maine, and shortages of rubber, gas, and oil were creating problems transporting students. Patten students were asked to walk to pick-up points to reduce the number of stops the bus had to make. Mount Chase had to close the Owlsboro School when its teacher resigned and another teacher could not be found to fill the position. The Shin Pond School was being taught by an uncertified teacher. Superintendent Hulbert stated that from December 1942 to spring 1944 he had lost nine teachers within the towns he served. But patriotism was still strong, and students were urged to buy war savings stamps. Superintendent Hulbert wrote, "We should keep in mind that the public school is the cornerstone of democracy, and the training of our boys and girls for the responsibilities of citizenship is one of the real essentials even in this period of stress."

In 1941, the Patten Academy Alumni Fund raised more than enough money to supplement the insurance money to build Founders' Memorial Hall on the same site where the Town Hall had stood. I was impressed with how quickly the town built new structures in those days even though they went up with manual labor.

As the depression eased in the early 1940s, Superintendent Hulbert made an appeal to the towns to restore teachers' salaries to what they had been before 1931. He stated that the cost of living was going up and wages in other places of work were being increased. There was a shortage of teachers throughout the state. He also made an appeal to the town that the roads be better plowed. He said students were missing school because the bus could not pick them up. He also wanted the school yards plowed as a convenience to teachers and students trying to enter the buildings. An ample and nutritional school lunch was available to students who didn't go home for lunch. There were about 340 students enrolled in Grades 1-8, with 57 of them being conveyed by bus. Sports programs at the Academy, including basketball, were cut, partly because a significant number of eligible players quit school and enlisted.

1943: The agricultural instructor at Patten Academy, Mr. Crouse (photo from Bradford), had been appealing to the town to build a new farm-shop building. He warned that the state would take back $1,200.00 worth of tools it had provided to the agriculture program if an adequate shop was not constructed. He said that the building could be used by local farmers to repair their farm machinery. He got his new building in 1943 when a previously-built structure was hauled to the Academy lot, although it took several years more before the building was finished and even longer to get a heating system installed in the building.

1943-44: In the Mount Chase Plantation Report, Hulbert criticized the plantation for not heeding his recommendations for the school budget. He wrote: *You have a large overdraft in your school account this year which is always an eye sore to me and I can't see what a town gains by doing anything like that, especially when the recommendation is high enough. A budget is very carefully worked out for you and included in this report and the recommendation made is in my opinion very conservative.*

Is it just me, or did Superintendent Hulbert like to get his little digs in from time to time? I shouldn't have said that, because on reflection, Mr. Hulbert served the area very capably as Superintendent of Schools from 1927 until 1944, throughout the extreme economic hardships of the Great Depression and the onset of World War II.

1944-1945: A new superintendent took over the job of running the schools. Mr. Ernest Tupper (who had formerly been the Academy principal) immediately made an appeal to build a second story on the Primary Building to create more classrooms. He cited the cases of Miss Reed, the 3rd and 4th grade teacher and also a principal, who had 61 students in her classroom and Mrs. Curtis who had 40-50 students in her 7th and 8th grade classes. The normal or recommended load for a teacher at that time was 30 pupils. The South Patten School had been closed.

Mr. Willis Phair became the principal of Patten Academy. The students and townspeople were pleased when he reinstated the sport of basketball. Soon the basketball schedule was back in full swing. Iowa Educational Development Tests had been given to Grade 9-12 students, and everyone was pleased that their average scores compared favorably with the nationwide averages.

1945-47: In the Mount Chase Plantation Report, Superintendent Tupper stated that the Myrick School was the only school open for Mount Chase students; its enrollment was 32 students from sub-primary through Grade Eight. Eight Mount Chase students were attending the elementary schools in Patten, and Mount Chase was paying tuition for seventeen students enrolled at Patten Academy. The next year, Mount Chase sent ten Shin Pond elementary students to Patten and paid tuition for thirteen secondary students. Barbara Sargent, daughter of Carroll and Florence Sargent, was attending Ricker Classical Institute.

1946: The Patten voters evidently decided it was time for real action and that they needed to go beyond adding a floor to the Primary Building. A building committee was formed, and a sinking fund was established for the purpose of saving money to build a brand new school. In 1946, Superintendent Tupper urged the town to get started on the plans for the new school so that the town would qualify for state funds which would amount to one-fourth the cost of the building.

1947: The problem of Patten's large classrooms was eased somewhat by hiring one teacher for each grade. A temporary solution for needed classroom space was achieved by taking over the Commercial room in the Academy and dividing a room at the Primary school. Unfortunately, the Commercial students were moved into the Agriculture building, displacing those students, who had just been celebrating because their building had finally been set on a concrete foundation.

In an effort to ease the overcrowded classrooms, the superintendent considered having a "platoon" schedule, in which half of the elementary students came in the morning and half came in the afternoon. He also broached the idea of doing away with the sub-primary class. Neither idea passed muster with the townspeople.

The boys' basketball team, coached by Principal Willis Phair, won the New England Championship game in Boston. (See Chapter Six for more information and a photo of the team.)

1948: $15,119.08 had been saved for the new school building.

1949: The Grammar School, located on the north side of Patten Academy, was built at a cost of $38,325.26. The builder in charge was Carl Grant, but many local residents helped in the project through labor and donations. It was a one-story building with a full basement. It would house grades four through seven. After it was built, all the cafeteria meals were prepared and served in the Grammar School basement. A nice baseball field was constructed behind the building.

1949: There were 334 students enrolled in Patten Primary (grades sub-primary through three) and Patten Grammar (grades four through seven), and 108 students were attending Patten Academy (grades eight through twelve). Clive Hatt and Vinal Heath were bus drivers, and Talmadge Bishop was the janitor. The high school had a successful magazine drive, and scholarships were awarded to students who had shown the most improvement in their schoolwork.

1951-1953: Hersey students started attending Patten Primary, Patten Grammar, and Patten Academy in 1951. There were now 475 students enrolled in school; this increased to 488 in 1952-53. (Evidently area couples had been doing their fair share to create the baby boomer generation.) The average yearly salary for a teacher was around $1,500.00. The English Department at the Academy had decided to split the English courses into four divisions based on ability. The principal felt this would eliminate frustration for some students and provide challenges for others. Playground equipment was purchased for the primary school. Bus drivers from these years were Robert Drew, Vinal Heath, Clive Hatt, Hazen Rogers, and H.R Robinson.

1952-1953: Food from government surpluses and the Farm Bureau and donations from the Patten Lion's Club and the Patten Women's Club helped the school lunch program continue to be a great success. By 1953-54, 260 lunches were being served daily. Students who could pay were charged twenty cents, while needy children got free lunches. Leftover food was donated to poor families.

1954-55: In the Patten Town Report, Superintendent Tupper responded to criticism of the schools' reading programs by encouraging parents to visit school and by urging the town to consider hiring a teacher skilled in teaching remedial reading. There were fifteen teachers teaching 452 students, which is an average of 30 students per teacher. Mr. Tupper said the ideal class size was 20-25 students. Physical education was added to the curriculum for fourth grade and up in 1955, and the school took over ownership of Founders Memorial Hall to take advantage of the state's reimbursement of 55% of expenses other than repairs. Class dues were abolished. The sub-primary class was discontinued.

1956: There were 30 boys enrolled in the agriculture program. New equipment had led to increased time spent in shop work, although the shop was still not being heated and couldn't be used when the weather was cold. The FFA was involved in many extra-curricular activities such as participating in Farm Home Week in Orono, attending Agricultural District meetings, and holding an annual Father and Son Banquet. At the Farmers Fair at the University of Maine in Orono, the Patten boys won a trophy for finishing first place in the sheep judging.

1957-1958: Evening agriculture classes were being offered to the public, with a specific goal of reaching out to those boys who had dropped out of school.

The primary school went from a three-grade system to a five-group system. Students would progress through the groups according their reading ability. Therefore, it could take three to five years to get through primary school. (I started school in 1957 and went through Group Two (taught by Mrs. Lois Brown), Group Four (taught by Mrs. Mary Campbell), and Group Five (taught by Mrs. Cordelia Brooks.) Mrs. Nedra Nightingale was usually the Group Five teacher, but she didn't teach that group that year because her daughter Carolyn was in the class. The other teachers at Patten Primary when I was there were Miss Anna Hanson and Mrs. Ella Bishop.

Half of Patten Academy's seniors were going on to higher education. A testing system for the freshman class was implemented to help them select appropriate courses and reduce the number of students who dropped out of school.

In Mount Chase Plantation, voters authorized the appointing of a school committee to study the benefits of school consolidation.

1959-1960: The Aggie shop finally got a heating system! Edwin Plissey, the agriculture teacher, reported that the Patten Academy agriculture students had been chosen to participate in a National Young Farmer Training Study. The boys took a trip to Kansas City, Missouri to attend a National FFA convention. As projects in town, they did some landscaping on the school lot, operated a seed sales outlet, established forage demonstration plots on land owned by Perley Harris and Patten Academy, and maintained a skating rink in the winter. The rink (photo above courtesy of Jennifer Bates Ryan) was on the fire pond behind Morse's garage and even had a hut where you could buy hot chocolate, chips, and candy (and get warm).

1960-1961: $2,000.00 worth of scientific equipment had been bought, as well as five new typewriters and a new fluid duplicator for Patten Academy. The FFA was awarded a trophy by the New England Meat and Wool Growers for having won the sheep judging contest four years in a row. The boys went to a Farmers Fair at the University of Maine in Orono and took a trip to central Maine to visit dairy and poultry farms. They also raised two acres of seed potatoes and sold light bulbs, seeds, and tractor cushions to raise money for their activities.

I started Grammar School in 1960. My teachers in Grades Four through Seven were Mrs. Violet McIntire, Mrs. Madelyn Howes, Mrs. Judy Heath, and Mrs. Dorothy McPhee.

1961-1963: The Academy curriculum was enriched by adding French III and a fourth year of math. Two biology courses were now offered, one for the general course of study and one for the college course of study. Ancient and Medieval History replaced Civic Government. Reading was added to the Grade Eight program. Lloyd McKenney replaced Talmadge Bishop as janitor, and cooks at this time were Eva Deschane, Agnes Campbell, and Virgie Willett. Students from Crystal, Mount Chase, Hersey, Moro, Stacyville, and T6R6 were paying tuition to attend Patten's schools.

1961-1962: As far back as 1956, consolidation had been a hot topic of discussion, and it became even more so with the passage of the Sinclair Act in 1957. The goal of the Sinclair Act was to save money by consolidating schools into districts, thus closing many small schools and reducing teaching and administrative staffs. In 1961-1962, a study was done to examine the feasibility of forming a Maine School Administration District made up of the towns of Mount Chase, Patten, Sherman, and Stacyville.

1963: At their town meetings in March of 1963, the citizens of the four towns approved by vote the forming of a district, and MSAD #25 was created. Mr. Ronald Susee was the first superintendent for MSAD #25. The towns selected the Horseman lot on Route 11 a few miles north of Stacyville as the site for the new high school. It was located halfway from the farthest points within the district, it had adequate drainage, it had ample space for the school and an athletic field, and it was naturally sheltered from wind and snow. The chart below gives data for the enrollment of students in 1963.

Myrick School (Mount Chase)	22	418 total students, north end	Total district enrollment: 862 students
Patten Primary School	119		
Patten Grammar School	133		
Patten Academy	144		
Sherman Elementary School	136	444 total students, south end	
Sherman High School	180		
Sherman Station Elementary School	128		

1964: The second superintendent of MSAD #25 was Robert Jones, who had been the high school principal in Patten. He outlined the way the towns were responsible for financial support of the schools. Using a formula based on each town's evaluation, each town's contribution to the MSAD #25 budget in 1964 is shown in the chart below, along with other revenues.

Town	Rate of apportionment	Amount of revenue	Total amounts
Mount Chase	8.5%	$9,174.00	$114,675.00 from towns
Patten	39.95%	$45,870.00	
Sherman	23.30%	$27,522.00	
Stacyville	28.35%	$32,109.00	
Tuition students		$20,373.11	$159,840.80 from other sources
State of Maine		$138,391.12	
Miscellaneous		1,076.57	
TOTAL REVENUES FOR 1964 $274,515.80			

Expenditures in 1964 amounted to $293,725.11, thus ending the year with an over-expended balance of $19,209.31. Mr. Jones blamed unexpected emergencies related to the existing buildings and bus expenses. He asked the town to come up with $121,581.64 for the coming school year.

1965-1967: Money problems continued to plague the new SAD. When the plans for the new building (drawn up by Allied Engineering from Gorham, Maine) were put out to bid to building contractors, the lowest bid was $507,558.00 by A.E. Flewelling Company of Crouseville. However, the district did not have enough money to meet the bid, so construction had to be delayed a year to raise more money.

The Neighborhood Youth Corps was established in 1966. The Stanford Achievement Test was given to elementary students, and the Iowa Test of Educational Development was given to secondary (high school) students. The results were used to evaluate current curriculum and plan for future curriculum.

1967: The consolidation of the high schools was a practical move from an economic and educational standpoint, but it was by no means a unanimously popular notion. Besides the usual reluctance to give up a home town school, Patten and Sherman were fierce competitors on the basketball court. In fact, the two teams played against each other in the Eastern Maine Basketball tournament championship game during their last year as separate schools. The photo below was printed in the 1967 edition of the Patten Academy yearbook, *The Mirror*. Both teams are shown—the team with the bigger plaque (Sherman High School) won the championship game. Al Pulkkinen was the coach for the P.A. Eagles, and Ron Marx coached the Sherman team.

But it all finally came together, and in 1967, Patten Academy and Sherman High School held their last graduation ceremonies.

1968: High school students began attending Katahdin High School, located on Route 11 in Stacyville, between Patten and Sherman. It only took a couple of months before Sherman and Patten kids were best of friends, and Katahdin High School began producing some great basketball teams!

Back in Patten, Grade Seven joined Grade Eight in the Academy building to become Patten Junior High School.

Kindergarten classes had been reinstated in Patten and Sherman, and Headstart provided a pre-school program.

The Neighborhood Youth Corp was still providing employment for young people. The pay scale was $1.25 an hour for in-school projects and $1.40 per hour for summer work. The teens painted the exterior of Patten Primary School, sanded floors in Patten and Sherman Station Schools, did landscaping at KHS, cleaned buildings, and organized the library at KHS.

Title I money from the state funded the Developmental Reading Program for Stacyville Elementary, Patten Grammar, and Katahdin High School. Title II money was used for library books and for science, language arts, and vocational materials.

1969: I was a member of the second class to graduate from Katahdin High School. The cougar had been chosen as our school mascot, and our school colors were black and red.

1975: The consolidation movement kept moving forward, and in 1975, Sherman and Patten students in Grades Six through Eight began attending Katahdin Junior High School. This was located in the former Katahdin High School building on the east side of Route 11, and a new high school building was built directly across the road on the west side of Route 11.

Patten Academy was torn down.

1976: A group of local citizens opened the Calvary Christian School on Ash Hill on the South Patten Road.

1977: The 1970's were a difficult time financially for the Patten and Mount Chase area, and the school budget was directly affected as well. In 1977, Superintendent of Schools Albert Ellis revealed in a report that MSAD #25 was $277,000.00 in debt. He immediately tackled this deficit and started a recovery process by reducing staff hours, laying off staff, putting jobs out to bid, and implementing a new accounting system.

1978-1981: Mr. Ellis reported that some of the money had been paid back on the deficit. By 1979, it had been reduced to $68,000.00. In 1980, the district towns unexpectedly had to provide funds to go along with energy audit grants for energy saving renovations, but in 1981, Mr. Ellis reported that the deficit had been erased. It was decided to keep the elementary schools in the district open for the time being, and the buildings were being renovated.

1982: Calvary Christian School had 35 students.

1986: Harvest recess was discontinued.

1987: The Patten Women's Club created a beautiful park on the Academy lot. Named Patten Academy Alumni Park, it has a bandstand, walkways, picnic tables, benches, and lots of flowers. The centerpiece of the park is a monument with the bell from the Academy building. Located between the park and Main Street is a tennis court. The park has become a community center for church services, Patten Pioneer Days events, and other activities.

1995: Calvary Christian School closed.

1997-1998: In a two-step process, Patten Primary and Patten Grammar Schools consolidated with Sherman and Stacyville Elementary Schools. They moved into the former Katahdin Junior High School building, which was renamed Katahdin Elementary School. It was time of transition for me personally; I had been teaching at Patten Grammar and now had to move my classroom from a big room to a smaller room, plus I had to leave home in the morning ten minutes earlier than I was used to! I survived and grew to love being a teacher at Katahdin Elementary School.

The junior high students moved into the high school building, now called Katahdin Middle and High School (photo at right).

2004: Patten Grammar School was burned down by the Patten Fire Department. This lot is now Patten Community Playground and a parking lot. The athletic field is still used on a regular basis; in fact, games can be played after dark there since new lights were installed in 2006.

2009: The Patten Primary building burned down. At that time, the Will family had purchased the building and was living there. It was the town's last visible link to the school system that had educated Patten and Mount Chase students for 160 years. This photo of Patten Primary was taken around 1980. The sign on the front of the building states the year that Patten Primary was built: 1905.

2011: Further consolidation occurred when the state once again put on a big push to combine school districts, even threatening schools with hefty fines for not attempting to consolidate. Although the local schools did not want to further consolidate, they felt they had no choice in the matter. The most logical consolidation scenario was to combine Southern Aroostook Community School with MSAD #25. In 2011, Regional School Unit #50 was formed; it included students from Island Falls, Oakfield, Dyer Brook, Merrill, Smyrna, Sherman, Benedicta, Stacyville, Patten, Mount Chase, Hersey, and Moro. No schools were closed, but administrative and some teaching services were combined across the two schools. The RSU served about 750 Pre-K to 12 students. Although negativity threatened staff morale, at no time did the education of children in the RSU suffer. Both schools continued to address the curriculum seriously and worked hard to keep up with state and federal mandates. Workshops provided opportunities for both parts of the union to share what was working well.

2014: The recent consolidation continued to be an unpopular movement, especially when talk turned to closing the Katahdin schools and bussing students to the Southern Aroostook building. The biggest problem was geography: RSU #50 was one of the largest geographical districts in the state, encompassing 460 square miles. The Southern Aroostook building was not centrally located within the RSU. Katahdin students were already putting in a great deal of time just getting to and from school, and parents understandably didn't want to add more hours to those bus trips.

With mixed feelings, I retired from teaching in June, 2014. I knew I would miss being around children and would miss my colleagues, but teaching had become a very demanding job. The Common Core Curriculum was being established, KES was going to be implementing a new math program, the reading program needed to be updated, and I was going to have to learn how to use a Smart Board! Listen to me whining; I should have been grateful that I wasn't one of those teachers in 1900 who had to teach fifty students in three different grades in one classroom!

2015-2016: A formal proposal to close Katahdin Middle/High School and send its students to the Southern Aroostook building created even further dissent in the former MSAD #25 communities. In a local grass roots movement, representatives from Patten, Mount Chase, Hersey, Moro, Sherman, Benedicta, and Stacyville formed a committee named *Leading Our Communities' Access to Learning*. LOCAL immediately began garnering support for keeping KMHS open. Besides the geographical challenges of consolidation, LOCAL was also frustrated at the school board's inability to pass a budget that sustained and satisfied all the member towns. LOCAL's first success was the part they played in convincing the school board to keep Katahdin Middle/High School open. At the time of this writing, the committee is exploring a withdrawal from the RSU and the formation of an Alternative Organizational Structure which would keep the Katahdin Schools open.

Controversy is the norm when public affairs are discussed. It makes a lot of people uncomfortable (me included), but it is bound to arise when people are sincerely concerned about the issues. And that is always better than apathy. Over the years in Patten and Mount Chase history, many heated discussions have taken place on the topic of education. It always comes back to the same questions: How can the town best provide a quality education for its young people while not over-burdening its taxpayers? What constitutes a *quality education*? What is the best scenario for our children?

Obviously, the area citizens have always come up with good answers to these questions. The area's elementary schools educated children well enough for them to attend area high schools, and the high schools educated teenagers well enough for them to attend college. The schools have provided rigorous and appropriate curricula and have expected their students to meet high standards.

This concern to provide a quality education was also the biggest consideration as consolidation began to occur. It has never been about neglecting education to save money. Many generations of students have been proud to say they attended Mount Chase, Patten, and Katahdin schools. I hope that wherever Patten and Mount Chase students go to school in the future, the people of the communities will feel that love for and pride in their schools that they have always felt in the past.

COLLEGES IN MAINE

If they wanted to further their education, students who graduated from Patten Academy or Katahdin High School had plenty of colleges to pick from. The chart below gives some information about some of the colleges that have been established in Maine.

NAME OF COLLEGE	DATE EST.	LOCATION/COMMENTS
Bowdoin College	1794	Brunswick
Colby College	1813	Waterville
Bangor Theological Seminary	1814	Bangor, closed in 2013
Bates College	1855	Lewiston
Farmington Normal School U of M at Farmington	1863	Farmington
University of Maine	1865	Orono
Eastern State College (buildings now part of Maine Maritime)	1867	Castine, closed in 1942
Western Normal School University of Southern Maine	1878	Gorham
Madawaska Training School University of Maine at Fort Kent	1878 1970	Madawaska, Fort Kent
Beal College	1891	Bangor
Thomas College Maine Criminal Justice Academy	1894 1970	Waterville/Vassalboro
Husson College/University	1898	Bangor
Aroostook Normal School Aroostook State Teachers College Aroostook State College U of M at Presque Isle	1903 1952 1965 1968	Presque Isle
Washington State Normal School U of M at Machias	1909	Machias
Maine Maritime Academy	1914	Castine
Northern ME Comm. College Northern ME Vocational Technical Institute	1961	Presque Isle
Unity College	1965	Unity
Eastern ME Comm. College	1966	Bangor
Washington County Community College	1969	Calais

I mentioned earlier that the students at Patten Academy had Greek organizations, which were eventually outlawed by the state at the high school level. However, Greek fraternities and sororities remain standard institutions in most colleges and universities today, and their members have a strong loyalty to their organizations and each other. At the time he enlisted in the Union Army during the Civil War, Edwin Searle Rogers, the second son of Dr. Luther and Hannah Rogers, was a member of the Delta Kappa Epsilon Fraternity at Colby College, and he proudly wore his fraternity pin on his soldier's uniform. In 1864, as he lay dying on the battlefield after being shot in the battle at Cold Harbor, Virginia, he was attended by a Confederate doctor. This doctor recognized Edwin's fraternity pin as the same fraternity he himself had been a member of at an Alabama college. The doctor removed the pin and sent it to his parents in Maine with a note explaining the circumstances. In 1897, a Bowdoin College DKE member named John Clair Minot heard this story and was moved to write this poem about Edwin and the Confederate doctor.

BROTHERS IN DKE

Upon a southern battle-field the twilight shadows fall;
The clash and roar are ended, and the evening bugles call.
The wearied hosts are resting where the ground is stained with red,
And o'er the plain between them lie the wounded and the dead.

And out upon the sodden field, where the armies fought all day,
There came a group of soldiers who wore the rebel gray.
But peaceful was their mission upon the darkened plain:
They came to save their wounded and lay at rest the slain.

And tenderly their hands performed the work they had to do,
And one among them paused beside a wounded boy in blue,
A Northern lad, with curly hair and eyes of softest brown,
Whose coat of blue was red with blood that trickled slowly down.

A bullet hole was in his breast, and there alone he lay
At night upon the battle-field, and moaned his life away.
The rebel paused beside him, and in the lantern's light
He saw upon the soldier's breast a fair familiar sight.

It was the pin of DKE, the diamond, stars and scroll,
The emblem of a brotherhood that bound them soul to soul.
He raised his hand and quickly tore his coat of gray apart,
And showed the wounded soldier a Deke pin o'er his heart.

Then close beside the Yankee dropped the rebel to his knee,
And their hands were clasped together in the grip of DKE.
"I'm from Theta," said the Yankee, and he tried to raise his head.
"I'm from Psi, in Alabama," were the words the rebel said.

"Brothers from the heart forever"—nothing more was left to say,
Though one was clad in Northern blue and one in Southern gray.
But the Northern lad was dying; his voice was faint at best
As he murmured out his messages to "mother and the rest."

And as the rebel soothed him, with his head upon his knee,
He heard him whisper "Bowdoin" and "Dear old DKE."
And he bandaged up the bosom that was torn by rebel shot;
And bathed the brow with water where the fever fires were hot;

And kissed him for his mother, and breathed a gentle prayer
As the angel's wings were fluttering above them in the air.
And to a lonely country home, far in the heart of Maine,
A letter soon was carried from that Southern battle plain.

It told about the conflict, and how he bravely fell,
Who was the son and brother in that home beloved so well.
It told the simple story of the night when he had died—
All written by the rebel Deke whom God sent to his side.

And when it all was written, the letter sent within
A little lock of curly hair and a battered diamond pin.
And thirty years have passed away, but the simple relics are
Of all a mother's treasures dear, the dearest still by far.

THE WCTU READING ROOM AND VETERAN'S MEMORIAL LIBRARY

Although I could find no exact dates or locations, there has been a library in Patten since the mid-1800's. In 1915, the Women's Christian Temperance Union (WCTU) set up a library and reading room in the town hall. In 1919, this library had 1,218 books. The WCTU made a formal request for a librarian, which was granted by 1921.

In 1928, the Patten Memorial Library opened in the building that had once been the Baptist Church. This building is the oldest public building in Patten, dating back to 1845. The renovations to the church to turn it into a library were paid for the most part by donations amounting to $1,500.00. In spite of its age, the library is still a beautiful building and has been well-maintained over the years.

The librarians since 1929 have been Nora Palmer (1929-1934), Mrs. I.G. Finch (1934-1959), Mrs. Mildred Grant (1959-1963), Mrs. Katherine K. S. Rogers (1963-1974), Mrs. Christine Shorey (1974-2001), Ms. Susan Hess (2001-2003), and Ms. Doris DeRespino (2003 to present). Over these years, the librarians have amassed a remarkable collection of books, from very old books to books hot off the press. They have encouraged children to visit the library by offering story hour at various times and inviting the local school teachers to bring their classes to the library. Here are some other important events in the life of the library:

1964-1965: The library was renamed Veterans Memorial Library.

1970: The library sponsored a Traveling Art Collection.

1974: The Patten Town Report was dedicated to Kathleen K.S. Rogers (photo at right), who had recently died. Mrs. Rogers, like all the librarians, had been a devoted public servant who worked hard to make life better for local citizens. She instituted story hour for preschoolers and invited classes from Patten Primary and Patten Grammar to visit the library weekly. Mrs. Rogers continued to stock the shelves after her death: in her will, Mrs. Rogers left $2,000.00 to the library. Christine Shorey took over librarian duties.

The library underwent a major renovation when the wall separating a back room and the main library was removed. With this extra space, a very nice children's area was created in the back part of the library.

1982-1985: The outside north wall of the library had to be repainted due to a fire in the house next door. The inside of the library was painted. The foundation was repaired and painted. The library began holding an annual book sale during Patten Pioneer Days. Computers were now available for public use. Mrs. Shorey continued the practices of story hour and weekly student visits.

1989: Christine Shorey reported that a new furnace had been installed and the building was in good shape. The library had won a grant from the Rose and Sam Rudman Library Trust Fund. Around this time, the National Starch and Chemical Foundation in Island Falls gave a hefty donation to the library every year.

1991: New shelves were built, and the floor and woodwork were painted. The World War I memorial was cleaned. Chris and Don Shorey chose a piece of granite for a new memorial. The Patten Women's Club decorated a tree in front of the library with the names of soldiers who were serving in the Persian Gulf.

1994: The outside of the library got a facelift with new vinyl siding, and the brickwork was painted black. The town erected the new war memorial, which honored veterans from conflicts from 1941-1994. Names of veterans from conflicts between 1994 and 2001 were added later.

2001: Christine Shorey retired from her position as town librarian. She had run the library very capably for twenty-seven years. She promoted use of the library by holding story time, by inviting school classes to visit the library regularly, by setting up computers, and by filling shelf after shelf with books, magazines, and videos that appealed to every age group.

2002: Librarian Susan Hess reported that the library got a $10,000 New Century Grant which was used to catalogue the books into a computer system.

2004: Librarian Doris DeRespino reported that the library got a $20,000 grant from the Stephen King Foundation. It was used to create shelving and storage.

2005: Using money the library got through a grant from the Maine State Library, two new computers and DSL high speed internet were installed in the library. The library also got a $500.00 grant to purchase materials to use to preserve older books.

2006: The library had 10,000 books entered into its computer system. Another computer was added for public use.

2008: The library was awarded a $5,000 grant from the Stephen and Tabitha King foundation. This was used to build new front steps and a ramp. A $300 grant from the Libri Foundation was matched by the family and friends of Wendell Harvey.

2009-2010: The library's chimney was rebuilt, and a new roof was put on the library.

2011: Using grant money, the library purchased three new computers and was offering free access to Skype and Ancestry.Com. A Stephen and Tabitha King Foundation grant of $10,000 paid for new carpeting. A $400 Libri grant, matched by $200 from individual donations, bought new books.

Patten is indeed fortunate to have this beautiful library. Patten's citizens have always supported the library financially to keep the building in excellent condition and to purchase books and other library materials, and the library has always been staffed by capable and dedicated librarians who have kept it a vital part of the community through the years.

THE LIBRARY OF MY CHILDHOOD

On a mid-summer day when it was too hot to do most anything,
I would walk the shaded street to the library.
I would climb the steps two at a time carrying an armload of books
I'd already read.

I'd push open the heavy church door
And step into the magical coolness of a room full of treasures,
A space full of thousands of books,
I hadn't already read.

I'd shyly hand my returns over to the librarian—
Mrs. Rogers with her snow white hair or Mrs. Grant with her poor gnarled hands.
I'd walk quietly to the back of the library and scan the shelves to find some books
I hadn't already read.

Did I want to solve mysteries with Nancy Drew,
Or learn about Jewish traditions with All-of-a-Kind Family?
Maybe I'd be a nurse with Sue Barton or pick out a Little House Book
Although there weren't any I hadn't already read.

Did I want to laugh with Beverly Cleary,
Or get to know characters from the past with Lenski or Speare?
And I must check out the special table where the librarian put new books
No one had already read.

So many books…. but it was time to check out my choices
And hurry back home with hours of enjoyment in my arms,
Hours that I could spend reading books
I hadn't already read.
(And maybe even some I'd already read.)

CHAPTER ELEVEN: HEALTH CARE AND EMERGENCY SERVICES

DOCTORS, HOSPITALS, AND CLINICS

Can you imagine how uneasy Patten's first settlers must have felt during the years before there was a doctor in town? They didn't have to wait too many years for health care, though; around 1841, Dr. Luther Rogers established a practice in the community. The chart below lists some of the other doctors and physician's assistants who have served the communities of Patten and Mount Chase throughout the years. The headings are the time periods that I used to divide the first part of this history into chapters. A doctor under a particular heading practiced medicine at some point during that time period, but not necessarily throughout the whole period.

1865-1889	1890-1917	1918-1945
Luther B. Rogers	Benjamin C. Woodbury	Elmer J. Farnham
Jesse Howe	Benjamin Woodbury	G. Frank Woodbury
Fisher	G. Frank Woodbury	Millard P. Hanson
Sandford	O.F. Best	George Hoekzema
H.A. Bascom	Elmer J. Farnham	Bernard Gagnon
E.W. Berry		
Frederick Bigelow		
O.F. Best		
Hubert Best		
William T. Merrill		
Benjamin C. Woodbury		
1946-1968	**1969-1999**	**2000-2016**
G. Frank Woodbury	Craig Sponseller	Ronald Blum
David Ascher	Gus Konturas	Ted Pettengill
John Dennison	Ted Pettengill	Martin Hrynick
Joseph Herson	James Guanci	Robert LaMorgese
Maniuchehr Mozaheney	Ronald Blum	Lisa Neilsen
J.B. Leith Hartman	Martin Hrynick	David Thao
	James Ryan	KVHC
	David Caron	
	Audie Horn	
	Cecilia Pinter	

The doctors or P.A.s who served the area for long periods of time and actually made their homes here were Luther Rogers, Benjamin C. Woodbury, G. Frank Woodbury, Ted Pettengill, Ron Blum, and Martin Hrynick. O.F. Best and Elmer J. Farnham also owned Patten Drug Company. Dr. Best was responsible for Patten's first public water system, and Dr. Farnham sold automobiles!

The first hospital built within a reasonable distance of Patten and Mount Chase was the Aroostook General Hospital, which opened in 1903 in Houlton. The Madigan Hospital in Houlton was established around 1912. Aroostook Hospital closed in the early 1970s, and Madigan closed around 1976, when Houlton Regional Hospital (photo at left) was built. The Millinocket Community Hospital (now Millinocket Regional Hospital) opened in 1955. For many years, the closest hospital to Patten and Mount Chase was the Emma V. Milliken Memorial Hospital in Island Falls. It opened in 1937 and closed in 1974. Most of the local baby boomers were born in this hospital. Patten and Mount Chase supported the Milliken Hospital with yearly appropriations and in 1971 joined a Hospital Administrative District along with other towns in the area.

In the days before immunizations, antibiotics, and good sanitation practices, an infectious disease could cause practically a whole village to become sick at the same time. Complications from the common cold, the flu, tuberculosis, diphtheria, whooping cough, polio, typhoid fever, and measles could cause death. As medical researchers studied these diseases, they learned that isolating an ill person could prevent the spreading of the illness. Patten had a "pest house" in the early 1900s where people with an infectious disease could be quarantined. Researchers also learned that some of these diseases were preventable through immunization. The Patten Town Report for 1917 states that 546 people were vaccinated by Dr. G.F. Woodbury and Dr. E.J. Farnham. In 1921, a sanitation law for schools was passed, which was another giant step forward in preventing communicable diseases. In 1928, the first known antibiotic, penicillin, helped people fight off some of these diseases, and soon other types of antibiotics were discovered. These discoveries and practices gave humans the edge over many germs and viruses that had once been deadly.

Up until around the 1960s, Patten and Mount Chase were well-served by doctors, but during the 1960s and early 1970s, there were periods when residents had to go out of town for medical attention. Doctor William Daniels of Sherman and Dr. Clyde Swett of Island Falls and Smyrna capably served the whole Katahdin Valley area during those years.

Seeing the need for local health care, the Patten Town Report for 1961-62 contained this article in the warrant for the March 1962 town meeting: *Article 13: To see if the town will vote to elect a committee of five whose duty it will be to carry out the plans of erecting a medical center under the direction and assistance of the Sears Roebuck Community Medical Assistance plan.*

This idea did not become Patten's solution to the need for health care, but a few years later, the Patten Medical Center committee enticed a doctor to come to Patten by remodeling the Gould house to make a combination medical office and home residence. In 1965-1966, the committee hired Dr. Maniuchehr Mozayeney. Unfortunately, the doctor left the next year to pursue higher education and seek employment elsewhere.

There had been no luck getting a federal grant, so a fund drive to raise $50,000 was undertaken to build a medical center. After a year of seeking donations, the town realized that they would not be able to raise the full amount in that manner and decided that $20,000 would have to be appropriated through taxes. A Medical Center Construction Committee was established in 1968.

Finally, in 1974, Katahdin Valley Health Center was established. The first office was in the back of Merrow's Department Store. Gus Konturas and Craig Sponseller were the first P.A.'s who worked for KVHC; Ruth Brooks was the nurse and Jean Edwards was the secretary and bookkeeper. By 1974, there was an M.D. on staff, and P.A. Ted Pettengill and Dr. Ronald Blum joined the staff in 1978. KVHC saw 5,043 patients that year and did immunizations and physicals for pre-school and school-age children. KVHC also sponsored a cancer screening clinic. Dr. James Guanci was hired in 1980.

In 1981, KVHC moved into a new building at the site on the corner of Houlton and Gardner Streets where the Oddfellows Hall had stood. The building included three examination rooms, an emergency/trauma room, and x-ray facilities. A new fund-raising effort was successful in raising $14,500.00 to contribute to expenses. The clinic saw over 6,000 patients in 1981 and held a hypertension clinic, a diabetes workshop, and glaucoma testing. Immunizations and free flu shots were offered as well. At various times throughout the years, KVHC has also offered dental care with Dr. Richard Engroff and mental health services.

The building was expanded in 2009.

KVCH was so successful that it was able to establish clinics in Island Falls, Houlton, Ashland, Millinocket, and Brownville. KVHC now offers a wide variety of services, including primary care, dental care, optometry, podiatry, and behavioral and occupational health care. Several KVHC sites also have pharmacies.

In 2016, KVHC opened an administration building on Ash Hill on the South Patten Road.

PUBLIC HEALTH NURSES

As I read the Patten and Mount Chase Town Reports, I was increasingly impressed with the contribution made to rural Maine communities by the Public Health Nurse organization. Beginning in the 1940s, these nurses visited each community on a regular basis and provided several essential services, including immunization. School-age children were inoculated in the schools, and pre-school children got their immunizations at clinics, many of which were sponsored in Patten in the 50s and 60s by the Women's Society for Christian Service (WSCS) of the Methodist Church. Public Health Nurses did skin tests for tuberculosis and referred people who had a positive result for a lung x-ray. In later years, they did diabetes screenings. The Visiting Nurse also made home visits for prenatal and postpartum care and care of the elderly. They educated people about communicable diseases, including venereal diseases, and the importance of good sanitation habits. Working closely with the schools, they initiated dental clinics which screened children for problems with their teeth and gums and provided the first fluoride treatments in the area. They did vision and hearing tests for preschoolers and school-age children. They assisted local doctors in giving physicals and referred children with physical problems to doctors or to organizations for "crippled" children. They educated educators about physical, emotional, and mental problems affecting their students. Katherine Donley was the first Public Health Nurse to serve the Patten and Mount Chase area. Around 1955, services were disrupted because of a shortage of nurses, but they resumed a few years later and continued until 1972 with the services of Carol Foss, Mary Crosby, Audrey McReady, and Jeannette Sherman. The towns helped fund the Visiting Nurses program with yearly contributions appropriated at town meetings, but the amount of money they came up with could never pay for all the services provided through the program. I think it is safe to say that the visiting nurses were literally life-savers.

DENTISTS AND DENTAL CARE

The first dentist in Patten was Martin B. Smiley. He was followed by June B. Robinson and Manson D. Brown in the late 1800s and early 1900s. Mrs. Robinson was married to H.G. Robinson, who was a fire warden in the Northern Penobscot area. Dr. Brown, who was from Quebec, married Annie Carpenter of Patten; she was the daughter of Ira and Ella Carpenter and the granddaughter of Emeline (Scribner) and Simeon Carpenter. Following them was Justin N. Rogers. Dr. Rogers was not related to the Patten Rogers family, but he did marry a Patten girl named Maud McLeod. They were killed in a car accident in 1913 while on their honeymoon. Dr. George Banton of Island Falls began practicing dentistry in the 1940's and had an office in Island Falls and also in the second story of the Gardner building (over Merrow's). Dr. Richard Engroff came to Patten in the 1970s, practicing first at Katahdin Valley Health Center and then opening his own office in 1995. Dick and his wife Peggy were former missionaries. They raised a family of four children in Patten and Mount Chase.

In the 1950s, the Public Health Nurse oversaw dental care for school children. Her services included sodium fluoride treatments, mouth exams, and instruction in mouth care. In the 1970s, Penquis CAP and the Chester Dental Clinic provided dental care for qualifying children.

UNDERTAKERS AND FUNERAL HOMES

This might be a good place to mention those people who made death a little easier to handle: undertakers and funeral homes. Jerome Frye was Patten's first undertaker; he arrived in town in 1844 and probably worked most of the years until 1901, when he himself died. He and his son Preston also manufactured caskets and coffins. In 1893, the Patten Town Report states that W. W. Woodbury was paid $17.00 for painting the hearse. The next undertaker I found was N. O. Raymond, who worked in Patten sometime between 1917 and 1945. Mr. Raymond also manufactured caskets and coffins. By the way, a casket is rectangular in shape and is of better quality than a coffin, which was narrower at the head and foot and widest in the shoulder area. Brown Funeral Home (owned by town dentist Manson Brown) opened sometime after 1946. Brown was bought out in 1957 by Bowers Funeral Home. The Patten branch of Bowers remained open until 1996.

TAKING CARE OF THE ELDERLY

Patten's current nursing home was once a party home! It was built in 1910 by Halbert P. Gardner, son of Ira and Helen (Darling) Gardner. Hal Gardner had served in the Maine House of Representatives from 1899-1902 and in the Maine Senate from 1903-1906. He also ran for governor of Maine in 1914, so he was something of a bigwig in those days and knew a lot of other bigwigs. He built his home with entertaining in mind. The first floor had a music room, dining room, kitchen, and living room. The second floor had six bedrooms, and there was a ballroom on the third floor! Mr. Gardner, his wife Adelaide (a Darling from Ashland), and their daughters Helen and Dorothy entertained governors, other state dignitaries, and even the ex-Vice President, Hannibal Hamlin.

The home was sold to Dyke Howe in 1916 and passed on to his son, Burton Howe. It was then sold to Clive Hatt in 1947. Mr. Hatt ran a boarding home there until 1949, when Joseph and Marjorie Nash bought it and completely redecorated it.

In 1951, the home was sold to Bob and Opal Goodall and became Rest Haven Nursing Home. In 1952, a maternity unit was established. Babies from Patten who were born here include Susan Coolong York, Gayle Bossie Noyes, and Cathy Ballard Perrin. In 1954, the building was sold to Mr. Sullivan from Lewiston. At some point after that, Howard and Marion Parker bought the building and operated it as a nursing home. Justine (Glidden) Michaud served as an LPN and administrator for forty-two years in the last half of the 1900's. The building is now owned by Dr. Steven Weisberger and managed by North Country Associates and is now known as Mountain Heights Health Care Facility. A unit called Baxter Apartments has been added on. The present staff (which coincidentally includes Gayle and Cathy who were born there) provides professional and compassionate care for the clients.

Edna Rigby of Patten also provided care to local elderly people at Friendship Manor.

AMBULANCE SERVICES

The first mention of ambulance services for Patten and Mount Chase appeared in the 1973 Patten Town Report when it was noted that George Dunn had made 56 trips with a new ambulance. In 1974, the Patten Ambulance Service was established with six participating communities: Benedicta, Hersey, Moro, Mount Chase, Sherman, and Stacyville. George Dunn was hired as a full-time attendant, and his salary was paid through a grant from CETA. Jeff Lord and Gary Bishop assisted Mr. Dunn. Listed below are other important events in the history of the Patten Ambulance Service.

1975: Kay Violette became the full-time driver and attendant, and she was assisted on 161 calls by Betty Patterson, Peggy Craig, Ruth Lane, John Roy, Iva Johnson, and Jeff Lord.

1976: The ambulance made 144 calls, 111 of which were emergencies. That year, ten new people were trained as first responder ambulance attendants. The Penobscot Consortium paid for the training and also paid for medical kits for them.

1977: A new ambulance was purchased.

1978: In 1978, the ambulance was called out 182 times. Obviously, the ambulance was being summoned on a regular basis. However, in 1978, Town Manager Donald Grant revealed that the service was carrying a consistently growing deficit because it was costing more to maintain the service that it was receiving in appropriations from the cooperating towns. The towns were charging a per capita yearly rate, which just wasn't enough to maintain the ambulance service. Inflation was rampant at that time; it cost $5,571.76 in 1974 and $28,435.97 in 1978 to keep the service operating. People who didn't pay their ambulance bills contributed to the problem. Due to the rising cost of health insurance, many of the calls were for uninsured or underinsured patients. The process for billing insurance companies of insured patients was complicated and the service did not always get reimbursed. As a solution to these financial woes, the selectmen recommended an increase to $5.00 per capita to start reducing the deficit.

1979: Even $5.00 a head wasn't enough to support the Ambulance Service, so the per capita rate was increased to $8.65.

1981: The Patten Ambulance Service Advisory Committee was established to oversee operations and the budget. The town manager would be the director of the ambulance service.

1982: The ambulance deficit was declared paid off. A new ambulance chassis was bought; $7,000.00 of its cost was already paid for.

1983-1984: An equipment reserve fund for purchasing new or used ambulances was established with an initial deposit of $6,000.00. Ironically, now that the service was in the black financially and could afford new equipment, there was a desperate need for additional drivers.

1985-1987: The per capita fee for the participating communities had gone down to $5.75. The ambulance made 155 runs in 1985, 192 in 1986, and 189 in 1987.

1988: The per capita fee was raised. There were two problems that ambulance services around the state were facing: the high cost of operation and the lack of personnel to provide medical care. The ambulance made 172 runs in 1988.

1989-1992: Patten Ambulance personnel included six Emergency Technicians (EMTs) and two drivers. They made 179 runs in 1989, 213 runs in 1990, 159 runs in 1991, and 197 runs in 1992.

1993: The Ambulance Service was still operating in the black, and a new ambulance was purchased. 151 runs were made.

1994: The ambulance made 174 runs. The EMTs were taking courses to become Intermediate Care Providers. Houlton Regional Hospital was footing the bill for this.

1995-1997: Ambulance and fire calls were now being handled by the Penobscot County Sheriff's Department, which allowed for much quicker response time. Three to five EMTs and two drivers responded to 185 calls in 1995, 177 calls in 1996, and 212 calls in 1997. Houlton and East Millinocket ambulance crews were providing Advanced Life Support services to the area covered by the Patten Ambulance Service.

1998: The Patten Ambulance Service was restructured and Edward Noyes became the director. He supervised 220 runs his first year; over 50% of those required assistance from Houlton or Millinocket's Advanced Life Support services.

1999: The ambulance made 248 runs and was now able to provide Advanced Life Support services. The ambulance was now housed at the fire house.

2000: A new ambulance and upgraded equipment were put to the test with 256 calls. By using the old ambulance for non-emergency transfers and back-up, they saved some miles on the new ambulance. The personnel continued to take courses in order to provide the best health care possible to their clients.

2001: The service was in good shape financially and was actually able to pay off a new ambulance ahead of schedule. There were 248 runs in 2001.

2002: The ambulance responded to 306 calls, 237 of which were emergencies. Kim Morse and Sylva-Jo Gallagher earned their paramedic licenses. The service got a $7,982.50 grant to provide half the cost of a Lifepak-12 Defibrillator/Cardiac Monitor.

2003: The ambulance made 354 runs, 264 of which were emergencies. There were six people providing medical services.

2004: The ambulance made 406 runs, 274 of which were emergencies. The service bought a new ambulance and updated their equipment.

2005: The ambulance made 520 runs, 298 of which were emergencies. Director Ed Noyes reported that they would not need to ask the town for any money and could in fact reduce the per capita rate to $2.00. The budget was getting a boost from the income earned through patient transfers. The service had two paramedics, two intermediate EMTs, one basic EMT, and two drivers.

2006: Director Ed Noyes was called to active military duty in June and deployed in September. Kim Morse was appointed as interim director and kept the service running smoothly. Brett Morse got his paramedic license. The service acquired another ambulance and now had three ALS systems.

2007-2010: The ambulance made about 600 runs a year with five ambulances. Personnel included three paramedics, three intermediate EMTs, two first responders, and one driver, and Ed Noyes returned from active duty.

2011-2016: Under the resumed leadership of Ed Noyes, the Patten Ambulance Service continued and still continues to provide a vital service to Patten, Mount Chase, Hersey, Moro, Stacyville, Benedicta, Sherman, and Island Falls. They continue to make transfers between medical facilities and respond to emergency calls, many of which are in remote areas outside of the villages. The staff is well-trained and professional. Those of us who live in the area greatly appreciate their services.

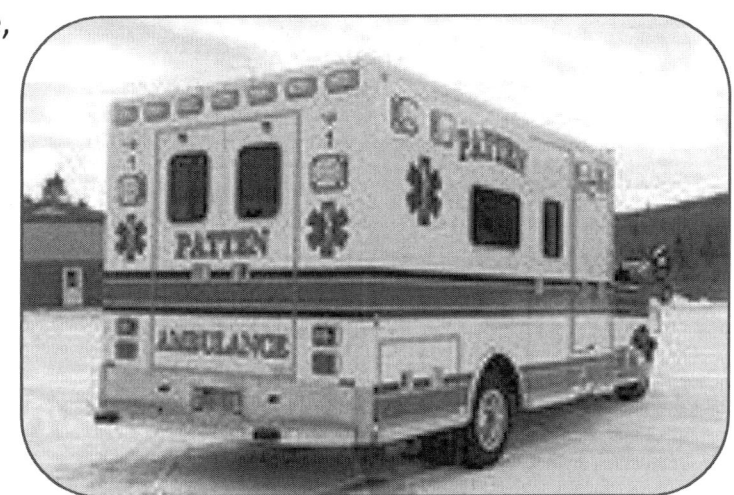

FIRE PROTECTION

Fire is one of the forces of nature that man has to some extent harnessed, but even now in the 21st century, it still causes great death and destruction. We have used technology and modern inventions and human knowledge to gain better control over fire, and we know that the number of fires and the severity of fires within communities have decreased over the years, yet we still fear fire. That fear must have been magnified for the early citizens of Patten and Mount Chase, who dealt with structure fires and forest fires on a fairly regular basis. Along with roads and education, the citizens of the towns always made sure to appropriate money for fire protection.

Patten has had a Volunteer Fire Department since 1875. Since then, the town has faithfully supported fire protection through yearly appropriations for equipment and payment of fire fighters and, in later years, a fire house. Until 1993, the town of Mount Chase depended on the Patten Fire Department and appropriated money yearly for fire protection, although the Mount Chase Fire Department was established in 1974. Besides the expected structure fires, the fire departments also dealt with forest fires from time to time. Some of the major events in Patten and Mount Chase fire protection history as well as some of the major fires are listed below. (If no town is mentioned, consider the item to be about the Patten Fire Department.)

1867: Fire destroyed buildings on Houlton Street owned by Ira Fish and Samuel Wiggins. Only the work of a bucket brigade saved other buildings in the area.

1871: The Jonathan Flanders farm buildings burned.

1874: Another Jonathan Flanders building burned.

1875: The first fire company, complete with uniforms, was established.

@1885: Charles Quincy's *Oyster Saloon*, residence, and barn burned.

1897: The first Patten Academy burned down.

1902: The town had a fire engine and a fire house.

1905: The Maine Forest Service installed its first lookout tower, and within a few years there were lookout towers scattered across the whole state, including one on Mount Chase and one at Trout Brook Farm. These towers were manned throughout the summers with the goal of detecting forest fires before they got too large to fight effectively. Several local men manned the Mount Chase tower and others in the area. James Coady of Patten was the chief fire warden for the area around Trout Brook Farm. Joseph Ingraham and John Mitchell worked at the tower on Spoon Mountain in Penobscot County and W.B. Hussey of Patten was a watchman at the Number Nine Mountain Tower in Aroostook County. At one point, Warren Darling of Smyrna manned the Mount Chase Fire Tower (photo at left).

1907: The Palmer House and the Horse Stables burned.

1911: The Shin Pond House burned. This was also the worst year for forest fires for many years. In total, 178 fires burned 99,654 acres at a cost of $289,052 in damages. (Just for comparison, 1912 was a more average year, with 94 fires burning 16,198 acres at a cost of $57,152 in damages.) The budget for 1911 was spent for the most part by mid-August, and the Forest Service had to lay off workers. Thankfully, the weather finally turned rainy near the end of August. Some of the forest fires in 1911 and 1912 were caused by lightning strikes, locomotive sparks, portable mills, landowners clearing land or burning grass. One fire in 1912 even started from a hot air balloon, and another started from a burning nest. On the plus side, the wardens were discovering fires in their early stages, the trails to the lookout towers were in good shape, and there was telephone service to many remote areas. The public was also beginning to be more careful with fire.

1917: The east side of Main Street burned flat.

1924: The Town Hall and Forrest Smith's garage burned. Fire destroyed the Merrill Mill.

1940: The Patten Town Report included the text of a new town ordinance which was designed to decrease the loss of property due to fire. It included regulations for building or placing hearths, chimneys, boilers, furnaces, ranges, and stoves; for disposing of ashes; and for electrical wiring. It warned citizens against leaving debris in public roadways. New buildings had to be inspected before a building permit would be granted. No explosives would be allowed other than on the Fourth of July.

1942: The town of Mount Chase purchased six Indian pumps from the Maine Forest Commission. These pumps proved their worth in fighting an Ackley Pond fire and a Cody (Coady? Cote?) place fire.

1948: The town water system was not meeting the minimum fire safety requirements for pressure and pipe diameter, and the system also needed to reach more parts of the town and be able to protect the plywood mill and the potato houses from fire. As these problems were addressed, forty fire hydrants were installed, as well as a standpipe and reservoir.

1953: Patten citizens voted to appropriate $15,000.00 to build a town garage and a fire house.

1954: A new Patten fire house was built on Dearborn Street. Several fire ponds had been dug around town, and work was still being done on the Shin Pond Road fire pond. A new 500 gallon-per-minute pump was purchased. A fire in Patten destroyed the homes of Stan Johnson and Eltha Mitchell and the Beehive. The Beehive was a boarding house owned by Edna Rigby. Three families were living in the boarding house at the time.

1954-1957: Because of improvements in fire safety, insurance premiums for residential and business properties within a three mile radius of the Patten fire station were reduced 30%. The fire pond at the corner of Route 11 and the Shin Pond Road was completed and was open during the winter for ice skating. Leonard Gould was the fire chief during these years.

1957-1958: A fire at the Patten town garage caused about $2,000.00 worth of damage. Gilbert "Mike" Campbell was the fire chief from 1958 to 1966. The Patten Fire Department was part of the Katahdin Valley Mutual Fireman's Association.

1958-1959: There were thirty active members of the Patten Fire Department. Fourteen members attended Fire Fighting School. This was a bad year for fires, with 43 calls, four of which were out of town.

1961-1962: A new fire truck had been bought at a cost of $8,792.00. Firemen's bells were installed in the homes of the firemen, saving valuable time in alerting them to report for duty. Two-way radios also improved communication.

1962-1963: Mount Chase started paying for fire protection from Patten through a yearly appropriated amount rather than by paying per fire.

1967-1970: Granville "Spike" Conrad was appointed Patten fire chief. Firemen attended two fire schools and first aid training in 1968.

1971-72: Gilbert Campbell was the Patten fire chief.

1973: Granville Conrad served as chief.

1974: Patten purchased a new fire truck. Gilbert Campbell returned as chief.

The Mount Chase Fire Department was established with Craig Hill as its first chief, a position he has held since then. The town bought a fire truck and equipment with money received from Federal Revenue Sharing. The residents still appropriated $600.00 for fire protection, but doesn't seem to have given Patten the lump sum of the money from 1975-1977; they were probably paying per fire. In 1974, a fire at Shin Pond put both departments to the test when a barn, an apartment, a Laundromat, and two stores burned.

1976-1979: Robert Somers was the Patten fire chief. The fire department now had two-way radios. The fire alarm siren was being used to alert the public of the location of fires and also of school cancellations.

1978: The Mount Chase Fire Department had built another truck and purchased more fire equipment, but paid Patten $1,000 for fire assistance.

1980: There were ten members of the Mount Chase Fire Department, which responded to 9 calls, including two fires in Patten. Mount Chase appropriated $1,000 for fire protection, but only paid Patten $636.00.

1980-1984: Waldo Harvey was the Patten fire chief. There were two bad fires in Patten in 1980, including the J.M. Huber fire. Mr. Harvey reported that there was a 70% increase in the number of fires that year, and that they were dealing with arson as the cause of some of those fires. The firemen attended a fire school in Orono and hosted a school in Patten. In 1981, several firemen worked on restoring a 3,000 gallon water tank to be used as an emergency water supply. The department also bought a 1,000 gallon tanker, allowing them to take up to 2,300 gallons of water to a fire. The department did woodstove and chimney inspections and burned grass in the spring. There were four bad structure fires in 1982. The fire in the house on Main Street beside the library started in a wood stove, leaving the Parsons family homeless. Ken and Sherri Cheeseman and their three children were also homeless after their home on the Shin Pond Road burned down. Just down the road from the Cheeseman's, Ray Porter's woodworking shop burned. The fourth fire was at County Forest Products on the Crystal Road.

1985: Chief Waldo Harvey reported that there were 59 fires in town and 14 out of town in 1985.

1986: An all-time high of 90 calls kept the Patten Fire Department hopping. The largest fire within town limits was the Judson and Doris Cunningham farm on the North Road. Their house and barn burned, and 38 cows died in the fire as well. There was also a forest fire near the East Branch of the Penobscot which burned about 300 acres.

1987: Patten's fire chief Jeff Lord reported there were 51 in-town fire calls and 13 out-of-town calls. In Patten, Bob and Patricia Morrarty lost their home in a fire, and in Mount Chase, a fire destroyed a house and trailer owned by Al DeGregorio. The Fire Department did save a newer house that Mr. DeGregorio was living in.

1988: The Patten Fire Department responded to 38 fires, including nine structure fires in Patten.

1989: The Mount Chase Fire Department held its first chicken barbecue and fireworks celebration in conjunction with Patten Pioneer Days. The Mount Chase Fire Department was also able to install a fire alert paging system, which then resulted in a reduction in property insurance premiums for the residents.

1989-1991: There were 35, 52, and 46 calls in Patten during these three years.

1991: The Mount Chase Fire Department was honored in a write-up which appeared in a national news magazine. The article was titled *Mount Chase ME Knows How to Save the Taxpayers' Money*. It described how the fire department bought a surplus truck and redesigned it to use as a fire truck.

1992-1993: In Patten, a new foam machine was purchased, as well as an army surplus 4X4 power wagon. 34 calls were handled in 1992 and 32 calls in 1993.

1993: The Mount Chase Fire Department applied for a Community Development Grant to be used to build a fire station. Mount Chase no longer paid Patten for fire protection, but the two towns worked cooperatively in responding to fires. A major project for Mt. Chase was mapping out camps/residences on camp roads and putting up signs. This enabled emergency services to respond to calls more quickly.

1994: The Patten Fire Department was in desperate need for more volunteer firemen. Fortunately, in 1994, the department had to respond to only 13 calls. Other communities in the Mutual Aid system frequently had to be called to help Patten out. The fire department received, at no cost, some expensive equipment from a fire department in New Jersey.

1995-1997: John Roy replaced Jeff Lord as Patten fire chief. There were eight new firemen, and more new equipment had come in from the New Jersey fire department. There were 30 calls in 1995, 24 calls in 1996, and 24 calls in 1997.

1996: Mount Chase built a fire station on a piece of property purchased by the town of Mount Chase. In 1999, an addition was built onto the building.

1998-1999: The lot next door to Patten's fire station was purchased in 1998, and a large addition was built on to the fire house in 1999. A controlled burn got rid of the house on the lot and provided a training opportunity for the firemen. The firemen did their first annual Santa Run. Several firemen donated their year's earnings to start a fund to buy a Thermal Imaging Camera.

2000: The Patten Fire Department was able to buy a Thermal Imaging Camera. They passed an OSHA inspection with a perfect score. Thirty-one calls were answered.

2001: A new pumper was purchased. The Towns of Mount Chase and Patten were now covered by 9-1-1.

2002: Town residences within a certain radius of the Patten fire station saw another decrease in insurance premiums because of the quality of service offered by the fire department. 27 calls were responded to. Grants were received from the following:

DONOR	AMOUNT	USED FOR
Maine Forestry	$1,190	Jaws of Life, OSHA approved turnout gear, Eight Scott 4.5 Air Packs, a breathing air compressor to refill air packs, other miscellaneous equipment
MMA	$2,000	
FEMA	$71,549	
MMA	$2,000	
Totals	$76,739	Cost of items purchased: $87,463

If you do the math, that left only $10,724.00 for the town to contribute. The department also bought a new pumper truck with a compressed air foam system.

2003: The Patten Fire Department used another grant to buy an automated external defibrillator and some other equipment. 37 calls were responded to.

2004-2008: The Patten Fire Department responded to 54 calls in 2004, 50 calls in 2005, 38 calls in 2006, 46 calls in 2007, and 43 calls in 2008. In 2008, the department got two grants. A $2,555 grant from the Maine Forest Service was used to buy radios and foam, and a Maine Municipal Association Safety Enhancement Grant of $955.37 was used to buy traffic safety equipment. The Fire Department did a controlled burn on Patten Grammar School.

2005: The Mount Chase Fire Department was able to buy a new fire truck through a grant of $169,000 and a matching sum of 10% ($16,900) from the town.

2008: The Gardner building on Main Street (which had housed Merrow's Department Store) burned down. The structure was built in 1885, making it 123 years old.

2009: Patten Primary School, last owned by the Will family, burned. No one was injured, but the building was demolished. All three school builidings were now gone.

2010-2011: The Patten Fire Department responded to 33 calls in 2009, 55 calls in 2010, and 27 calls in 2011.

2012-2015: Jordan Landry became the Patten fire chief. The department responded to 27, 31, 36, and 32 calls during these years.

At the time of this writing: The towns of Mount Chase and Patten currently maintain good fire protection services. Response time is still a problem because neither department has full-time firefighters and because of the geographical distances the departments have to cover, but the firefighters are well-trained and dedicated, and their equipment is well-maintained and up-to-date. Hopefully, the town will never again see the devastation caused by fires such as the one that burned the whole east side of Main Street, but if a serious fire does get started, our firemen will be able to reduce the damages significantly.

CIVIL DEFENSE

From the 1930s through the 1960s, the United States was concerned about foreign attacks. Before and during World War II, these attacks might have come from Germany, and after the war they might have been initiated by the US.'s Cold War enemy, Russia. Canada and the U.S. jointly established NORAD (North American Aerospace Defense Command) for the purpose of early detection of missiles being launched toward the countries. In 1953, Loring Air Force Base near Fort Fairfield was established. It continued to be the home base for the 42nd Bomb Wing until 1994, and from 1955-1994 it was also the 42nd Refueling Wing. Because of its location on the east coast and near the Canadian border, Loring was also part of the early warning system in the event of a missile, bomb, or other air attack. The Emergency Broadcast System was also established. These organizations also assist in the preparing the public for an impending natural disaster.

Communities throughout the U.S. created bomb shelters and educated their children about what to do if the air raid siren went off. I can remember as a child in the late 1950s being quite afraid that the siren would go off while I was walking home from school and I would have to go into the house of someone I didn't know. We also practiced hiding under our desks at school. Patten and Mount Chase maintained Civil Defense accounts and personnel throughout these years. Founders Memorial Hall was designated as the bomb shelter in Patten. Some people had their own shelters and stockpiled food and water. The Patten Civil Defense Team purchased a one-ton panel truck for $45.00 and got it in working order with $37.29 worth of repairs. They also bought a generator and two-way radios. In 1954, they did patrols during Hurricane Edna. However, that was about the extent of the civil defense presence in the town. By the mid-1970's, no money was being appropriated for it, and it finally transferred its balance of $412.13 to the town's surplus account in 1977.

LAW ENFORCEMENT

By 1840, law enforcement had been established in T4R6, in the person of a sheriff. (Perhaps the fact that the town already had two taverns led to the need for the sheriff.) Throughout the 1800s and 1900s, constables were consistently appointed at annual town meetings to enforce laws and assist other law enforcement officers if there were any. Up until 1962, Patten dealt with its own warnings, tickets, arrests, fines, and jail confinements. After that, most offenses were dealt with in district courts in Millinocket or Houlton. There were occasional serious crimes, including assault, murder, and theft, but most of the work of law enforcement dealt with drunk and disorderly offenses, vandalism, truancy, excessive noise, enforcing laws related to dogs, and collecting dog taxes. After cars came into use in the early 1900s, officers and constables enforced traffic and parking laws.

Some of the events in Patten related to law enforcement include the following.

1906: Patten had built a jail with two cells.

1915: The Patten Town Report stated that the town had a truant officer and five constables.

1954-1957: A new jail had been installed. Amos Steen was the local sheriff. He prosecuted 56 cases in 1956-57, most of which were traffic or vehicle offenses. Randolph McLean and Eugene Campbell were the jailors during these years.

1957-1958: Russell Arbo was appointed as Patten's first chief of police. He dealt with 41 cases, including one manslaughter case. Leo Grant was the jailor. The town continued to employ several constables as well.

1960-1961: Lloyd McKenney was the chief of police for a year. In the town report for 1960-1961, Officer McKenney reminded citizens of a new dog ordinance and stated that he would enforce it. Eight robberies were committed that year.

1961-1962: Russell Arbo returned as chief of police. He reported that all the robberies had been cleared except the ones at the Patten Hardware and Morse's Esso. In 1962, a new district court system went into effect, and Officer Arbo had to take 75% of his cases to Millinocket to be prosecuted. However, Patten still maintained a jail. Ronald Campbell, Jr., Russell Lee, and Walter Tosh served as jailors. In1965, Arbo handed out three snowsled violations.

1966-67: Officer Arbo reported that he was dealing with a lot of problems with teenagers and dogs. He suggested that parents set rules for their unruly offspring and keep their teens home after dark. He also suggested that dog owners keep their dogs at home before and after dark.

1967-1972: Frank Violette was appointed as chief of police in 1967. He served partway through 1969, when Manley Brown took over the job. New regulations on jails said that the jail couldn't be used in its present location at the town garage, so they moved the jail to the fire station. A new parking ordinance had been enacted after Main Street was rebuilt in 1967-68, and Officer Brown reminded citizens he would enforce the ordinance. The police force had the use of two-way radios furnished by the Maine Sheriff's Department. From 1970 on, there was also a state policeman in the area who assisted the local police force and vice versa. 1971 was a busy year with 23 accidents and 24 intoxication cases, but in 1972, Officer Brown said in the Town Report that his biggest problems were dogs and family brawls.

1973-1975: Orrie "Bunny" Hunt served as chief of police. In 1974, a new communications center was established at the Penobscot County Sheriff's Department in Bangor; it handled emergency calls for the town of Patten. In 1975, a curfew was established in response to problems with delinquency, abuse and damage to schools and other properties, reckless and noisy operation of motor vehicles, and other noise disturbances. The curfew mandated that there would be no loitering between 10:30 P.M. and 6:00 a.m. Minors were not allowed out after 10:30 unless they were attending a special school, church, or club function. Excessive noise was also prohibited.

1976-1985: In 1976, Officer Hunt assisted in investigations into five unattended deaths and several vandalism cases. He stated that he was thankful for the help given him by the state police, and he felt that they appreciated his help in return. Additional constables had to be hired in 1977 to handle problems with dogs, hot rods, arsonists, and vandals. After the J.M. Huber mill fire in 1980, Officer Hunt arranged for full time security at the site. In 1981, he reported that criminal activity in the area was way down. In 1982, he dealt with domestic complaints, burglaries, criminal mischief, harassment, theft, illegal possession of alcohol, traffic accidents, and traffic violations. In 1983, he had a new type of case to deal with: he had to harvest and destroy $6,000.00 worth of marijuana plants growing in a field in Patten.

1985-1988: Officer Hunt resigned in 1985 for health reasons. Since then, law enforcement coverage in the Patten and Mount Chase area has been provided by the Sheriff's Department and/or the Maine State Police. In 1986, Sheriff Gary Doliber spent most of his beats doing security checks at businesses, homes, and schools and dealing with traffic violations.

1988: The Drug Abuse Resistance Education (DARE) program was established in fifth grades across the state. Law enforcement organizations were beginning to use computers to get quick access to information about people they were dealing with. There were 38 non-routine calls in 1988.

1989-2016: Patten surveyed other police departments throughout the state to gather information about providing its own police protection. It was found that initiating such service would cost around $42,000.00, while the Penobscot County Sheriff's Department charged the town around $37,000 a year. The town voted to continue with sheriff coverage. Since then, either the Sheriff's Department and/or the Maine State Police have provided law enforcement services for the towns.

MAINE WARDEN SERVICE

When the first settlers arrived in T4R6 and T4R5, Maine had already begun efforts to manage the state's valuable wildlife. Open and closed seasons had been established, but no bag limits had been set. In 1867, the first fisheries commissioners were appointed by the governor. A caribou season from October to January was established in 1870. Beginning in 1873, hunters could only bag three deer a year, and seasons were established for fishing landlocked salmon, trout, and togue.

The Department of Fish and Game was established in 1880, and just three days later, on March 12, 1880, the first warden arrest was made when two men were apprehended for shooting a pregnant doe deer out of season. In the early years, most of the wardens were fish wardens, but they were expected to handle game violations as well. In 1881, they earned $25.00 a year. Commissioner Stanley's report to the Governor in 1881, stated:

Game wardens receive no regular salary at all. They are expected to be sustained by enthusiasm alone in game protection, to abandon home and the occupations that give bread to their families, and go forth to the forest for the reward of one-half of the penalties that they may obtain from captured and convicted law-breakers and the soul-stirring privilege of shooting on sight any dog which they may observe chasing deer.

The two biggest problems facing the new Fish and Game Department were dogs and crusters. Deer were being harassed or killed by dogs allowed to run free or by dogs used specifically for hunting. Crusters were poachers who took advantage of snow crust to poach and sell deer or moose hides and meat. Laws were quickly enacted to get a handle on both of these problems. 1882 saw the first fish stocking event. By 1900, there was no open season on caribou, but that wasn't a problem for hunters because there were no caribou left in Maine. Trapping seasons were established in 1900. As automobiles came into use in the early 1900s, a law was passed making it illegal to shoot from a vehicle. By 1917, resident and non-resident hunting and fishing licenses were required. In 1926, a one-deer bag limit was set. Moose seasons began being opened and closed depending on moose populations.

In 1928, wardens earned $25.00 a month! The first Warden Academy was established in 1936, and in 1938, warden pilots joined the effort to control fish and wildlife. In 1947, all seasons were curtailed because of a severe drought. Since 1959-1960, wardens have been supplied with vehicles. In 1961, illuminating laws were passed. An attempt to return caribou to Maine failed in 1964 when all the caribou brought in migrated back out of the state within a couple of years. A later experiment was even more disastrous when all the caribou died of brain worm disease while being held at the University of Maine. 1973 was the year blaze orange showed up in all parts of the state. In 1975, the name of the warden service was changed from *Department of Fish and Game* to *Department of Inland Fisheries and Wildlife*. Deb Palman became the first female warden in 1978, and in 1980, she helped establish the first K9 team. Turkey season was established in 1985, but antlerless deer restrictions came into effect. In 2008, the first Fallen Officer Memorial Run honored wardens lost in the line of duty. Maine has lost more wardens in the line of duty than any other state, and many more have been seriously injured on the job.

YEAR	WARDEN	EVENT
1886	Charles Niles, Lyman Hill	Shot and killed by poacher
1921	Arthur Deag	Capsized canoe and drowned
1921	Leslie Robinson	Auto accident in snowstorm
1922	David Brown, Mertley E. Johnson	Disappeared while investigating illegal beaver traps, bodies recovered at ice-out in May
1927	Lee Parker	Shot and killed by night hunter
1933	Jean Baptiste Jalbert	Capsized canoe and drowned
1935	Robert Moore	Railroad car and automobile collision
1946	Randall Shelley	Heart attack while on duty
1956	George Townsend	Pilot: crashed plane near Winthrop
1968	Lyle Frost	Killed in dynamite explosion while getting rid of beaver dam
1972	Richard Varney	Pilot: crashed helicopter in Maranacook Lake and drowned
1992	Bill Hanrahan	Heart attack while pursuing suspects
2011	Darryl Gordon	Pilot; plane crashed in Clear Lake

Besides continuing to enforce hunting and fishing laws which protect Maine's wildlife, wardens also enforce environmental laws and safety laws, including laws having to do with operation of recreational vehicles such as boats, ATVs, and snowmobiles. They are on the scene for motor vehicle accidents involving wildlife, for accidents involving recreational vehicles, and for hunting accidents. They conduct search and rescue operations, sometimes using specialty teams such as the dive team or search dog teams. They patrol woods and waters with the use of trucks, ATVs, snowmobiles, boats, and planes. Since wardens are assigned to districts based on population and not on geographic size, the wardens in our neck of the woods have large areas to cover. Some of the wardens who have served in northern Penobscot County are Amos Steen, Sherwood Howes, Caleb Scribner (who was also a warden supervisor), Carroll Bates, Danny Watson, Randy Probert, Chris Dyer, Alvin Theriault, and Scott Martin. Danny Glidden grew up in Patten and had a district in Northern Maine, and Alan Dudley, who grew up at Matagamon, is a game warden in Aroostook County.

****

Since 9-11 in 2001, the public has become very aware of the value of our emergency and medical services. Our firefighters, law enforcement officers, ambulance crews, and hospital staffs are trained for catastrophic events, especially natural disasters and terrorist attacks. We might not expect to have to deal with hurricanes, earthquakes, tornadoes, or volcanic eruptions, and living in a remote geographic area might give our citizens a little more peace of mind about the likelihood of a terrorist attack affecting us directly, but we still must maintain a state of preparedness. In the meantime, you can rest assured that our emergency and medical personnel will be on the scene whenever you need them, whether your house is burning down, or you're in a car accident, or if you accidently get shot in a hunting accident, or when you've fallen and can't get up. They'll also be there if you exceed the speed limit, if you shoot a deer out of season, if you catch too many fish, or if you've fallen down drunk and can't get up. Hey, they're just doing their jobs!

DEATH DATA AND DEADLY DISEASES

I'm going to finish Chapter Eleven a little morbidly (death data and deadly diseases), but let's have a little humor first. There are many witty quotes about dying, but I like these ones, from funeral helper.org and www.workinghumor.com/quotes/death.shtml.

- "We all have to die some day, if we live long enough. "—Dave Farber
- "Die, my dear doctor! That's the last thing I shall do!"—Lord Palmerston
- "There is nothing which at once affects a man so much and so little as his own death."—Samuel Butler

I spent several hours one day at my computer researching mortality statistics I experienced a lot of emotions that day, including confusion, surprise, disbelief, sadness, and relief.

I was confused as I tried to decipher charts and figures galore, as I realized I didn't know what a lot of medical terms mean, and as I struggled to fit everything into neat little sensible categories so I could make a chart. I wanted to include statistics from before 1890, but the charts I found were so old-fashioned that I could not translate them to more modern-day categories. The 1850 data I found listed deaths by these categories: zymotic diseases (infectious diseases; 27% of deaths which occurred in 1850), uncertain seat (included abscesses, Addison's Disease, atrophy, cancer, debility, diabetes, dropsy, gout, hemorrhage, inflammation, mortification, sudden death, and ulcers; 12% of deaths), nervous organs (10%), respiratory organs (30%), circulatory organs (2%), digestive organs (6%), urinative organs (<1%), generative organs (1%), locomotive organs (<1%), integumentive organs (skin, hair, and nails; <1%), old age (5%), and violent causes (4%). I just couldn't get this data to fit into the categories I was planning to use!

I was surprised at how often diarrhea was a cause of death in the 19th century. Dysentery was a common disease which caused bloody diarrhea (or bloody flux as it was also called). Cholera infantum and flux infantile were terms which referred to diarrhea in an infant. Summer diarrhea was often caused by the effect of heat on unpasteurized milk. Diarrhea could also be caused by drinking milk from cows with certain diseases. And of course, diarrhea was and is often a symptom of influenza and other diseases.

I couldn't believe the 1812 data I found: it listed 54 different causes of death, plus *other*, for 942 deaths in Hyde Park Massachusetts. This list was way too detailed; some of the causes of death it listed were *abscesses, apoplexy* (fainting), *a cramp in the stomach, debility, drinking cold water, dropsy* and *dropsy in the head* (edema, accumulation of fluids), *being struck by lightning, insanity, intemperance, mortification* (necrosis and gangrene), *old age, palsy* (paralysis or tremors), *pleurisy* (inflammation or collection of fluid between layers of lung tissue, *puerperal fever* (after childbirth), *quinsy* (abscess behind tonsils), *rupture of blood vessels, spasms, white swelling* (tuberculosis arthritis), *worms, teething, near misses from cannonballs* (concussive injuries), and *spontaneous combustion* (what a mess that must have been). It even said that *sudden death* was a cause of death in 3% of the cases. I did figure out that the leading causes of death were *consumption* (tuberculosis), *fever* (which was broken down into five kinds of fevers), and *diarrhea*. Of course, fever and diarrhea could both have been a symptom of other illnesses.

Naturally, I experienced sadness as I learned more about death and diseases. On the next page is a chart listing the percentages of death caused by various diseases in various years. I think it's pretty simple to understand, but I'll give you a few tips.

- Here's how to read the chart. In 1890, 11% of deaths were due to pneumonia, 12% were due to tuberculosis, etc.
- Statistics are for the United States only.
- Cerebrovascular means strokes.
- Respiratory: same as pulmonary; does not include pneumonia.
- Accidents: includes motor vehicle accidents after 1920.
- Kidney disease includes nephrosis, nephritis, and nephritic syndrome.
- Liver disease includes cirrhosis.
- Intestinal disease includes diarrhea, ulcers, and dysentery.
- Keep in mind: many illnesses have been eliminated or occur more rarely, so they are less of a factor when figuring percentages in modern years. For example, in 1890, a lot of people died of TB, so the percentages of deaths for other illnesses was lower. If TB hadn't been around, those percentages would have been higher.

LEADING CAUSES OF DEATH BY PERCENTAGE — ALL AGES, BOTH SEXES, ALL RACES, UNITED STATES

Cause of death	1890	1900	1910	1920	1930	1940	1950	1960	1970	1980	1990	2000	2010	2014
Heart disease	5	8	11	12	19	27	37	39	38	38	34	30	24	23
Cancer	2	4	5	6	9	11	15	16	17	21	24	23	23	23
Cerebrovascular	2	6	7	7	8	8	11	9	7	7	5	5	5	5
Respiratory									2	3	4	5	6	6
Accidents		4	6	5	7	7	6	5	6	5	4	4	5	5
Pneumonia/flu	11	12	11	16	9	7	3	4	3	3	4	3	2	2
Diabetes						2		2	2	2	3	3	3	3
Suicide								1		1	1		2	2
kidney disease		5	6	7	8	8		<1		1	1	2	2	2
Liver disease								<1	2	2	1			2
Septicemia										<1	1	1		
Arthrosclerosis									2	1				
Early infancy	3						4		2	<1	<1			
Tuberculosis	12	11	10	9	6	4	2	<1	<1	<1	<1			
Premature birth	1	2	3	3	3	2								
Intestinal	6	8	8	4	2									
Senility/Alzheimer's		3	2									2	3	4
Diphtheria	3	2												
Typhoid	3													

In the past, there were many causes of death for children, including those listed in the chart. It was also not unusual for a child to die from complications from a common childhood illness such as diarrhea, measles, mumps, or whooping cough (pertussis). Premature babies were common; if the baby was born with respiratory problems, he or she was referred to as a blue baby. Albert and Sadie (Waters) Chase kept their daughter Annie alive by putting her in the warming oven of their wood stove. In 2010, some of the leading causes of death in American children were unintentional injury, congenital abnormalities, cancer, pneumonia, and flu.

An epidemic is the occurrence of a disease over a large area. A pandemic occurs when an epidemic moves from continent to continent. Such was the case of the flu pandemic of 1918. This flu *pandemic* rates as one of the deadliest natural disasters in human history. While the peak of the pandemic was in the summer and early fall of 1918, there were cases of this H1N1 virus making people sick as early as 1917 and into 1919. The first wave was a fairly typical flu which was deadliest for infants, sick, or elderly people. However, the second wave was a mutated virus which struck young healthy people who died because their strong immune systems overreacted and did more damage than the virus itself. The virus then mutated again, but the third wave was a milder version of the flu. Nicknamed "the Spanish Flu" for no legitimate reason, this virus was also unusual in that the second wave occurred during the summer season. Particularly vulnerable were pregnant women. Many of them died before giving birth; if the woman did manage to survive through childbirth, there was a one in four chance the baby would not live. Also vulnerable were the troops fighting in Europe, who were living in unsanitary conditions, in close contact with each other, and with medical personnel and hospital space stretched to the limits. When the pandemic finally ended, the statistics were staggering.

- Worldwide, 500,000,000 people caught the flu.
- Worldwide, 50,000,000-100,000,000 people died from the flu.
- 3-5% of the world's population died.
- Life expectancy in 1918 dropped by twelve years.
- In the U.S., 28% of the population caught the flu and 500,000-675,000 people died. Native Americans were particularly vulnerable to the virus.
- Entire populations of villages in Alaska and the South Pacific died.
- More troops were killed by the flu than died in battle.

The actual numbers of people who died may be even greater. It was difficult to arrive at an accurate count because in many places, no one was keeping track of the data.

Many of the diseases prior to the 20th century were spread during epidemics or pandemics. Here are a few which would have affected people from Mount Chase and Patten.

- Cholera is a disease caused by bacteria getting into food or a water supply, often from unsanitary habits such as allowing feces to get into the water supply. Its primary symptoms are diarrhea, vomiting, and dehydration. In the last 200 years, there have been pandemics of cholera in seven different waves (with the last wave still going on). Hardest hit areas are places where poverty persists, as these areas still lack modern-day sewage and water treatment systems. Cholera also is common in areas that have been hit recently by earthquakes or tsunamis; the last cases seen in the U.S. were as a result of eating seafood from Haiti after the 2010 earthquake.

- Typhoid fever is also caused by contaminated water and food. It was probably the plague that killed so many Athens citizens in 430 B.C. that it caused the downfall of a government. Typhoid and dysentery killed more Union soldiers in the Civil War than were killed in battle. The worst outbreak of typhoid fever in the U.S. came in 1891, when the death rate was 174 per 100,000 people. The symptoms of typhoid are fever, rash, weakness, abdominal pain, constipation, and headaches. It is possible to be a carrier of the disease without showing symptoms. In 1907, a carrier named Mary spread the disease to hundreds of people. She got fired as a cook, but got another cooking job later under a different name. She was finally apprehended, and she was forced to spend the rest of her life in quarantine. A vaccine has been available since 1896, but an important defense against the disease is good hygienic habits.

- Smallpox is a viral infection passed from person to person. Its symptoms are fever, vomiting, body aches, and a rash of pus-filled blisters. Smallpox has been around since 10,000 B.C. The first preventative treatments date back to the 6th century, when people deliberately exposed themselves to smallpox by placing a small amount of fluid from a blister into an open cut. In 1796, Edward Jenner discovered that using cowpox fluid was safer and just as effective. In 1967, the World Health Organization started a campaign to eliminated smallpox worldwide. It met its goal in 1979.

- Typhus is an entirely different disease from typhoid fever. Typhus is a bacterial infection that was first documented in 1083. It is transmitted by lice, mites, fleas, ticks, and squirrels and also by person-to-person contact. Its symptoms include fever, body pain, falling blood pressure, rash, and death. It occurs in several different forms, some milder than others. Historically, epidemics have often occurred during times of war and deprivation. Hundreds of thousands of soldiers and citizens being held in death camps died from typhus during World War II. The first vaccine was developed around 1930 using ground up lice; in 1938 the vaccine began being made from egg yolks. If treated aggressively with antibiotics, intravenous fluids, and oxygen, chances of survival are high.

- Diphtheria is a bacterial infection with mild to severe symptoms, including sore throat, fever, and cough. In some patients, a white patch in the throat blocks the airway. Other severe symptoms include heart problems, inflammation of nerves, paralysis, and death. The earliest documented epidemic of diphtheria occurred in 1613, and epidemics remained common until 1943. It was prevalent during times of deprivation, after disasters such as earthquakes, and during wars. 50,000 people died from diphtheria in Europe during World War II. An antitoxin was developed in the late 1800s using serum from horses. Diphtheria still occurs in isolated cases, usually where vaccines have been unavailable or refused.

- Tuberculosis, also called consumption, is a bacterial infection which usually affects the lungs. It has been around since ancient times and is still a major health concern throughout the world. It is estimated that 1/3 of the world population is infected with TB, although 90% of those infected have the inactive form of the disease. In the past, treatments included collapsing the infected lung to allow it to heal and placing infected persons in a sanitorium for extended rest. A caccination has been available since the early 1900s, and aggressive use of antibiotics has reduced the number of deaths from the disease.

- Dysentery is characterized by fever, abdominal pain, and extreme diarrhea with blood and mucus in the stool. Dysentery in various forms can be caused by bacteria, viruses, parasitic worms, or protozoa. It can be treated with oral rehydration therapy, intravenously if necessary. There is no vaccine currently available, but researchers are working on one.

- Pneumonia can be caused by a virus, a bacterial infection, or fungi. It attacks the air sacs known as alveoli in the lungs, causing symptoms such as coughing, difficulty breathing, chest pain, and rapid breathing, and it can lead to death, particularly in young children and the elderly. It often occurs after an initial illness such as a cold or the flu or in people who have cystic fibrosis, COPD, or any illness which weakens the immune system. Most people (with the exception of the elderly) recover from pneumonia if it is diagnosed early and treated aggressively with antibiotics. A vaccine has been around since 1977 for adults and since 2000 for children, but pneumonia is far from eradicated world-wide. It is still the leading cause of death in parts of the world (four million deaths in 2015) and along with flu is the 8th leading cause of death in the United States (55,227 deaths in the U.S. in 2015).

Infant mortality refers to the death of a baby before or during birth or in the first year after birth. The rate of miscarriages (death of a fetus before 20 weeks) has improved somewhat but is still estimated to be somewhere around 25-30% of all reported pregnancies in the U.S. The leading cause of miscarriages is abnormality in the fetus, although smoking, drinking, or drug use cause miscarriages as well. For deaths of a fetus over 20 weeks (which would include stillborn), the statistics have gone from 4% of pregnancies in 1922, 3% in 1970, to less than 1% in 2013. Reported abortions in the U.S. have gone from two a year in 1930 to around a million a year since 2010. The largest number of reported abortions was 1,608,620 in 1990. There was a marked increase in the number of abortions during the Great Depression and again during World War II, and a marked decrease in the number of abortions the year after World War II ended. It is ironic that abortion rates climbed after birth control methods became widely available.

I was most relived to see how dramatically the infant mortality rates during the first year of life have gone down. The percentages given for each year are the percentages of infants who died before their first birthday.

year	percentage	year	percentage
1900	16.5%	1950	2.9%
1915	10.5%	1960	2.6%
1920	10.2%	1970	2%
1920	7.5%	1980	1.3%
1940	5.4%	1990	<1%

We've come a long way in treating and preventing many illnesses that were once killers. We have better hygiene habits, our surroundings are more sanitary, our milk and water are not likely to be contaminated, we know more about how diseases are spread, we have all kinds of effective medications, we get enough to eat, and we have more accessible and better health care. And because we're healthier, we are living longer. Below is a chart of life expectancy rates since 1700. The data is based on mortality since birth, for both sexes, and for all races. All ages are rounded.

YEAR	LIFE EXPECTANCY	YEAR	LIFE EXPECTANCY
1700	35	1940	62
1750	36	1950	69
1800	37	1960	70
1880	40	1970	71
1900	47	1980	74
1910	50	1990	75
1920	54	2000	77
1930	60	2010	79

This increase in life expectancy has changed the leading causes of death lists; we have more old people around now, and they tend to die of things like heart attacks and strokes, pneumonia and flu, and Alzheimer's disease.

An obituary is an important piece of writing. First of all, it lets everyone know you've died. Second, it tells people when and where your funeral will be held. Third, it gives your relatives a chance to brag about you. I found obituaries to be very helpful in putting together information for this history, especially the family charts I included at the end of Chapter Four. And once again, I stumbled on a website that gave me more than I had hoped for. This one is: http://freepages.genealogy.rootsweb.ancestry.com/~howefalto/aom.htm. Here are a few samples of some old time obituaries, some of which were written after the funeral. (I have corrected some errors in spelling, grammar, and punctuation.

NORTH LAKE, June 2 - The funeral of the late Mrs. W. Van Tassel, took place on Saturday, June 1st. Rev. Mr. Thompson preached the funeral sermon. The choir from Forest City rendered some very beautiful and appropriate music. A large concourse of people in teams and on foot followed the remains to their last resting place, where they were tenderly laid beside those of her little boy who died last November. This death is especially sad for the deceased's grandmother, Mrs. Alexander Boone, with whom she lived from a child, and who on account of illness was unable to see her during her last sickness and death.

It is reported that the wife of Mr. Forest Howe, formerly of this place but now of Island Falls, Maine, is dead from poisoning, whether by accident or intentional has not been definitely learned. Oil of cedar was the fatal drug.

Jan. 10, 1908 An old lady by the name of Salome Dewitt, residing with Mrs. O Buckingham, was found dead on the floor of her room on Sunday evening 10th The deceased had been blind for a number of years. She was always very cheerful and would converse freely with anybody who would talk with her. The interment will take place on Wednesday 13th.

(1907) It is with sadness we record the death from la grippe of Mrs. Enoch Buckingham, which took place on Wednesday evening, Feb 13, 1907. The funeral service was conducted by the Rev. Mr. Weed of Danforth, on Saturday afternoon at 2 o'clock, the 16th. Her husband, who was taken sick about the same time as the deceased, lies critically ill and was unable to attend the service.

Fosterville, March 11, 1907: The sad news was received here last week of the death of George Foster, who went to Colorado with the hope of regaining his health, but he never rallied, and died in that far-away place aged 28 years old. He left a loving wife and two children to mourn their sad loss. Mr. Foster was a kind and loving husband, a fond and indulgent father, and an obliging neighbor. He was a man of remarkable even temper, always calm, thoughtful and cheerful, looking on the best side of life. He will be missed by his friends and acquaintances, but mostly by his brother and sisters. He was tenderly cared for by his younger brother, Grover, who went with him. All that could be done to alleviate his sufferings was done by loving hands, but the Angel of Death came and guided him to the heavenly mansion, where there is no sickness or death; and where an eternal day reigns forever and ever.

(May 11, 1906) The people of this place were shocked when they learned that Mr. Hugh McMinn died at an early hour this morning. Although the deceased had been very poorly for some time, the news was a surprise to many. He was in his usual health when he retired on Thursday evening and slept until 3:30 am. On Friday he arose and sat on the side of the bed. His wife, who was in bed, called to him and receiving no answer, she started to get up when the deceased fell over, partly on his wife and partly on the bed. Mrs. McMinn rapped on the wall and aroused her nephew and his wife who immediately hastened to the bedside but on arrival found life was extinct. The funeral will take place from the home of his nephew, with whom he has lived for a year past, at two o'clock, on Sunday afternoon. At the church, funeral services will be conducted by Rev. Mr. Phelan of Danforth, Me. The deceased left no family but a number of nieces and nephews and one sister, Mrs. D. Wood, to mourn the loss of a kind relative.

Millinocket, Feb. 12 - A familiar figure will be missed by the passing of John Barrie, died 53 years old. Since several automobile accidents in which he as injured, his health had failed and on Jan. 7 he had a severe shock.

Okay, that takes care of disease and death, although you have to admit that we're getting better at keeping people alive and healthy! I promise the next chapter will be more fun. But first I have to get in a little more dark humor. Here are some humorous headstone inscriptions I have come across:

- I told you I was sick.
- Izzy Dead Yet.
- Died from not forwarding that Facebook Post to ten people.
- I came here without being consulted and I leave without my consent.
- Here lies Scotty Fife for fooling around with the marshall's wife.
- Here lies Clyde. His life was full until he tried to milk a bull.
- Unknown man. Died eating library paste.
- Ma loved Pa, Pa loved women. Ma caught Pa with two in swimmin'. Here lies Pa.

And here are a few more quotes:

- Old people at weddings always poke me and say, "You're next." So I've started doing the same thing at funerals.
- I would like to think I will die a heroic death, but it's more likely I'll trip over the dog and choke on a spoonful of frosting.
- Live each day like it's your last. One day you'll get it right.
- Death is not the greatest loss in life. The greatest loss is what dies inside us while we live. ~Norman Cousins.

But one of my favorite quotes was a serious one:

   No one is actually dead until the ripples they cause in the world die away.

I hope that this history keeps those ripples going for the Patten and Mount Chase citizens who now rest in peace!

CHAPTER TWELVE: RELIGION, ORGANIZATIONS, AND RECREATION

We often see the words *mind, body,* and *soul* grouped together as the three facets of human existence. Chapter Ten took care of the mind (schools and libraries), and Chapter Eleven handled the body (health care and emergency services). So Chapter Thirteen will take care of the soul.

RELIGION

Patten has always had religion, even in the days when worship services were no more than a group of worshippers meeting in someone's home. By 1837, the Baptists had begun to meet for worship. By 1838, a Methodist Society had been formed, and the Congregationalists began meeting in March, 1841.

On October 5, 1839, Reverend J.G. Pingree was appointed as the community's first circuit preacher. Rev. Pingree's area included communities as far north as Presque Isle. On October 12th, he rode into town with his black robes flapping in the wind" (to quote Irene Bradford) to hold the first official Methodist church service in Elbridge Stetson's cabin (where Ellis's parking lot is now). By the following August, the congregation had outgrown the cabin, so Ira Fish offered his newly constructed sheep barn at the top of Mill Hill as a meeting place. The Methodists held Sunday School Services in the schoolhouse

The Baptists built their church in 1845. The building was paid for by selling 42 shares for $45.00 per share ($1,890). The buyer of a share could donate the cash or could pay off the $45.00 through lumber, building supplies, or labor. The result was a beautiful and sturdy structure which still graces Patten's Main Street. The Baptists graciously shared their sanctuary with the Methodists, who found the sheep barn a little drafty in cold weather.

The Congregational Church was built on the corner of Church and Main Streets in 1865. Their first minister was E.G. Carpenter. Another minister who served there was Reverend William Sleeper. The bell in the church has been donated to Rev. Sleeper by his former parishioners in Massachusetts. After the church closed, Caleb Scribner made arrangements to have the bell placed in the belfry of Patten Academy. That bell is now the centerpiece of the Patten Academy Alumni Park. The building was later occupied by the Grange and was rented out for wedding receptions, reunions, etc. In its last years, it was the site of the Katahdin Community Center. It was torn down in 1989.

In 1854, the Methodists built a parsonage. In 1871, the Methodists built Stetson Memorial Methodist Church, named for one of the original founders of the congregation, Elbridge Stetson. The building was designed by architect Thomas Clark of Cross, Illinois. He and Reverend John Morse supervised volunteer workmen in the construction of the $6,000.00 building. A bell was cast in a Bangor foundry, hauled to Mattawamkeag on a flatbed car of the European and North American Railroad, and transported to Patten by Timothy Woodbury's ox team. The church has been repaired, redecorated, and remodeled with additions over the years. The beautiful stained glass windows were donated and installed in the 1940's. Cushioned pews have replaced the wooden pews, and the steeple was replaced and dedicated to the memory of 2nd Lt. Leslie Dickinson in 1991. However, one feature of the church that has not been replaced is the beautiful tin ceiling and walls. The photo at left shows Madelyn Howes's choir singing in 1991 as part of the town's 150th anniversary. Mrs. Howes was incredibly talented musically and led the choir for many years in the last half of the 1900's.

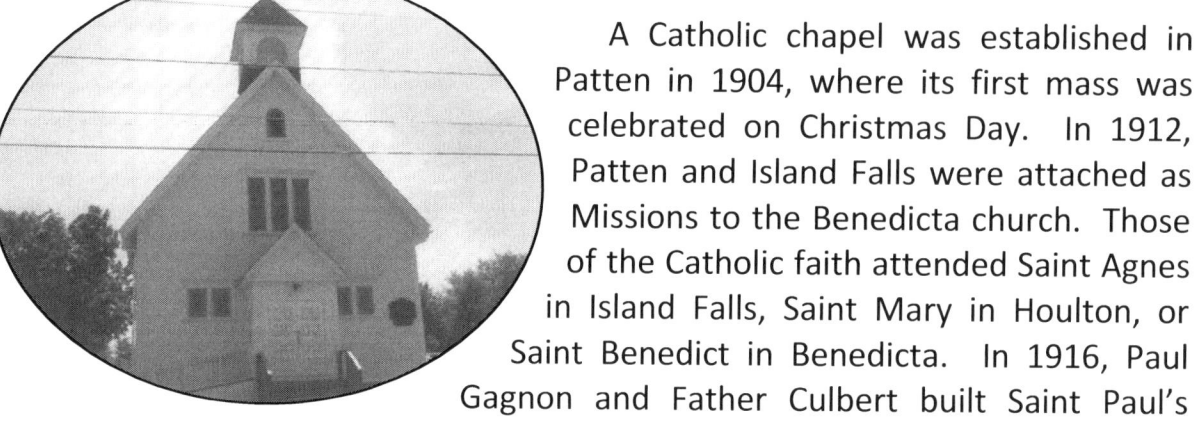

A Catholic chapel was established in Patten in 1904, where its first mass was celebrated on Christmas Day. In 1912, Patten and Island Falls were attached as Missions to the Benedicta church. Those of the Catholic faith attended Saint Agnes in Island Falls, Saint Mary in Houlton, or Saint Benedict in Benedicta. In 1916, Paul Gagnon and Father Culbert built Saint Paul's Roman Catholic Church on the corner of High and Katahdin Streets. In 1920, Saint Paul's became a Mission of the Island Falls church and subsequently grew into a lively and active church. Worship services became even more uplifting in the 1960s and 1970s with the development of a choir led by John Pond.

Patten Pentecostal Church was built on upper Main Street in 1931. The congregation, which included quite a few people from Mount Chase, Hersey, and Moro, had been meeting in homes and the rural schools. The lot they chose to build their church on had an old building on it which was torn down. The original church building was the part of the church you see on the left side of the photo above. In 1980-1981, a large addition was built on to the church, paid for entirely by donations.

The church has always had an active youth program and hosts a very popular Bible School week every year in August. Over the years, the church has been home to many talented musicians who have led the congregation in worship.

The Kingdom Hall of Jehovah's Witnesses building was constructed on Houlton Street in 1968. However, a congregation of Jehovah's Witnesses had been established in Patten some time previous to 1968. Jehovah's Witnesses were originally known as the Watchtower Society, which was established in 1884 in Pennsylvania. When that organization split in 1931, the Watchtower Society became Jehovah's Witnesses. Their churches were called Kingdom Halls. Right from the beginning, the church was the object of both verbal and physical attacks to the point of religious persecution, including the vandalism and burning of the Kennebunk, Maine, Kingdom Hall in 1940. Although the Patten congregation did not experience any overt physical attacks, there were community members who belittled and criticized them or found fault with some of their beliefs and practices. Actually, the beliefs and practices of all the congregations in Patten have been criticized at one time or another. But for most people, the door you darkened on Sunday morning didn't matter; actually, it didn't even matter if you didn't darken any door. All residents were integral members of the community, working together, shopping at the same schools, and going to school together.

Other religious groups in town in the past were the Universalists and the Seventh Day Adventists. However, they did not have large enough congregations to warrant building their own churches. Congregations in other churches have also been reduced in size. The Baptist Church stopped having services in 1910, and the Congregational Church closed in 1928. The Kingdom Hall of Jehovah's Witnesses closed in 2009. Saint Paul's Catholic Church does not have a priest now, but does offer Mass on Saturday afternoons. The Pentecostal Church and the Methodist Church have both seen declines in attendance but continue to offer worship services to their congregations. The two churches often hold special services together, including community prayer and services in the park. They also are involved in supporting the community as a whole, with public events and benefit dinners.

SOCIAL AND COMMUNITY ORGANIZATIONS

Humans are social creatures, and so they need to socialize. Patten residents have been no different. By 1845, a Social Library had been established in town. School activities have in many ways been a big part of social life for the community. Some of the school sponsored events that people have enjoyed over the years are talent shows, speaking contests, one act plays, school programs, and dances. Basketball and baseball games, as well as various other sports activities, have always drawn big crowds of fans. Churches also offered opportunities for socializing, especially through men's, women's, and youth clubs that they sponsored. Soon after the early residents got their schools up and running and had formed their religious congregations, social organizations began to be established. Many of these groups have endeavored to benefit the whole community through their activities.

Organizations which were established by 1889 in Patten included:

- Masons: Katahdin Lodge No. 98
- Independent Order of Oddfellows: Pamola, No. 87 International Organisation of Good Templars (a fraternal organization which had as its primary mission the promotion of abstinence from alcohol. And I did not make a spelling error here for the word *Organisation*—that's how it was spelled in those days!)
- Grand Army of the Republic: Edwin Rogers Post 114 (named in honor of Edwin Searle Rogers, who lost his life during the Civil War)
- Women's Relief Corps (auxiliary to G.A.R.)
- Patrons of Husbandry Advance No. 275 (Grange)
- Ancient Order of United Workmen: Anvil (an early version of a union)
- Patten Brass Band (F. E. Arnold, Sylvester Huston, leaders)

Organizations from 1890-1917 included:
- Masons: Katahdin Lodge No. 98
- Eastern Star: Pleiades No. 7 (women's auxiliary of the Masons)
- Independent Order of Oddfellows: Pamola No. 87
- Ideal Rebekah No. 93 (women's auxiliary of the Oddfellows)
- Grand Army of the Republic: Edwin Rogers Post 114
- Women's Relief Corps
- L.O.L. Patten No. 30 (I could not figure out what this was, although I very much doubt that LOL stands for Laugh Out Loud, League of Legends, or Locks of Love)
- Patrons of Husbandry Advance No. 275
- Ancient Order of United Workmen: Anvil
- Knights of the Maccabees (a fraternal organization dealing with life insurance)
- Independent Order of Foresters (a fraternal organization dealing with insurance)

Organizations from 1917-1945 included all the organizations listed above as well as these:
- Sons of Veterans
- Loyal Legion (Could be a patriotic order of Civil War military officers or an association for Loggers and Lumbermen)
- American Legion
- Board of Trade: C.E. Lord, Secretary (similar to a Chamber of Commerce)
- Women's Christian Temperance Union
- Patten Lion's Club

The Patten Lions Club was an international service organization which was founded in 1917. Its mission is to improve communities around the world. LIONS stands for Liberty, Intelligence, Our Nations Safety. A club was formed in Patten before 1931 and had a meeting place on Main Street. Although there is no longer a club in Patten, the Lions Club is still an active organization with over 46,000 clubs around the world.

The American Legion was a veterans' organization formed in Paris, France, in 1919 by Thomas Roosevelt, Jr. and members of the American Expeditionary Forces. It has supported veterans in many ways, such as sponsoring the GI bill, promoting better medical care, and lobbying on behalf of veterans. Its motto is "For God and Country" and membership is open to any veteran who served during war time. The American Legion existed in Patten at some point between 1919 and 1945.

Following World War II, a Veterans of Foreign Wars (V.F.W.) was established in Patten. It was named the Grant-Gardner post in honor of Wallace Blackwell Grant and Everett Kelsey Gardner, who lost their lives during the war.

Between 1945 and 2016, the Patten Women's Club, the Triple Link Club (a spin-off from the Oddfellows), Girl Scouts, Boy Scouts, and 4-H were established at one time or other. Penquis CAP organized a Senior Citizens Group in the 1970's. It offered ceramics lessons, bus trips, and other activities. Seniors who had begun meeting through Penquis CAP organized the Katahdin View Senior Citizens group and started having regular meetings in the community room at Meadowbrook Manor.

Since 2004, the Patten Historical Society has provided a place to collect artifacts and photos related to the history of Patten. The house itself dates from the 1840s, when it was built by John Gardner. Through the years, the home was owned by John Gardner, Calvin Bradford, Halbert and Cora (Chapman) Robinson, Charles Vaughn and Dove (Soule) Chapman, Bill and Helen (Chapman) Garton, and Ervin and Dawn (Hotham) Tower. The Towers donated the house to the society. An open house is held during Patten Academy Alumni Days and Patten Pioneer Days, and refreshments are offered to area veterans each year after the Memorial Day parade. Other events happening at the site have been presentations by various speakers, a writing contest, and presentations or skits about Patten's history. In 2006, a calendar with photos from Patten's past was published. A special item on display at the house is the flag given to Leslie and Dorothy Dickinson after their son Dickie was killed in Vietnam.

Music is often the focal point for a social organization. In 1884, the Patten Silver Cornet Band entertained crowds and performed at ceremonies such as the Memorial Day ceremony at the cemetery. The Patten Brass Band was led by F. E. Arnold, then Sylvester Huston, and then W.W. Woodbury, who was nicknamed the Father of the Band. The Patten Juvenile Band was organized around 1932. There was once a bandstand on Main Street between the Peavey Block and the Gardner Block, and now there is one at Patten Academy Alumni Park. Local schools have produced fine bands and choruses which have competed in All Aroostook activities. Church and community choirs have produced many cantatas over the years. We have enjoyed the musical gifts of the Golden Chariot Singers, the Good News Singers, Madelyn Howes, Marguerite Sinclair, and Chuck Loucka. Other local musicians have entertained crowds at dances and concerts. In the 1960s, Helen Garton offered dance lessons to local youths, and around the 1970s, there was an active square dancing group in town.

In modern times as well, some of our organizations have fun as their mission, but they also serve the communities in various ways. The Rockabema Snow Rangers and the Patten ATV club are two of these groups.

Many of these organizations have disbanded over the years. As the 20th century continued, people seemed to prefer to stay home and watch television rather than attend evening meetings! At the present time, organizations which remain active are church men's, women's, and youth groups, Mason's, Patten Women's Club, Patten Historical Society, Patten ATV Club, Rockabema Snow Rangers, and Scouts. There is also an active musical group which plays gospel and country music. These organizations offer their members a great deal of enjoyment, but they also contribute in many ways to the communities of Patten and Mount Chase as a whole.

RECREATION

There was a popular song a few years ago titled "Girls Just Wanna Have Fun." Well, people in general—not just girls—do want to have fun. They want to exercise and enjoy the great outdoors. They want to participate in celebrations and get together with other people. They want to laugh and forget about the trials of life, at least for a little while. Patten and Mount Chases are good places to live if you just wanna have fun!

We'll begin with the site of a great deal of fun over the years—the gym in Patten. This building on Founders Street has a long history. Built around 1914, It was first known as the Town Hall, and most of the high school extracurricular activities took place there, including dances, basketball games, graduation ceremonies, one-act plays, variety shows, school programs, etc. The Town Hall burned in 1940, but was quickly rebuilt and opened back up in 1941. It was renamed the Founders Memorial Building, although many people still just called it the gym or the town hall. It continued to be a focal point of activities for the town. In 1954, it was turned over to the school department. It was also used for physical education classes until 1998.

The Patten Parks and Recreation Department was established in 1979 to study ways to renovate Founders Memorial Hall and implement a recreation program. Patrick McAvoy was hired as the first Rec Director: his first duty was to oversee renovations. A furnace (donated by SAD #25 from the Patten Academy building) was installed, windows and floors were repaired, floors were sanded and varnished, painting was done inside and out, new bathrooms were installed, and the building was rewired. The building was renamed the Patten Parks and Recreation Building.

In 1980, Sadie Heath took over the job of director. In 1981, an advisory board was created to make decisions and handle the financial business of Patten Rec, and Gerry Giles became the director. Later directors included Glenda Bossie, Darlene Ordway, Mari Birmingham, Dottie Tucker, Michelle Sherman, Beth Somers, Kelly Birmingham, Melissa Strang, Krista McGraw, Karen McGraw, Michele Roshto, and Paula Sweeney.

In 2002, the Rec Department had one full time (40 hours a week) director and two assistant directors. This staffing was reduced in 2003 to one director working 25 hours per week. In their annual reports, the directors always thanked the many volunteers who helped with all the various activities of the Patten Rec. and also thanked Patten and Mount Chase for financial support through annual appropriations. In that way, the Rec was able to continue its services to the citizens—young, old, and in-between— of Patten and Mount Chase.

This chart shows some of the programs which have been sponsored by the Patten Parks and Recreation Department.

SPORTS	CHILDREN AND TEENS	ADULTS
Basketball for all ages
Baseball/softball for all ages(incl. Little League, T-ball, and First Pitch)
Volleyball for all ages
Soccer for children
Cheerleading for children
Kickball for children

(Children's teams were provided with uniforms by the Rec Dept and sponsors) | Roller skating
Movies
Whiffle Ball
Gymnastics
Swimming lessons
Halloween parties, hay rides
Ice-skating on the fire pond
Dances
Chem-free graduation party
Patten Pioneer Days
Little Miss Patten Pioneer
Summer playground
Hunter Safety
Fingerprinting
ATV safety course
Karate
Storytime
Easter Egg Hunt
Preschool program
Toys for Tots | Crafts
Classes
Flytying
Slimnastics
Aerobic dance
Beano
Dances
Live music
Gospel Nite
Adult Ed
Rabies clinic
Community activities
Walking
Zumba |

Patten Parks and Recreation also oversaw renovations and upkeep of the building. Although the programs and building were maintained by yearly appropriations from the towns of Patten and Mount Chase, Patten Rec contributed to its own upkeep by holding fundraisers. Some successful fundraisers over the years have been talent shows, flea markets, bike raffles, a roll-a-thon, a t-shirt sale, toy auctions, comedy basketball games, fishing derbies, Children's Fairs, and Christmas Fairs. In 2015, Patten Rec brought a carnival to town. Additionally, the hall has been rented out for a wide variety of functions, especially birthday parties, and has been used for other events such as town meetings and Patten Pioneer Days.

Between 1985 and 1990, a new furnace and a new sewer system were installed, a new lighting system was installed (thanks to a large donation from Sherman Wheelabrator), the furnace room was renovated, and the east side of the roof was re-shingled. At the athletic field, two dugouts were built and a fence was put up, thanks to donations from local businesses and labor from the National Guard and community members. In 1991, the gym was repainted, new front doors were installed, and new mats were purchased for gymnastics classes. A Community Development Block Grant paid for a new floor, a small kitchen area, a new scoreboard, new backboards, new bleachers, new carpets and linoleum, and new lights in the bathroom and entry way. The west side of the roof was re-shingled. In 1998, a new roof was put on the back of the gym and the floor was refinished. The bathrooms were renovated the next year, and in 2000 the office was redone, new cabinets were put in the kitchen, and a metal roof was put on. New tables were purchased in 2001.

The building was closed in 2013, but was reopened in 2014 after additional work was done on the building to bring it up to code. At the time of this writing, the building continues to be a focal point of activities for the communities of Patten and Mount Chase.

There are many other opportunities in the area for recreational activities in all the seasons of the year. As soon as the snow melts and the ball field dries up, locals start playing baseball and softball. In the past, men's and women's town teams competed against other area towns. Around 1913, they played at the Paul Gagnon Race Track, Fairgrounds, and Ball Field, and in more recent years at the ball diamond on upper Main Street. The schools and Patten Rec offer spring sports opportunities for children of all ages, including T-ball and pee-wee teams for the youngest athletes right up through the high school teams. Patten also has a Little League organization.

This might be an appropriate place to recognize all the adults who support youth sports activities by volunteering to be a coach. These coaches put in many hours organizing their programs, scheduling games with other communities, setting up photography sessions, and attending practices and games. The conclusion of a season often includes a party. But their biggest service is offering children opportunities to engage in physical activity, build self-esteem, improve sports skills, and learn how to be a team player. The coaches walk a fine line between accepting each child at his or her level but challenging the child to improve and do his or her best. They have to have patience and self-control, and they have to know a hundred different ways to say, "Good job!"

Summer activities tend to be more family oriented, as many families go to camp or go on camping trips. Local residents as well as "outsiders" enjoy hiking and mountain climbing, swimming, canoeing, and fishing. The picture at the left shows a sign in Mount Chase for the Owlsboro Road, which is part of the Appalachian Trail. Off and on throughout the years, a carnival or circus may have come to town for several days in the summer. Local churches have sponsored Bible Schools. In the past, horse racing and horse pulls were popular. Patten and nearby communities have annual celebrations in summer, complete with parades, food, and a wide variety of activities. And some locals might even venture out of town to go to the annual fairs around the state.

A summer activity which is definitely fun but which is also a great service to the children of Patten and Mount Chase is swimming lessons. Prior to 1969, swimming lessons had been sponsored for many years directly by the town. From 1969 to 1979, they were sponsored by Penquis CAP. Since 1980, swimming lessons have been provided by the Patten Parks and Recreation Department. Instructors taught thousands of children (as many as 140 in one season) to swim. In years past, lessons were held at Shin Pond, but in recent years local residents offered their pools as sites for lessons.

In recent years, ATV riding has become a favorite activity for many locals. The Patten ATV club has developed over a hundred miles of trails in the Patten and Mount Chase area. Over 60 landowners have graciously allowed trails to cross their property. In 2014, the ATV club had 81 members and 15 supporting businesses. They urge riders to respect the environment and drive safely.

Fall has always been the favorite time of the year for hunting enthusiasts. Partridge season opens in October, and deer season commences in November. There is a bear season as well. Moose season has been modified over the years and now occurs in three one-week sessions in the fall. Football never took off as a fall sport in the area, but field hockey and soccer have become popular in recent years. Halloween has long been a fun holiday for local kids. When Patten Primary and Patten Grammar school were still open, students painted the windows of businesses in town and paraded up Main Street in their costumes. The kids still enjoy trick-or-treating and going to Halloween parties. The high school usually sets up a haunted house. Another popular sport which commences in the fall and goes throughout winter and spring has been bowling. Patten men's and women's teams travel to Birch Point in Island Falls to compete against other area teams.

Mainers don't let winter keep them indoors, and the more snow the better! Winter activities include sliding, skating, skiing, ice fishing, snowmobiling, and snowshoeing. In the 1950s and 1960s, the Aggie Boys (the Future Farmers of America) kept the skating rink at the fire pond behind Morse's Garage cleared off. They even had a little concessions booth. In recent years, a skating rink has sometimes been built at the playground. During the 1900's, Willow Street was often closed during the winter months to provide a sliding area. There is currently a popular sliding area at Shin Pond. Over the years, many local youths have made the dangerous sliding trip down Killer Hill. There are cross-country ski trails nearby, and ice-fishing and snowmobiling are also popular winter activities. The Rockabema Snow Rangers Snowmobile Club (photo above) keeps trails beautifully groomed for many miles around Patten and Mount Chase as well as being a rental site for various private and public events.

The most popular indoor activity in the winter is basketball. The Rec Department offers basketball to children (complete with round robins and tournaments with teams from neighboring communities) and at times have adult games as well. Katahdin Middle and High School programs have varsity and junior varsity basketball teams, and the highlight of a successful season is a trip to Bangor to play in the Eastern Maine tournament.

Television has created the opportunity for fans to cheer for their favorite big league teams. Although there are some exceptions (C.G.—you know who you are), most locals cheer for the Boston Red Sox, the Boston Bruins, the New England Patriots, and the Boston Celtics, as well as the University of Maine Black Bear Teams. And of course, in February, we get to watch Maine basketball tournament games thanks to MPBN or one of the other Maine stations.

In 2006, a group of interested citizens formed the Patten Playground Committee which has focused on keeping the playground as an important service to the community. The committee has replaced and added equipment at the playground, kept mulch in place under the equipment, erected fencing around the playground area, and built skating rinks during the winter months. In 2009, the committee sponsored a winter carnival. In 2010, the committee built a hot dog stand on wheels which has been a great fundraiser for the playground. The hot dog stand has been hired out during Patten Pioneer Games and athletic events. In 2012, a beautiful Patten Community Playground sign was erected.

Many parades have processed up Main Street over the years, including serious parades on Memorial Day and fun parades on annual town celebrations. I found pictures showing Labor Day parades from as far back as 1920. For many years the Oddfellows held an annual Labor Day celebration. This included a parade and games and food on the school grounds. (Do you remember Mr. Fenlason, a teacher from the area who ran games and concessions all over Maine?) In 1983, Patten Pioneer Days was established to coincide with the Lumberman's Museum annual Beanhole Bean dinner. Jon Ellis was instrumental in making Patten Pioneer Days a local tradition. Again, a parade, games, and concessions are part of the fun, along with a progressive dinner, sports contests, a flea market, music, dances, and the crowning of Little Miss Patten Pioneers Days. Several of these events take place at Patten Academy Alumni Park. A chicken barbecue and fireworks bring the festivities to Shin Pond for an evening of fun.

Mount Chase hasn't been mentioned a lot in this chapter. Mount Chase has never had any churches, and all the Mount Chase schools closed long ago. You definitely can't play basketball in the Mount Chase town hall, and there are no social or recreational organizations based in Mount Chase. However, I've already mentioned—more than once—that in many ways, Patten and Mount Chase are one community. Residents of both towns pass back and forth across town lines without even thinking about it. As one community, Mount Chase and Patten residents worship, belong, contribute, participate, attend, organize, sponsor, and have fun together.

Although there are some people who are true loners, most of humanity wants to belong. So people form clubs. Sometimes they make rules for their clubs. Sometimes they decide who can and cannot belong to their clubs. As a teacher, I know that children as young as six years old have this urge to form to clubs. Most clubs have a lot of positive qualities. They provide opportunities for like-minded people to contribute to society in many different ways. However, there are some clubs that are exclusive—you have to meet certain requirements to belong. For example, you might have to be male or female, or athletically gifted, or a certain age. There are groups just for veterans, just for certain ethnic groups, just for really smart people, and the list goes on. Most of the time, the exclusivity is not a big deal—why would a twenty-year old want to join a Senior Citizens group? Thankfully, we're getting better at the inclusion factor. We've become more aware that exclusion of others is not acceptable in society.

There are also informal clubs which bring together people who have something in common. Young mothers form playgroups to help their children acquire social skills. People who work together often socialize together. People who like to ski or hike or bowl or sew or sing get together to share the fun.

And then there are the coffee clubs that gather regularly at a local restaurant or coffee shop. They don't hold meetings—they just show up. They don't have a mission—they just socialize. They don't elect officers, have eligibility requirements, prepare an agenda, or have sub-committees. The poem on the next page is dedicated to all those little coffee groups, especially the Coffee Babes at Shin Pond Village, the guys who meet every morning at Weezie's Snack Bar in Shin Pond, and the gang at the Deli in Patten.

JUST MOVED TO TOWN

Just moved to town, had nothing much to do.
Was feeling kinda lonesome, and wanted some fun, too.

Thought I'd join a club and get to meet some folks,
Give me something to do, might even swap a few jokes.

Tried out the snowsled club. Thought that'd be a group I'd like.
Pot-luck suppers were good, but can't do a poker run on a bike.

Attended a meeting of the PTA and asked what that'd entail.
Turns out I'd have to sell little candles and cook for the bake sale.

Couldn't join the choir—can't sing. Couldn't play baseball—too fat to run.
Couldn't join Boy Scouts—too old. Didn't think Chess Club'd be much fun.

Said no to the Book Club, and Garden Club'd be too hard on my knee.
And the Breast Cancer Survivor's Group? Uh, not really.

Tried to join the Mayflower Club, but when they checked my pedigree,
Turns out my ancestors were the first Americans the Pilgrims diddeth see.

Then happened one mornin' to crave a sweet, drove down to the local rest'raunt,
And found the perfect gang for me—everything in a club I'd ever want.

Bunch of old men just sitting around, hashing over the latest news,
Noticed my plaid shirt and camo pants, said, "Sit down, Stranger, if ya choose."
I felt right to home and pulled up a chair, happy I'd found my niche at last!
Just had to be able to shoot the breeze and recall the days gone past—

No dues, no fancy dress code, no rules, no standards to meet.
Just order a coffee and a bear claw and grab the nearest seat.

While I was editing Chapter Ten, I was doing some online research to see if I could find some extra information about some of Patten Academy's teachers. I googled Emma Bradford Lane, who provided music classes for Patten students around 1915-1920. But I also found out that she played for special events around town, including the wedding of Ruth Rogers and Angus MacLean (or McLean). That made me think about how people enjoy parties such as wedding receptions, anniversary and birthday celebrations, holiday get-togethers, and so on. So it was with great interest that I read about Ruth Rogers's wedding.

Ruth was the youngest daughter of Colonel Luther Bailey and Mary (Barker) Rogers. I was surprised at how similar this wedding was to more modern-day weddings. This description of the wedding was submitted online by Ruth and Angus's granddaughter; I have taken the liberty of combining two different wedding announcements as they most likely appeared in newspapers. Neither announcement included the year, but the wedding probably took place sometime between 1915 and 1920, at which time Angus would have been 23-28 years old and Ruth would have been 21-26 years old. She was born in 1894 and graduated from Patten Academy in 1913. She had attended McGill University and had been working at the time of her marriage. Her first child was born in 1924. Beth Rogers, the maid of honor, was the daughter of Ruth's brother Edwin (therefore Ruth's niece), who lived with his wife Mattie Jane (Barker) and their daughters Beth (born in 1897) and Justine in Andover, New Brunswick. You can learn more about the Rogers family at the end of Chapter Four and at this website: https://www.geni.com/people/Ruth-MacLean/5674253567030033363

This website also includes photos of many of the Rogers family members. I would have loved to include them in this history, but I was a little nervous about copyright laws.

The Congregational Church of Patten, Maine was the scene of a very pretty wedding of unusual interest on Monday, May 29th, at 2:00 p.m. Miss Ruth Rogers, daughter of Colonel and Mrs. Luther Bailey Rogers, was united in marriage with Mr. Angus MacLean of Montreal by Rev. I.H. Lidstone of the Methodist Episcopal Church. The single ring service was used. The church was beautifully decorated with apple blossoms, evergreens, and flags, the Canadian flag conspicuous beside the Stars and Stripes.

Promptly at 2:15 to the strains of the Bridal chorus from Lohengrin, played by Miss Emma Lane, the bridal party passed down the aisle and took their place. The bride, who was given away by her father, looked very sweet and charming in a gown of delicate pink Georgette (flesh crepe de chine) with panels of white "Princess Mary" lace and wore a conventional veil of white tulle caught with lilies of the valley. She carried a shower bouquet of white bride's roses and sweet peas. The maid of honor, Miss Beth Rogers of Andover, New Brunswick was very attractive in a charming gown of pink organdy, with a large white organdy hat and carrying a shower bouquet of lilies of the valley and painted trilliums. The groom was attended by Mr. Robert Hall of Montreal, a college friend of the groom. Both men wore conventional black. Following the ceremony a reception was tendered to a large gathering of relatives and friends, including all of the girls from the Academy, and refreshments of fruit punch and assorted cakes, including the wedding cake, were served. The wedding gifts were many, among them handsome pieces of silverware and cut glass, linen, and several generous gifts of money. Mrs. McLean is a graduate of Patten Academy and McGill University at Montreal and after special training entered the Y.W.C.A. work as county secretary, a position in which she has been very successful and has thoroughly enjoyed. Mr. McLean, also of McGill University, is pastor of the Federated church and after spending a few days at the Rogers camps at Shin Pond, will return to Patten for the summer.

Among the out of town guests were: Mr. and Mrs. Edwin S. Rogers, Miss Beth Rogers, Miss Justine Rogers of Andover, N.B., Luther Rogers, Jr., of New York, Mr. and Mrs. Wesley Elliot of Montreal, Rev. Robert Hall of Montreal, Mr. and Mrs. Beecher Sleeper, Royce Sleeper of Sherman.

The wedding announcement also included this information about the church service the day after the wedding.

Memorial Sunday was observed by a union service at the Congregational Church, which was beautifully decorated by the young ladies with flags and apple blossoms and was filled to its capacity. The G.A.R., American Legion, Sons of Veterans, and Woman's Relief Corps were represented. The prayer and Scripture reading were by Rev. I.H. Lidstone of the M.E. church, and Hon. Verdi Ludgate sang The Recessional, by Kipling, arranged to music by De Koven. The pastor of the Federated church, Angus McLean, delivered a most impressive sermon on American patriotism, which was rather remarkable from the fact that he served overseas in the Canadian army and speaks from the Canadian point of view. The speaker in the evening was Rev. Robert Hall of the Presbyterian Church, Montreal, also a veteran of the World War, who served four years at the front. It was certainly a privilege to listen to two young men on our National Memorial Day who have thus earned the right to speak on patriotism."

CHAPTER THIRTEEN: RECOLLECTIONS

Note: This chapter is entirely my own recollections of life growing up in Patten in the 1950s and 1960s and living as an adult in Mount Chase since then. Please bear with me as I take a trip down memory lane.

The town of Patten looks very different now than it did when I was growing up there. There were no empty lots on Main Street at that time. There were four active churches, three school buildings, at least two and sometimes three gas stations, a large general store and a couple of convenience stores, clothing stores, two hardware stores, an insurance company, a movie theater, and two grocery stores, besides the drug store, the bank, the library, and the post office. You could buy a dairy cream in two different places or a regular ice cream at the drug store. Family reunions and wedding receptions were held at the Grange Hall (photo at right)

From the library to the cemetery, huge elm trees lined both sides of the street, creating a shady walk to town on a hot summer day. On Friday and Saturday nights, the town was bustling with activity as people did their shopping (Friday was payday) or went to the movies. However, on Sundays, the town was shut down while church parking lots were full. On Labor Day, Main Street was clogged with traffic as the Labor Day parade and celebration took place. Main Street was magical at Christmas time, with carols broadcast so you could hear them all over town. Stores and the streets were decorated brightly, and the fire truck brought Santa Claus to town.

Even the smells and sounds were different in those days. You could smell burning leaves and arsenic in the fall, "Stinkin' Lincoln" on overcast days, a freshly cut fir tree at Christmas time, and burning grass in the spring. You could hear the train whistle as the train pulled into the station and the drone of a chain saw in the distance. The mill whistle blew three times a day, and school bells rang to keep children on schedule. The fire station siren let you know where a fire was or if school was cancelled. Cars backfired, jets broke the sound barrier, and tractors putted down Main Street.

In the 1950s, children began school at Patten Primary. There was no kindergarten, and the classes were organized into five groups rather than three grades. Students might therefore finish primary school in three, four, or (rarely) five years. From there, students moved to Patten Grammar School, which housed grades four through seven. Eighth graders attended Patten Academy along with grades nine through twelve students. High School students were divided into groups based on what they would probably do after graduation: College Course, Business Course, Home Economics, and Agriculture.

Some of the people who worked at the Patten Schools when I was growing up were:

Patten Primary	Patten Grammar	Patten Academy
Anna Hanson Lois Brown Mary Campbell Mrs. Fenlason Nedra Nightingale Cordelia Brooks Ella Bishop	Violet McIntire Madelyn Howes Judy Heath Lillian Lougee Dorothy McPhee	Margaret Davis Jeanette Harvey Chester Chase David Michaud Joe Wilcox Jim McKenna Stan Pullen Lois Jones Jon Fenlason Fern Clements Laurene Blodgett Hill Al Pulkkinen Katherine Rogers Peter Viles

Administration, Band and Phys. Ed.	Bus drivers and janitors	Cooks
Ron Susee Clarence Pelletier Merle Rainey Bob Jones Dick Burr Bob White Larry Godsoe Laddie Deemer	Talmadge Bishop Lloyd McKenney Manley Brown John Brown Clive Hatt	Eva Deschane Virgie Willett Agnes Campbell Joyce Hunter Mahala Rogers

Our lives were pretty much contained to a radius of ten miles in those days. We could get most anything we needed right in town, or we shopped out of the Sears, Penney's, or Montgomery Ward catalogs. We waited impatiently for the Christmas catalogs to come in the mail. When they arrived, we looked through them from cover to cover, amazed by all the wonderful toys and the pretty clothes. We went to Houlton once in a while to shop at Penney's or Woolworth's, and we went to Bangor in the fall after harvest was over and in February if our team made the tournament.

The school year started in mid-August. Students attended school for a few weeks before having a harvest break of three weeks (or more if the weather had been bad). Most students in Grades 4-12 worked for a farmer picking potatoes. This was not considered child labor, but rather an opportunity to earn money to buy winter clothes or other items or just save. Sometimes whole families worked in the field during harvest. My father was a potato farmer, and I loved being a part of his harvest. You can read more about picking potatoes in Chapter Fifteen.

Girls were not allowed to wear pants in school. This could be a problem in the winter, especially for the town kids who walked to school. The high school girls preferred to freeze, but the younger girls often wore ski pants, pants under their skirts, or the ugliest light brown stockings you could imagine. They were thick and heavy and covered the legs up to the thighs, where they attached to a suspender system which had shoulder straps as well as a chest strap. Every girl whose mother forced her to wear these stockings lived for the day when she no longer had to wear them. I was mad at my mother for a long time because she let my younger sister Lynn stop wearing them the same year she let me stop wearing them. (Please excuse my art work. I tried to find a picture of that suspender device online, but could not locate one anywhere. Evidently it was such a hated thing that it has been deleted from clothing history.)

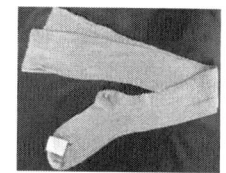

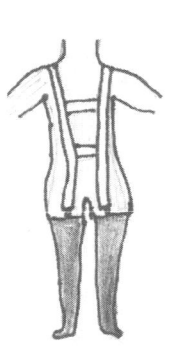

There was a bit of division between the town kids and the bus kids. The town kids often did not go straight home after school. They would slowly walk home with their friends and might make a stop somewhere in town. One popular gathering spot was the soda fountain at the drug store. (Unfortunately, I lived north of the school buildings and did not get a chance to participate in this fun.)

After arriving home from school, kids often went outside to play. (Of course, this was after changing from their school clothes to their play clothes.) We played croquet, badminton, softball, basketball, tag, hopscotch, jumprope, Chinese jumprope, marbles, hide-and-seek, Simon Says, Red Rover, and Alley Alley Over. We went sliding and skating in the winter. I was a teenager when we got our first snowsled. (We always called it a snowsled, not a snowmobile). It was a big heavy Polaris (photo at left) that got stuck fairly easily, often quite a ways from home. (My father was a patient man, though, and always came to our rescue.) Indoor recreational activities included playing cards and board games. Younger kids played with paper dolls, baby dolls, and toy trucks. My dad built us kids a playhouse (photo at right) where Lynn and I played with our dolls. My little brother Scott always played with his toy trucks and tractors in the dirt. He could imitate all the different sounds of different trucks and tractors.

My childhood home was located on the north corner of Main and Carver Streets. My parents, Rodney and Esther (Boynton) Harris, were potato and dairy farmers, although Dad got rid of the cows when I was about ten years old. We enjoyed playing in the barn. I was a little scared about going up into the haymow, but Lynn and I loved our little riding tractors and rode back and forth behind the cows while Dad did the milking. Mum had a big vegetable garden and spent late summer and early fall canning and pickling until the shelves in the cellar were lined with good food to eat all winter. And of course, we ate a lot of potatoes! In this photo, my mother and I are standing in front of our home. My parents lived in that house for over fifty years.

Although Lynn and I were expected to do household chores, we really preferred working outdoors. Lynn, Scott, and I helped plant potatoes in the spring, picked rocks in the summer, picked potatoes in the fall, and worked in the potato house in the winter. We helped with the firewood and the garden. We had lots of opportunities to drive the tractors and farm trucks. The photo at left shows my Dad teaching me to drive the tractor when I was 6 weeks old. We learned to drive a car with a standard shift long before we took driver education and got our licenses. The photo at right shows my Dad and me planting our garden.

My father's parents (Perley and Sadie Harris) moved to Patten from Fort Fairfield in the 1940's. They bought Traveler View Farm on the top of Finch Hill and lived in the same house where John and Faye Brown now live. They were potato and dairy farmers, although they got rid of the cows when I was still a child. Gram always had chickens, turkeys, and geese, and I can remember her cooking pig slop on the kitchen stove. (One of her geese was quite the watchdog and always attacked my father when he got out of his truck in her yard.) She kept her pigs in the orchard that my brother's wife now keeps looking so nice. My grandmother was famous for her green thumb; people would travel from all over the state to see her flower gardens. But if we wanted to visit our Harris cousins, we had to go "over home" across the border to New Brunswick, where my grandparents lived before they immigrated to the states as a young married couple. I remember an occasion when the cousins came to Patten and we took a camping trip to the base of Mount Chase. Dad covered the body of the farm truck with canvas and all eleven of us slept on the truck body. The next morning we climbed the mountain.

My mother's parents (Leo and Damaris Boynton) and my uncle (Laurel) lived on a farm about 6 miles south of town, in Stacyville. This farm is now owned by an Amish family. They were potato and dairy farmers, although they stopped raising potatoes when I was a child. The photo at left shows my brother Scott helping out during haying season. They also raised chickens and sold eggs. I can remember my grandmother inspecting the eggs with a candler, a special light that let you see the inside of the egg. My mother went to elementary school in Stacyville, but graduated from Patten Academy in 1949 as the valedictorian of her class. We had a camp in the woods behind the Boynton farm where we would spend time.

We didn't have a lot of vacation time in the summer because of the potatoes, but we did make time occasionally to do a little traveling. My dad built a camper on the back of the pickup truck, and the five of us rode in the cab—on one seat, of course. We went to New Hampshire one year and down on the coast one year. Our last family trip was taken the year before Lynn and I got married—we went to Prince Edward Island.

My husband's parents, Hadley and Pat (Cunningham) Coolong both grew up in Patten, as did Kemp and his sisters Glenda and Susan. As a young child, Kemp lived in a small house on Pleasant Street and then in a larger house on the east corner of Pleasant and Houlton Streets along with grandparents and various aunts and uncles. When he was about ten, his family moved to Shin Pond. Hadley's father, Tellis Coolong, had a cabin about two miles east of Shin Pond; Hadley added on to the cabin until it made a comfortable home for their family, which now included Kemp's brother Dan and sister Marie. Hadley and Pat were the caretakers of Point of Pines Camps for many years; there were times during the school year when Kemp and his siblings had to travel across Upper Shin Pond in a boat before catching the bus out on the main road. Later in life Hadley worked for Baxter State Park.

The Coolongs all loved to hunt and fish. (I was a big disappointment to them, as I couldn't shoot a gun worth a darn, although, in my own defense, I did learn to cast a fishing rod.) While I grew up in the fields, Kemp grew up in the woods. The Coolongs were storytellers, so Kemp heard all the old stories about the old time characters who lived and worked in the woods. Working alongside his father, he became a jack-of-all-trades: carpenter, plumber, electrician, logger, mechanic, and inventor.

The radio was a common household item in the fifties. You could listen to music (I remember hearing Curly O'Brien and Dick Curless on Saturday morning) or catch the news. As a teenager, I listened to 45s and LPs on my record player. My favorite singers were Elvis, Bobby Vinton, and Leslie Gore. The first televisions showed up in the 1950s. My husband remembers when his family got their first TV. It was the only set in the neighborhood, so his grandfather often invited friends over to watch sports events and wrestling. We watched stations broadcast from Bangor, Presque Isle, and New Brunswick. Some of my favorite shows from those years were *The Donna Reed Show*, Ed Sullivan's variety show, Walt Disney's show, *Leave It to Beaver*, and the Canadian show *Time for Juniors*. Kids watched cartoons on Saturday mornings, teenagers tuned in to *American Bandstand* with Dick Clark on Saturday afternoons, and adults watched the news. Men watched westerns such as *Wagon Train*, *Rawhide*, and *Gunsmoke*, and women got hooked on soap operas.

You could also go the movies in Patten and see the same shows everyone else in the U.S. was watching. For my generation, there were Elvis movies, *The Sound of Music*, and *Dr. Zhivago* . I was quite shy as a teenager and had pretty strict parents as well, so my social life was somewhat limited. I went to a few dances in town, where everyone had a great time learning the twist and the mashed potato. We went bowling in Island Falls and rode around.... and around.... and around Patten and Sherman and Island Falls. Everybody would chip together and you'd buy a dollar's worth of gas for the evening.

There are many people whom I remember fondly from that era. Rev. Herman Grant was my favorite minister; when I was a teenager and the Beatles became popular, some friends and I went to visit Mr. and Mrs. Grant in Presque Isle and sang Beatles songs to them. Irene Bradford (photo at left) was my Sunday School teacher when I was in high school, and she taught me many valuable lessons about life. I took piano lessons from Agnes Howes and Marilyn Somers, and Madelyn Howes taught me how to sing alto in the choir. Florence Sargent helped Dr. Banton take care of my teeth. Mrs. McIntire read us all the Little House books and had us learn poetry. Mildred Grant and Mrs. Rogers helped me find good books at the library. George and Rose Merrow sold the fabric and sewing supplies that my mother used to make many of my clothes. Dick Dickinson filled our prescriptions for penicillin when we had bronchitis. I looked up to Willard McIntire, Dan and Verna Woodbury, Amy Curtis, and Carroll Sargent.

I don't remember being too concerned about world events in those years other than the threat of nuclear war that shadowed my years at the Primary School. I was afraid whenever we practiced hiding under our desks, when I was walking home from school and worried about having to go into a stranger's house if the air raid siren went off, whenever I heard a plane fly overhead, or when I thought about going to the shelter at the town hall. But that threat subsided as I got to be around nine or ten years old and I went back to being content in my own little world of Patten, Maine. Even as a teenager, I didn't think too much about the war in Vietnam until local boys started enlisting or getting drafted. I wrote letters to a friend while he was serving and married a Vietnam vet after the war. The photo at the right is a picture of my husband Kemp while he was in Vietnam in 1968-69. Our boys were supported locally—we were disgusted with the treatment veterans were getting in other parts of the United States. There were a lot of veterans from previous wars living in town who supported the military as the means for keeping the world safe for democracy.

Let's see how well you remember this era of life in Patten. Do you remember......

- Soda coolers with ice cold water
- The wainscoting and the smell of lunch cooking at Patten Grammar School
- The big climb up the steps and the fast trip down the slide at the Primary School
- The huge study hall room, the dark dingy basements, and the two-headed calf at Patten Academy
- The dark oiled floors in the stores
- The metal railings at Merrow's (And did you ever put your tongue on those railings in the winter?)
- Going on picnics, often to picnic areas constructed by CCC crews in the 30's or in Baxter State Park
- Mr. Fenlason's cotton candy and baton twirlers on Labor Day
- Learning to do the Grand March in the gym
- Sammy and his peddler's wagon
- Picking fiddleheads in the spring, wild strawberries and raspberries in the summer, and blueberries and apples in the fall
- Going to Peavey's to get ice to make homemade ice-cream
- Calling the operator to make a phone call to anyone who wasn't on your party line (My family phone number was 10 ring 21.)
- Going to tournament games in Bangor the old way in a snowstorm
- Making paper dolls with the models pictured in the catalogs
- Knowing when Mrs. McPhee was coming back to the classroom because you could hear her jingling bracelets
- Playing croquet and badminton on your lawn
- The steam from canning vegetables and the sharp smell of vinegar from making pickles
- Green stamps at the grocery store
- Going to Ken Lord's store to get candy bars to go in your dinner pail during harvest
- Climbing that dark staircase to see Pearl Main, Phyllis Harrington, and Elizabeth Harvey Boynton at Patten Insurance Agency

As you can see, I get kind of nostalgic about my hometown and my growing-up years. I think I had a wonderful childhood: a good mix of work and play, family close by, a neighborhood to supply playmates, lots of things to buy at the stores, and great schools. It wasn't ideal: I wasn't always happy, I got mad at my parents and my sister sometimes, I witnessed bullying at school and took my share of teasing as well, and I got sick or fell down and skinned my knees up on a regular basis. But it was as good as it gets, and better than what a lot of kids experience. Looking back now, I realize I was a lucky girl.

And now I get to live in one of the most beautiful spots I could imagine: Mount Chase, Maine. My husband was already living here when we got married in 1972. Our house is about two miles southeast of Shin Pond, a half hour drive to Matagamon, and just a little further to Baxter State Park. We raised our two kids (Tellis and Melissa) here, playing in and appreciating the great outdoors. We lived just up the hill from Kemp's parents, and the kids' cousins lived just down the road. They played in the woods and in the field. Melissa brought me home a nice snake one day, and Tellis and his cousins Ryan and Carroll got in big trouble with their grandfather for throwing rocks at an old car.

We were fortunate to have free use of a camp on Upper Shin Pond that we looked after, and we had wonderful times there while the kids were growing up. We had a big old boat that we used to go fishing. Melissa loved to fish and didn't even mind catching eels! The kids swam in the pond off and on all day, toasted marshmallows over the campfire, and played poker with their father in the evening by gas light. We also spent many hot summer afternoons at the swimming beach on Lower Shin Pond. The kids took swimming lessons there, but really learned more about swimming just from being in the water often. The great challenge at the Shin Pond Beach was swimming out to "the rock."

We visited South Branch Pond in Baxter State Park often, as the ranger there was related to us. We tented, climbed Traveler Mountain, and canoed on the pond. Melissa fed a tame deer, and Tellis found $20.00 at the bottom of the pond! Kemp's parents lived in a camper all summer at Matagamon, and it was great fun to visit them. The kids and I tubed a ways down the East Branch of the Penobscot—the most fun I've had as an adult! One summer when Kemp was away with his National Guard unit, the kids and I stayed in one of Don Dudley's brand new camps at Matagamon.

In the winter, we ice-fished at Hay Lake. Kemp's father built a "ski-boose" (pulled by the snowsled) that the kids and their grandmother could ride in across the lake to the best fishing spot. I enjoyed cross-country skiing on the lake.

Every year, the Mount Chase Town Office hosted a Christmas party for the Mount Chase kids, and Santa came in the fire truck. The day even came when Tellis was Santa!

When the kids got to be teenagers, I gave them driving lessons on the Owlsboro Road. Can you imagine learning to drive on a section of road called the *Devil's Gulch*? We actually were glad when the kids got their driver's licenses; the only drawback to living out in the boonies was (and still is) the time and distance involved in getting to town and school.

Now that we've retired, Kemp and I are enjoying Mount Chase just as much as ever. We have a beautiful view of Mount Chase from our front window in the winter when the leaves are off the trees. Since we really don't care for traveling, we bought a side-by-side. We can ride for hours on ATV trails in the area. Kemp ice-fishes in the winter, and I ski and snowshoe on trails in the woods behind our house. I love to walk along the Shin Pond Road and have met the challenges of climbing Mount Chase, Sugarloaf Mountain and Mount Katahdin.

CHAPTER FOURTEEN: LOGGING, THE MILLS, AND THE MUSEUM

PART ONE: LOGGING

It is probably safe to say that every town and city in Maine has a logging heritage. Patten and Mount Chase definitely do. Even before Amos Patten bought T4R6, there were logging operations established in the region. As Patten and Mount Chase developed into towns, they began to serve as important gateways to logging operations. Local businesses provided goods and services, local men worked in the woods and on river drives, and local mills bought some of the wood. The towns were the last settled areas before you reached the dense forests to the west and north. Route 159 ended at Shin Pond.

Author's note: You may notice that I do not use the term lumberjack to identify men who worked in the woods. This was not a widely used term among Maine woodsmen, although it was used in other states. Even today you rarely hear a Maine logger referred to as a lumberjack. I also do not use the terms "lumberman" and "lumbering" as much as I used the terms "loggers" and "logging." That's probably just a personal quirk. To me, logs are trees that have been cut down and lumber is the stuff you buy that has already been cut to certain sizes.

In the 1800s, most of the wood was cut during the fall and winter months, and woods workers lived in logging camps for the duration. A logging camp was a self-contained community in the woods. Most of its supplies were hauled in during the fall months, although some camps had their own gardens to provide fresh produce and kept beef cattle and milking cows for fresh meat and milk.

A logging camp offered several different kinds of employment. The owner of the operation might be called a **lumber baron**. If you recall from Chapter One, Amos Patten was considered a lumber baron at the time he bought T4R6. The man in charge was called the **camp boss**; if he was in charge of more than one camp, he was called a **walking boss**.

Cruisers and **surveyors** were the first men on the scene of a logging operation. They evaluated the stand of timber and planned locations for the lumber camp, roads, and log yards. Next on the scene were **teamsters** and **swampers** who made roads and twitch trails. Teamsters also took care of the animals (oxen in the earliest days, then horses) and transported supplies into camp. Sometimes a camp would hire a **barn boss** as well. The photo at the left shows a woods crew working with horses in 1911.

The men who cut down the trees were called **choppers**, **loggers**, **lumbermen**, **sawyers**, or **limbers**. A good chopper could lay a huge tree right where he wanted it, sometimes on a bed of boughs to prevent the tree from splintering. Choppers used axes to fell trees until around 1890, when bucksaws and crosscut saws replaced axes. After the tree was down, the branches were sawed off. Horses or oxen pulled the logs through the woods on twitch trails to a yard, where they were loaded onto sleds. Men who worked in the yard were called **sled-tenders**, **yard rollers**, or **cant-dog men**. From there, the logs were moved to another yard, sometimes called a landing. This yard was located next to a body of water—a river or sometimes a lake.

Before a fellow took a job in a lumber camp, he might ask who the **cook** in the camp was. There are those who swear the cook could actually make or break a logging operation. A cook and his helper (called a **cookee**) prepared three huge meals a day. Breakfast and supper were served in a dining camp (photo above, Katahdin Woods and Waters ad), but lunch was carried into the woods so the loggers didn't lose time getting to and from the camp.

In many camps, there was a rule against talking in the dining camp. The cook wanted the men to eat and leave so he and the cookee could clean up. Baked beans, biscuits or brownbread, and huge pancakes were served often. In fact, one lumberman complained about the cook in the camp where he worked, saying that they had beans and brownbread for breakfast, brownbread and beans for lunch, and leftovers for supper. On the other hand, a good cook might even serve cakes and cookies for dessert.

A clerk, sometimes known as an **inkslinger**, kept track of the supplies and also oversaw the workers' wages. Choppers were usually paid by the cord, so the clerk also kept track of how much wood was being cut throughout the season. The **blacksmith** kept the animals shod and made things with metal. A **wood butcher** made things from wood.

Loggers worked from sunup to sundown. Their days consisted of working, eating, and sleeping. There was not much need for recreational opportunities or creature comforts in a logging camp. The men slept in camps lined with bunkbeds. These buildings were sometimes called ram pastures. (Usually, lice also lived there with the men.) There was a wood stove for warmth in the center of the room, and lines were hung so the men could dry their clothes. One logger complained that the horse hovels were built better than the camp he had to sleep in. In later years, some efforts were made to make lumber camps more pleasant places to live.

The last job that had to get done before the spring breakup was getting the wood to the mills: the river drive. Being a river driver was the most exciting woods-related job there was. All winter, the logs had been piled near a body of water. In the spring, when water levels were at their peak, the logs were pushed into the water and floated downstream to a mill. At times, dams were built to raise water levels and create stronger currents. River drivers were a special breed of men. It was dangerous work as the men scrambled around the logs to keep them moving down river. They wore special boots with cleats for better footing on the logs.

If there was a log jam, they had to use pick poles or peaveys to pry the logs apart. (Joseph Peavey of Stillwater, Maine, was the inventor of the peavey, which was an improved version of a cant-dog.) If all else failed, they would dynamite the dam. River drivers were considered to be a rather wild breed of men, especially since they tended to do a lot of celebrating when they got the logs to their intended destination. If a driver did not survive the trip, his cleated boots were hung on a tree near the place where he met his demise.

In the Patten and Mount Chase area, some logs were driven down Fish Stream into the Mattawamkeag River and then on to the Penobscot River. West of Mount Chase, logs were driven down the Sebois River into the East Branch of the Penobscot or directly down the East Branch of the Penobscot River from Matagamon. The Penobscot Log Driving Company was formed in 1846; it could be hired to oversee the whole drive. The company hired the best log drivers, chose the best water routes to use (or creatively altered waterways with dams), and handled the many problems that went along with this dangerous job.

The state of Maine was developed from south to north as logging operations moved northward in search of uncut forests of pine. By the early 1800s, logging operations had been established in northern Penobscot County and in Aroostook County. Logging became such big business in northern Maine that a war with Canada almost began in 1838. The northern border of Maine with Quebec and New Brunswick had never been established to the satisfaction of either side. Maine loggers insisted the border was further to the north than the Canadian loggers maintained. In 1826, Jim Chase was sent north to the Mount Chase area to burn the hay supply for a Canadian logging operation. (The fire got away from him and burned an extensive area as Mr. Chase was forced to take refuge on the mountain, henceforth called Mount Chase.) Other acts of sabotage were committed by both sides, and finally, around 1838, both sides prepared for war. Fort Kent and Fort Fairfield were hastily built, and American soldiers marched north through Sherman and Houlton, to northern Maine. One of my sources said that a large group of soldiers camped out for a time in Patten. The army did a lot of camping out over the next several years as the two sides entered into negotiations to try to settle the matter without going to war.

As it turned out, Daniel Webster of the U.S. and Lord Ashburton of Great Britain (on behalf of Canada), arrived at a compromise. The Webster-Ashburton treaty was signed in 1842, establishing the border at its present day location. The conflict was called *The Bloodless Aroostook War*, since no battle-related fatalities occurred. Well, that is, except for the cow which wandered onto the field during target practice. Many of the soldiers involved in the war decided they liked the area and settled in Northern Maine after the treaty was signed; one of these was A.G. Baker, who became a schoolteacher in Patten.

Throughout the rest of the 1800s, logging remained the vital force behind the state's economy, and the economy of Patten and Mount Chase as well. There were logging operations established all around the area, particularly west of Shin Pond towards Mount Katahdin. There were as many as 26 lumber camps in the area at one point. By the late 1800's, logging was such big business in Maine that Bangor was known as "the lumber capital of the world."

The photo at the right (1991 Patten heritage calendar) shows a 12.3 cord load of wood. In 1871, there were about 600 men working in the woods around Patten and Mount Chase. They worked with 298 horses. In 1899, crews cut 43 million feet of wood, and in 1900 they cut 66.9 million feet.

Supplies were "toted" from Patten to logging camps as far away as Chamberlain Farm, which was about seventy miles west of Patten. There was a great demand for tote teamsters, blacksmith shops, and supplies. In Patten, the Cooper, Quincy, and Rowe store and the Ira B. Gardner & Sons store sold a lot of those supplies around the turn of the century. There was a steady parade of horse teams back and forth between Patten and the camps. The first leg of the trip was the ten miles to Shin Pond. From there it was about another ten miles to Sebois Farm.

From Sebois Farm a trip might follow these routes:

- Sebois Farm to Grand Lake Matagamon to Trout Brook to Black Brook to Sourdnahunk, where the headquarters for Great Northern Pulp and Paper was located.
- Sebois Farm to Bluff Cove on the Eagle Lake Trail to the Swing, where the tote team was met by teamsters from the Eastern Manufacturing Company in T9R14.

As the final stop-off before entering the wilderness, the Shin Pond area prospered during these years. The first Shin Pond House was built in the 1870s and catered to lumbermen and sports. (You can read more about the history of the Shin Pond House in Chapter Sixteen.) About a mile or so west of the Shin Pond House was Crommett Farm, which provided many services to logging operations around the turn of the century, including raising and selling hay and potatoes, storing hay and grain in their barns, providing stables for horses and cattle, and maintaining an ice house and a blacksmith shop. They also boarded woods workers and operated a sporting camp.

In the last half of the 1800s, the logging industry got a big boost as paper mills were established around the state. One of the earliest paper manufacturers in Maine was the S. D. Warren Company, established in Congin Falls, Maine, in 1854. By 1880, S.D. Warren was the largest paper mill in the world. International Paper Company was established in 1898, and Great Northern Paper Company (the biggest paper mill in the world at that time) built the town of Millinocket in 1900. The paper mills preferred pulp wood to full-length logs, and species other than pine came into demand. In 1912, there were over fifty species of wood being used by Maine manufacturers.

The early 1900s saw great changes in logging operations as mechanization came to the woods. In 1901, Alvin Lombard of Waterville, Maine, patented the Lombard Log Hauler, a machine that could haul tremendous loads of logs in the woods. Other machines followed: tractors, caterpillar tractors, bulldozers, and skidders.

By the 1940s, axes and hand-held saws were replaced by the chainsaw. In areas where the logs had to be moved from one side of a lake to the other, steamboats pulled booms of logs over the water. Special boats called bateaus were used to get around in water. Men began traveling to work each day in pickup trucks rather than staying in logging camps.

Mechanization also led to changes in the way logs and pulp were transported from the woods to the mills. In the early 1900s, trains became an efficient way to transport wood, and after World War I, trucks came into use for getting the job done. By the mid 1920s, many logging operations had done away with the annual spring drive. The last long log river drive on the West Branch of the Penobscot was in 1928. Pulpwood drives continued into the 1960s, but environmentalists were working on laws to prohibit drives, as many of Maine's waterways were suffering the effects of bark and wood in the water. The last pulpwood drive on the West Branch of the Penobscot was in 1971, and in 1976, a law was passed which ended log drives for good.

River driving was tough, dangerous work, but so is driving a log, pulp, or chip truck. Logging roads tend to cover rough, rutty, hilly terrain, have sharp corners, and get muddy at times. Truck drivers put in long days. They have big payments to make, so they want to haul as much wood as possible. They often arrive in the woods before daylight and deliver their last load after sunset. Some of these hardy men who have gotten the job done over the years are Dan Baker, Fred Brownlee, Travis Brownlee, Ronald Campbell Sr., Ronald Campbell, Jr., Michael Detour, David Gardner, Jodi Gardner, David Gardner, Jr., Brian L. Glidden, Chester Glidden, Jr., Mike Hanson, Scott Harris, Carroll Heath, Brenden Landry, Dana Landry, Frank Landry, George Landry & Sons, Johnny Landry, Paul Landry, Richard Landry, John Marr, Calvin McCarthy, Jr., Brett Morse, Craig Morse, Rick Morse, Cody Morse, Randy Probert, Eric Raymond, Gregg Smallwood, Kerry Swallow, Graydon Watson, Scott Willett, Sr., and Scott Willett, Jr.

Logging continued to be an important part of the area's economy throughout the last half of the 20th century. With modern equipment, more wood could be cut in a shorter period of time. Logging operations varied from small one- or two-man operations to companies which employed multiple crews. Many of the larger mills throughout Maine had logging crews in the northern Penobscot County area throughout the years. Some of the logging operations owned trucks to haul their logs or pulp, while other companies hired independent truckers to haul their logs or pulp.

Below are some of the prominent names and businesses in the logging and trucking industry in the Patten and Mount Chase area over the years. Dates are approximate and an operation may precede or continue on from the dates provided. Some of these woods operations were privately owned, some were large companies who hired crews, and some were outfits that contracted woods work through a larger company.

NAME	DATES	COMMENTS
Zenas Littlefield	1840s	Cut at Trout Brook, ran a sporting camp there
Henry Averill	@1878	Scaler for the next five men
Elijah Webster	1860s-70s	Cut onT5R9 (Trout Brook), four horses, 16 men
S.L. Kimball	@1870's	From Mount Chase; cut on T5R8
Ezra Myrick	@1871	From Mount Chase
S.L. Hackman	@1871	From Mount Chase
Samuel Harvey	@1871	From Mount Chase
W. E. Myrick	@1876	From Mount Chase
Eli Kellogg	@1878	Cut on T6R8
J. and A. Hammond	@1878	Cut on T5R10
B.C. Hammond	@1878	Cut on T5R7
Lawler	@1900	Chamberlain Lake
Murphy	@1900	Chamberlain Lake
Marsh	@1900	Chamberlain Lake
Leen Brothers	@1900	Chamberlain Lake, Grand Lake Matagamon to Whetstone
McNulty	@1900	Third and Fourth Lakes

Gardner and Finch	@1900	Grand Lake Matagmon, 2nd & 3rd Lakes
Landry and Sousie	@1900	Grand Lake Matagmon, 2nd & 3rd Lakes
Katahdin Pulp & Paper	@1900	Grand Lake Matagmon, 2nd & 3rd Lakes, Wassataquoik
Ira B. Gardner & Sons	@1900-1930	Cut at Grand Lake Matagmon, 2nd & 3rd Lakes around 1900
B. W. Howe	@1900-1930	Cut at Grand Lake Matagmon, 2nd & 3rd Lakes and at Sebois around 1900
Hugh Cunningham	@1900	Grand Lake Matagamon to Whetstone
J. Kimball	@1900	Grand Lake Matagamon to Whetstone
M. Tracy	@1900	Grand Lake Matagamon to Whetstone
Edwin Rogers	@1900	Wassataquoik
J. Cunningham & Son	@1900	Sebois
L. F. Russell	@1900	Sebois
Tozier Brothers	@1900	Sebois
E.B. Brown	@1900-1930	Cut at Sebois around 1900
M. Jordan	@1900	Soldier Brook
Berry	@1900	Mud Brook
Eagle Lake Co.	@1900-1930	
Ira Carpenter	@1900-1930	
Paul Gagnon	@1900-1930	
George French	@1900	
Maynard Darling	@1900	
Luther Hall	@1918-1930	
Lincoln Pulpwood	@1918-1930	
W. H. Murphy	@1918-1930	Out of Old Town
E. G. Bryson	@1918-1930	Out of Houlton
American Thread Co.	@1918-1930	
Barker Lumber	@1918-1930	Out of Milford
Bangor Lumber	@1918-1930	
Penobscot Development	@1918-1930	Out of Great Works
M. B. Wadleigh	@1918-1930	Out of Old Town

Below is a list of men or companies who have established logging operations which have been active at some point between 1930 and 2016.

Cliff Webster	Buck, Rick, and Shawn McAvoy
Arnold Shorey	Jack, Mike, Kevin, and Shawn Craig
Hollis Shorey	Jim, Jamie, and Doug Cunningham
Hollis and Kent Ordway	Cal McCarthy
Farrell Lumber Company	Arnold Porter
Chamberlain Lumber Company	Norm Perkins
Katahdin Lumber Company	Randy Cyr
Adrian, Dana, and Jimmy Carver	George and Barbara Landry
John, Scott, and Mike Savage	The Libby family

I most sincerely apologize for leaving out any names of truck drivers and logging operations. And I would love to list every man (and woman, too) who has worked in the woods over the years, but there have been too many. These workers deserve our recognition for making Maine the great state it is today. They worked and still work outdoors year round in the heat and the rain, the cold and the snow, and even during blackfly season. And while logging is somewhat safer in the 21st century, it still remains the most dangerous job in the United States, and loggers often have the scars to show for it. Look around at everything made out of wood, including the paper in this book. Now thank a logger! And remind him or her to wear safety equipment.

PART TWO: THE MILLS

Equally important to the economy of Maine towns and cities were the mills which processed the wood. Patten had sawmills from its very early years. Although there were almost certainly other wood mills in Patten's early years, my research did turn up the following information. [Note: Grist mills and starch factories are also included in this list.)

1831: A grist mill was built to grind grain.

1833: David Haynes had a lumber and floor business

1835: Samuel Leslie built the first sawmill in Patten for Ira D. Fish.

1843: Samuel Darling manufactured furniture, cabinets, blinds, doors, and sashes.

1850: Joseph Heald built a grist mill on Ellis Brook (now called Webb Brook).

1870: Jacob Frye built a steam lumber mill where the Patten Playground is now located. Samuel Darling was manufacturing furniture and caskets out of a building on the west side of Mill Hill (photo at right).

At various times: Caskets and coffins were manufactured by Jerome Frye and his son Preston, the Huston brothers, and N. Raymond.

1882: John and Ira Gardner built a steam lumber and grist mill.

1894: Sherman Lumber Company in Stacyville was established by Frank L. Robinson and his son Walter.

Around 1900: Gilman, Finch, and Stevens manufactured cabinets, furnishings, sleds, and wagons. This establishment was located on Houlton Street. This was later sold to the Patten Planing Company, which burned in the 1930s.

1900: Great Northern Paper Company was established in Millinocket.

1903: The Carding Mill was building furniture.

1920: The Red Saw Mill (photo at left) was operating. It was located where Paul Morse's house is now on the bottom of Mill Hill.

Around 1920: The Leon Stevens Mill (photo at right) was located on Houlton Street and made furniture, and skis. Skis cost 25 cents a pair or 10 cents each. (Why would you want one ski?) This mill burned in 1932.

1950's: Chester McManus was operating a sawmill where Meadowbrook Manor is now located. This mill burned in 1964. Around this time Ordway and Son also operated a sawmill.

1970's: Austin Lord operated Double A Sawmill (later Double A and CG). Other mills in the area during the 1970s were County Forest products (Bobby Porter) and Northern Mill and Lumber Company.

1987: Ray Porter set up a quonset building and another building on the Shin Pond Road where he operated Porter's Paddle Shop (photo above). Porter sold out to Jim Carson of Millinocket in 1994; he later moved the operation to Millinocket. Since then, Ricky Keim has been manufacturing paddles at Dri-Ki Woodworking at a location just a mile or so west of Porter's shop.

1978-1986: Ervin Tower owned and operated Crystal Lumber Company (photo at right) just over the town line in Crystal. At one time, 37 people were employed in the production of railroad ties, cedar shingles, and cedar fencing. Tower shipped the last loaded railroad car from Patten before the tracks were torn up. After 1986, the mill was sold to Holly Ward, a fourth generation lumberman from Vermont. After being operated by other managers, Cecil Gallagher became manager of Ward Clapboard, a position he holds through 2017. The mill is currently owned by Rob Brownlee of Patten.

The most popular site for a mill in Patten was at the foot of Mill Hill, where Fish Stream ran through town, a logical site since early mills used moving water to operate the mill machinery. The mills that were established here were as follows.

1831: A grist mill was built.

1835: Samuel Leslie built a grist mill and saw mill for Ira D. Fish.

1867: William Gifford bought the grist mill and converted it to a lumber mill. He later sold it to F.F. Weymouth, who later sold it to Jerry Foote.

1879: John and Ira Gardner built a starch factory on the south side of Fish Stream. The factory processed potatoes to make starch, which was shipped to Kingman. When John died in 1903, the factory was sold to T.H. Phair, who sold it to Piper and Libby, who sold it to C.E. Clark. It burned around 1915. (T. H. Phair was a "starch baron" who at one time owned fourteen starch factories in Aroostook County.)

1900: Edwin and George Merrill bought the former Gifford Mill and named it Merrill Mill Company. They manufactured long and short lumber and spools.

1902: The Huston Brothers built a dam by the mill and opened an electric light plant.

1904: The light plant was sold to Merrill Mill.

1920: The photo at right shows the Mill Pond. On the right is Norm Arbo's house. On the left is a blacksmith shop, and behind that are Fred Quint's apartments.

1924: Fire destroyed the Merrill Mill. It was rebuilt but was not successful and was closed for a few years. This photo shows Merrill Mill in 1920.

1936: American Thread Company was using the mill to take in birch to be shipped to Milo to be used in the manufacture of spools for thread. American Thread also had an operation on Kimball Brook.

1939: Sam Antworth bought the mill and converted it from a lumber mill to a plywood mill (photo at right). Several families from Northern Maine who were familiar with the manufacture of plywood moved to Patten to work at the mill. These included the Corriveau, Bishop, Roy, Rossignol, Skidgell, and Bossie families.

1944: Atlas Plywood bought the mill. Atlas also had mills in Houlton and Greenville, but the Patten mill was the most successful.

1959: Atlas sold to Joe Sewell and J.M. Huber.

1962: Joe Sewell left, but the mill was kept by Huber. This photo shows the Huber Mill.

1980: Fire destroyed the Huber mill and put 100 people out of work

1981: Using the new steam chest that had been built by Huber and which had not been damaged in the fire, a group of local men formed Patten Veneer Mill.

1982: Patten Veneer Mill closed.

1985: Calley & Currier Co., Inc. of New Hampshire bought the mill to manufacture veneer. The veneer was used to make crutches at the New Hampshire plant. Some of the veneer was also sold to a company which made bleachers.

1988: Calley & Currier sold their mills in Patten and New Hampshire to Woody Sponaugle and Bill Bischoff. The business was still called Calley & Currier.

1998: Sponaugle bought out Bischoff.

2005: Calley & Currier closed.

2006: Appalachian Engineered Floors (a division of Anderson Floors from South Carolina; Shaw Industries) bought the mill. It was named Appalachian Katahdin.

2010: The last strip of veneer was peeled and Appalachian Katahdin closed.

2011: The mill equipment and buildings were auctioned or sold off.

2013: An anonymous investor bought the mill, which is now called Haymart. Haymart is involved in organic farming, but at the Patten site they currently manufacture wood pellets called "hotties" for use in pellet stoves. The pellets became available for purchase in 2016. In the future they plan to manufacture feed pellets. The mill is managed by Matthew and Adam Fronczak.

Indirectly contributing to the economy of Patten were mills outside of town; paychecks from Sherman Lumber Company and Great Northern Paper Company were deposited, cashed, and spent in Patten for over a hundred years. Sherman Lumber Company, owned by the Robinson family of Stacyville, operated from 1894 to 2003. Great Northern Paper Company was actually responsible for creating the town of Millinocket when it opened in 1900. Once the largest paper mills of its kind in the world, it provided good jobs for many Patten men until the late 1990s, when the sagging economy forced the sale and eventual closing of the mill.

PART THREE: THE MUSEUM

Lore Rogers and Caleb Scribner recognized the important of the logging industry to this area of Maine. In the 1950s, they began a collection of information, artifacts, and displays having to do with logging. This was housed in a back room at Veteran's Memorial Library until 1962, when the present day Lumberman's Museum was built. The museum houses a Lombard Log Hauler, a bateau, a road sprinkler, and boom boats. It has full-size replicas of logging camp buildings, including a men's bunkhouse, a cookhouse and dining room, a sawmill, a blacksmith shop, a horse hovel, a tool shed, and an equipment shed. Some of the buildings were actually moved from woods sites to the museum lot. There are hundreds of displays and artifacts. A beautiful reception area sells books, t-shirts, etc. The museum has also become a center of activity in general. Each year, the museum serves a traditional baked bean meal as part of the Patten Pioneer Days celebration. It hosts local events such as the Fiddlers and Fiddlehead Fest, the Patten Academy Alumni Banquet, and book talks.

The economy of the Patten and Mount Chase area has always been driven by the logging industry. It has been responsible for the success of local businesses, the enrollment in local schools, and the population of the towns in general. It has provided employment for a good percentage of the population of the towns. It has contributed directly to the vitality of the towns and in many ways has created the character of the towns.

The logging industry in Maine has survived many challenges. As the tall pine forests were depleted across the state, a demand for spruce and other species kept logging operations going. The depression of the 1870s was a difficult time, but the demand for wood for paper mills helped keep the industry thriving. The depression of the 1930s was another challenge, but through those years and the years following, logging remained big business in the Patten and Mount Chase area. But the logging industry has never completely recovered from the nationwide economic "recession" of the 1980's. Coinciding with the recession was a decreased demand for paper, in part because of the increased use of electronic technology. As one Maine mill after another has closed, the future of the logging industry is shaky to say the least. Jobs have been lost by the thousands. Some have been lost directly through the closing of mills and fewer employment opportunities for woods work. Others have been lost indirectly because of the effects the poor economy has had on other businesses and school enrollment. Young adults particularly have left the area to find better employment opportunities elsewhere.

Change comes hard to many people. But no one can deny that things are changing in Patten and Mount Chase. We can remain hopeful that the woods industry will make a comeback or at least not get any worse, but if these communities want to stay alive, the residents will have to find other ways to bring money into the area. Although some residents of Patten and Mount Chase saw the establishment of the Katahdin Woods and Waters National Monument in 2016 as a further threat to the logging industry, others saw this development as a possible boon to the economy of the area. Regardless of what the future holds for us, no one can take our logging heritage away from us. It is indelibly ingrained in the history and the character of these two towns.

THE DAILY NEWS — MILL CLOSURES HIT MAINE'S ECONOMY HARD

LEGENDS OF THE NORTH MAINE WOODS AND RIVERS

Logging in the late 1800s and early 1900s was a hard and dangerous occupation, and riverdriving was even more so—just the kind of work that creates legends, both fictional and nonfictional. Of course, all Mainers are familiar with that famous logger, Paul Bunyan; after all, there is a 31-foot statue of him right in front of the Cross Insurance Center in Bangor, Maine. Paul was born in Bangor, although the folks of Bemidji, Minnesota, claim he was their child. At any rate, Paul was responsible for much of the natural layout of the land (between his giant footprints and his habit of dragging his axe) and broke all records for his logging abilities.

So was Paul Bunyan completely a tall tale, or was he a real logger whose accomplishments got a little blown out of proportion? It is believed that his character might be based on one or two real-life loggers. One was Fabian Fournier, a French-Canadian logger who worked in Michigan after the Civil War. Fournier earned himself the nickname "Saginaw Joe" and was said to have two sets of teeth with which he could bite through wooden rails. He was murdered in a brawl in Michigan. Paul might have also had his origins in the life of Bon Jean (whose name sounds a lot like Bunyan). Bon Jean was also a French-Canadian logger; he was involved in the patriot revolt at Saint Eustache, Quebec, Canada.

Just as there is disagreement about Paul Bunyan's birthplace, there is disagreement about who told the first Paul Bunyan tall tale. The first tales were part of our oral storytelling heritage, but James MacGillivray may have written the first published account of Paul's exploits in 1906 for a Michigan newspaper. Another early written account came in the form of a promotional pamphlet for the Red River Lumber Company in Minnesota written by William B. Laughead.

Eddie Clark from Ashland earned the respect of the older loggers in a woods camp when he walked 30 miles to begin his new job as a cookee. The crew was mostly French-Canadian, and they nicknamed Eddie "Bonne Homme." Eddie, being one of the few in camp who could read and write, read books such as *Robinson Crusoe* and *The Adventures of Tom Sawyer* to the men at night. He would read a passage, another fellow would translate it into French, and then the men would discuss it. As I did some research on Eddie, I finally realized that he was the fictional main character in a book named *Bon Homme,* written by Leonard Hutchins of Ashland and Presque Isle. However, Mr. Hutchins did base Eddie's character on a real-life woodscaler who worked in one of Edouard La Croix's lumber camps in the 1920s. Mr. Hutchins also wrote about the adventure of Umcolcus Charlie.

At first I believed that the legendary Jigger Jones was a fictional woodsman and riverdriver, but it turns out there really was such a man. From Fryeburg, Maine, Jigger began working in the woods at the age of twelve, when he proved himself by putting down a much-larger logger who had committed the terrible sin of talking at the supper table. Jigger was a hard-working, hard-fighting, and hard-drinking character. Kendall Morse, a Maine folk singer, sang a song about Jigger in which Jigger was a lumber camp cook who was tired of the complaints about the food. In revenge, he baked up a moose-poop pie (a poopie pie?) to serve as a special desert. (I'm going to guess that even though Jigger was real, some of the stories that have been told about him may have been just slightly exaggerated for the sake of telling a good tale.)

Joe Attien, of French and Penobscot Indian heritage, was a legendary but real-life river driver. He also served as Henry David Thoreau's guide on Thoreau's visits to Maine. He was the last hereditary chief and the first elected chief of the Penobscot tribe. Joe died the way he lived—on the river driving logs. He died while trying to steer a bateau through rapids on the West Branch of the Penobscot River, desperately trying to save the lives of the other men in the bateau. His cleated boots were hung from a tree near the site of his death.

John Ross of Bangor has been called the greatest riverman and river boss in the world. He was the master driver of the Penobscot Log Driving Company for many years. He had a reputation for accomplishing what seemed to be impossible drives. He was well-respected by the men who worked the drives under him, including the group of men known as the Bangor Tigers.

Shepard Boody was the engineer who designed "the dam-in-the-woods, now known as the Telos Dam. In 1841, Boody dug a canal called the Telos Cut, built a dam between Telos and Eagle Lakes there, and built another dam between Eagle and Chamberlain Lakes. For the first time in history, the waters of the Chamberlain and Telos Lakes flowed south, through the Telos Cut, into Webster Lake, and into the East Branch of the Penobscot.

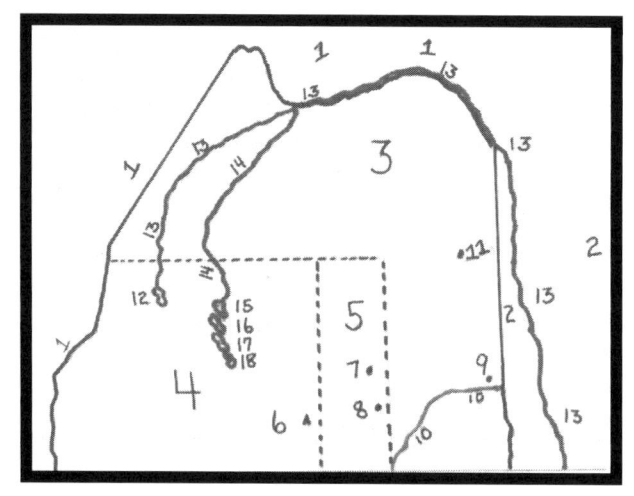

Ebenezer Coe was another engineer who also used his brain more than his brawn to get the logs to the mill. In the 1850s, he built a series of lock dams which raised the levels of Eagle and Churchill Lakes in order to reverse the flow of water in those lakes from northward to southward into the Penobscot.

MAP CODE

1. Quebec, Canada	10. Interstate 95
2. New Brunswick, Canada	11. Presque Isle
3. Aroostook County, Maine	12. Baker Lake
4. Piscataquis County, Maine	13. Saint John River
5. Penobscot County Maine	14. Allagash River
6. Mount Katahdin	15. Churchill Lake
7. Mount Chase	16. Eagle Lake
8. Patten	17. Chamberlain Lake
9. Houlton	18. Telos Lake

Edouard LaCroix was one of those lumbermen who wore a suit and tie. Lumber barons, as they were known, were businessmen and often politicians who made money in the logging business. They were men of vision, knowledge, and ability. I said they wore a suit and tie, but they probably felt more comfortable in a plaid shirt. Here are a few of these real-life legends of the Maine woods.

- Edouard LaCroix began his successful career at the bottom at the age of twelve and worked his way up in the lumbering business. He also established successful sawmills, a woolen mill, and a shipping company. He was from Quebec, but his influence was felt in Maine, Ontario, and New York. He, like other lumber barons, provided jobs for thousands of people. He served as a member of Parliament in Ottawa, Ontario.
- Amos Patten was a lumber baron from Bangor who bought the tract of land that became the town of Patten. He also bought other land in various parts of Maine for the purpose of logging it. He was a Maine Representative from Penobscot County to the General Court of Massachusetts in 1815 and served on the Council of Maine after that. He was one of Bangor's first settlers.
- Shep Cary came from Houlton and is credited with being a driving force in the development of Aroostook County. He served in the Maine Legislature and was a leader in the Democratic Party. His voting habits were a testimony to his good common sense. He was an important player in the battle with Canada that was later called *The Bloodless Aroostook War*. He made a fortune with logging operations and mills.
- John Goddard was another lumber baron from Houlton who, while famous because of his logging businesses, was also well known for being a braggart who used a pair of captive moose in place of horses.
- David Pingree was a land investor who owned more than a million acres of land in Maine and several other states, including a great deal of land in the Allagash region. He was an innovator in finding efficient ways to drive logs to the mills.

There are many more legendary loggers, river drivers, and lumber barons who could be mentioned here. I will mention some of them in Chapter Sixteen. As I worked on my book *Letting Daylight Into the Swamp*, almost every book I read as research mentioned with awe the men who logged the north Maine woods. The woodsmen of Patten and Mount Chase can be included among those larger-than-life men. Robert Pike had this to say about loggers in his book *Tall Trees, Tough Men* :

> *"...we see the lumberjack...who had a passion for the wild and toilsome life, who was reckless, generous, and social. A man generally recognized as a separate species, as is shown by a newspaper account of a steamboat accident in 1912, which reported that three men and a logger were drowned. "*

LOGGING A CENTURY LATER

What did Maine logging look like a hundred years after Bangor was the lumber capital of the world? You read about the logging camp era and what that was like for the men who worked in the woods in those days. Let's take a look now at logging in the last half of the 20th century.

We are talking about the backbone of Patten and Mount Chase economy. The paychecks went into the pockets of forest landowners, owners of logging operations, truck drivers, skidder operators, choppers, mill owners, and mill workers. But it didn't stay long in the pockets of the local woods and mill workers and truck drivers. It went quickly into the cash drawers of local stores and gas stations, or back to the bank as payments of one kind or another. It went to the town office for taxes, but it didn't stay there long, either, as it was moved to the accounts of schools and water systems and sewer systems and road repairs and so on and so on. In short, there was a lot of money floating around town, but it wasn't making anybody very rich! This is Gus's story—fictional but certainly based on fact!

****

The winter of 1985-1986 was your typical Maine winter: cold and snowy. Gus owned a skidder and worked in the woods west of Shin Pond for a company which employed ten skidder crews. He got up really early five or six days a week and drove his pickup to where he was cutting.

On Friday, February 20, he picked up Ora, his chopper, around 4:00 a.m. and started driving west on Route 159. Ora immediately went back to sleep, and Shin Pond was still asleep when they passed through. Around 5:00, they got to the log yard where he had parked his skidder the night before. He got out and got it started. It started hard 'cause it was twenty below, but finally the motor caught and stayed running. Gus got back into his truck and had a doughnut and the rest of his coffee while he waited for the skidder to warm up. At 6:00, he said, "Time's a'wastin'." They got out of the warm pickup into the cold and put on their helmet liners and hard hats. Gus and Ora were both wearing long johns, long-sleeved Henley shirts, flannel shirts, Canadian pants, winter jackets, woolen socks, and their winter steel toe boots. Ora liked lined gum rubbers, but Gus preferred lace-ups. In spite of the cold, the men would have to shed their jackets later on as their work generated a lot of body heat.

Ora went off with his chainsaw to start cutting down trees while Gus fueled up the skidder. He looked around the yard and noted that three of the other skidder crews were already at work, but another skidder was sitting there with parts spread around on the snowy ground. Poor Wes. He just couldn't catch a break. Gus had heard the bank was breathing down Wes's neck and was about ready to repossess the skidder. Not that it was worth much. And it wasn't like Wes wasn't a good worker. But if he didn't have bad luck, he wouldn't a'had any luck atall.

Gus noticed there had already been two trucks there since he had left the yard the previous day. Probably Pete and Hank. They put in long hours, trying to get as many loads as possible hauled into the mill. The trucks which picked up wood out of this yard had their own loaders, but other logging operations had a loader truck which stayed in the yard. The trucks that hauled wood from those yards didn't have their own loaders.

As the morning progressed, Ora cut down trees and limbed them, and Gus hauled them to the yard with the skidder. Ora had to stop a few times to file his saw, but they did a fair mornin's work.

Around noon, they stopped for lunch. Gus ate quickly, then greased the skidder and fixed a chain that kept breaking. His wife Mae was going to Houlton that day to pick up a couple of parts that he needed to replace. He tried to keep it in good repair because a broke-down skidder reversed the flow of cash in his pocket. Mae had figured out that they lost a hundred dollars a day when the skidder wasn't running, not counting the cost of repairs.

After the noon break, the men went back to work. Trucks came in and out of the yard. At least in the cold of winter, the ground stayed pretty froze and you didn't have to worry so much about getting stuck. The scaler for the operator Gus and Ora worked for came around to scale logs in the yard and hand out paychecks. Finally, around 4:00, Gus hauled the last twitch to the yard. Tomorrow was Saturday. Ora would take Saturday and Sunday off, but Gus would spend Saturday working on the skidder.

Before Gus went home Friday, he went to the gas station. He gassed up his pickup and filled the gas drum that was in the body of the pickup. (This gas was used to fuel up the skidder.) He went into the garage to pick up the tab for the fuel and oil and what not that he had gotten during the week. When he finally got home at supper time, he handed his pay check to his wife and showered and ate quickly. His daughter Jen had a game that night at the school, and Gus didn't want to miss a single dribble. She was only a sophomore, but she had made the varsity team and was actually seeing quite a bit of floor time.

Saturday, Gus headed back into the log yard. He took his son Sam with him. Mechanicking went a lot faster if you had someone to hand you tools or help you hold on to something. Sam liked working with his father, but Gus didn't know if that was a good thing or not. Sam was pretty smart. Maybe Gus should encourage him to go to college and find a safer and easier job that paid more money. On the other hand, woods work wasn't all that bad as far as jobs went.

At home, Gus's wife Mae got her baked beans in the oven and made a double batch of bread. Gus liked homemade bread for his sandwiches, so she made bread two or three times a week. After she picked up the house, she got out the checkbook and the bank statement and the calculator and sat down at the dining room table to take care of business. She was pleased with the amount of wood Gus and Ora had cut that week. She was trying to get a couple of skidder and pickup payments ahead because it would soon be spring break. And according to the Main Street newscasters, the mill quotas were filling up fast. Spring break started either when the quotas were full or when the bans went up on hauling logs over the town roads. (Hauling on thawing roads wreaked havoc on them.) She knew Gus would try to find a private lot to cut on while regular woods work was suspended, but he wouldn't be able to get the wood hauled until the bans were lifted.

After Mae balanced the checkbook with the bank statement, she made checks out to the bank for the payments, to the gas station for gas and oil, and to the insurance company for the insurance on the skidder and the pickup. She subtracted the amount of the bill for the parts she had picked up the previous day. Then she made out checks for the regular household bills. If she skimped on the grocery bill by serving macaroni or potatoes or hamburger more often, she should have enough next week (counting her biweekly paycheck) to make an extra skidder payment. That's if the skidder didn't break down. That's if neither Gus nor Ora got that flu that was going around. That's if that storm they were predicting didn't dump two feet of snow on them. That's if…she didn't even want to think about Gus or Ora getting hurt.

She knew she and Gus were lucky. They both had good jobs. There were lots of people around who didn't have good jobs, and some who didn't have any job at all. They had a warm, comfortable home, a brand-new second hand car, family that could loan them fifty bucks in a pinch, and two good kids who didn't throw a hissy fit when they had to wear store brand clothes and sneakers instead of Levis and Nikes. And you could make some pretty tasty meals with macaroni and potatoes and hamburger.

They'd get by.

CHAPTER FIFTEEN: PATTEN'S FARMING HERITAGE

Along with the forests, the fields have also been an important part of Patten and Mount Chase life. From its formative years, local residents have grown and harvested crops and raised livestock. The first settlers of Patten and Mount Chase were subsistence farmers; that is, they farmed to provide for their own needs, with little or no surplus for trade. In those days, most families kept a cow or two to provide milk for their own use. Milk was also used to make butter and cheese. They had oxen for work animals and raised sheep, chickens, beef cattle, and hogs to be slaughtered for meat. The chickens would also provide eggs, and the sheep's wool could be used to make cloth. They also relied on what the natural environment provided, such as berries, fiddleheads, moose, deer, partridge, rabbits, and maple sap to be made into syrup and sugar.

As the years passed and more and more men worked away from the home place, dairy farming in the Patten and Mount Chase area changed from subsistence farming to farming as a business. Families were less likely to have a cow or two, preferring to buy their milk from a dairy farmer. In 1855, Jacob Frye opened a cheese factory in Patten. Therefore, we can deduce that by then there were farmers who were tending big enough herds so they could sell some of their milk. Throughout the last half of the 19th century, milk and milk products were generally sold to households or to a store.

One of the big problems in those days was keeping dairy products cool and fresh. Because it didn't take long for milk to spoil, it was rarely transported too far from the farm. For refrigeration, people used ice cut from brooks and ponds during the winter and stored in sawdust throughout the summer. However, by the early 1900s, dairy farmers were benefiting from new ideas about keeping milk fresh. Linwood Palmer and Ray Gardner opened the first creamery in Patten in 1920, providing another market for local milk.

The advances in keeping milk products fresh were due in part to the work of Dr. Lore Rogers of Patten. Dr. Rogers was a noted bacteriologist who made several important discoveries in the early 1900s about maintaining and using dairy products. After a brilliant career which took him to top research facilities and colleges in the United States and to seminars in Europe, Dr. Rogers returned to Patten and opened Katahdin Creamery in 1931. It remained open until 1958.

Farmers could tend even larger herds when milking machines and other mechanized equipment (tractors, trucks, conveyors, etc.) became available from the World War I era on. Using data published in Town Reports, trends in farming were clear. The number of cows taxed as personal property increased steadily throughout the 1900s, while the number of horses dropped.

What these statistics don't show, however, is how many farmers owned those cows. By the late 1950s, when milking machines came into use and trucks began hauling milk directly from the farm to a dairy such as Hood's, farmers had either increased their herds or sold them off to farmers with large herds. So there were fewer farmers owning more cows.

Like lumbering, dairy farming was a job that started before sunup and ended after sunset. Milking had to be done twice a day, so a dairy farmer could not travel very far from home. People sometimes wrinkle their noses at the smell of cow manure, but most dairy farmers are very careful about the cleanliness of their equipment and the milk produced. I can remember my grandmother *doing the milk dishes*; every day she had to sterilize the equipment in the milk room used for handling and storing the milk. Throughout the day, farmers did other jobs—cleaning the barn, repairing equipment, and so on. Many dairy farmers were also potato farmers in the mid-1900s.

Dairy farmers also had to harvest hay so the cows would have food all year around. The photo at the right shows a horse-drawn wagon piled high with hay. Horses and manual labor were replaced by tractors and baling machines, and trucks could be used to haul the hay to the barn, where it was put in on conveyors and moved up into the hayloft. In the 1900s, hay was compacted into rectangular blocks and tied with baling twine. Late in the century, farmers had the option of baling their hay in much larger cylindrical bales.

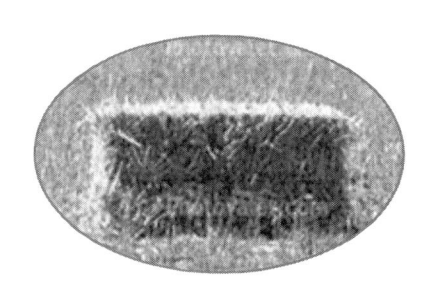

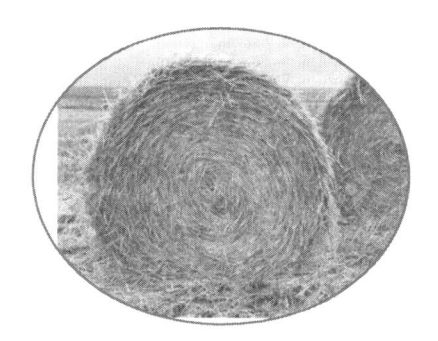

Some of the dairy farming names from the 1900s in Patten, Mount Chase, and Stacyville were Boynton, Willigar, Guptill, Townsend, Glidden, Cunningham, Harris, Brawn, Beattie, Slauenwhite, Webb, Donovan, Heath, Crouse, Harrington, and Bradford. I only list last names because many dairy operations were multi-generational. Also, if I listed first names, I would have to include all the names of the farmers' wives and daughters. Farming has always been a family business!

Donis Willigar is the only dairy farmer living in Patten at the writing of this book. Just south of the Patten/Stacyville line is the farm which used to be owned by my grandparents and uncle, Leo, Damaris, and Laurel Boynton. After sitting vacant for a few years, the farm is now owned by an Amish family; they have a dairy herd, build storage sheds, and sell various items.

Now we'll stray outside of Penobscot County as we turn our attention to crop farming. Patten and Mount Chase are pretty much surrounded by Aroostook County and in many ways fit better with their northern and eastern neighbors than they do with their southern neighbors. This is particularly true when you talk about growing crops, since the soil in this area is more like Aroostook soil than Penobscot soil.

The first settlers arrived in the Aroostook County area around 1782; they were French-speaking immigrants from Canada. Houlton saw its first settlers in 1807, and Maysville was settled in 1820. In 1831, Houlton became the first town in northern Maine, before Aroostook County even became a county in 1839. Presque Isle became a town in 1859, and Maysville was annexed to Presque Isle in 1883.

Around 1829, when the first settlers arrived in Patten, growing crops was not a simple matter; a lot of work had to be done before a crop could even be planted. Settlers found that the easiest way to develop a field for planting was to cut down a bunch of trees and set them on fire. They not only cleared the field, but the ashes made good fertilizer for the crops. By 1831, Patten had a grist mill where corn and grains such as wheat, barley, rye, oats, and buckwheat were ground into flour or meal. They also raised garden crops such as squash, turnips, carrots, potatoes, and peas.

The Aroostook War (1838-1842) accomplished more for northern Maine than just settle the boundary dispute. It led to improvements in roads throughout the area, which in turn led to greater settlement along those roads. The Aroostook Road in particular was a boon to the development of the towns of Patten and Mount Chase. It provided much easier access to points north and south. It also meant that if a farmer grew more of a crop than his family needed or than he could sell locally, he could get his crops to other markets.

Also contributing to increased settlement of Aroostook County was the fact that land in northern Maine was cheap and the soil was good. The population of "the crown of Maine" grew rapidly in the 1830s, and in 1839, the area officially became Aroostook County. In 1839, Ezekial Holmes (considered the Father of Maine Agriculture) praised Aroostook soil, stating it was good for growing corn and grains such as barley, rye, oats, buckwheat, and wheat. Aroostook and northern Penobscot soil was also ideal for growing potatoes. By 1840, Maine was producing more potatoes than any other state except New York. Some of the species from those years were:

Russet potatoes   Irish Cobblers   Katahdins   Kennebecs

In 1852, the towns of Patten, Mount Chase, and Golden Ridge (Sherman) established the Penobscot and Aroostook Union Agricultural Society, which was the region's local unit of the Maine Board of Agriculture. The towns held annual exhibits at which crops and livestock were shown and judged. I found a couple of the annual reports on line. The reports produced by the convention were lengthy, detailed, and written in the style of reporting in those days. They included reports from each of the societies across Maine. Ira Fish's report in 1859 stated that several Patten or Mount Chase farmers had fine grade Durham bulls and other stock. The wheat crop was almost a failure due to weevil and rust. Jonathan Palmer was reported to have an excellent farm, elegant farm house, and strong armed boys who had helped him make his farm from the unbroken wilderness. Abner Weeks had commenced clearing a farm in Patten twenty years prior and now a nicely cultivated farm and an elegant farm house. Henry Blake also had an excellent farm and had raised a couple of staunch sons, models of industry, perseverance, and economy. The report also printed the text of a speech which included this comment: *We are carried back to the times when faith and hope...cheered the labors, hardships, and privations of pioneer life, that they fainted not, but laid the foundations of what they today doat* [sic] *upon, and say to their children, "These are my bequests."*

In 1879, Alfred Cushman of Golden Ridge prepared the report for the Penobscot and Aroostook Union Agricultural Society. (Dr. Luther Rogers was the secretary for the Society.) Mr. Cushman and the other leaders of the various societies announced the premiums (prizes) for livestock and crops which had been awarded at the most recent exhibitions. In the Patten and Sherman area, a stallion owned by J.S. Stacy of Golden Ridge and reared by Ira Fish, Esquire, was awarded first premium. Henry Blake and Thomas Myrick won awards for sheep, Joseph Heald and Thomas Myrick shared first place for swine, and Charles Fish and H.N. Darling won awards for their apples. J.S. Mitchell, Eli Kellogg, and Jonathan Palmer won awards for butter and cheese. For their crops of corn, potatoes, or beans, Joseph Heald, James Mitchell, and Dr. Luther Rogers won premiums. Other members of the society from Patten and Mount Chase included Jacob Frye, Andrew McCourt, Samuel and William Waters, John Hammond, William Hunt, Samuel Wiggins, James Hill, and J.S. Hall.

Other reports in the document covered a wide variety of agricultural topics, including soil, manure, cultivation practices, agricultural implements, plant diseases and insect problems, animal breeds, and fruit and crop species.

There was also a lengthy section in the document on the merits of agriculture colleges. A statement by Mr. N.T. True, Chairman of the Maine Board of Agriculture, included these remarks:

> *In our changeable climate, confining a young man within the walls of a school-room for any length of time almost invariably enervates his system, and he loathes the sight of agricultural labor....We must then come to the conclusion that....it will not be the best policy to pursue to establish agricultural schools with the expectation of directly educating the farmer.....*

Mr. True went on to say that it might be all right if a few men attended agricultural colleges and then served as models for the rest of the farmers. He did feel that most farmers would benefit from following these model famers, reading books and periodicals about agriculture, and belonging to agricultural societies where issues related to agriculture could be discussed.

One factor which held farmers back from planting even larger crops of potatoes was finding an efficient way to get the potatoes to market. That problem was greatly remedied by the arrival of the railroad in northern Maine. By the 1870's, northern Maine had rail access to Quebec and New Brunswick, and by 1895, the Bangor and Aroostook Railroad stretched from Bangor to Maine's northern border, with stations in Sherman, Oakfield, Houlton, Presque Isle, Caribou, Fort Fairfield, Ashland, and Van Buren. In 1895, tracks were laid to connect Patten to Sherman and in 1896, the BAR reached Patten. Now Aroostook and Northern Penobscot potato farmers could expand their markets for their potatoes.

Another boon to the potato farming industry was the establishment of starch factories throughout the area. Aroostook County's first starch plant was built in 1871 and was followed by many more. Patten's first starch plant was built in 1879 by John and Ira Gardner. In 1903, they sold it to T. H. Phair, who was a big name in starch factory history in Aroostook County. (Phair later sold it to Piper and Libby.) Now farmers had a guaranteed local market for their potatoes. They generally sold their best potatoes as table stock and sold culls (second-rate potatoes) to the starch factories.

Newly invented or redesigned agricultural implements let the farmer plant more in a shorter period of time, and the use of Western draft horses instead of oxen also was working well. The days of burning down the forests to create a field for crops were gone—now it was possible to plow fields on a yearly basis.

Here are some interesting statistics for you to mull over.

- In 1869, 380,701 bushels of potatoes were grown in Aroostook County. In 1889, that figure had increased to 2,746,765 bushels, and in 1910, it was even higher at 17,514,491.
- In 1890 in Aroostook County, 16,641 acres were planted in potatoes. In 1900, 41,953 acres were planted, and in 1910, 75,738 acres were planted. Aroostook County was growing more than half of Maine's potatoes.

Throughout the logging camp era, farms around Patten and Mount Chase and even further into the woods made money by supplying produce for the lumber camps. Potatoes were a popular food with hard-working lumberjacks and their cooks, and of course they wanted lots of milk, butter, and cheese as well!

Up until World War I, most crop farming was done with horse-drawn equipment. After tractors became available and affordable, farmers began to plant larger crops, and potato farming became an important business in the Patten area. By 1915, Charles W. Wescott was selling farm implements in Patten.

Potato farming was a very risky business. A farmer could find himself making good money one year and deeply in debt or even bankrupt the next. One bad year because of drought, disease, or low prices could wipe a farmer out. The market prices for potatoes can vary greatly from year to year and even from place to place. For example, in 1912, the U.S. crop was doing well, but Maine's crop was down. This meant that Maine farmers got lower prices for their potatoes. From 1916-1919, the reverse was true, and Maine became the leading state in potato production. 1920-1924 saw a downward turn again, then 1925-1930 were better years. Then came the great depression. Farmers everywhere racked up huge debts and got extremely low prices for their crops.

In 1935, a Potato Branding Law was passed. This regulated the quality and grade of potatoes being sold. In 1937, the Potato Tax Act was passed. A one or two cent tax on each barrel of potatoes created revenue that was used to support advertising and research. The war years from 1941 to 1945 were actually good for potato farmers, as they sold their crops to the federal government for the military. The government wanted lots of potatoes, and the farmers were getting a good price for them. However, there was a serious shortage of labor, in spite of the law that said that farmers could be exempted from the draft. German soldiers held in P.O.W. camps throughout Maine provided some help with farming and logging operations during the last couple of years of the war.

The post-World War II era saw a tremendous boom in potato farming as farming became increasingly mechanized. Tractors were now used instead of horses to pull equipment, meaning farmers could plant and harvest bigger crops. Besides increases in the amount of acreage being planted, farmers were using new ideas in farming to increase their yield per acre. These developments included ideas such as crop rotation and products such as commercial fertilizer, insecticides and herbicides. Potato houses were being built which allowed for better potato storage, even into spring and summer when prices were better. By the 1980's, the need for manual labor was greatly reduced when many farmers started using potato harvesters. The small farmer who planted under a hundred acres of potatoes disappeared. And eventually even the farmers who had invested in a harvester could not compete against even bigger farming operations.

In the years from 1946 to 2000, there was a long list potato shippers and farmers in the Patten and Mount Chase area, including Ralph Robinson, Fred Quint, Freeman Bradford, W.S. Edwards and Son, John Hanson, Robert Anderson, Wendell Kennedy, Merritt Everett, Ora Beattie, Boyd and Edgar Harrington, Philip Nightingale, Robert McNally, Perley and Rodney Harris, Joe Brawn, Webb Farms, Arthur Crouse, Willard McIntire, Charles and Judson Cunningham (photo of their farm on the North Road at right), Ola and Arnold McLaughlin, Lester and Thurston Townsend, Bob and Wayne Heath, and Qualey Farms.

Potato farming continues to be big business in Aroostook County in the 21st century, but it is no longer is a major business in Patten and Mount Chase. One by one, the farmers in the list above retired or went out of business. Only Qualey Farms still raises potatoes to be sold outside of the area. Arthur Crouse's son Steve raises potatoes to sell in the area, as does Kerry McNally of McNally Farm Produce.

So the era from 1940-1970 was the heyday of potato and dairy farming in Patten and Mount Chase. I feel fortunate that, as part of a farming family, I was part of that heritage. We joke in my family that I was born during cultivating season (July), my sister was born during shipping season (February), and my brother was born just before planting season (May 1st). We celebrated my mother's birthday in June during rock picking season and my father's birthday in September during harvest (or digging, as we also called it). The photo at the left shows us bringing Dad's birthday cake to the field. My parents told me that as a 3-month old baby, I was taken to the potato field and placed inside a potato barrel so my mother could help with the harvest. However, I didn't really start picking potatoes until I was a little older. I loved being in the potato field and was very upset the year I had to stay home with the chicken pox during harvest.

The photos below show my sister Lynn, my brother Scott, and me picking potatoes in 1958.

Three generations of Harris farmers: my brother Scott, father Rodney, and grandfather Perley during harvest sometime in the 1970's.

A year in the life of a potato farmer went something like this. After the fields dried out enough in the spring (around mid-May), they were plowed and harrowed, breaking up the soil which had compacted throughout the winter. In late May and early June, we cut seed: each potato had to be cut into halves or thirds with an eye on each piece. The potatoes were then planted in rows by a machine that also dispensed fertilizer and lime. Throughout the summer, the farmer cultivated the potatoes, keeping the soil mounded up around the potato plants. This also controlled weeds that grew between the rows. To protect the plants, he sprayed pesticides and insecticides on them. In the fall, he killed the tops by spraying them with arsenic or another herbicide or by rotobeating them, just to make digging the potatoes easier. The earliest potato diggers were one row diggers, then two-row diggers came along. By the mid-1960s, potato harvesters were being used to dig the potatoes. In modern times, a combination of windrowers and a harvester are used to dig the potatoes.

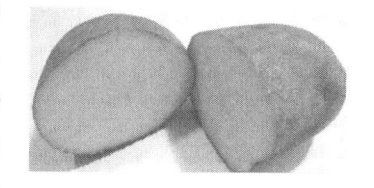

During the winter, the potatoes were stored in a potato house until they were sold. To prepare a load for shipping, the potatoes were run over a conveyor so that rotten and sunburned potatoes could be discarded and so the potatoes could be sorted according to size.

Prior to the mid-1960s most potatoes were shipped to market by railroad, which is why the potato houses were built near the railroad tracks. Since then, most potatoes are shipped by tractor-trailer truck. My brother Scott didn't want to be a farmer, but he always wanted to be a truck driver; he has been delivering potatoes to markets as far west as Ohio since the mid-1970s. We loved it when Dad's potatoes were delivered to the Lay's Potato chip plant; we often got to keep the test samples done at the plant to make sure the potatoes were good enough to be made into chips.

Potato farming was so important to the community during those years that it governed the school calendar! Students went back to school in mid-August so that they could have a potato recess of three weeks (or even longer if it had been a rainy season) to help with the potato harvest from mid-September to early October.

A day in the potato field during digging in the 1950s and 60s went like this. After being transported to the field on the back of a pickup truck (That's right—how did we survive without car seats and seat belts?), you found your section. This was a part of a potato row marked off by the farmer. He placed a branch with leaves at each end of a section. As he continued to dig rows, you moved your stick across the field. If you were a good picker, you got a long section. I usually got a fairly short section, and as the day wore on, it would get shorter and the section of the girl who picked next to me would get longer.

After the farmer went by digging up two rows of potatoes, you picked up the potatoes and put them in a basket. When your basket was full, you dumped the potatoes into a barrel. When the barrel was full, you put a ticket on it and set up a new barrel. A farm truck would drive around the field picking up the full barrels using tongs. They put the tickets in a box and rolled the barrels into place on the truck body. When the truck was loaded, they would head to the potato house. They would dump the potatoes onto a conveyor which took them into bins where they would be stored until they were sold. Then the truck driver would bring his load of empty barrels back to the field.

Good pickers stood up to pick; I always picked kneeling on the ground. 'Nough said. On frosty mornings, you would be pretty cold for a while, and some days it would get pretty hot by mid-afternoon. We also picked in the rain and even snow once in a while. We carried our lunches and used the woods for a bathroom. If you got behind, usually someone would help you get caught up. Often whole families would be in the field together. Finally, towards 5:00, the farmer would dig the last rows of the day and you could go home, tired and dirty but thinking of how much money you earned that day.

As a farmer's daughter, I helped my parents each evening as they counted tickets and recorded the number of barrels each picker had filled. (The picture at right shows what a ticket looked like.) At the end of the week, the farmer gave each picker a check for the week's work. I remember being paid anywhere from $0.25 to $0.75 a barrel, although it went up to $1.00 or more a barrel after I stopped picking.

When I was in high school, my father bought a harvester. Instead of hiring several dozen pickers, he needed only four teenagers or adults (usually female) to work on the harvester. Other farmers in the area also converted their operations to using a harvester, and gradually the need for school-age children to help with the harvest diminished. By the mid-1980s, the harvest recess was discontinued for MSAD #25 schools. However, potato harvest remains a special memory for many people from northern Maine, and kids who participated in potato harvest learned some valuable lessons about hard work and handling money.

This photo shows one of my father's hard-working crews—his four oldest grandchildren. As you can see, there wasn't a one of them who minded getting a little dirty!

This picture might explain why my father chose potato farming over dairy farming—we had a tendency to make pets of the cows. Dad and Gramp are making sure those calves don't take off with me in the little cart between them. Farming isn't all work and no play!

The last summer my Dad was alive, he and I took a ride around the Happy Corner Road and he told me who had planted what and where during the years he was farming. Now those once productive farms are just picturesque fields. It is always sad to see the end of an era, but, as the old saying goes, you can't stop progress.

I wrote this poem in 1988 for my father, but I think the words are true for any farmer who plants, nurtures, and harvests crops.

THE FARMER

He goes out into the early morning freshness.
With practiced eye, he measures the day:
Notes the dew, scans the sky, tests the soil,
And girds himself up for the toil of the day.

But his work is more than a job to do—
It is part of his very soul.
He knows his craft, knows it risks,
But knows, too, it has made him whole.

So, without fanfare or fumbling,
He goes about his livelihood:
Restoring to earth what he has removed.
And he knows in his soul: This is good.

And when the final harvest is gathered up,
He will finally take his day of rest.
So many years of a labor of love
Surely deserve to be blessed.

No one can see God or know His mind,
But the farmer, more than most, might understand
How the Creator felt on the seventh day
As he surveyed water, sky, and land.

JOHN DEERE: NOT THE INVENTOR OF THE TRACTOR

John Deere. Tractors, right? Combines and harvesters. Skidders. Bulldozers. Even lawn mowers and ATV's.

John Deere did not invent the tractor.

In fact, John Deere died before tractors even came into use.

John Deere was born in 1804 in Rutland, Vermont. At age 17, he was apprenticed to a blacksmith. After learning the trade, he started his own blacksmith shop in 1825. He married Demarias Lamb in 1827, and they raised a family of nine children: six girls and three boys.

In 1837, the Deere family moved to Illinois where John opened another blacksmith shop. Being a very observant man, he noticed right off quick that the plows that were being used by the farmers were not doing a very good job plowing up the tough prairie soil. He reasoned that they would work better with a polished steel plowshare. John made his first such plow in 1837 and sold it to a local farmer. It worked so well, all the other farmers wanted a John Deere plow. By 1841, he was making 75-100 plows a year. In 1848, he opened a factory, and by 1855 he was yearly manufacturing 10,000 of these plows "that broke the plains." John insisted that every plow he made was of the highest quality.

In 1868, John established Deere & Company, of which he was president. However, most of the operations were handled by his son, Charles Deere, and his son-in-law, Christopher Webber, and John turned his attention to other matters. He was the President of the National Bank of Moline, Illinois and the director of the Moline Free Public Library, and he served as mayor of Moline for two years. He died in 1886.

So if John Deere didn't invent the John Deere tractor, who did? Hold your horses…or your horsepower. I'll get to that in a minute.

The business continued to do well in the hands of Charles Deere and other family members. When Charles died in 1907, his son-in-law, William Butterworth, replaced him. In 1912, Deere and Company began experimenting with tractors. In 1923, the John Deere Model D tractor was introduced. In 1927, Deere produced their first combine harvester.

By the 1940s, Deere & Company was being run by John Deere's great-grandson, Charles Deere Wiman. Charles served as a colonel during WWII and steered the company into manufacturing military tractors, transmissions for tanks, aircrafts parts, and ammunition.

Oh, I forgot to mention. The tractor was invented by John Froelich in 1892 in Waterloo, Iowa. Mr. Froelich's business was bought out in 1918 by Deere & Company for $2,350,000.00. And *then* the John Deere tractor was introduced. Not invented. Introduced.

Since then, John Deere has continually introduced new machinery and improved its line of equipment, but the name John Deere still stands for quality. The John Deere logo and bright green paint are popular symbols of America's hard-working farmers and loggers and heavy-equipment operators. Oh, yeah, and all those people who mow acres of lawn so they can justify buying a John Deere lawnmower. After all, "Nothing runs like a Deere." Which you have to admit sounds a lot better than, "Nothing runs like a Butterworth" or "Nothing runs like a Froelich."

Oh, another thing I forgot to mention. My Dad also drove Massey-Harris and Farmall tractors.

CHAPTER SIXTEEN: OUTSIDERS AND OUTDOORSMEN

Patten and Mount Chase have been a "destination" for tourists for many years. *Outsiders*, as the locals call anyone who didn't grow up in northern Maine, have been visiting the area since the early 17th century. These early tourists were impressed with the flora and fauna and the opportunity to have a true wilderness experience. (By the way, we also call outsiders "people from away.")

Mount Katahdin has always been a major drawing card for the area. Rising 5,267 feet in elevation and visible from many locations, the mountain is a breathtaking scene. The Wabanaki people named the mountain *Ktaadn*, which means *greatest mountain*. Native lore told stories of the storm god Pamola, who inhabited the peak of the mountain. The white clouds often seen hovering over Katahdin's peaks were called *The Plumes of Pamola*. John Gyles may have been the first white man to see Katahdin. As a captive of the Wabanakis in 1689, he traveled up the East Branch of the Penobscot with a hunting party. He remarked in his journal that *Teddon* was higher than the White Hills above the Saco River. The first recorded account of climbing the mountain dates back to 1804, when Zackery Adley and Charles Turner bushwhacked their way up the mountain. Dr. Luther Rogers of Patten climbed the mountain in 1856.

Mount Katahdin is located within Baxter State Park in Piscataquis County, west of Shin Pond. Between 1931 and 1962, Governor Percival Baxter created Baxter State Park by buying land around Mount Katahdin in 28 different parcels and deeding them to the state. The park covers more than 200,000 acres which have been kept in their natural wild state, which was one of Baxter's stipulations. The park attracts around 60,000 campers, hikers, mountain climbers, and sightseers each summer. These words written by Governor Baxter demonstrate how he felt about the mountain: *Man is born to die, His works are short-lived. Buildings crumble, monuments decay, wealth vanishes. But Katahdin in all its glory forever shall remain the mountain of the people.*

In August, 2016, Roxanne Quimby donated 87,563 acres of land and $20 million to the United States Federal Government to create a national monument. Katahdin Woods and Waters National Monument is located along the east side of Baxter State Park, within Penobscot County, including a section along the East Branch of the Penobscot River. While there was some opposition to the creation of the monument, local residents hope the economy of the area will benefit from an influx of visitors to the monument.

Some considerably famous people have fallen in love with the area around Patten and Mount Chase. Henry David Thoreau (photo at right) visited the area more than once between 1846 and 1857 and wrote his book *The Maine Woods* about his experiences in the Maine wilderness. Artist Frederic Edwin Church produced scenes of Katahdin, including his 1860 painting *Twilight (Katahdin)*, which in 2011 was sold at an art auction for $3.1 million. Another famous artist, Marsden Hartley, painted Katahdin scenes in the 1930's.

Artist and photographer Maurice "Jake" Day produced scenes from the Katahdin region. In recognition of Jake's love for Maine and his efforts to promote conservation, Governor Baxter gave Jake the title of *Artist in Residence of Baxter State Park*. Several of Jake's paintings can be seen at Park Headquarters in Millinocket, Maine.

Carl Sprinchorn was another artist and Edmund Ware Smith another author who spent spent considerable time in this area. I will write more about them later in this chapter as they actually managed to get past the stigma of being considered *outsiders*!

Besides Baxter and Katahdin, there are other tourist destinations in the area. Shin Pond Village and Matagamon Wilderness Campground offer camping sites for RVs as well as cabin rentals. Other businesses provide lodging and meals for travelers who want to spend a few days in the area. Many *outsiders* own camps in the area, especially around Upper and Lower Shin Pond. Tourists buy groceries, gas, souvenirs, and supplies at Patten and Shin Pond businesses. Many also visit the Lumberman's Museum to see its impressive displays of Maine's lumbering heritage. Patten is also a stop-off point for tourists traveling further north to explore Aroostook County, canoe down the Allagash, or do some *leaf peeping* (enjoy the colorful fall foliage) or moose peeping. In recent years, the popularity of snowmobiling has been a benefit to the local economy.

A surprise visitor to our yard.

Below, a special houseguest for Kemp's sister Marie—she and her husband rescued a baby moose who had been swept downstream away from its mother.

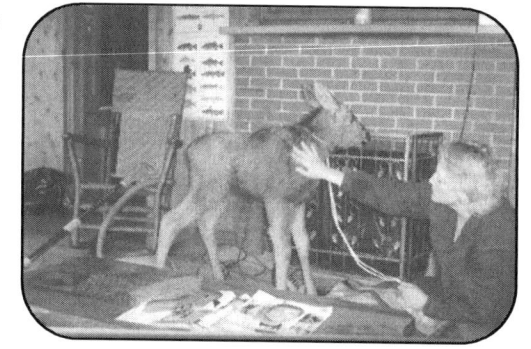

So far we've been talking about *tourists*. Another group of outsiders are the *sports*, which is what the natives call people who come here to hunt and fish. Since the mid-1800s, many businesses in Patten and Mount Chase have also catered to sports. As the last communities before entering the wilderness of Piscataquis County or the sparsely settled Aroostook Scenic Highway, they have become important stop-offs for sports. Margaret Bates's collection included this picture of Ira B. Gardner's business card from 1899. It advertises his store and shows the numbers of game killed from 1896-1899. The G.T. Merrill store in Patten also catered to sportsmen. Lodging was available at Frye's Inn, Paul Peavey's establishment, the Patten House, the Patten Exchange, and the Pomeroy House.

How About Your Hunting Trip?

Going to Northern Maine?
That's Right.

Now, your Outfit? Don't send needless weight. Save trouble, time, money. Buy on the spot with practical help. We furnish everything needed.

Ammunition, Provisions, Proper Teams, First-Class Guides, Safe Canoe Men, Reliable Information.

Write us,

Ira B. Gardner & Sons, Patten, Me.

Game shipped from PATTEN, MAINE:

Year	Deer	Moose	Caribou
1896	120	13	20
1897	230	13	17
1898	244	31	15
1899	406	36	Close time

"Patten, Nearest The Big Game Country"
IRA B. GARDNER & SONS,
Headquarters.

The photo to the left shows a moose which was taken in the area around 1906. The photo shows the scene as you look north on Main Street. (Margaret Bates collection)

But the real draw for hunters and fishermen from outside the area were (and still are) the sporting camps. These camps provide not only lodging, but also meals (sometimes even bag lunches) and guides who could lead them to the best sites for hunting or fishing. Several sporting camps have operated in Patten and Mount Chase or further north on Route 11 over the years. These include Lyman's Hillside Lodge (Lyman Botting), the Sportsman's Edge/Eager Beaver Lodge, Dri-Ki Lodge (the Keim family) Bear Mountain Lodge (Carroll and Deanna Gerow), Conklin's Lodge (Lester and Marie Conklin), Patten Hunting Lodge (Bill Finney), North Country Lodge (the Goodman family), and Katahdin Lodge (Arthur and Eugenia Sharpe, Finley and Marty Clark, and Chuck and Chris Loucka). Raymond Lorentz also operated sporting camps in the Patten area at one point.

The area from Shin Pond to Matagamon has also long been a destination for hunters and fishermen, as well as other people who are looking for an outdoors experience. In 1895, Colonel Luther B. Rogers built a sporting camp on the East Branch near Wassataquoik. This had previously been known as the Patterson place. Bowlin Camps, located in T5R8 off the Matagamon Road, also opened in 1895. In the years around 1912, sportsmen could stay at William McKenney's Birch Point Lodge on Upper Shin Pond, Charlie Wren's Fairview Camps on Lower Shin Pond, Stevie Giles and Pearlie Joy's Sawtelle Brook Camps, the Sebois Bridge Camps, or Elijah Arbo's Hay Lake Sporting Camps. Forman Smith operated Lower Shin Pond Camps around 1931. Another area business which catered to sports was the Point-of-Pines camp on Upper Shin Pond. It was originally operated by G.F. Root, but was eventually bought by the Riley family for private use. Hadley and Pat Coolong were the primary caretakers of Point-of-Pines during those years. G.F. Root also operated Birch Point Camps. Sebois Farm and Trout Brook Farm advertised for fishing, hunting, and family vacation resorts.

During the years 1870-1923, Matagamon was a mini logging town, complete with a post office, school, and store, as seen in the diagram at right. In 1895, Sam Harvey built a lodge on Matagamon Lake, and Chub Foster took it over in 1941. Chub and his wife Fran operated Foster's Wilderness Camps until 1970. Since 1971, the site has been a Boy Scout camp. It is now a base for Maine High Adventure, an outdoor program for Boy Scouts.

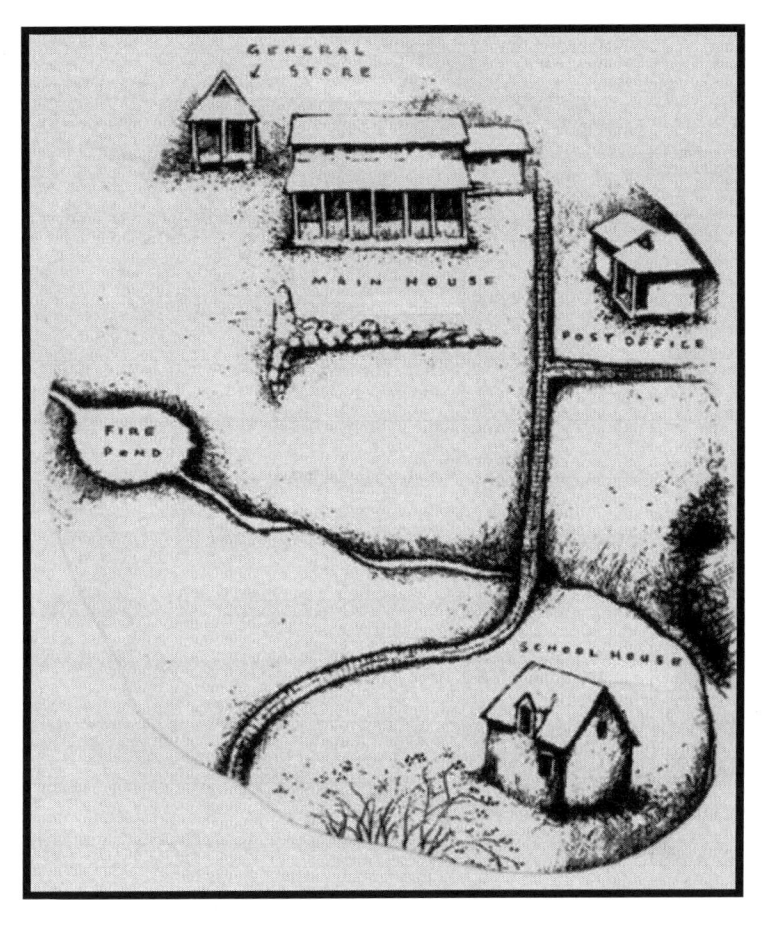

Irving B. Myrick first operated Trout Brook Hotel before opening up Myrick Sporting Camps on Grand Lake, Matagamon. His ad in the Field and Stream magazine claimed:

> *Grand Lake, Matagamon, the Sportsman's Paradise is situated on the head waters of the East Branch of the Penobscot River. It is reached by stage from Patten, Maine (Bangor and Aroostook Railroad). Good automobile roads to Shin Pond. Practically virgin country, waters alive with trout, salmon, and togue. Wonderful fishing. Deer, Moose, Bear, Partridge, Duck are plentiful. Comfortable camps, good beds, wholesome food. Detached camps. Come and invite your friends. No disappointments. Fish and game are here. Full particulars by writing.*

By the 1950s and 60s, there were as many as seventeen sporting camps in the Patten, Shin Pond, North Road, and Matagamon area. Nowadays, sporting camps and lodges cater not only to sports, but also to hikers, sightseers, snowmobilers, and ATV enthusiasts who are visiting the area. Many of these destinations have been bought and sold repeatedly over the years. They include Jerry Pond Camps (Vernald and Freda Stubbs), Shin Pond Camps, Camp Wapiti (Roger J. Bail [around 1946], Harold and Martha Schmidt, Jerry and Glenda Snow, Frank and Anita Ramelli, Ryan and Jennifer Shepard, Travis and Brandy Libby), Pleasant Lake Camps, Mattagamon (or Matagamon) Camps, Foster's Wilderness Camps (Chub and Fran Foster), Shin Pond Lodge, Bradford Camps (Dave Youland), Driftwood (Harold Schmidt, Paul and Tracy Reed), and Matagamon Wilderness Campground (Don and Di Dudley, the Christianson family).

In 1960, Mount Chase Lodge was built by Henry and Mary Schmidt. Rick and Sara Hill took over in 1976, and since 2015, their daughter Lindsay and her husband Mike Downing have operated the lodge.

Scott and Louise Skinner's Wilderness Variety store, opened in 1985, sells hunting and fishing licenses, tags game, serves food, and sells groceries and supplies. And the Shin Pond Pub, operated by Vicki Hashey-Nanni, provides a great place for outsiders and locals to swap yarns about their outdoor experiences.

And then there was the Shin Pond House, right at the top of the hill which rises from the bridge that spans the thoroughfare between Upper and Lower Shin Ponds. The first Shin Pond House was built in the 1870s by Charles Sibley. Its next owners were Lewis Cooper, then Ted Crommett. This building burned in 1911, but by the following year it had been rebuilt by Zenas Harvey, who also added cabins for sports to stay in. Some consider this the heyday of the Shin Pond House. The photo here (courtesy of Mount Chase Town Office Collection) shows the Shin Pond House in 1929. Harvey and his son Vernon and their families provided lodging for sports and for lumbermen who were working at nearby logging camps. However, the sports were treated differently than the lumbermen. The sports had individual quarters, while the lumbermen slept in a type of bunkhouse on the top floor. Sports and lumbermen were even served meals in separate areas and at different times. The lumbermen followed the logging camp rule of no talking during a meal, but the sports liked to socialize and actually had a room where they could sit around and talk. There were occasions, however, when the sports enjoyed listening to the yarns of the lumbermen and the guides. Tad Peavey and Tellis Coolong were skilled storytellers who also served as guides to the sports.

Other workers at the Shin Pond House during those years were Zenas's wife Minnie, Vernon's wife Alice, Florence Sargent and her daughters, Aggie Lord, Nola Wilson, Jim and Dean McKenney, Curtis and Flora Hatt, and Hadley Coolong. Vernon Harvey was considered to be a mechanical genius. He was a creator, inventor, and repairman. Harvey's sister-in-law, Lula Hatt helped out and also ran the post office across the street. The post office handled all the mail and the payroll (which consisted of silver dollars) for the lumber camps to the west of Shin Pond. From 1925 to 1933, Leon Crommett operated the Patten/Matagamon Stage, which made two trips a week hauling passengers, mail, and silver dollars between Patten and Trout Brook. There were two phones. One phone connected Shin Pond with the outside world, while the other one connected Shin Pond with the woods. Its single wire reached into fire towers, lumber camps, and remote cabins.

Harvey's Shin Pond House burned in February, 1949. On July 4th of the same year, Edna and Arthur Augustine opened Augustine's Hotel on the site. They also owned a store across the street; this was operated throughout the next 20 years or so by Fred Artell, Ken and Irene Lord, and Ola and Emma McLaughlin. The drawing pictured here is an advertisement for the hotel.

In 1964, Dale and Margaret Bates took over the hotel and restaurant, renaming it the Shin Pond House (1967 photo at left, courtesy of Mount Chase Town Office collection).

The next owners were Richard and Teddy Schmidt, who bought the hotel in 1968. They also owned a sporting goods store in the vicinity. John and Filena (Anderson) Desaulniers took over ownership in 1972 and ran the hotel until 1977. In 1974, a fire destroyed the store, a barn and garage, and a Laundromat, all owned by the Desaulniers, and the sporting goods store owned by Dick Schmidt.

In 1979, the Shin Pond House burned down for the third time. In 1981, Craig and Terry Hill built Shin Pond Village on the site, operating a store, snack bar, meeting room, public laundry, and showering services. The Hills also maintain several guest cabins and guest houses and provide catering services, often to events which take place in large tents in the field atop the hill.

Less than two miles further along on the Shin Pond Road was Ted Crommett's operation, called Crommett Farms. There is a description in Chapter Twelve of how Crommett served logging operations in the area, but his set-up was also a sporting camp. The picture above is a sign which has been erected on the Crommett Farm site.

A frequent guest at both the Shin Pond House and Crommett Farms—actually more a boarder than a guest—was an artist named Carl Sprinchorn. He spent at least half of his time in the Patten and Shin Pond area between 1937 and 1952. He did paintings of the scenery of the area (although interestingly enough, he never finished a painting of Mount Katahdin), but he was also interested in portraying the woodsmen at work. He was a close friend of Caleb Scribner.

Another outsider who stayed for extended periods in the area was Edmund Ware Smith. Smith was an author of some note and wrote several books set in the Maine woods, including *For Maine Only, Upriver and Down, A Treasury of the Maine Woods*, and *To Fish and Hunt in Maine*. He also wrote several books based on a character called The One-Eyed Poacher. Smith and his wife built a cabin on Matagamon Lake and became close friends with Elmer Wilson, Nat Hudson, and Zenas Harvey. Smith wrote that when he asked Harvey if he had lived in Shin Pond all his life, Harvey replied, "Not yet, but I aim to."

This chapter is titled *Outsiders and Outdoorsmen*. While most of the outsiders who visit this area are outdoorsmen (and women and children), Patten and Shin Pond have been home to a unique breed of outdoorsmen. These are the men about whom stories are told, and they include bush pilots, dam tenders, game wardens, guides, loggers, and hermits. They tended to be slow talkers and deep thinkers and were physically fit well into their senior years. Many of them were family men in spite of the fact that they were often away from home for long periods of time.

Throughout the decades from 1940 to 2000, Shin Pond was the home site for several bush pilots. Included in this list of daring and hardworking pilots are Randolph Mulherin, Buck Sherman, Ray O'Donnell, Elmer Wilson, Clint Porter, Ray Porter, Virgil Lynch, and Scott Skinner, who opened Scotty's Flying Service in 1973. Taking off from Lower Shin Pond, they would transport hunters and fishermen to remote backwoods areas. They were also invaluable in assisting with search and rescue missions and flying fire patrols. Ray Porter (photo at right). started his flying service at Shin Pond in 1950 with a PA II Piper Cub. Business was so good that he was able to buy two more planes and hire pilots to fly them. Porter flew from May to October with float skis, and in the winter he put snow skis on his plane and used it to trap beaver. Since he could get to remote areas that other trappers did not have access to, he was a very successful trapper. Ray, his wife Madelyn, and their children Linda, Judy, and John lived in the house just west of the Shin Pond Bridge until Ray opened his paddle shop nearer to town. At the time of this writing, Ray and Madelyn are living in their own home in Patten. Although in his nineties now, Ray makes beautiful packbaskets.

Local game wardens through the years have been Caleb Scribner, Amos Steen, Sherwood "Shinny" Howes, Sherm Clements, Jack McPhee (see also page 213), Carroll Bates, Chris Dyer, Alvin Theriault, and Scott Martin. Alan Dudley grew up at Matagamon and became a game warden who has worked in northern Maine and is also a member of the Forensic Mapping Team. Danny Glidden also had a district in Northern Maine. These outdoorsmen earn their pay as they enforce hunting and fishing laws, assist in search and rescue missions, and do public outreach programs. The wardens in the Patten and Mount Chase area had (and still have) a huge district to cover, and local hunters and fishermen have always included a number of poachers and jackers. A story about Amos Steen relates that he was out one night on the trail of a poaching ring. He drove into a wooded area near an open field, and he watched as the poachers killed a deer. The poachers then ran helter-skelter for their friend's vehicle to get away from the scene of the crime. Unfortunately for them, they bailed into the back seat of Warden Steen's vehicle and excitedly related their success in getting the deer. That was an easy arrest for Warden Steen. In the past, a warden might overlook a deer taken illegally if it meant a family would have meat for the winter, but those days are gone by. And rightly so: without fish and game laws to protect Maine's wildlife, the wildlife populations would decline and disrupt the food chain. And we would eventually even lose those dollars spent by visitors to the area.

Many Mainers are good storytellers (there's definitely an art to it), and there are a lot of good tales which have come out of the Maine woods around Patten and Mount Chase. I have already mentioned Tellis Coolong and Tad Peavey, who entertained the sports and the lumbermen at the Shin Pond House in the early 1900's. Tellis (photo at left), who was born Telesphore (or Tellesforte) Coulombe in Baker Lake, Quebec, most likely came to the Patten area to work in the woods, but he also generated income as a guide. His son, Hadley, followed in his footsteps as a woodsman, guide, and storyteller. Hadley shared many of his stories with the public on Bud Leavitt's Woods and Waters Show in the 1970's.

The storytellers' tales told of the great days past, hunting and fishing tales and recollections of those great Maine woodsmen. Here are a few of these local folk heroes.

- The four Steen brothers: Pat and his wife Mildred lived in a remote cabin at Black Brook near Matagamon and tended the dam for Bangor Hydroelectric Company there. Pat also trapped and guided. Amos was a game warden, and Herschel and Maurice were trappers and guides.
- Johnny White was a river driver, guide, pulp cutter, and railroad tie maker. He was a foreman for American Thread Company and also served as the CCC foreman who supervised the building of the road between Shin Pond and Matagamon.
- Henry Red Eagle (Henry Perley) was a full-blooded Maliseet guide based at Moosehead Lake. However he was much more than that—he was also an actor, entertainer, and author. He became the youngest licensed guide in the state of Maine at age 14. He was the valedictorian of his Greenville High School class in 1902.
- Roy Dudley was a noted Maine guide and had a camp at Chimney Pond on Katahdin. He is considered by some to be the best hunter and trapper in the area. He was responsible for opening several of the trails on Katahdin, including the Dudley Trail and the Cathedral Trail.
- Charlie Marr lived at Trout Brook Farm and worked for Eastern Woodlands. He drowned in Trout Book while guiding some fishermen.
- Nat Hudson had a camp on the East Branch of the Penobscot. Nat was a trapper and woods worker, but what he really liked to do was build things. As a child, he built himself a small car. He also built a snowmobile and a boat which was equipped with an airplane motor; the boat would travel on the East Branch whether the water was open or frozen. Nat's sister, Frances, was married to Hal Nason, who worked for the Crommetts.

Storytellers might also mention the names Leo King, Louis Rowe, Hadley McDonald, Clair Desmond, and Scott Davis.

Mel Craig was a woodsman who cut wood for Atlas Plywood and Old Town Canoe using his horse Prince for years after skidders started being used in the woods. This photo from the Mount Chase Town Office collection shows Mel and Prince at work. Prince was a show horse from Ontario, but Mel trained him to pull logs between the woods and a yard near the road. Prince could even make the trip without Mel alongside him. Prince liked tobacco—he chewed up at least 12 of Mel's pipes and the tobacco that was in them. Mel allowed that horses were better than skidders because they were not prone to breakdowns and they burned hay, not oil. Mel lived in a cabin near Shin Pond with his dogs Pat and Mike well into his 70s. He had no electricity, phone, or running water.

One of the more sensational stories told by local storytellers was the story of Wesley Porter (photo at left) a skilled Maine woods guide from Patten. He was killed at Webster Lake in 1943 by Alfred Maurence (or Alphonse Morency), a Canadian draft dodger. Maurence was nicknamed *The Phantom of the Allagash* as he proved to be quite elusive. Finally, after a 66-day manhunt, Maurence was captured by Porter's son Clint and Chub Foster (photo left) after Foster shot Maurence in the leg in a stand-off in the Allagash woods near the Canadian border. Maurence defended his actions by saying he was just firing warning shots over Porter's head. Wesley Porter was the father of eight children and only 46 years old when he died.

I want to pause here and say something about the *women* who married these outdoorsmen. In some cases, the women stayed in relatively-civilized Patten or Mount Chase, raising children and taking care of the homeplace. They saw their husbands only during off seasons—summers for woods workers or outside of hunting or fishing season for guides. Their lives were not easy, but very few of them actually divorced their husbands. It was the kind of life they expected when they got married, and they weren't the only women around that had a "part-time" husband.

In other cases, the wives went to the woods with their husbands, especially those who operated sporting camps. These women also worked hard cooking, cleaning, gardening, and doing whatever else they could do to help make their camps successful. They often went months without talking to another woman. The photo here is of Fran Foster. She was also a wonderful cook and some of the guests at Foster's Wilderness Camps came more for the meals than the hunting or fishing, but it looks like she was pretty fair at fishing, too.

The dam tenders tended to be husband and wife teams. Matagamon Dam, owned by Bangor Hydro, was tended over the years by Pat and Mildred Steen, Wendell and Madelyn Kennedy, and Don and Di Dudley. The Dudleys brought their two children out to Shin Pond every morning and picked them up later in the day so they could attend school.

Whether they stayed at home in town or went to the woods with their husbands, both kinds of wives made it possible for their husbands to do what they loved to do. And there are still many women who are married to wardens, rangers, sporting camp owners, woods workers, and so on. Their lives may be easier in many regards, but they still have to deal with many of the same issues that women from earlier times dealt with.

A TRIBUTE TO WIVES PAST AND PRESENT

- to the wives of bush pilots
- to the wives of dam keepers
- to the wives of forestry wardens
- to the wives of game wardens
- to the wives of guides
- to the wives of park rangers
- to the wives of river drivers and woodsmen
- to the wives of sporting camp owners
- to the wives of trappers
- to the wives of woodsmen

AND ALL THE THINGS YOU WORRIED (WORRY) ABOUT

- getting all the work done that needed to be done
- having enough money to feed your children
- keeping the farm going
- keeping your house warm and in good repair
- making a go of your sporting camp business
- taking care of your kids by yourself
- your husband drowning while on a river drive
- your husband getting shot by a careless or angry hunter
- your husband not being able to get needed medical attention
- your husband losing his life in a woods accident
- your husband's plane going down in the wilderness

Many stories have been told about the hermits who retreated into the Maine woods to live out their lives in solitude. We think of hermits as anti-social recluses, scarred by some event that left them hating humanity, who took to the woods to get away from it all. Most Mainers are familiar with the story of the North Pond Hermit, Christopher Knight. This man simply walked away from his home in Albion and lived the life of a hermit for 27 years, surviving by stealing what he needed from camps in the area. Charles Coffin was a hermit who hung out around the Desert of Maine, near Freeport. He was remarkable mostly because of his strange get-up: a Grover Cleveland bandana and Civil-War era forage cap. Even Henry David Thoreau of Walden Pond was considered a hermit, although he also doesn't quite fit the description of hermit.

When we talk about the hermits who lived in the woods west of Patten and Mount Chase, we find men who don't fit the typical description of hermit either. Fred Harrison was the hermit of Hudson Pond for forty-five years. He was born in 1890 in Ohio and spent some time in New York. After reading about northern Maine in a trapping magazine, he decided that was where he wanted to live out his life. His camp was remote to say the least, located in the northern part of Baxter State Park. In his younger days he would walk the forty miles to Patten, but in later years Elmer Wilson and Ray Porter ferried him in and out of Hudson Pond.

He was almost entirely self-sufficient, but liked to make occasional trips into Patten, where he would stay for a few days or a week before deciding it was time to head back to the woods. At one time, he owned a dog named Dixie Two-Spot, who was his faithful companion as he hunted, fished, and trapped. However, he was forced to shoot Dixie when she began chasing deer. Fred was heartbroken and did not get another dog for many years after that. Sadly, in 1961, Fred's next dog began chasing deer as well, and Fred was forced to shoot it. By chance, a few days later, Ray Porter decided to fly to Hudson Pond to check on Fred. Porter discovered that Fred had committed suicide out of grief over what he had had to do.

The hermit of Matagamon was Fred Walker, born in Patten in 1895. He was a shell-shocked World War I vet who had seen his brother killed in action; this could certainly be considered a legitimate "scarring event." He settled in the Matagamon area after the war. But he was not anti-social.

Greenleaf "Hunter" Davis, was the Hermit of Shin Pond (photo at right). So many stories have been told about him that it was a little hard to decide what information about him was fact and what was fiction. All resources agreed he was originally from Lincoln, Maine and that he took off for the gold fields of California in 1849. I found various scenarios as to why he left Maine. One of these said he had fallen in love with his stepsister, and the parents disapproved of the relationship. Another source says his love interest was the daughter of the postmaster, who intercepted Davis's letters to her. Both sources say Davis returned home to find his sweetheart married to another man, so he headed for Shin Pond with a broken heart. After arriving here, he cleared over 40 acres of land and possibly owned squatter's rights to 160 acres on the lower pond. He built a cabin and a mill, farmed, hunted, fished, and trapped. He owned two guns, which he called Napoleon Bonaparte and Alexander the Great; he used these guns to kill over 360 bears. He was well-known as a guide, and he even guided Henry David Thoreau on occasion. He often canoed across Shin Pond and walked to Patten to take part in debating. In the winter, he would make the trip on snowshoes. He also played the violin and wrote poetry. After he became unable to care for himself, he was taken to the Patten Almshouse and then to Crommett Hotel, where he stayed in a private camp until he died at the age of 96 in 1916.

Obviously, these hermits of the Maine woods didn't mind going for long stretches of time without other human contact, but they were not antisocial men. They all enjoyed spending time with friends, family, and visitors to their neck of the woods. Their adventures in the Maine woods have most likely been exaggerated over time, but they have definitely added to the mystique of the Maine outdoorsman.

A SHIN POND HUNTING TRIP

It amazes me to think of all the information that you can get from the internet! As you can see in my bibliography, I used the internet very frequently while I was writing this book; who would have thought that you could type in the name of a person who lived in Mount Chase, Maine in 1860 and find out data such as when he was born, when he died, who he married, even what street he lived on! Of course, I wasn't successful every time I tried this, but I hit the jackpot several times. And sometimes, while researching one topic, I stumbled across something else that caught my attention; that was how I found the letter written by Civil War soldier William Jackman to his wife back in Patten. The following is one of those accidental finds, but I found it so pertinent to this chapter that I had to share it with you.

My discovery was a three-part article by Edward Evan Backus that appeared in the January 23, January 30, and February 6, 1902, editions of the *Shooting and Fishing Magazine* (which could be bought for ten cents a single copy or a year's subscription for $3.50). Mr. Backus's article was titled *A Shooting Trip in Maine*, and it was naturally about a hunting trip in Maine that he and a friend named Lane had recently taken. (In fact, the destination for the trip was Charlie's Wren's Camp Fairview on Lower Shin Pond in Mount Chase.) Mr. Backus was from New Jersey, but his story began in Boston, where he was supposed to meet up with Lane and another fellow named Norton at the train station. Lane was there waiting for him, and finally Norton showed up at the last minute with a considerable amount of gear. They were all ready to board the train when Norton got a telegram. He had to attend to an urgent business matter, he said, and asked Backus to take all his gear with him and said he would try to catch up with Backus and Lane in Portland. So the two continued on their trip by rail. Upon arriving in Portland, they waited two days for Norton to arrive, but he never did show up, so they got on the northbound train, still hauling along Norton's gear. The trip was exceedingly monotonous until after they passed through Milo and caught their first glimpse of Mount Katahdin. From that point on, the scenery more than made up for the monotony. They met some fellow travelers named Barker, Hathaway, and Smith who were also going hunting, but they didn't seem to have a particular destination in mind.

In Millinocket, a badly wounded man was loaded onto the train. He had accidentally shot one of his hands completely off, and the other one was in pretty bad shape. He was bandaged up, but the bandages were blood soaked and blood was actually pooling on the floor of the train. He was headed to Houlton to get medical attention, but Backus said he already looked like a corpse. At this point, the man named Hathaway started showing his true colors; by the time they reached Sherman, he was quite ill. They had to switch trains in Sherman, onto what Backus called a "little jigger of a train." So they hauled their gear (and Norton's as well) onto the train and set off on the twenty-minute ride to Patten that Backus said "I can liken to nothing within my railroad experience." In Patten, they had to transfer to a stage, which took them to the Palmer House. Backus said that both the Patten House and the Palmer House were not much to look at and had no amenities, but he had a comfortable stay and an excellent meal at the Palmer House.

The next morning they looked around for Herbert Brown, who was supposed to take them to Camp Fairview on Lower Shin Pond. Brown wasn't around, but his man Mitchell picked them up with a horse and a three-seated buckboard. Hathaway, Barker, and Smith decided they wanted to go to Shin Pond as well, so they all got on the wagon with all their gear—and Norton's as well. They rode five miles quickly and easily on a good road to Sibley's, where they turned onto a tote road. The next ten miles were torturous; in fact it was recommended that they walk the ten miles to Shin Pond rather than ride. But Backus and Hathaway decided to ride. By the time they got to Shin Pond, Hathaway was once again in pretty bad shape, but the fellows who had walked were already there.

Camp Fairview was owned by Charlie Wren. It was a two story frame and shingle house located near the lower end of Lower Shin Pond. There was another hunting party there already when they got there. Maria, the cook, served them supper (which Hathaway did not eat). When Charlie Wren arrived, he looked at the thirteen sportsmen crowded around the dining table and then beckoned for Backus to come outside with him. Wren said he didn't have room for everyone and wondered why Backus had brought a larger party than he had made reservations for. Backus explained that Hathaway, Barker, and Smith were not part of their party but had tagged along anyway.

Wren decided to let everyone stay if they didn't mind sleeping on the floor. It was a long night. Mr. Backus snored extremely loudly. It got so bad that the other men started throwing things at him. Finally everyone settled down...except Hathaway, who didn't sleep at all.

In the morning, there was five inches of fresh snow on the ground and it was still snowing heavily. Backus was outside looking things over when he saw Hathaway heading off down the tote road with his rifle and suitcase. During breakfast, Mr. Barker shared a note which he said Hathaway had written. It said:

> *Hathaway ran away,*
> *Dawn of day, scairt away.*
> *Said him nay—terrors sway.*
> *Man of clay wouldn't stay.*
> *Gruesome day! Lack-a-day!*
> *Hathaway, Go away!*
> *Get away! Run away!*
> *Hathaway!*

Backus and Lane had pre-arranged to be guided by Charlie Wren. They took off towards Sebois River. They later split up, and Backus shot and wounded a doe. Luckily, he was able to track it and kill it. He field dressed it and blazed his way back to camp. Barker also got a deer on their first day.

The next morning, the sportsmen gave Backus a special written award for not snoring during the previous night. Barker had written it up and all the sports had signed it. It read in part, "Whereas, the inmates of Camp Fairview...in council assembled in a foot and a half of snow at 5 o'clock this morning after a good night's rest, being exceedingly grateful to the fattest man in camp for said good night's rest and refraining from his ability to sound the moose call...thereto present this award to said fattest man." They all had a good laugh about it, but Backus noticed that the handwriting was the same as on the note that Hathaway supposedly left!

It snowed all day that day as well. Barker shot his second deer that morning, which was the legal limit for deer at that time. The next day, Wren sent word to town to send in a horse and wagon, and on the fourth day several of the men, along with Maria (who had been at the camp since spring) and Wren left for town.

The men who were left divvied up the camp chores, and Backus became the cook. By now there was two-and-a-half feet of snow on the ground. The men stayed busy cutting firewood and exploring the area around the camp. Backus shot a buck and the men ate venison for their suppers thereafter.

The men spent quite a bit of their time visiting an old fellow who had a camp about 70 yards away from Camp Fairview. The old fellow had built his camp forty years ago and lived there by himself year round. This remarkable 82-year-old man was none other than Hunter Davis, the Hermit of Shin Pond. In his article, Backus included two stories about Davis. One story began by telling about a French wood chopper who had taken ill. He was out walking around one day near Sugarloaf Mountain (west of Shin Pond) when he came upon a spring. He drank the water from the spring and was cured of his illness! Unfortunately, no one had ever been able to find the spring after that...no one, that is, except Hunter Davis. And that spring water was the reason that Davis at the age of 80 years had the body of a 30-year-old man.

The other story told about the day Davis came upon a bear which had been caught by one foot in one of Davis's traps. As Davis approached the bear, it gave a mighty lunge, broke free of the trap, and headed towards Davis. Davis ran, but fell, and the bear was almost on him. Suddenly, Davis's little dog attacked the bear's hind quarters, giving Davis a chance to pull his knife. He drove the knife into the bear's neck and severed its spinal cord.

The men enjoyed many hours with Davis until it was time to leave. Davis entertained them with stories, played his fiddle, and sang songs he had written himself. One of the songs went like this:

HURRAH FOR SHIN POND
(TO THE TUNE OF ARTHUR MCBRIDE)

Hurrah for Shin Pond! Hear the steam whistle blow,
Hear the ring of the axes as trees are laid low,
Hear the rattle of wagons as they come and go,
Oh! The scene is most pleasant and charming.

Hurrah for Shin Pond! Hear the surge and the roar
Of bright glistening wavelets that break on the shore,
Hear the clang of the engine that trips evermore.
Oh! The scene is most pleasant and charming.

Hurrah for Shin Pond! Hear the shout and the ring,
As laborers wield their broadaxes and sing.
Hear the tones of the fiddle, with its ting-a-ling-ling,
Oh! The scene is most pleasant and charming.

Hurrah for Shin Pond! Hear that incoming train
As it thunders along o'er valley and plain.
To check that wild horse 'twer idle and vain,
Oh! The scene is most pleasant and charming.

Hurrah for Shin Pond! See that old hunter stand
With eye on the scene and his pen in his hand,
To paint that fair scene so gladsome and grand
Oh! The scene is most pleasant and charming.

Hurrah for Shin Pond! The great west is here,
We know that success is now drawing near
So get up your steam without any fear
Oh! The scene is most pleasant and charming.

Hurrah for Shin Pond! For many years past
A byword't has been, but booming at last.
The wild wealth is growing and growing so fast
Oh! The scene is most pleasant and charming.

Hurrah for Shin Pond! The birch and the ash
And the poplar are bringing a nice lot of cash,
So go into business with a rush and a dash,
Oh! The scene is most pleasant and charming.

When Wren returned to camp, he used his horse Dandy Jim to haul all the deer back to camp. The men packed up all their gear—including Norton's— and began their journey in reverse. The trip out was much easier; snow had filled in all the ruts and holes and covered the logs and boulders on the tote road. When they got to Patten, they arranged to have the deer shipped to their homes, and they began their trip south.

A strange thing happened one night in a hotel along the way. Backus was checking in when a man and woman walked across the lobby and up the stairs. The man looked rather familiar, but Backus couldn't see his face. He asked the desk clerk if he could look at the hotel register. He read that the couple had signed in a little over two weeks ago as Mr. and Mrs. R. Notmar Reid, Overlook It. It appeared that Norton had had his own good luck those two weeks during the hunting trip after all!

No one personifies the Maine outdoorsman better than Chub Foster, a Maine guide, sporting camp owner, and storyteller. Chub was born in Bar Harbor, Maine, in 1897. After his mother died when Chub was young, he was adopted by a family named Foster. He attended Gould Academy in Bethel, where he acquired the nickname Chub. In 1916, he joined the army. He spent time in the cavalry in Texas, where his outfit searched for Poncho Villa. In 1917, Chub was deployed to France during World War I. After the war, he stayed in Paris, working with the military and going to school.

But his missed the Maine woods and bean-hole-beans, so he returned to Maine and took a job as a teamster in a pulpwood camp. Around 1920 he got his guide's license and began working for various sporting clubs and camps which took in sports. At one point he worked for Virgil Lynch, who ran a set of sporting camps on the Machias River in southern Aroostook county near Ashland. In 1941, Chub and his wife Fran (Smallwood, from Patten) opened a sporting camp business on Matagamon Lake.

Foster's Wilderness Camps provided lodging, meals, and guide services for almost 40 years. Following are some excerpts from an article called *When a Guide Was a Storyteller*, written by Roger Price for Salt Magazine.

In the bullet list below, Chub's actual words are printed in bold italics.

EXCERPTS FROM *WHEN A GUIDE WAS A STORYTELLER*

- Chub is a real Maine guide, not today's version with a fancy patch and red wool jacket, but a true woodsman and storyteller. With his canvas cone and spruce pole he opened the woods to hundreds of sportsmen in the more than 40 years he lived and worked in the forest.
- Out of these camps on Grand Lake Matagamon, Chub paddled on almost all the waterways of northern Maine. On the Allagash River, he trekked north toward Allagash and Saint Francis. On the branches of the Penobscot, he journeyed south as far as Millinocket and Medway. On the Aroostook River, he headed east toward Ashland and Presque Isle. The headwaters of the Saint John took him west almost to Quebec. I can visit the places Chub talks about, but the experiences he had there are gone. I can travel the same rivers, but his descriptions are of another place. Time is erasing Chub's woods.
- Listening to Chub takes me back to when the woods were foreboding and mysterious, when guides took sportsmen days away from any sign of civilization, when the woods of Maine seemed as impenetrable as any Amazon rain forest. For people like Chub this was never the case, but for his sports, the Bostonians and New Yorkers, it was. ***"The woods---it's just like a damn fever or something. If you go into it once, you never can leave it."***
- ***"I don't know what muddles them up so. They know there's not a thing in the woods that's going to hurt them, and I'm sure you're not going to die just staying out one night,"*** Chub leans forward and takes a fatherly tone as he talks about lost hunters. ***"Make yourself as comfortable as possible, and the next day try to figure it out. But you can't tell them that. Would you believe the antics? I've had them actually tell me the compass points to camp... I couldn't imagine anyone as dumb as that."***
- Guiding has changed. While today's guides still protect their clients from harm, Chub and the rest of the older guides did much more. They cooked, they set up camp, they paddled the canoes, they dressed the game, and they were the fireside entertainment.

- When a guide went into the woods, he had his compass and his pole, but the tool he relied on the most was himself. He knew the woods and he had the skills. With these, other tools were not always necessary.
- In travelling through the North Woods, Chub came to know the country better than any atlas. He knows the geography, but he also has a story to go with each place.
- *"Yeah, that was quite a gang that used to be around here."* Chub describes the other guides and woodsmen who used to live around Matagamon. Just beyond the dam on the East Branch was Fred Walker, a guide and *"a clown if there ever was one."* Charlie Marr lived at Trout Brook Farm just off Matagamon Lake and worked for Eastern Woodlands. *"No matter how much he drank, he was a gentleman all the time, very soft spoken and very nice."* Pat Steen lived at the dam. *"He was harmless, but he was so … big. He'd grab hold of you and he could pick you right up off the ground."*
- He knew Percival Baxter who gave the Baxter State Park to Maine. *"Baxter, he was a very nice, soft-spoken person, the few times that I met him. An old gentleman. I thought he was doing a wonderful job buying that [land] and giving it over to the state…Moose over there, they died from old age."*
- Tellis Coolong was a French-Canadian guide who worked for Chub. Although he spoke in broken English, he made his name as a storyteller. *"By God, if he were alive today, he could make a fortune just telling his experiences. He always had sickle tobacco that you whittled off. He always cut off just enough so that it would fill his pipe. He'd start telling you a story and that pipe would go round and round."*
- What separated guides from other woodsmen was their ability to tell stories and keeps their sportsmen entertained. When I was talking to Carroll Bates, a retired game warden and longtime friend of Chub's, he said, "The old saying that the Maine guides are ten percent Bean boots and ninety percent bullshit is not all that far out. Not that they didn't do a good job, because they did, but the ability to talk with people and tell a good story and to entertain, that was where they really shone. They were woodswise and very capable…But the ability to entertain and to keep people entertained, that was where the few like him really caught on."

- Chub is modest about himself as a storyteller. *"I learned young that I couldn't compete with those guys. They could tell a story and varnish it up in good shape. You saw a lot of guides on the rivers. They were good entertainment."*
- Chub told about Roy Dudley, a guide who had a camp at Chimney Pond at the base of Mount Katahdin, Maine's highest peak. *"I think he's the best hunter I ever saw, and the best trapper. Now, he, back along there, he and Ray Porter was trapping together. That is, they wasn't in the same country, but they were selling together…God he had some great stories,"*
- Chub says one of the guides he always enjoyed seeing was Henry Red Eagle. *"He was a full-blooded Indian, and a very well-educated man. I used to like to have him drop by, or get to the same camp site with him because he was entertaining, and you learned a lot from his talk. The sportsmen enjoyed it."*

These are only snippets from the article. You can read the whole article online at http://www.saltstoryarchive.com/articleview.php?id=2475

Over the years, Chub and Fran met many "bigwigs." One of these was Chief Justice William O. Douglas, who took a fishing trip down the Allagash with Chub and Fran. A friendship developed as they subsequently exchanged letters.

Chub and Fran had two sons, Halton (who predeceased Chub) and Kerry, who lives in Glenburn and provided the photos and some of the information about his parents. Foster's Wilderness Camp became a base for a Boy Scout Maine High Adventure camp in 1971. Chub died at Matagamon in 1995 with Fran caring for him until the end, and Fran died in 1999 at Resthaven Nursing Home in Patten. If it's true that you are never truly dead until your life stops making ripples, then the Fosters are certainly still making ripples in this neck of the woods. They are true icons for those unique characters who played such a big part in our outdoor heritage.

I was lamenting the demise of the true Maine outdoorsman, thinking about those who no longer live their lives in the woods. Then I read an article about Jeffery Martin, a young boy from Patten who had a grand slam in 2015 when he was eleven years old. Although he's a good baseball player, his grand slam was achieved by his hunting skills. He started off by getting his bear and a wild turkey. His dad got a moose hunting permit in the annual moose lottery and named Jeffery as his sub-permittee. Jeffery got his moose—three down, and just a deer to go. And he got it with plenty of time to spare. Then I got to thinking about all the young people in the Patten and Mount Chase area who are taking hunter safety courses and learning from their parents or grandparents or aunts and uncles about how to get around the woods and how to hunt and fish and trap. I have to conclude that our outdoor heritage is alive and well in the forests of Patten and Mount Chase. Hopefully, our young people will put their own stories in print so that future generations can enjoy reading about their experiences in the Maine woods.

I will close this chapter with another Hunter Davis song which tells why he—and all Maine outdoorsmen—love the woods.

The Wild Woods of Maine

How dear to my hear is my own native forest
Where through sunshine and storm as a hunter I roam.
Oh! Picture the forest, the mountain and valley,
And the sweet little brooklet, all fondly my own.
How sweet to retire from the cares and vexations
That spring from a world of contention and strife.
The sweetest, the dearest, the happiest moments
I have ever known through a storm-riven life.
Then away let me fly in the bright days of autumn
And range with delight through the wild woods of Maine.

CONCLUSION

As I am writing the conclusion to this history in January 2017, I am hearing a lot about how 2016 was the worst year ever. The news was pretty dismal throughout the year: Zika virus, the economy, mistreatment of minority groups, cops killing and getting killed, the homeless, drugs, terrorist attacks, American boots on the ground, bullying, war in the streets of Syria where innocent children are dying, families desperate to find refuge, creepy clowns, hacking, fake news, dirty elections, politicians who…well, I'm not even going to go there. Yes, it's tough living in the 21st century.

Some of my readers may think I have painted life in days gone by through rose-colored glasses. Older people like myself tend to be fondly nostalgic about the past (as I was in Chapter Thirteen, *Recollections*). But at the same time, I've written about many very hard times in the history of Patten and Mount Chase. I wrote about losing our soldiers in war after war. I wrote about the town poor and devastating fires. I wrote about times of economic depression. I added information about natural disasters and assassinations of good people. I told you about the deaths of children from disease and other tragic deaths within the communities. So, no, 2016 wasn't the worst year ever for most of us.

Every community experiences change. Every community goes through times of struggle and times of prosperity. Sadly, Patten and Mount Chase have been struggling economically in recent years. Farming and the logging industry have both fallen on hard times. Main Street has big empty gaps, and there are far fewer stores in town than there were in the past. The town schools are gone. Patten's population declined from a high of 1,548 in the 1940 census to 1,017 in the 2010 census. Mount Chase has more than a hundred fewer residents now than it did in 1880, when the town had 310 residents.

Now I'm sounding like a television reporter on the nightly news. But let me put my rose-colored glasses back on and take a look at the positive side of life in Patten and Mount Chase.

- ✓ You can fill your prescription at the Drug Store or fill-er-up at the gas station of your choice.
- ✓ You can pick up a 2 X 4 at Richardson's Hardware or pick a quart of blueberries at McNally Farms.
- ✓ You can buy lobster at Ellis Family Market or an order of flat clams at Craig's Clam Shop. Both places sell ice cream, too.
- ✓ You can choose a nice Maine gift at Red Moose Trading Post or Shin Pond Village with the cash you get when you go to the Redemption Center.
- ✓ You can pick out a really good book at the library or a really cute top at a really good price at the Daisy Boutique.
- ✓ You can get your physical, get your fillings, and get your feel-better meds at Katahdin Valley Health Center.
- ✓ You can get your taxes done at Calculations, mail your return at the post office, and deposit your refund in your account at KTCo.
- ✓ You can hire a carpenter to build you a house and an electrician to do the wiring.
- ✓ You can hire someone to plow your dooryard or someone to dig a hole in your backyard.
- ✓ You can order a bouquet of roses from Georgia at the Drug Store or buy a rose bush at Richardson's Greenhouse.
- ✓ You can pay someone to cut your grass or cut your hair or clean your car.
- ✓ You can hire somebody to haul off your trash or your poop.
- ✓ You can eat in or order out at Deb's Deli or you can get a beer with your meal at the Shin Pond Pub.
- ✓ You can eat in, order out, or fly in at the Hangar.

- ✓ You don't have to drive very far at all to get to Baxter State Park or to Katahdin Woods and Waters National Monument.
- ✓ You can park your RV at a campground or rent a cabin or pitch a tent or stay at a lodge where the beds are comfortable and the food is good.
- ✓ You can get your bait for open water fishing or ice fishing at Wilderness Variety. Then you can head out to Upper Shin or Lower Shin.
- ✓ You can hire a guide for hunting or go hunting for berries and fiddleheads.
- ✓ You can hike the Appalachian Trail or ride the snowsled and ATV trails.
- ✓ You can watch a Little League game at the ball field while your kids play at the Patten Community Playground.
- ✓ You can watch a parade and watch the fireworks during Patten Pioneer Days.
- ✓ You can visit the Patten Historical Society, the Lumberman's Museum, or the Bradford House to get a glimpse of life in the past.
- ✓ You can buy Hotties at Haymart or a fine paddle from Ricky or a handcrafted packbasket from Ray.
- ✓ You can watch the local kids play ball or play an instrument at Katahdin Elementary, Middle, and High Schools. You can go to their super student-led conferences or watch the super confer a diploma on them.
- ✓ You can have a ball or dribble a ball at the Rec Department.
- ✓ You can slide, ski, snowshoe, or swim.
- ✓ You can go to meetings at Patten Women's Club, the ATV Club, the Rockabema Snow Rangers, the Historical Society, the Masons, or a church group. If you really like meetings, you can be a school board member or a selectman.
- ✓ You can worship at your choice of three churches or praise God from the top of a mountain. (Here is the view of Mount Katahdin and Lower Shin Pond from the top of Mount Chase.)
- ✓ You can live on Main Street if you like to be around people or in a cabin in the woods if you want some peace and quiet.

I have used the word community often throughout the text of this history. So what were the goals and interests of the people who made up the combined community of Patten and Mount Chase? In many instances, the goals were the interests, so I will just make one list:
- To provide for their families: food, shelter, safety, health care, and the basic necessities of life
- To provide opportunities for people to earn the money needed to provide for themselves and their families
- To provide a quality education for their children
- To ensure the right to worship as one pleases
- To govern the town as a democracy, in a fair and effective manner
- To offer ways for people to enrich their lives

Patten and Mount Chase seem to have met all these goals/interests in the past and are continuing to meet them in the present. But the towns are even more than that. They have always been and still are communities where people care about each other. When a need becomes apparent, people step up to meet that need. The towns might not look the same as they did fifty years ago, but the people of Patten and Mount Chase still want to make these towns great places to live and work and play.

It's probably not hard to figure out that I love Patten and Mount Chase and hope to live here for a good long time yet. I want to be able to introduce my grandson to both of my hometowns someday, and I want him to appreciate their many assets. I want him to be impressed by how these little towns grew up in the wilderness and survived through hard times. And I want him to feel like he knows the pioneers and the merchants and the woodsmen and the farm families and the town leaders who were responsible for this history. I certainly have grown to know them and love them and admire them!

I hope this history has been interesting to you. I hope you learned a little more about the towns of Mount Chase and Patten. I hope it will inspire you to appreciate your community even more, whether that community is Patten or Mount Chase or New York City or Lick Skillet, Tennessee. And I hope it will motivate you to do what you can to help your community continue to meet the goals and interests of its citizens.

APPENDIX A: TIMELINE OF MOUNT CHASE DEVELOPMENT AND GOVERNMENT

YEAR	EVENT
1826	The Great State Bonfire; Mount Chase the mountain got its name (see pgs. 29-30 for the story of Jim Chase and the fire)
1837	First settlers arrived
@1852	The Mount Chase Cemetery on Route 11 was established.
1860	Mount Chase was known as Monterey Plantation.
1862	Monterey Plantation became Mount Chase Plantation.
1864	Mount Chase was incorporated as Maine's 415th town. The town had at least one school by this time.
1867	The Mount Chase Cemetery on the Shin Pond Road was established.
1870's	The first Shin Pond House was built.
1881	Mount Chase had a Methodist Society.
1875	See page 56 for a map of property holders in 1875.
Late 1800's	The first sporting camps were established.
Early 1900's	A fire tire was installed on top of Mount Chase. There were as many as six schools in Mount Chase at this time.
1907-1908	Ted Crommett was the Shin Pond Postmaster, and William Howes was the Myrick Postmaster.
1911	The first Shin Pond House burned, but was rebuilt and reopened within a year.
1924-1927	Mount Chase had been divided into six road districts: State Aid Road #1, State Aid Road #2, Aroostook Road, Mountain Road, Owlsboro Road, Shin Pond Road.
1925-1933	A stage was operating between Patten and Matagamon.
1926	A fish hatchery was established on the Owlsboro Road.
1936	The Town of Mount Chase was deorganized and returned to being a plantation.
1949	Zenas Harvey's Shin Pond House burned. It was rebuilt the same year.
By 1960	All the Mount Chase schools had closed except the Myrick School.

YEAR	EVENT
1962	The dump was established.
1974	The Mount Chase Volunteer Fire Department was established.
1979	Mount Chase returned to being a town. The Shin Pond House burned for the third time.
1981	Shin Pond Village opened.
Prior to 1983	Town government was handled by a town clerk, a tax collector, and tax assessors.
1983	The town hall was refurbished and put into use as a town office. A new form of government was introduced: the town now had an administrative assistant and three assessors (selectmen). Annie Lord was the first administrative assistant. Randy McKenney became the Public Works Director (Road Commissioner).
1984	Susan Bates became the administrative assistant.
1985	Wilderness Variety Store opened.
1986	Hadley McKenney became the Road Commissioner.
1990	Susan Sheehan became the administrative assistant.
1991-1992	Mount Chase joined the Northern Katahdin Valley Solid Waste Committee. Mount Chase resident Tom Sheehan served as the director around this time.
1994	The dump closed.
1996	The Mount Chase Fire Station was erected.
2001	The Mount Chase Town Hall was refurbished and a computer system was installed.
2002	Rhoda Houtz became the administrative assistant. The fire tower on top of Mount Chase was moved to the Lumberman's Museum.
2007	A salt-sand Quonset building was erected.
2010	Jutta Beyer became the administrative assistant.
2013	Lora Ryan became the administrative assistant.
2014	Mount Chase celebrated its sesquicentennial anniversary.

APPENDIX B: TIMELINE OF PATTEN DEVELOPMENT AND GOVERNMENT

YEAR	EVENT
1828	Amos Patten purchased T4R6; it was surveyed by Ira Fish, Eli Kellogg, and Samuel Wiggins
1829	The first settlers arrived.
1830	The Aroostook Trail was blazed between Mattawamkeag and T4R6.
1831	The first mill was built.
1834	The first family moved to T4R6. The first frame house was built.
1835	The first baby was born in T4R6.
1838	The first school was built.
1839	T4R6 was incorporated as a plantation. It was probably called Fish's Village, Fish's Mills, or Fish's Plantation. Ira Fish built a barn on the site of the present Methodist church. The barn was used for Methodist church services. The Patten Cemetery was established.
1840-1842	The Bradford barn and home were built. The house now owned by Cecily and Al MacKinnon was built.
By 1841	The town had several businesses, a doctor, and a sheriff. Three congregations (Baptist, Methodist, and Congregationalist) had begun meeting.
1841	The town of Patten was incorporated.
1842	The first Patten House was built.
1845	The Baptist Church was built. A Social Library had been formed. Around this time, the house that is now Patten Historical Society was built.
1846	The house now owned by Marty Arbo was built.
1847	Patten Academy was incorporated.
@1848	The house that was most recently Chickadee Realty was built.
1852	Patten belonged to the Penobscot and Aroostook Union Agricultural and Horticultural Society.
1856	A militia group called the Patten Rifle Company was established.
1860	A newspaper called *The Voice* was being published.

YEAR	EVENT
1861	A post office was established and a mail coach was delivering mail. Some of the first postmasters were Joseph Heald, Calvin and Mary Bradford, and W.S. Kellogg.
1861-1865	177 men from Patten and Mount Chase served in the Civil War. 35 of them died in battle or of disease.
1863	The Scribner house was built.
1864	The house now owned by Craig Greenier was built.
1865	The Congregational Church was built.
1867	A stage traveled between Mattawamkeag and Patten.
1871	The Methodist Church was built.
1875	The Patten Volunteer Fire Department was established. See pages 55 and 57 for maps of property holders in 1875.
1878	A newspaper called the *Katahdin Kalendar* was being published.
1883	Water was being piped from springs at the top of Finch Hill to Main Street.
1886	The Ira B. Gardner store (later Merrow's) was built. The Mason's Hall was built in the late 1800's.
1888	The Quincy, Cooper, and Rowe building was built.
1890	The Patten Telephone Company was organized.
1891-1893	Patten Drug Company was built.
1894-1896	Railroad tracks were laid between Sherman and Patten, a railroad station was built, and the Bangor and Aroostook Railroad arrived.
@1895	There were eight elementary schools, a grammar school, and a high school in Patten.
1897	The first Patten Academy building burned.
1898	The second Patten Academy opened. A newspaper called *The Light* was being published. Roland Sampson Scribner died while serving in the Spanish-American War. The Oddfellows Hall was built.
By 1900	Gas street lights had been installed. The first car dealerships in Patten were opened in the early 1900's.
1902	Electric street lights were installed.
@1904	Sewer lines were installed. The Katahdin Farmers Telephone Company was established and Patten had long-distance phone service.

YEAR	EVENT
1905	The first Patten House burned and the second one was built. Patten Primary School was built.
1907	Patten had a pest house, which was used to quarantine people with serious infectious diseases.
1909	The first hardware store owned by the Richardson family opened.
1910	Hal Gardner built the building that is now Mountain Heights Health Care Facility. The Baptist Church closed.
1914	A town hall had been built. A public dump had been opened.
1916	Saint Paul's Catholic Church was built. The Peavey Block was built.
1917-1918	86 Patten and Mount Chase men and women served in World War I. Raymond Walker died in battle. John Daley, John Coote, and Jessie Mariner died while serving because of the influenza epidemic which swept the world during those years.
1917	The east side of Main Street burned, including the Patten House and the Quincy, Cooper, and Rowe building. Patten was publishing a newspaper called *The Katahdin Herald*.
1918	Katahdin Trust Company opened. The first president was Henry Rowe. Between 1918 and 1935, Jacob Hersey, Stanley Wescott, and Theresa Tozier served as postmasters.
1919	The Henry Rowe building was erected.
1920	The Quincy building which later housed Ken Lord's grocery store was built. A creamery had been established. Miss Main had a post office. The Chase Opera House had been built. At some point during this era, Henry Main operated a moving picture theater.
1922	There were five different automobile dealers in town.
1927	A flood took out all three bridges in Patten and was the cause of the drowning deaths in Shin Pond of five Patten Academy students.
1928	The Congregational Church closed. The library was established in the former Baptist church.
1931	The Pentecostal Church was built. Dr. Lore Rogers opened the Katahdin Creamery. Baxter State Park had its beginnings.
1933	A CCC camp was established in Patten.
1935	Hubert Nevers was appointed as postmaster.

YEAR	EVENT
1936	The building that now houses Magic Wand Car Wash was built.
1939	A movie theater was opened by Ira and Sherwood Howes. The plywood mill was established.
1940	The town hall and Forrest Smith's garage burned. Lloyd Morse opened a garage on the corner of Main Street and the Shin Pond Road.
1941	The second town hall was built. This building is now the home of the Patten Parks and Recreation Department.
1941	The town established a government led by a town manager. The first manager was Archer Scribner. The town celebrated its centennial anniversary.
1941-1945	Around 250 Patten and Mount Chase men and women served in World War II. Six of them died: Frank Johnson, Samuel Smith, Wallace Grant, Everett Gardner, Philip Smallwood, and Paul Peavey.
1943	Elden Shute became the town manager.
1946	WW II vets Gillie Brown, Ken Lord, and Dudley Olsen opened businesses in Patten. Joseph McGillicuddy was the town manager.
1947	The Patten Academy boys' basketball team won a regional tournament in Boston, Massachusetts.
1948	Richardson's Hardware opened.
1949	Patten Grammar School was built.
1950	T.R. Bartlett was the town manager. 75 Patten and Mount Chase men and women served in the Korean War. Frank Kilgore was killed in action in the war.
1951	Resthaven Nursing Home (later Mountain Heights Health Care Facility) was established.
1952	Stanley Johnson was the town manager.
1953	Robert Anderson was the town manager. A fire station was built on Dearborn Street and a town garage was built on Katahdin Street.
1954	George and Rose Merrow took over management of Stratton's. Around this time, the first clam shop opened at its current location.
1956	The Lumberman's Museum was established.

YEAR	EVENT
1957	The Patten Police Department was established with Russell Arbo as its first chief.
1958	The creamery closed.
1960	James MacArthur was the town manager.
1962	Robert Anderson was the town manager. The post office was moved to its current location. The Lumberman's Museum was moved to its current location.
1963	James Hannigan was the town manager. MSAD #25 was formed.
1965	Firth Smallwood was the town manager.
1967	The reconstruction of Main Street began. The last class graduated from Patten Academy.
1968	Leslie Dickinson was the only Patten native to die in the Vietnam War. Around 86 local men and women served in the war.
1969	The last train passed through Patten. Kingdom Hall of Jehovah's Witnesses was built.
1970	Marian Guptill was appointed as postmaster.
1972	Kathleen Rogers was the town manager. The movie hall closed.
1974	The Patten Ambulance Service was established. The new high school was built. Patten Academy was closed. Katahdin Valley Health Center was established.
1975	Donald Grant was the town manager.
1976	Meadowbrook Manor was established. Hathaway's Motel/Apartments was built; a home that stood on that site was torn down.
1977	Patten Academy was torn down.
1980	The plywood mill burned.
1981	Katahdin Valley Health Center moved to its present location.
1982	Rhonda Harvey was the town manager. Philip Wyman, then Harriet Campbell were appointed as postmaster. Calvary Christian Academy was established.
1983	Ellis Family IGA was established. Patten Pioneer Days was established.

YEAR	EVENT
1984	The Patten Town Office on Katahdin Street opened. A new town garage was erected there as well.
1985	The Patten Police Department was discontinued.
1986	Dianne London, then Sandra McNally were appointed as postmaster.
1987	Patten Academy Alumni Park was created. The building that had been Gillie Brown's grocery store and the Laura Scribner store was torn down. The garage beside it was also torn down.
1989	Merrow's closed. The Grange Hall was torn down.
1990	Margaret Daigle was the town manager.
1991	Paul Beattie was the town manager. The town celebrated its sesquicentennial anniversary.
1992-1994	A new system and a new water system were installed. The dump closed.
1995	Downtown Deli/Deb's Deli opened at its current location. Calvary Christian School closed.
1996	Paul Caruso was the town manager. Houlton Street was reconstructed.
1997	Ken Lord's grocery store closed.
1997-1998	Patten Grammar and Patten Primary Schools closed. Katahdin Elementary School was established. The high school became Katahdin Middle and High School. The building that had most recently housed Al-E-Oop Restaurant was torn down.
1998	Rhonda Harvey was the town manager.
1999	Morse's garage closed. An addition was built on to the fire station.
2001-present	At least 23 men and women with ties to the area served in the Iraq and Afghanistan Wars, including Dustin Harris, who was killed in Iraq in 2006.
2002	The Henry Rowe building was torn down.
2004	Patten Grammar School was burned. The Patten Historical Society was established at its current location.
2006	Ruth Peters, Deborah Bivighouse, and Terri Conklin were town managers.
2007	Hangar Pizza opened.

YEAR	EVENT
2008-2009	Magic Wand Car Wash/Main Street Outback Garage opened. The Merrow's Department Store building burned down. Rhonda Brophy purchased the Red Moose Tradiing Post and the lot that had been Merrow's. Daisy Boutique opened. The building which had housed Ken Lord's grocery store and the Post Office was torn down. Kingdom Hall of Jehovah's Witnesses closed. The Primary School burned down.
2010	Stephanie Berry was appointed as postmaster. The buildings on the corner of Main and Founders Streets were torn down. The building between the Deli and Patten Rec was torn down. The veneer mill closed.
2011	RSU # 50 was formed.
2012	John Jamo was appointed as postmaster.
2013	Richardson's Greenhouse opened. A new town garage was erected.
2016	Raymond Foss was appointed as the town manager. Cody Pond was appointed as postmaster. The town celebrated its 175th anniversary. Haymart was established. Katahdin Woods and Waters National Monument was established.

APPENDIX C: THE POPULATIONS OF PATTEN AND MOUNT CHASE ACCORDING TO CENSUS FIGURES

YEAR OF CENSUS	PATTEN	MOUNT CHASE	TOTAL
1837	114	12	126
1850	470		470
1860	639	250	889
1870	704	262	966
1880	716	310	1026
1890	936	284	1220
1900	1172	299	1471
1910	1406	227	1633
1920	1498	239	1737
1930	1278	210	1488
1940	1548	198	1746
1950	1536	250	1786
1960	1312	179	1491
1970	1266	197	1463
1980	1368	233	1601
1990	1256	254	1510
2000	1011	247	1258
2010	1017	201	1218
2014 (EST.)	1002	199	1201

APPENDIX D: HONOR ROLL LISTS

HONOR ROLL

IN RECOGNITION OF THOSE PATTEN AND MOUNT CHASE MEN AND WOMEN WHO WERE KILLED OR DIED OF DISEASE DURING WARTIME

CIVIL WAR   1861-1865

Alexander Bigger	Ebenezer Bigger	Wallace Blackwell
Bradish Brown	Alonzo Clark	Samuel Crommett
Edward Cunningham	Owen Cunningham	Lyman Dolloff
Isaac Donham	James Fairfield	Jeremiah Farewell
Aden Hackett	Walker Harriman	William Jackman
Marcellus Kellogg	Charles Kimball	Martin Kimball
James Kyle	Joseph Lurvey	John McKeen
Wyman Morgridge	Ira Morrill	Winslow Morrill
Gardner Pierce	Joseph Preble	Henry Ricker
Edwin Rogers	Miles Scribner	John Troop
Ira Wadlin	Loammi Wadlin	Byron Waters
Hartson Weeks	Daniel Wescott	Isaac York

SPANISH-AMERICAN WAR   1898

Roland Scribner

WORLD WAR I 1914-1918   U.S. INVOLVEMENT   1917-1918

Raymond Walker

WORLD WAR II 1939-1945   U.S. INVOLVEMENT   1941-1945

Frank Johnson   *Samuel Smith*   *Wallace Blackwell Grant*
Everett Gardner   *Philip Smallwood*   *Paul Peavey*

KOREAN WAR   1950-1953

Frank Kilgore

VIETNAM WAR   1965-1973

Leslie A. Dickinson

IRAQ AND AFGHANISTAN WARS   2001-2017

Dustin Harris

HONOR ROLL FOR PATTEN AND MOUNT CHASE

YEARS	WAR	# KNOWN SERVED	# KNOWN CASUAL-TIES	POPULATION: PATTEN & MOUNT CHASE*	% OF POPULATION SERVING
1812	War of 1812	1	0	1810—0	--
1861-1865	Civil War	177	35	1860—889	20%
1898	Spanish-American War	8	1	1900—1,471	0.5%
1917-1818	World War I	113	4	1920--1737	6.5%
1941-1945	World War II	178	6	1940—1746	10%
1950-1953	Korean War	75	1	1950—1786	4%
1968-1973	Vietnam War	86	1	1970—1463	6%
1991	First Gulf War	6**			
2001-2017	Afghanistan & Iraq	23***	1		

* The first number is the census date; the second number is the combined population of Patten and Mount Chase
** Undoubtedly there were more who served.
*** Includes any veteran with ties to Patten or Mount Chase and/or who graduated from Katahdin High School. There are most likely more than

During the Civil War, these families had three or more with same surname serving.
    Bigger—3 (2 died)
    Blackwell—3 (1 died, 1 discharged for wounds or illness)
    Brown—4 (1 died, 1 wounded)
    Chesley—3 (1 discharged for wounds or illness)
    Hackett—4 (1 died)
    Kimball—4 (2 died, 1 wounded)
    Legrow—3 (1 wounded)
    Myrick—3
    Sargent—3 (possible 1 died)
    Scribner—7 (1 died, 1 POW, 2 wounded; includes father and son in same unit)
    Wadlin—2 (brothers, died)
    Weeks—3
    Wescott—3 (2 died)
    Woodbury—4 (father and three sons)

During World War I, these families had three or more with same surname serving.

    Campbell—4   Carpenter—3
    Drew—3   Porter—3
    Smith—3   Walker—1 died, 1 wounded

During World War II, these families had three or more with same surname serving.

    Bates—7 (3 were brothers)
    Birmingham—5
    Coolong—3 (brothers: Chester, Hadley, Henry)
    Gagnon—3
    Goodine: 3 (brothers: David, Eugene, Frank)
    Harrington—4 (3 brothers and a sister: Edgar, Joseph, Boyd, Mary))
    Hatt—3
    Hunter—3 (brothers: Adrian, Anthony, James)
    Johnson—3 (brothers: Frank, Maurice, Stanley)
    Kennedy—3
    Landry—3 (brothers: (Clifford, John, Joseph)
    Lord—4
    McKenney—3
    Mulligan—4 (brothers: Claude, Ernest, Herman, Melvin)
    Palmer—4 (includes 2 brothers and a cousin who was wounded)
    Peavey—4
    Rogers—3 (2 brothers and a sister: Percy, Winfred, Frances)
    Roy—3 (brothers: Clarence, Leonard, Walphy)
    White—4

26 pairs of brothers not included above
Highest ranking officer from Patten: Major Lawrence Willett
Nurses: Barbara Harnden, Mary Harrington, Ruth Smith, Marian Philpott,
    Frances Rogers

WAR OF 1812: Daniel Scribner

SPANISH AMERICAN WAR

Bragg, Carroll
Brown, Hadley F.
Elliott, Wesley
Hackett, Arthur
Hackett, Offin
Hackett, Pearl
Hackett, Ralph
Scribner, Roland

CIVIL WAR

Akely, Caleb
Bailey, Ephraim
Beals, Waldo
Bigger, Alexander
Bigger, Archibald
Bigger, Ebenezer
Blackwell, Charles
Blackwell, E.I.
Blackwell, Joshua
Blackwell, Wallace
Brackett, Elijah
Bradford, Columbus
Brown, Bradish
Brown, Byron
Brown, Charles
Brown, Orrin
Butterfield, Lowell
Buxton, Stillman
Carpenter, Lafayette
Chase, John
Chelsey, Jefferson
Chesley, Hiram
Chesley, John
Clapp, Carleton
Clark, Alonzo
Clark, Joseph
Clements, Lewis Jr.

Coburn, George
Conant, Charles
Craig, Augustine
Craig, William
Cramp, Charles
Crommett Samuel
Cunningham, Owen
Cunningham, Edward
Curo, Edward
Daley, James
Doloff, Lyman
Donham, Charles
Donham, Isaac
Fairfield, Hadley
Fairfield, James
Farewell, Hannibal
Farewell, Jeremiah
Farwell, Charles
Fitzpatrick, John
Fowler, Timothy
Gardner Ira
Gemo, Peter
George, John
Gerry, John
Gifford, Benjamin
Gilman, Charles
Goff, Edmond

Gonier, David
Grant, Amza
Guptill, Isaiah
Hackett, Alden
Hackett, William
Hackett, Charles
Hackett, Lorenzo
Harriman, Walker
Hayes, John
Haynes, Thomas II
Heald, Charles
Hersey, John
Hill, James
Hill, Joseph
Hopdela, Francis
Husey, John
Ingerson, Lewis
Jackman, William
Jameson, Nathan
Kellogg, Horace
Kellogg, Marcellus
Kimball, Andrew
Kimball, Charles
Kimball, Martin

Kimball, Samuel Jr.	Parker, James	Smart, Robert
Kyle, James	Perow, Benjamin	Smiley, Martin
Legrow, Daniel	Perry, Charles	Smith, Adoniram
Legrow, Erastus	Perry, Jonathan	Soule, John
Legrow, Samuel	Pierce, Abner	Stacey, Robert
Leslie, Melvin	Pierce, Gardner	Tripp, Alonzo
Lincoln, George	Poor, Austin	Troop, John
Lowell, Hiram	Powers, Thomas	Twitchell, Joseph
Loyal, Russell	Preble, Joseph	Vance, Robert
Lurvey, George	Ricker, Barzilla	Wadlin, Ira
Lurvey, Joseph	Ricker, Henry	Wadlin, Loammi
Lurvey, Joseph	Rines, George	Walton, Abram
Mancy, William	Robbins, William	Walton, America
Marshall, Jimmo	Rogers, Edwin	Warren, Lorenzo
McKeen, John	Rogers, Luther	Waters, Byron
McKenney, William H.	Rowe, Albert	Weed, Martin
McLellan, Sylvester	Royal, Russell	Weeks, Alonzo
Miles, Horace	Sanders, William	Weeks, George
Mitchell, Horace	Sanders, Woodbury	Weeks, Hartson
Moody, Frank	Sargent, Edward	Wescott, Daniel
Morgridge, Wyman	Sargent, Lewis	Wescott, Harry
Morrill, Ira	Sargent, William	Wescott, John
Morrill, Winslow	Savage, Cyrus	Whalon, Peter
Muncy, William	Sawtelle, Daniel	Wilcox, William
Myrick, Ezra	Scribner, Daniel	Wilson, William
Myrick, Melville	Scribner, Francis	Woodbury, Edwin
Myrick, Richard	Scribner, George	Woodbury, Timothy
Noyes, Charles	Scribner, Levi	Woodbury, W.Worthly
Noyes, Frederick	Scribner, Miles, Jr.	Woodbury, William
Ordway, Augustus	Scribner, Miles, Sr.	York, Isaac
Orr, Samuel	Scribner, William	Young, Spencer
Palmer, Moses Jr.	Shaw, Joshua	
Palmer, Uriah	Shaw, Martin	

WORLD WAR I

Ambrose, F.S.
Ash, H.A.
Bates, F.A.
Boynton, F.H.
Boynton, W.C.
Brown, F.E.
Brown, R.H.
Campbell, D.L.
Campbell, H.
Campbell, H.E.
Campbell, O.
Carlisle, E.D.
Carpenter, F.H.
Carpenter, Miss F.W.
Carpenter, R.J.
Carver, A.
Clark, H.
Clark, L.
Coady, D.L.
Coady, K. J.
Cobb, O.R.
Cobb, R.L.
Conrad, Pete
Coote, J.E.
Coote, W.F.
Cunningham, R.C.
Daigle, A.
Daley, John
Davis, George
Deschane, L.P.
Desmond, C.
Desmond, C.R.
Downing, F.A.
Drew, G.A.
Drew, H.D.
Drew, T.W.
Gagnon, A.
Gagnon, A.H.

Gagnon, C.
Gardner, E.K.
Garnet, R.S.
Glidden, H.D.
Glidden, H.L.
Gomm, A.
Grant, C.H.
Grant, L.E.
Grant, V.H.
Gudreau, Joe
Hagar, R.K.
Hall, B.G.
Hall, W.H.
Harrington, E.
Harris, J.F.
Hotham, C.E.
Howe, D.B.
Huston, C.B.
Kimball, A.L.
London, G.
Lord, G.E.
Lord, H.T.
Lord, R.A.
Marriner, Miss J.B.
McGibney, J.I.
McKenney, A.
McLellan, D.
Merrill, R.E.
Michaud, A.
Michaud, O.
Mitchell, Edw.
Morse, F.P.
Myrick, B.L.
Nelder, F.C.
Noonan, F.A.
Oaks, W.G.
Palmer, Guy
Palmer, H.H.

Parker, R.E.
Parson, F.A.
Pelkey, H.
Pomeroy, L.
Porter, C.E.
Porter, D.V.
Porter, W.F.
Proctor, E.D.
Proctor, J.
Ranks, M.H.
Ranks, W.F.
Ribgy, J.
Richmond, Miss T.I.
Rowe, B.A.
Sargent, C.G.
Sargent, H.D.
Shay, Dan
Shean, P. R.
Sibley, R.F.
Silverman, Max
Smallwood, H.
Smith, G.M.
Smith, L.O.
Smith, S.A.
Steen, A.C.
Steen, Amos
Stevens, W.L.
Stimpson, H.
Twitchell, E.H.
Walker, Fred
Walker, Ray
Waters, C.W.
Waters, W.J.
Webb, E.T.
Weeks, E.
Whitney, A.W.
Willett, R.

-458-

WORLD WAR II

Arbo, Sterling
Asher, Harland
Asher, Rexford
Bailey, Chester
Banks, Howard
Bates, Delmont
Bates, Harold
Bates, Harvey
Bates, Herbert
Bates, Leon
Bates, Merle
Bates, Scott
Birmingham, Carroll
Birmingham, Howard
Birmingham, Richard
Birmingham, Robert
Birmingham, Vida
Blackmore, Robert
Boyle, Charles
Campbell, F. Clayton
Campbell, Neal
Castine, M. Palmer
Chamberlain, Lewis
Chamberlain, Richard
Chapman, Charles
Chute, Ralph (Shute?)
Cochran, Alfred
Cole, Herschel
Coolong, Chester
Coolong, Hadley
Coolong, Henry
Corriveau, John
Corriveau, Rosaire
Craig, Philip
Cratty, Arthur
Crommett, Hiram
Cunningham, Jerrold
Desmond, Clair
Desmond, Ralph
Dow, Leland
Dunn, Erland
Dunn, Leon
Dyer, Edward
Dyer, Leslie
Estabrooke, Ora
Finch, Cecil
Finch, Lawrence
Foster, Halton
Freve, Edward
Gagnon, Charles
Gagnon, Donald
Gagnon, John
Gardner, Everett
Gardner, H.P.
Getchell, Wesley
Giles, Stanley
Glidden, Alston
Glidden, Keith
Good, Ralph
Goodine, Dave
Goodine, Eugene
Goodine, Frank
Gormer, Ledger
Grant, Leon
Grant, Wallace
Guptill, Evan
Hall, William
Hanson, Harold
Harnden, Barbara
Harrington, Boyd Jr.
Harrington, Edgar
Harrington, Joseph
Harrington, Mary
Hatt, Clifford
Hatt, Gordon
Hatt, Herbert
Howe, Cecil
Howes, Philip
Hulbert, Charles Jr.
Hulbert, Wayne
Hunter, Adrian
Hunter, Anthony
Hunter, James
Huntley, Orrin
Ingerson, Oma
Jones, John
Johnson, Frank
Johnson, Maurice
Johnson, Stanley
Jones, Kenneth
Jones, William
Keddrel, Arlie
Kennedy, Arthur
Kennedy, Edward
Kennedy, Ralph
Knox, Vernon
Lander, Charles
Landry, Clifford
Landry, John
Landry, Joseph
Lord, Austin
Lord, Carl
Lord, Kenneth
Lord, Manley
Lunt, E.W.Jr.
Lunt, Harry
Martin, Roland
McCarthy, Harry
McCourt, John

McDonald, Kenneth	Peavey, Arthur	Shean, Wayne
McDonald, Vinal	Peavey, George	Shean, Wesley
McKenney, Gerald	Peavey, John	Smallwood, Elmer
McKenney, Leland	Peavey, Paul	Smallwood, Philip
McKenney, William	Philpot, Marian	Smith, Ruth
McManus, Robert	Porter, Raymond	Smith, Samuel
Miles, Arthur	Porter, Wesley	Steen, Maurice
Miles, Leroy	Purvis, Donald	Tozier, William
Morse, Howard	Purvis, Warren	Violette, Joseph
Mulligan, Charles	Richardson, Chester Jr.	Webster, Clifton
Mulligan, Herman	Richardson, Robert	Webster, Leland
Mulligan, Melvin	Rigby, Elden	Weeks, George
Noonan, Merle	Roberts, Fred	Wescott, John
Nott, William	Rockwell, James	Wescott, Stanley
Noyes, Halbert	Rogers, Frances	White, Chester
Olsen, Dudley	Rogers, Percy	White, Ernest
Olsen, Henry	Rogers, Wilfred	White, John
Ordway, Richard	Rossignal, Clarence	White, Vaughn
Ouellette, Vernard	Roy, Clarence	Willett, Chester
Palmer, Darrell	Roy, Leonard	Willett, Lawrence
Palmer, Evan	Roy, Walphy	Winship, Edward
Palmer, Philip	Shakespeare, Noel	Wood, Raymond Jr.
Palmer, Robert	Shaw, Avon	Woodbury, Walter

KOREAN WAR

Bates, George
Bates, Wesley
Botting, Delbert
Brackett, Richard
Campbell, Don
Campbell, James
Chamberlain, Dana
Corriveau, Abel
Corriveau, Albert
Corriveau, Leon
Grant, Donald
Harvey, Wallace
Howard, Ira
Lebel, Arthur
Lent, Edward Jr.

Lent, John
Lord, Rodney Sr.
McElroy, Keith
McElroy, Rodney
McKenney, Hadley
Noyes, Adelbert
Noyes, Archie
Noyes, David
Noyes, Frederick
Noyes, Laurie
Ouellette, Kenneth
Purvis, Lawrence
Twitchell, Elmer
Willett, Darrell

VIETNAM

- Adams, Donald
- Adams, Richard
- Anderson, Fleetwood
- Anderson, Robert
- Arbo, Martin
- Beane, Jon
- Bell, Richard
- Birmingham, John
- Birmingham, Kerry
- Bishop, Gary
- Boone, Donald
- Botting, Calvin
- Botting, Paul
- Bouchard, Anthony
- Brown, Robert
- Brownlee, John Jr.
- Cameron, Richard
- Campbell Vernon
- Campbell, Bruce
- Campbell, Charles
- Campbell, Danny
- Campbell, Rufus
- Cole, Dana
- Cole, Gregory
- Conrad, Jack
- Coolong, Kempton
- Corey, Phillip
- Corriveau, Armand
- Corriveau, Clayton
- Cote, James
- Craig, Isaac
- Craig, Melvin
- Cyr, Ernie
- Cyr, Francis
- Dauphinee, Gordon
- Dauphinee, Peter
- Dennis, Donald
- Desmond, Donald
- Dickinson, Leslie Jr.
- Foster, Kerry
- Glidden, Colin
- Glidden, Donald
- Grant, Donald
- Grant, Michael
- Guirey, Richard
- Guptill, Robert
- Harrington, Gerald
- Harris, Harold Wayne
- Howes, John
- Howes, Ronald
- Hurlbert, Frederick
- Kleynen, Karel
- Landry, Frank
- Lebel, Arthur
- Lent, Edward Jr.
- Libby, Richard
- Lord, David
- Lord, Jeffrey
- Lyons, Glenn
- Lyons, Roderick
- MacArthur, James
- MacKinnon, Al
- Main, Leroy
- Main, Peter
- Marr, John
- McCarthy, Gary
- McCourt, Joseph
- McCourt, Michael
- McGraw, Donald
- McGraw, Glenn
- McIntire, Burtt
- McKenney, Randolph
- McPherson, George
- Melvin, Wayne
- Morse, Timothy
- Mulligan, Phillip
- Palmer, Richard
- Parker, Howard Gary
- Parker, Keith
- Pelletier, Damase
- Perkins, George
- Porter, John
- Porter, Robert
- Purvis, Lawrence
- Rideout, Delbert
- Rigby, Roderick
- Rockwell, James
- Ryan, Dennis
- Skinner, Richard Scott
- Somers, Spurgeon Jr.
- Tarr, Charles
- Tarr, Fred
- Townsend, Mark
- Tweedie, Clayton
- Watson, Kirkland
- Willett, Rayfield
- Willett, Wayne
- Williams, Daniel
- Young, Wilfred

FIRST GULF WAR

Dauphinee, Gregory
McCarthy, Marcus
Noyes, Edward
Palmer, Jessica
Whitney, Frederick Jr.

Coolong, Kempton (Med Evac unit stationed in Germany)

WARS IN AFGHANISTAN AND IRAQ (includes names of veterans with ties to Patten and Mount Chase and/or graduates of Katahdin High School)

Birmingham, Matthew
Conrad, John
Curtis, Steve
Hall, Aaron
Horton, Scott
Kelley, Carson
Libby, Aaron
McCarthy, Marcus
Melvin, Amber
Noyes, Edward
Robinson, Christian
Schmidt, Richard III

Campbell, Cyrus
Cummings, John
Falanka, Anthony
Harris, Dustin
Ireland, Robert
Lane, Travis
Lord, Corey
McNally, Andrew
Mulligan, Nicholas
Peavey, Jason
Savage, Matthew
Willett, Roger

BIBLIOGRAPHY

Author's note: Some of my research could not be fully identified in bibliography form. I have done my best to include below all the information I could find about my resources.

PART ONE: BOOKS, PERIODICALS, REPORTS, PAMPHLETS, ARTICLES

Backus, Edward Evan. *A Shooting Trip in Maine.* Shooting and Fishing: A Journal of the Rifle, Gun, and Rod. A.C. Gould, Editor. New York. Vol XXXI. Nos. 15, 16, and 17. Jan. 23, Jan. 30, Feb. 6.

Bradford, Irene. *The History of Patten Academy.* Furbush Robert Printing Company. Bangor, ME. (as Irene Olsen.)
It Took a Miracle. (an unpublished history of the Methodist Church in Patten).

Campbell, Donald. *Important Dates in the History of Patten, Maine.* Paper Talks, 1985 (Eighth Edition).

Chase, William. *The History of Penobscot County.* Cleveland, Ohio: Williams, Chase, & Co., 1882. (Available online through Google Books)

Coolong, Deborah. *Letting Daylight into the Swamp.* (an unpublished history of logging in Maine).

Field and Stream advertisement. May, 1921. Volume XXVI, No. 1.

Harrington, Rita. *The Development of Patten, Maine.* May 13, 1970. (written for coursework at the University of Maine in Orono, copy located at Veteran's Memorial Library in Patten).

Holbrook, Stewart H. *Yankee Loggers.* New York: International Paper Company, 1961.

Howe, Justin. *The First Hundred Years of Agriculture in Aroostook County.* Written through an EPSCoR grant under the supervision of Dr. Kimberly R. Sebold, PhD, Associate Professor of History, University of Maine at Presque Isle, presented in 2013.

Huntington, Chris. *Carl Sprinchorn News.* Volume 2 (Spring 1966),Volume 3 (Summer 1996), and Volume 4 (Winter 1997). (Self-published by Carl Sprinchorn Admiration Society).

Kephart, George. *Campfires Rekindled.* Marion, Mass: Channing Books, 1977.

Lloyd, Robert M. *Who Has Not Heard Them.* Colby Magazine, June 2000.
Maine Atlas and Gazeteer, The(Ninth Edition). DeLorme Publishing Company:Freeport, Maine, 1984.

Maine Register, State Yearbook, and Legislative Manual. [Note: I used various editions published between around 1850 and 2016. Some I read online and others I read at Veteran's Memorial Library in Patten or at Cary Library in Houlton. These were published annually by a variety of publishers throughout the years.]

Mitchell, Frances Robinson. *A Few Woodsman in the Patten Area of the 1920's and 30's.* Available at Veteran's Memorial Library.

Mount Chase Town Reports. Available at Mount Chase Town Office.

Noonan, Bob. *Maine's Main Beaver Man.* The Trapper and Predator Caller, April/May 2001.

Olsen, Irene. *See Bradford, Irene.*

Packard, Winthrop. *An Accidental Official Forest Fire.* The Thresherman's Review. March, 1905. Vol. XIV, #11. St. Joseph, Michigan. [Can be read online at *https://books.google.com/books?id=p0I1AQAAMAAJ*].

Paper Talks. Northern Penobscot County Editions.

Patten Town Reports. Available at Veteran's Memorial Library in Patten.

Price, Roger. *When a Guide Was a Storyteller.* Salt Magazine XI, #44, Dec. 1993.

Rolde, Neil and WCBB. *So You Think You Know Maine.* Harpswell Press: Gardiner, Maine, 1984.

Smith, Edmund Ware. *The Last Hermit.* Field and Stream, April, 1963.

Stanley, R. H. and Geo. O. Hall. *Eastern Maine and the Rebellion.* R.H. Stanley & Co., Bangor, Maine, 1887. (Available online through Google Books)

PART TWO: INTERNET RESOURCES

archiver.rootsweb.ancestry.com › PATTEN › 2011-01
bangordailynews.com/2010/04/11/.../bangor-tigers-drove-logs-down-the-connecticut/
bangordailynews.com/2014/12/18/living/blogs-and.../the-making-of-a-good-man/
bangormetro.com/Archive/1508/The-Best-Known-Small-Town.aspx
cbhf.ca/edouard-lacroix
content.time.com/time/magazine/article/0,9171,765867,00.html
credo.library.umass.edu/view/full/muph061-sl123-i001
Facebook Page *So You Think You Know Patten, Maine*
http://ccclegacy.org/CCC_Brief_History.html
http://digitalmaine.com/arc_civilwarportraits/
http://downeast.com/escape-spencer-lake/
http://drjasonwhite.com/symptoms/childhood-vaccinations/
http://en.wikipedia.org/wiki/Baxter_State_Park
http://en.wikipedia.org/wiki/Humid_continental_climate
http://en.wikipedia.org/wiki/Katahdin_Woods_and_Waters_National_Monument
http://en.wikipedia.org/wiki/Lore_Alford_Rogers
http://en.wikipedia.org/wiki/Mount_Chase,_Maine
http://en.wikipedia.org/wiki/Mount_Katahdin
http://en.wikipedia.org/wiki/Patten,_Maine
http://fam.eastmill.com/f444.htm#f79683
http://files.usgwarchives.net/me/cumberland/androscoggin/turner/bradford/bdrf-his.txt
http://findagrave.com
http://logos.wikia.com/wiki/Logopedia
http://louisdl.louislibraries.org/cdm/ref/collection/AAW/id/994
http://outthere.bangordailynews.com/2016/05/05/hunting/patten-11-year-old-celebrates-hunting-grand-slam/
http://maineanencyclopedia.com/governors/
http://maineanencyclopedia.com/mount-chase/
http://repository.cmu.edu/cgi/viewcontent.cgi?article=1070&context=hsshono
http://statelaws.findlaw.com/maine-law/maine-compulsory-education-laws.html
http://u.demog.berkeley.edu/~andrew/1918/figure2.html
http://wabi.tv/2013/01/24/60-years-of-wabi-tv-5-a-look-back/
http://www.american-rails.com/bangor-and-aroostook.html
http://www.colby.edu/colby.mag/issues/fall00/vietnam/
http://www.etravelmaine.com/region/aroostook/houlton-maine/
http://www.greatachievements.org/?id=3642
http://www.gsmmaine.org/wp-content/uploads/2010/02/A-History-of-non-ferrous-metal-mining-and-exploration-6.pdf

http://www.infoplease.com/ipa/A0779935.html
http://www.johnstonsarchive.net/policy/abortion/ab-unitedstates.html
http://www.maineafp.org/members-in-the-news
http://www.mainegasprices.com/retail_price_chart.aspx
http://www.maine.gov/ifw/warden_service/
http://www.mainelegislature.org/legis/lawlib/legbiog/webform1.aspx
http://www.mainething.com/alexander/community%20life/Making%20a%20living/Farming/A%5D%20BRIEF%20HISTORY%20OF%20FARMING.html
http://www.maryagnespaul.org/index.php/en/st-mary
http://www.oobject.com/category/dental-chairs-through-history/
http://www.pa-roots.org/data/read.php?1209,841243
http://www.pbs.org/fmc/timeline/dmortality.htm
http://www.potus.com/
http://www.rootsweb.ancestry.com/~meandrhs/census/maine/patten/1837.html
http://www.rootsweb.ancestry.com/~meandros/bradford.html
http://www.rootsweb.ancestry.com/~mearoost/CoburnDiary.html
http://www.school-for-champions.com/history/lincolnjfk.htm#.WJOh6Dig4rg
http://www.searsarchives.com/homes/index.htm
http://www.techetoday.com/lifestyle-columns/death-gulf-april-1951
http://www.thejumpingfrog.com/?page=shop/flypage&product_id=1206496
http://www.usgwcensus.org/cenfiles/me/1837/1837-03.txt
http://www.worldcat.org/title/personal-recollections-of-english-and-american poets/oclc/24427278
https://archive.org/details/historyofpenobsc00will
https://books.google.com/books?id=1tAUAAAAYAAJ&pg=PA284&lpg=PA284&dq=clifford+grindal+patten+maine&source=bl&ots=yfPQ3do4Ph&sig=TZSh6Jx7VaSO4cat6EqxMt4Un4&hl=en&sa=X&ved=0ahUKEwifrPm1rbnSAhUk0OmkhwkldoQ6AEIIjAD#v=onepage&q=clifford%20grindal%20patten%20maine&f=false
https://books.google.com/books?id=u3Q1AQAAMAAJ
https://books.google.com/books?id=4pkwAQAAMAAJ
https://books.google.com/books?id=cTpi2YI7_EoC&pg=PA16&lpg=PA16&dq=G. Root+Maine+Birch+Point+Camps&source=bl&ots=kq2BMBUxoA&sig=jJv755XS9J3zUQWE9Kb5H1EGCA&hl=en&sa=X&ved=0ahUKEwi5rLP1zJjPAhVq6YMKHY6vAc8Q6AEIITAB#v=onepage&q=G.F. Root Maine Birch Point Camps&f=false
https://books.google.com/books?id=duiE2cQSnvcC&pg=PA466&lpg=PA466&dq+%20Patten%20+%20Maine#v=onepage&q&f=false
https://books.google.com/books?id=Fn0YAAAAYAAJ&pg=RA1-PA192&lpg=RA1-
https://books.google.com/books?id=-kEUAQAAMAAJ

-467-

https://books.google.com/books?id=p0I1AQAAMAAJ&pg=RA1-PA63&lpg=RA1-PA63&dq=The+Great+State+fire+of+1826&source=bl&ots=D7sYdw2oaV&sig=Of3VRhPCFqgKHR99a7nlbGlagFs&hl=en&sa=X&ved=0ahUKEwjhsfz2qtvRAhVr1oMKHbjUCMsQ6AEILzAE#v=onepage&q=The%20Great%20State%20fire%201826&f=true-
https://books.google.com/books?id=rH95AAAAMAAJ&pg=PA197&lpg=PA197&=Halbert+P.+Gardner
https://books.google.com/books?id=swxFAQAAMAAJ&pg=PA226&lpg=PA226&dq=maineEIUTAI#v=onepage&q=maineregister 1900&f=false
https://books.google.com/books?id=vleDBAAAQBAJ&pg=PA153&lpg=PA153&dq
https://books.google.com/books?id=xFbbpKNM9icC&pg=PA746&lpg=PA746&dq=Isaac+York++Patten+Maine&source=bl&ots=zZwzxeYWPS&sig=v7SiRXVxu93-
https://en.wikipedia.org/wiki/1815_eruption_of_Mount_Tambora
https://en.wikipedia.org/wiki/1918_flu_pandemic
https://en.wikipedia.org/wiki/American_Legion
https://en.wikipedia.org/wiki/Bay_of_Pigs_Invasion
https://en.wikipedia.org/wiki/Bradford_Farm_Historic_District
https://en.wikipedia.org/wiki/Cold_War
https://en.wikipedia.org/wiki/Cuban_Missile_Crisis
https://en.wikipedia.org/wiki/Diphtheria
https://en.wikipedia.org/wiki/Édouard_Lacroix
https://en.wikipedia.org/wiki/Edward_Everett_Hale
https://en.wikipedia.org/wiki/Enrollment_Act\
https://en.wikipedia.org/wiki/Epidemic_typhus
https://en.wikipedia.org/wiki/Impeachment_of_Bill_Clinton
https://en.wikipedia.org/wiki/Jimmy_Carter
https://en.wikipedia.org/wiki/John_Deere
https://en.wikipedia.org/wiki/John_Deere_(inventor)
https://en.wikipedia.org/wiki/Lions_Clubs_International
https://en.wikipedia.org/wiki/List_of_counties_in_Maine
https://en.wikipedia.org/wiki/List_of_disasters_in_the_United_States_by_death_toll
https://en.wikipedia.org/wiki/Margaret_Chase_Smith
https://en.wikipedia.org/wiki/Patten,_Maine
https://en.wikipedia.org/wiki/Paul_Bunyan
https://en.wikipedia.org/wiki/Pennsylvania_Hospital
https://en.wikipedia.org/wiki/Pneumonia
https://en.wikipedia.org/wiki/Richard_Nixon
https://en.wikipedia.org/wiki/Robert_F._Kennedy

https://en.wikipedia.org/wiki/Space_Shuttle_Challenger_disaster
https://en.wikipedia.org/wiki/Space_Shuttle_Columbia_disaster
https://en.wikipedia.org/wiki/Twenty-fourth_Amendment_to_the_United_States_Constitution
https://en.wikipedia.org/wiki/Typhoid_fever
https://en.wikipedia.org/wiki/United_States_in_World_War_I
https://familysearch.org/search/collection/list
https://in.pinterest.com/pin/538039486718138257/
https://newengland.com/today/living/new-england-history/karenwood/
https://npgallery.nps.gov/GetAsset?assetID=65268c1f-e43a-4db3-8372-af887bab2868
https://ourworldindata.org/life-expectancy/
http://patentimages.storage.googleapis.com/pdfs/US1363930.pdf
https://priceonomics.com/how-the-lumberjack-became-such-a-deadly-profession/
https://www1.maine.gov/ifw/warden_service/pdf/History.pdf
https://www.bostonglobe.com/metro/maine/2013/05/...hermit...maine.../story.html
https://www.britannica.com/biography/Charles-E-Duryea-and-J-Frank-Duryea
https://www.cbc.ca/news/technology/cholera-s-seven-pandemics-1.758504
https://www.cdc.gov/injury/wisqars/pdf/101cid_all_death_by_age_group_2010-a.pdf
https://www.cdc.gov/mmwr/preview/mmwrhtml/mm4838a2.htm
https://www.census.gov/1940census/
https://www.findagrave.com/cgi-bin/fg.cgi?page=gr&GRid=133688851
https://www.findagrave.com/cgi-bin/fg.cgi?page=gr&GRid=68060518
https://www.geni.com/people/Jacob-Frye/6000000000088493057
https://www.geni.com/people/John-Gardner/6000000002641549181
https://www.geni.com/people/William-McKenney/6000000014047447259
https://www.google.com/maps/place/Allagash,+ME+04774/@46.1758299,69.7638402,241085m/data=!3m1!1e3!4m5!3m4!1s0x4cbc158aadcd4385:0x38cbc0d67f630251!8m2!3d47.0833103!4d-69.0417481
https://www.google.com/patents/US428340
https://www.google.com/search?q=Warden+service
https://www.maine.gov/dacf/parks/discover_history.../telos_dam_and_cut.shtml
https://www.mainememory.net/sitebuilder/site/193/slideshow/229/display?format=list
https://www.mainememory.net/sitebuilder/site/1982/display?use_mmn=1
https://www.mainememory.net/sitebuilder/site/903/page/1314/display?page=2
https://www.mauricejakeday.com/
https://www.stkfoundation.org/
https://www.youtube.com/watch?v=LhYwzdMq2Cg

maineanencyclopedia.com/patten/
mainecrimewriters.com/uncategorized/maine-hermits-and-how-i-used-them
mainefrontier.tumblr.com/post/.../a-story-about-jigger-jones-legendary-river-
    driver
myrootsplace.com/getperson.php?personID=I139580&tree=MRP
www.civilwar.org/education/history/faq/
www.history.com/this-day.../john-froelich-inventor-of-the-gas-powered-tractor
www.infoplease.com/cig/dangerous...epidemics/smallpox-12000-years-
    terror.html
www.nature.com/pr/journal/v55/n1/full/pr200425a.html
www.nber.org/vital-stats-books/vsrates1900_40.CV.pdf
www.outdoors.org/articles/amc-outdoors/exclusive-preview-desperate-steps/
www.outdoorsportinglibrary.com/the-authors-2/edmund-ware-smith/\
www.pbs.org/wgbh/americanexperience/features/general-article/death-
    numbers/
www.pem.org/library/blog/?p=2734
www.roadsideamerica.com/story/10327
www.scribnerfamilies.org/scribnerfamilies/ghtout2/gp345.htm
www.usclimatedata.com/climate/houlton/maine/united-states/usme0185
www.usclimatedata.com/climate/patten/maine/united-states/usme0738

Made in the USA
Middletown, DE
24 August 2022